D0934307

Honey and Wax

Honey

and Wax

PLEASURES AND POWERS
OF NARRATIVE

An Anthology
Assembled by

RICHARD STERN

Illustrated by

JOAN FITZGERALD

Chicago and London

THE UNIVERSITY OF CHICAGO PRESS

Library of Congress Catalog Card Number: 66–13889
THE UNIVERSITY OF CHICAGO PRESS, CHICAGO & LONDON
The University of Toronto Press, Toronto 5, Canada
© 1966 by The University of Chicago
All rights reserved
Published 1966
Printed in the United States of America

The anthology is affectionately and gratefully dedicated to the University of Chicago which, though a collective, and thus incapable of either benevolence or beneficence, has been for seventy-five years their container.

EPIGRAPH

Honey . . . . a sweet viscid liquid, obtained by bees chiefly from the nectaries of flowers, i.e., those parts of flowers specially constructed for the elaboraton of honey, and, after transportation to the hive in the proventriculus or crop of the insects, discharged by them into the cells prepared for its reception. Whether the nectar undergoes any alteration within the crop of the bee is a point on which authors have differed. . . . It is a popular saying that where is the best honey there also is the best wool. . . . The origin of the honey-yielding properties manifested specially by flowers . honey has been carefully considered by Darwin, who regards the saccharine matter in nectar as a waste product of chemical changes in the sap, which, when it happened to be excreted within the envelopes of flowers, was utilized for the important object of cross-fertilization. . . . To the ancients honey was of very great importance as an article of diet, being almost their only available source of sugar. . . . The KORAN, in the chapter entitled "The Bee," remarks . . . "There proceedeth from their bellies a liquor of various colour, wherein is a medicine for men" (Sale's *Koran*, chap. xvi).

Beeswax is possessed of properties which render it a most convenient medium for preparing figures and models, either by modelling or casting in moulds. At ordinary temperatures it can be cut and shaped with facility; and it melts to a limpid fluid at a low heat; it mixes with any colouring matter, and takes surface tints well; and its texture and consistency may be modified by the addition of earthy matters. . . . When molten, it takes the minutest impressions of a mould, and it sets and hardens at such a temperature that no ordinary climatic influences affect the form it assumes. . . . The facilities which wax offers for modelling have been taken advantage of from the remotest times . . .

Encyclopaedia Britannica, 11th ed., XIII, XXVIII.

PREFATORY NOTE

Narrative, a time art, proceeds by the orderly accumulation of special data into such patterns as the evocation and dispersal of tension and the serial stripping of illusion. Unlike music, a bit like the dance, a bit more like drama, narrative works by manipulating the more or less familiar events of most lives. It corrals attention by exploiting familiar sympathies and identifications, but almost never fails to extend or subvert them. The physical security necessary for the creation and absorption of the art may be related to the ease of such subversion, as well as to the narrator's special interest in disruption and extremity. Artists seem peculiarly aware that the only natural experiences sufficiently ordered to be easily grasped as wholes are those dominated by great passions and powers, love, hatred, ambition, mania, preservation. The connection of the arts, particularly the story arts, with revolutions in manners, feeling, and society is not accidental, and this despite the fact that their finest examples exhaust whatever emotions they arouse and overflow their interpretation.

All utterance, all expression, all art is response to alteration, of perception or condition. Lyric may begin as the articulation of immediate responses to such change, gasps of relief, cries of ecstasy, insight or pain. Its meters, fractured syntax, consonance, and rapid, idiosyncratic transitions from notion to notion also characterize the small discourse of powerful feelings and half-signal, half-express the emotional storm which the lyricist has experienced or imagined. Narrative is a delayed response to alteration. It is grounded by description, explanation, or a more or less careful rendition of events. Whether minimal transcription of a single event or oblique, many-sided registration of a thousand, it is defined by *what happened* rather than by *reactions* to what happened. Its discourse is, therefore, closer to the usual discourse of explanation (or, in the case of semi-lyric narratives, such as some of Joyce, Sterne, and Lautréamont, to the internal discourse of dreams or reverie). Tales are told, narratives are narrated to someone, even if the narrated to someone, even if the someone be but the narrator's own shadow, that inner doubter in quest of reassurance, clarity, or remembrance.

Narrative forms have bred and crossbred for millennia. Prose fiction, that form which "takes the minutest impressions," is linked with epic, chronicle, memoir, fable, essay, case history, biography, report, prose romance, and what have you, letter, rogue's tale, anecdote. It constitutes the bulk of the present collection, surrounded here not only by its brothers but by such cousins as drama and song; the notion is that the reader will not only relish the titular honey of particular works but enjoy the subtle, interstitial pleasure of comparative morphology as he perceives the remarkable properties of the medium, that wax which bears the sweet freight.

As in all collections, there are a number of other determiners of contents, some beyond the collector's control. The morphologist-reader will remark certain groupings: a cluster of first-person accounts ranging from straightforward reports to distortions so extreme as to derail interest from the events to their distorter; another cluster of works about writers, a third offering a spectrum of "improbables." Then too the collection is controlled by a desire to include less familiar material spread out over millennia and ten or twelve bodies of literature. A collector's materials are more obviously prefabricated than an artist's, but his serried preferences may make a peculiar impression on some readers (though "whether the nectar undergoes any alteration within the crop of the bee is a point on which authors have differed"). Such readers may notice that the present collector's taste is limited by a preference for the earthbound to the untethered, the oblique to the direct, the sweet to the medicinal; yet the hope remains that even readers whose preferences diverge sharply from these may find pleasure in the honeycomb.

CONTENTS

ILLUSTRATIONS

The Texts

GINO O

Danilo Dolci

What were my beginnings? I'll tell you. My mother was a *spicciafac-cende*.[1] She was a widow—her husband had been a shoemaker by trade. She had to keep going to the Town Hall, and amongst the other employees she met there was the man who was to become my father. She was a real good-looker, and he was crazy about her; by promising to marry her, he got her to do what he wanted. He didn't bother to tell her he was married already.

I was born in 1912, a bastard. Mother couldn't bring herself to part with me, and as I hadn't a name, she gave me hers. I remember very little about those early days; I've a dim recollection of playing in the street and of being left in charge of a neighbour while Mother was out at work, but that's all.

When the Spanish 'flu epidemic hit Sicily, Mother caught it and died. Her family had written her off because she'd gone wrong, and as I was a child of sin, none of them would give me a home.

I had a grown-up half-brother who was engaged, and he got his girl's family to take me in. There was a young pickpocket living in the house, and after a while, he started to teach me the tricks of the trade. He began by showing me how to pinch the contents of a woman's handbag (a *magghia appendente*, a trawling net, it's called in thieves'

[1] The word *spicciafaccende* is derived from *spicciare*, to attend to, sort out, and *faccende*, affairs. The *spicciafaccende* offers, for a fee, to fill in official forms for illiterates who cannot cope with them, obtain copies of birth-certificates, marriage-lines, legal documents, etc. The profession of *spicciafaccende* is carried on by large numbers of unemployed men and women in Palermo. *Trans. note.*

Gino's story first appeared in the review *Nuovi Argomenti*. Reprinting it in *Inchiesta a Palermo*, Danilo Dolci decided to omit the three lines which were held to constitute obscene matter, and for which he was prosecuted and sentenced to two months' imprisonment. He appealed his conviction, and when his appeal was heard a year later, the Court decided that as the matter contained in the offending lines was factual, it could not be termed obscene, and the conviction was accordingly quashed. (R.S.)

slang) in the *il frontino* way—that is, from the front. What I had to
do was this. I had to pass the victim, walk on five or six metres, then
turn round sharply so that I was face to face with her; as soon as I
came level with her handbag, I had to unfasten it in a flash. I had to
be able to cope with every kind of fastening: buttons (some handbags
fastened with buttons in those days), press-studs, clasps and zips. The
moment I'd opened the bag, I had to slip my hand inside and nick the
wallet or whatever else I could.

When a kid had mastered his trade, his problem was to convince
people he could be trusted and get someone to take him on. After a
bit, some chap who'd been a pickpocket himself in his young days
would get to hear about him. "There's a kid that knows his job and
one that won't split," he'd say to himself, and he'd hire him. The two
would travel all over the place, and work every city in Italy. My first
master was a certain B. I shall never forget the first day I went out
with him. I was in such a panic that I wet my trousers: I was terrified
out of my wits that the woman we'd picked out would tumble to what
I was doing, grab me and scream for the police. If I hadn't been still
more scared that B. would call me yellow and give me the chuck, I
never would have gone through with it. Lots of kids used to screw up
their courage and steady their nerves with drink or drugs; after that
first time, though, I was all right. B. gave half the money from the
hauls we made to his family; he didn't give me any, but he paid for
my board and keep. He never told me how much was in the wallets
which he always opened himself. I usually nabbed two or three a day
and while I was at it, B. made sure that none of the passers-by would
spot my game.

Almost every family in the street I lived in had a youngster like
myself who was learning to be a pickpocket. In Via Sant' Agostino,
Cortile Catarro, Cortile Salara (Scalilla) and in practically all the
streets around, there was either a master-thief or a school for thieves.
Here, in Ballaro, you'll find hundreds of young pickpockets; there are
swarms of them, too, in Via Montalbo, Via Castro, Rione Borgo—
half Palermo's alive with them. Some of the expert thieves emigrate
to America; others go to the big Italian cities—Milan, Turin, Genoa
—where they aren't known, and where they find things much easier
than they do here as the people aren't wise to their tricks—stealing
their wallets is child's play. In Rome, a prostitute will often lend
pickpockets a hand; she'll rub herself up against a chap while they're

frisking him, and so he doesn't notice what's going on. Well, I mustn't give away too much; I shouldn't like to see all the thieves rounded up and hauled off to prison. The authorities wouldn't dream of helping them to live differently, by finding them honest work, so once they were out of jug, they'd become far worse than when they went in. Things haven't changed since the days when the Saracens landed; men thought then, as they do now, that prison was the only cure for all the wickedness in the world, and what happened? They clapped, not only sinners, but saints, too, behind bars.

Nowadays squads of so-called "special" police patrol the city on the look-out for thieves and pickpockets, but the fact is, there's nothing very special about them. In my time, though, there were some famous squads—Sciabbica's, for instance. He was a holy terror, Sciabbica was; he's on the retired list now, but sleuthing's in his blood, you might say. He can't live without it, and he still does a bit on his own account. Sciabbica could run like a hare. Then there were the squads under the orders of a chap we nicknamed Lu Signorino because he smarmed his hair down with brilliantine.

One day—I shall never forget it—I was "going down," going to work with my gang, when all of a sudden, at the corner of the Via Sant'Agostino and Via Maqueda, where people lingering to look in the shop-windows are easy prey, I caught sight of one of Sciabbica's squads. "Sciabbica! Scram!" I got out, and we instantly scattered and hared for dear life up the side-alleys. I never stopped running till I got home; my side ached, I was panting, but I dared not slacken speed—I knew if they caught me I'd get at least three days in jug. Even when I did get back, I couldn't calm down—the thought that the cops might have spotted me was enough to make me tremble all over. The inmates of the house gathered round as they always did when one of us rushed home unexpectedly; they stood there, waiting for me to get my breath back and tell them whether the police were on to me or whether I'd made a bolt for it after nabbing a wallet. Alarms, flight, pursuit, panic, thrills and triumphs—that's the life of a pickpocket. When a gang sets out in the morning, so do the police squads.

So far, I've only told you about the pickpockets who pinch from *minule*, women; now I'll tell you about those who specialize in robbing *u vascu*, a man. These gangs work with a *sciammaru*, a kid of twelve to fourteen, who has to be the right height—that's to say, he has to come up to the victim's elbow. It's the *sciammaru's* job to move the man's arm without his noticing it to right or left, depending on which side he keeps his wallet—*u surci*, the mouse, as it's called in thieves slang. The *sciammaru* brushes against the chap, gives his waistcoat a tweak and makes sure that the "mouse" is there; then he touches one of the gang who's directly behind him, either on the right shoulder or the left to show him where the "mouse" is, gives the waistcoat a second tweak to turn it round a bit more, and his accomplice passes his hand under the chap's armpit and grabs the "mouse."

When the street's crowded, and the man the gang has marked down is trying to pass people or is waiting to cross the road, the whole thing's fairly easy. There are usually four or five in a gang, and sometimes, they work with hustlers whose job it is to create a spot of confusion so that the victim doesn't notice what's going on. The hustlers are old lags who've had more than enough of prison and prefer to do the less risky part of the business—they act as look-outs too. They've done with the active side of the game, but they haven't given it up. A hustler's rather like an old tart who's been on the bash in a quarter for twenty years, and who goes on making a living there, not by selling herself, but by washing down the doorsteps. The hustler either cannons into the victim, or he takes him by the shoulders as if he were in a hurry to pass him. When the gang's nabbed a wallet, the money inside it is shared out; one half is split between the *sciammaru* and the chap who actually pinched the "mouse"; the rest is divided between the others. The hustler gets whatever the gang chooses to give him—he isn't one of them, properly speaking, he hasn't any standing.

Most of the victims are *contadini* who've come to Palermo to go to the hospital, look for work or do some shopping; they always bring all their savings with them. Pickpockets also keep a sharp look-out for *fardaioli*, emigrants who've been in North and South America for years, and have just returned to Sicily; they're almost certain to have in their pockets *u surcu abbuzzatu*—a wallet stuffed with notes. As well as thieves, there are confidence tricksters who have their own particular ways of making *u coppo*, a packet—a *bidone*, they call it in Rome. There's the lone wolf, for instance, who rigs himself out in a blue jersey and peaked cap with an anchor on it, and makes out he's a Yank who's just landed. "Say, can you direct me to the Amurrican Consulate?" he'll say to some innocent, and then he'll mutter: "I've

GINO O
Danilo Dolci

got some real good 'English'² stuff in my valise—you can have it cheap if you like." It ends up, of course, with his unloading a lot of rubbish on the dupe. Then there are pickpockets who frisk passengers on the autobuses, but they don't always bring it off—in winter, for instance, it's not at all easy to get at the trouser-pockets of a man who's wearing an overcoat.

Well, now you know the sort of life I led as a very young pickpocket—the life I went on leading until I was twelve. Sometimes a master, to encourage his "apprentices" would promise to take them to a brothel. Once four of us were taken into the room of a prostitute who catered specially for kids like ourselves. She threw herself flat on the bed and . . . but let's leave it at that, talking about it makes me feel sick. There's one thing I must tell you, though, vile as it is: if we found out that one of the gang had turned squeaker, then the rest of us, in order to disgrace him, got hold of him and buggered him to show our contempt.

By the time I was twelve, I'd made quite a name for myself. There was a kind of thieves' hiring market, and one day, a big shot—let's call him X.—came to see the family I was living with, told them he'd like to take me on, and agreed to give them so much for me. So I left home, and began travelling around with him; I was on the up and up now—he even took me abroad. To do what? The very same thing, of course. It's enough to say I was bad. One dodge we worked between us was a regular tear-jerker. X. would stride along the street, leather belt in hand. "Have you seen a kid of twelve anywhere about?" he'd ask the passers-by. "My nipper's run away from home, been missing for three days—wait till I get him! I'll tan his hide off!" The next minute, he'd let out a shout. "There he is!" he'd exclaim, pointing at me, and away I'd bolt, with him at my heels. As soon as I spotted a chap who was sure to have a nice fat "mouse" in his pocket, I'd clutch at his legs and howl: "Save me! Save me! Don't let Father beat me!" I clung to him for dear life while "Father" raised the belt and began to slash at me; I grovelled and writhed, and while the kind gentleman was doing his best to shield me from the blows, X. would neatly nick his wallet. He then cleared his throat, the signal that he'd got the "mouse," and I'd leave go, get up, and go off with him sobbing and sniffling.

² The term "English" is applied indiscriminately in Sicily and parts of Italy to mean "super." *Trans. note.*

We often hired a *carrozza* whose driver was in the know to follow us along in case we had to make a quick getaway. Once, when we were in Palermo, on the Corso dei Mille, near the Mulino Pecoraro, a man came along carrying about ten empty bottles. X. was in the act of frisking him when he suddenly got wise to it and asked a chap who was passing to hold his bottles for a minute. "My trousers are coming down," he said. No sooner were his hands free than he whipped out a revolver, and began to fire at us; scared out of our wits, we made for the *carrozza*, jumped in, and off we went. The crowd who heard the shots thought it was the usual story, that a girl had been kidnapped, and that someone was firing at her abductors.

We stayed for a while in Naples where we had a room in a hotel; we wore decent suits and looked altogether respectable—X. made out he was a commercial. We went to Turin, Milan—all over the place. At one time, X. managed to get himself a press card and posed as a journalist. Every so cften, we'd return to Palermo, our base.

When I was fourteen, I joined up for a bit with two other pickpockets, both in their twenties. One evening, when we were working a certain city, we picked up a woman, and took her back to the place where we were staying. When my mates had had her, it was my turn; afterwards, as I lay in bed with her, she began to ask me questions, and before I knew where I was, I'd told her all about myself and what the three of us were doing. When I woke up in the morning, she wasn't there—while I was asleep, she'd flitted. The next thing that happened was that the police came along, and when they started to question me, I soon realized it was the tart who'd given us away. The cops kept asking me about a certain corporal in the *carabinieri*, a Sicilian from Palermo—he's a sergeant now—who'd helped us by hustling people around; if I hadn't told the woman about him, they couldn't possibly have known that he had any connection with us.

A year later, the authorities decided to send me to the reformatory of Santa Maria Capua Vetere in the province of Naples. I was put on the boat in charge of a policeman who had no idea that, amongst the passengers, was a pal of mine who was determined that I shouldn't be put away. When we landed, and the cop had seen me safely on the train, my pal gave me some stuff to rub into my eyes which would make them red and inflamed. "They'll think you've got something infectious and won't admit you," he said. I told myself that anything was better than losing my freedom, so I rubbed the stuff in. It made my eyes so bad that the doctor who examined me when I arrived told the superintendent that he couldn't pass me as fit. The trouble cleared up in a week, but to this day, I still suffer from conjunctivitis.

I went home for a bit, then I started roaming all over the place again. Twice I was arrested and hauled before the beak; the first time I got twenty days, and the second, thirty, but although both sentences were recorded in my dossier, I didn't actually serve them as I was under age. Then, when I was in Rome, the cops got hold of me once more; I was detained and finally sent to the Emmanuel III reformatory in the province of Mantua.

It was the time I spent in this reformatory that made a rebel of me. The superintendent was a swine; apart from thrashing us for the least trifle, he did things that I won't repeat. If we so much as dared kick a ball around while he was having his siesta, he gave us two or three days in the cells. We were always starving. We used to creep down at night, force the lock of the kitchen cupboard and pinch a bit of bread, or else we'd tiptoe out into the garden and grab some tomatoes and a melon or two. A day came when we were so sick of being everlastingly beaten and of being kept on short commons that we decided to write and complain to the Mayor. The letter was signed by all the seniors, and I was chosen to deliver it. When I got back, I found the superintendent waiting for me: he raved and cursed and threatened me with his revolver. But the Mayor investigated our complaints and in the end, the superintendent was dismissed.

I spent three years in the reformatory—three years of hell. We longed for a smoke, and we used to save a slice or two of our bread ration to swap with the *contadini* for one of their homemade fags. We had a long walk to school; people would look at us as we marched along and say: "Poor little devils—come on, let's give them a bit of bread and a drop of wine." As I could read a bit, I was put in the third class; I'd already started to shave, and I looked like the father of all the little country kids who were mixed up in the classroom with us. I still remember my first day at school. The master chalked a triangle on the blackboard and said: "To find the area of a triangle, multiply the base by the height and bisect the answer." He fixed me with an eye, and asked: "You, boy—do you understand?" "Yes, sir," I said, though I hadn't the faintest idea of what he was talking about. After geometry, we had dictation: "Oh pony trot—comma"—"comma," I wrote, and "You were good but you could not talk—full stop" and I wrote "full stop."

By the time I got into the sixth class, I was eighteen. I'd been put to work in the flower-garden which was close to the school; one day, I was caught kissing the Mayor's daughter amongst the bushes, and I was expelled on the spot. So there I was, left to face the world without a trade. What sense was there in teaching me, a city chap, country stuff? I ask you—did they expect me to grow gherkins in St. Peter's Square?

The Tribunal found a foster home for me in Rome; I lived there for three years, and during that time, I learnt the barber's trade. I hadn't forgotten my old friends, but I wanted to make a new life for myself. Then, although I begged to be allowed to stay with my mother by adoption, the Rome police transferred me to Palermo. The Palermo police, who didn't know what to do with me, finally solved the problem by exiling me for two years on the island of Pantelleria.[3]

I shan't dwell on the unspeakable corruption to which I was exposed on the island. Was that the way to make a decent human being of a chap—was that the way? Let me give you just a faint idea of what went on there. It was the regular thing for the village kids to come along to us and say: "Toss you off for a lira." Even to tell you about it makes me feel ashamed. The brothel was out of bounds, and we were so sex-starved that one chap even became jealous of his pet bitch. If I hadn't been through it, I'd never have believed that such things were possible. And this was what the authorities were pleased to call a centre for moral rehabilitation!

When I left Pantelleria, I was twenty-two. I was called up for military service, but was rejected because of my conjunctivitis. I went straight back to Rome, and started to work as a barber. I got customers, attended them at their houses, made new friends, and lived a normal life. I'd reached a point when I knew I must break with my past once and for all; I wanted a family of my own, I wanted, not only love, but responsibility. If a man doesn't feel the need for responsibility, where will he end up?

Gradually, I grew more and more homesick for the city where I'd spent my childhood, and so I went back to Palermo. But how

---

[3] Exile—i.e., *confino,* a means of getting rid of unwanted persons originated by the Fascists. The exiles were free to go where they liked within certain limits, but had to report morning and evening to the police. *Trans. note.*

different things were for me now that I'd become a respectable citizen and earned an honest living as a barber; now I could enjoy a drink in the Caffe delle Rose and saunter about at ease under the clock of the Massimo Theatre, the favourite rendezvous of the smart set. When I walked through the Capo, the miserable quarter where I'd been born, I felt like a stranger. Sometimes, I'd meet one of my former pals. "Listen," I'd say. "You'll pay dearly in the end for the easy money you make. I used to lie awake, trembling at the very thought of Sciabbica, but that's over and done with—I'm going straight now, and when I go to bed at night, I sleep soundly till morning." I hadn't yet solved the problem of my future, though; I was still too exhausted with all I'd been through to see things clearly, to make any kind of constructive plans.

I met a girl, fell in love with her and got engaged; I was desperately keen to get married, but I only made just enough to live on—I couldn't put anything by. At last, I asked a friend if he knew of any job that was going which would bring in a bit more; he said there might be one in a cement factory and promised to put in a word for me in the right quarter. The "right quarter" was a paralysed old rascal, an ex-*pezzo di novanta*,[4] who had the last word on which chaps were hired and which were fired. I got taken on, but the work was far too heavy for me; I toiled like a beast of burden, stoking up the furnace and carting loads of baked bricks about on a huge iron shovel. I simply hadn't the strength for it, and three, four, or five times a day I'd go to the bog, so that I could get a breather. It reached the ears of the *pezzo di novanta*, of course: "We've no use for lazy buggers like you," I was told, and was promptly given the sack.

I did everything I could think of to earn the money I had to have before we could get married. I worked on commission, trying to get orders for wax figurines, materials, watches, etc., I made a few lire as a *spiccia*, and did a bit of ladies' hairdressing, about which I'd learnt a little. But try as I would, I still couldn't make enough to put anything by—there seemed no way out. "Never mind the money, Gino—let's get married," my girl urged me. "Two can live as cheaply as one, and

---

[4] *Pezzo di novanta*—a heavy cannon—thieves' slang for master-thief. These criminal types are the paid "bullies" of the Mafia which controls labour in industry. They see to it that the protection money extorted from the employers is paid over, as well as collecting from the wretched workers, who grease their palms in the hope of getting hired or in their anxiety not to lose the job they are holding. *Trans. note.*

we'll be free to love each other." I wouldn't hear of it, though. "It's no use going on, then," she said at last. "We'd better break it off." But I couldn't bear to think that all the sacrifices I'd made were in vain, so I asked her if she'd leave Palermo and come away with me. "Yes, Gino," she said. People who knew us both thought she was crazy. "Poor girl—she must be out of her mind," they said. "Fancy running away with a chap who's got no work and who can't possibly keep her."

We went to Rome, and my mother by adoption who'd shown me the only kindness I'd ever known, took us both in; what little she had, she shared with us. So my girl and I got married; there was no show, no nothing, it was just the usual wedding of poor lovers. Not long afterwards, my wife fell ill, and had to go to hospital. I couldn't find a job, and things went from bad to worse for me; often and often, I went hungry to bed. But what I minded most was having to go empty-handed to the hospital to visit my wife. It made me bitterly ashamed of myself— I felt I wasn't a real man, a proper husband. What a red-letter day it was for me when I was able to take her an orange. An orange—what's an orange, you'll say. To me it was everything.

I felt desperately alone. I went from barber's shop to barber's shop in the hope of being taken on but I had no luck. I reached such a pitch that I was tempted to look up my former pals and go back to work with them; it was only the fear that I might lose my wife if I returned to that sort of life that held me back. One day, I ran accidently into one of my old pickpocketing chums who gave me five lire. I bought a present for my wife, and a bit of food for myself— I made it last out for two days. I tramped the streets looking for work in vain, and at last, in despair, I told myself there was no help for it— there was only one way out and I'd have to take it. I *would* have taken it if my mother by adoption hadn't guessed my thoughts. "Gino," she said, as I sat brooding over the bowl of *minestra* she'd set before me, "don't do anything stupid. Remember you've got a wife now—she's only a girl, you've got to look after her. I know what's in your mind, I know it seems the only thing you can do—but you mustn't do it." Her words comforted me and calmed me down—maybe they brought me luck, too, for a few days later, I was taken on by a Neapolitan barber. He paid me 25 lire a week, and allowed me to keep whatever tips the customers gave me; if he hadn't, he'd have had to pay me a weekly wage of 35 lire. Work—I'd found work at last, and I was happy.

When my wife left hospital, we went to live with a cousin of mine in the Marinella. I paid regular visits to my adopted mother, and now that I was earning a bit, did what I could to help her. Her husband had been an outside railway porter and those of his mates who were still working clubbed together and gave him a percentage of their takings. But it didn't amount to much, and he couldn't afford to buy himself a glass of wine or a cigar. I knew how much he craved for them, and was always glad when I had enough to treat him to these small pleasures. Sometimes, his wife would go for him hammer and tongs because he'd keep a few soldi for himself, and then I'd step in and do my best to restore the peace. He was seventy, poor old chap, and if he did tell a few lies over the money—well, you couldn't blame him. He could only buy himself one pipeful of tobacco a week; when he'd smoked it, he used to scrape out the dottle and chew it just to get a taste of the real thing. On Saturday nights, he'd come home a bit tight and rub his damp moustache fondly against my cheek. "Poor boy," he'd say, "poor boy. . . ."

We had a row with my cousin, and decided that we'd leave Rome. So we packed up and came back to Palermo.

I knew my father by sight because people had pointed him out to me, but I'd never exchanged a word with him. I was on speaking terms with my grandfather, though, and when I met him in the street, I used to beg a few soldi from him. I'd saved a little money in Rome, but not much, and as I had no job, and all my wife and I possessed in the world was a bit of household linen, I finally forced myself to go to my father. As we were strangers to one another, I'd no natural affection for him, I couldn't even feel that he *was* my father. He said we could come and live with him, but when we arrived, we didn't get what you could call a warm welcome from his wife. It was plain that she didn't want us, but she had to put up with us just the same—she couldn't go against her husband's orders.

My father had fallen on very hard times. He'd been fired from the Council because he was a constitutional Socialist; he hadn't been able to find another job and was on his beam-ends. When we moved in, I became the provider—out of my savings, I bought food for the whole household. Father had been driven into becoming a *spiccia*—it was lucky for him that he had friends at the Town Hall.

There's one particular evening that stands out in my memory. I'd been out, and the moment I got back, my step-sisters came to me crying with hunger; there wasn't a bite to eat in the place. "Papa's got some money, Gino," one of them said, "but he won't buy us any food." "We'll see about that," I said, so off I went in search of him. Well, I found him, and asked him straight out if it was true. "I've got a few lire in my pocket, Gino," he said, "but they don't belong to me —a client gave them to me to get him some papers he needs." I was amazed at his honesty, for I was well aware that most of the *spicciafaccende* in Palermo are crooks. They'll double-cross anyone; not only that, they're hand-in-glove with certain officials, and are quite prepared, if need be, to supply customers with false papers, documents, etc.

We only stayed for a very short time with my father. His wife was determined to get rid of us by hook or by crook, and what do you think she did? At night, as we lay on our mattresses on the floor, she used to chuck pebbles at us to make us believe the house was haunted! One night, my wife got up to go to the lavatory. "G-gino, are there gh-ghosts in this place?" she asked, her teeth chattering with fright. The "ghosts" had just pelted her with stones. But two could play at that game. Close to the bed where my father and stepmother slept, there was a tiny altar on which stood a lighted candle; the next time the pebbles came flying, I picked up a shoe, chucked it straight at the candle and put it out. "The ghosts! The ghosts!" I shrieked, then, wrapping myself in a sheet, I rushed over to the bed, and gave my dear stepmother a sound box on the ears! In the morning, I listened with a perfectly straight face while she told me of the fearful goings-on. "I saw it as plainly as I see you, Gino," she said. "A ghost— all in white, it was, and—" "A ghost!" I burst out. "I won't spend another night in a haunted house! Thanks very much—I'm off!"

So we moved out and I rented a barber's shop. You've no idea how careful a barber has to be not to give his customers the slightest cause for offence—for a mere trifle, they'll walk out on him and never come back. Many a time, I lost a customer simply because I hadn't helped him into his overcoat or straightened his jacket to his liking. Believe me, if you leave a single hair on a man's chin or don't bow to him as low as the barber next door, that's the last you'll see of him. Flattery's the barber's stock-in-trade. When a new customer came in to open an account, you should have heard me! "What is your honoured name, sir?" or: "Would you be good enough to give me your name, Your

Excellency?" I'd say obsequiously, poising my pencil over my book. If you're a barber's assistant, you work very long hours; one barber I worked for in Rome did at least stick to a timetable, but another chap, a Neapolitan, wouldn't put up his shutters before his rival across the way had closed his; often, I didn't get home till ten o'clock at night.

In my father's house, I'd noticed the photograph of a smartly dressed girl, and one day I asked him who she was. "Your sister," he said, "your real sister—your mother's daughter and mine. She's seven years older than you." You can imagine my surprise. He told me she was living with an uncle, and I thought I'd like to get acquainted with her, so I wrote her a letter and said I had a message for her from another uncle who lived in Rome. This was just a story I'd cooked up, of course, as I couldn't be sure she'd be willing to see me; people are so anxious to keep up appearances, to be thought "respectable" that they'll hide their natural feelings, deny their own flesh and blood, as well I knew. If only my father had had the guts to say "that's my son," as Mother did when I was born, mine would have been a very different story. But to go back. An answer came from my sister to say she couldn't very well invite me to her uncle's house, but that she'd arranged for us to meet at a cousin's place. Well, I went along, the cousin introduced us to each other, and left us alone. We sat down on the sofa in dead silence. After a minute or two, I began to fidget impatiently: was she waiting for me to speak, or was I to wait till she opened her mouth? At last, I plucked up courage, and broke the ice. "Why do you live with Uncle and not with Father?" I asked. "Uncle hasn't any children of his own," she said. "I've become a daughter to him—he loves me dearly, helps me with my studies, does everything for me. But tell me: where have you been all this time? Papa told me I had a brother—why haven't you been to see me before?"

"I didn't even know I had a sister till the other day," I said.

Then she began to ask me all sorts of questions: what school had I been to, was I a Catholic, was I a Fascist? (this was during the Fascist régime). I told her I hadn't got beyond the sixth elementary class, and that I'd never bothered my head about religion or politics. "What! You're *not* a Catholic, *not* a Fascist!" she exclaimed in a shocked voice, and promptly gave me a lecture on both subjects. She'd graduated in literature, and she was still more taken aback when I said: "My dear sister, if I'd had the same education as you, no doubt, with a bit of luck, I'd have graduated, too, and become both Catholic and Fascist into the bargain!"

I couldn't summon up a grain of brotherly affection for her. They talk of the call of the blood, but hers certainly didn't call to mine. Before I left, we agreed to see more of each other, but I really didn't care whether we did nor not.

However, we did meet again. One evening, she asked me to go with her to the Fascist HQ in the Piazza Bologni as she had to renew her party card. As we were on the way, she said. "If you see a short young man coming towards me, would you mind leaving me? He's my fiancé, and—well—he might be jealous. . . ." Although she didn't come straight out with it, it was plain what she meant: she didn't want anyone to know we were brother and sister.

That was the end of it as far as I was concerned. I left her abruptly, and it wasn't till years later, after the war, that I saw her again. We met at father's funeral; she was married, by this time, and I'd become a Communist. For a while, we were quite friendly, and I often went to her house. Then, one Christmas Day, when I'd turned up for dinner, there was a ring at the door. "It must be some of my in-laws— hide, Gino, don't let them see you," she said. I cleared out without a word, and never set foot in her place again.

It was mainly on account of all the misery and hardship I'd been through that I became a Communist. To me, Communism meant a new life for mankind, it meant work for all, salvation for all; it meant a world in which there'd be no need for a Sciabbica since no one would be driven to steal any more—there'd be no light-fingered gentry left, except kleptos. A world where men could live as men—that's what Communism stood for to me. Let me tell you how I became a member of the Party.

After the American forces had occupied Sicily, we all existed by dealing in the Black Market. I sold contraband cigarettes in my shop which I got direct from a customs guard, and as every barber in Palermo was doing the very same thing, I had no scruples about it. With the money I made in this way, I was able to buy food for my family. But all over the city, people were starving. The sight of so much misery, the awful injustice of it, stirred me to such a state of anger that at last I resolved I must try to do something about it. So I shut myself in the room at the back of the shop, and after much thought, wrote a manifesto which ended with the words: "Long live Stalin! Long live Roosevelt! Long live Italian Communism!" I scraped up enough money to have a number of copies printed, rallied some friends together and formed the Anti-Fascist Action Party. We plastered the walls with this manifesto of mine, and handed it to passersby in the crowded streets in the centre of the city.

One day, while I was busy in my shop, a gleaming American car drew up outside. "An important customer," I thought, and asked my wife to fetch me a clean towel. The next moment, in strode a party of US officers who told me curtly that they'd come to arrest me for disobeying General Alexander's directive. "Haven't you read it?" they demanded. "Don't tell us you didn't know what his orders were." But I didn't know what they were, all I knew was that people were dying of hunger. I was tried by the Military Tribunal and sentenced to a year's imprisonment, but this sentence was quashed.

Shortly after this, I received a visit from a schoolteacher who'd heard about my manifesto; he invited me to attend a Socialist meeting with him. As all political meetings were strictly banned, this was held in secret. I went to a few more meetings with him, and at one of them a certain resolution was put to the vote. I was against it, and was so outspoken that I was severely reprimanded. I'd applied for membership, but I'd grown heartily sick of the Socialist Party's jaw-jaw-jaw—it was deeds, not words, I wanted.

When the ban on political meetings was lifted, I started to attend them once more. I became active on my own account, and rallied a mass demonstration of barbers. On the day on which it was held, a Communist came up to me and said: "Why don't you join the Party?" This was in 1943 when anyone who wished to join the C.P. was free to do so. As soon as I got my party card, I was made responsible for a cell in my street, and a bit later on, was promoted to leader of a section. I read all the literature eagerly, not only because it helped me to understand the doctrine of the Party but because I'd always had a thirst for knowledge. I got up a workers' study group, and we began with Marx. I sweated over his dialectical materialism for months before I could get the full meaning of it into my head. We followed Marx with Gramsci's *La Città del Socialismo*, from which I learnt an enormous amount. It taught me, for instance, that society can be likened to a train made up of obsolete, dilapidated coaches drawn by a streamlined, bang-up-to-date engine. Each coach stands for a system of government that's been tried in the past, and each has its own characteristics, its own weaknesses. The journey's frightfully difficult and slow because now a door'll come unhinged, now a screw will work loose in one of the coaches; the driver has to stop, and the passengers have to join forces to put things right. When, thanks to their united efforts, the damage has been repaired, the train moves off again, and so, little by little, it draws nearer to its destination, the city where all men are equal. . . .

Well, I acquired a Marxist culture, and at the same time, went on working in my shop. But a barber can't make much in Palermo, and as I now had four children, I was badly in need of some other job which would help me to make ends meet. One day, a comrade who'd had a decent education, said to me, "Why don't you see the secretary of the Agricultural Workers' Federation?" I took his advice, and enrolled for the political correspondence course which the Party had recently started.

I took tremendous pains to learn and worked hard at my books; I realized that the more I knew, the more use I would be to the Party. "Learn all you can; the revolution is a revolution of men. The revolutionary movement needs new and responsible leaders." These words of Gramsci's had become my guiding light. I sat up to all hours of the night, and to save electricity studied by candlelight. But in my eagerness to go ahead, I drove myself much too hard; although I didn't realize it, I was on the edge of a breakdown. I grew more and more depressed. I told myself it was hopeless, that I was no good, that I should never get anywhere. Finally I wrote to the joint heads of the correspondence school in Rome to ask them whether they thought there was any use in my going on with the course; I was beginning to doubt, I added, that the revolution would take place in my lifetime. Nothing could have encouraged me more than the reply I received: "To continue studying in such difficult conditions as yours is a positive gain in itself," it ran. "As for the revolution, bear in mind that history cannot be measured by the span of a man's life." I pulled myself together, persevered, took the examination, and when the results came out was congratulated on having done remarkably well— I had passed sixteenth out of 4,000. From this time on, I worked on the committee of the Party, and became jointly responsible with the other members for all problems concerning agricultural workers.

The first time I was sent to address a meeting of peasants, there were looks of disappointment when I entered the gaily decorated hall. "We were expecting Comrade P., not you," I was told. Comrade P. was the party leader. They'd evidently made a fabled figure of him, and this was all wrong, so I did my best to impress on my audience that, in the class struggle, all men are equal, that it's the masses that count, not the individual. The individual must be subordinated to the masses, I said, above all, the individual who is incapable of understanding and furthering their interests. When I sat down, the warmth of the applause more than made up for the coolness of my reception; I went home full of joy knowing that, although I still couldn't express myself in technical terms, I'd succeeded in speaking straight from the heart to those who were struggling for the right to live—I'd succeeded because I'd made their struggle my own. In the past, I'd only fought for one person: myself. Now I'd learnt to identify myself with the cause of others, and so I'd taken the first step on the road to redemption.

In 1949, I was sent to Mantua to attend the National Congress of Agricultural Workers. It was then that I realized with a great thrill of happiness that the Sicilian peasants who were getting ready to take possession of the land, far from being alone in their struggle, had the full support of all the workers in Italy. I shall never forget the country woman from Lecce who sprang on to the platform, excused herself for not being able to speak Italian, and exclaimed in her patois: "As long as they won't give us land, as long as my children have to go barefoot, I'll fight side by side with my comrades. I'll never give up the fight— despite all the blows of the police!" I was so moved by her passionate sincerity that the tears came into my eyes.

Shortly after my return from Mantua, I was sent to Marineo where the struggle for the occupation of the land was in full swing. I had been chosen to replace a comrade who had proved himself incompetent to deal with the situation. On the morning following my arrival, I led the peasants onto the fief; it was then that I learnt a hard lesson, learnt that theory and practice are by no means the same thing. The night before, I had talked to the *contadini* about the *kholkozes* and they'd listened attentively when I said that, following the Russian example, we'd cultivate the fief collectively. The moment they set foot on the land, however, they forgot every single word I'd said, and rushed feverishly about, marking off plots for themselves by pegging out mule reins or piling up stones. They were exactly like passengers scrambling on to a train and reserving seats for themselves by dumping down newspapers and suitcases. I was completely taken aback. "This is all wrong, you know," I said to one man. "Excuse me, Comrade Gino," he said, "but I look at it like this. I've got a mule, my neighbour hasn't, so it stands to reason my crop'll be twice as heavy as his. It's only right, then, isn't it, that I should have my own bit of land."

But I've gone ahead too fast, I must go back to the evening of my arrival in Marineo. It had been agreed that the fief should be occupied in the morning, and we leaders had taken the greatest care to make the *contadini* feel that they were organizing the whole thing, that we were only there to help them in any way we could and to make sure that their plan succeeded. As soon as we had fixed on the meeting-place where we were all to assemble at daybreak, the meeting broke up. Morning came, and we leaders were the first to arrive, but in a few minutes, we were joined by a crowd of *contadini*, some of them carrying hoes, others leading mules. It was still dark when we started for the fief; men, women and children marched along chattering as gaily about the coming harvest as if the land was already theirs. It was deeply moving to see these peasants who'd already played their parts in the war of liberation setting forth to fight another war which they themselves had planned. They pressed round me eagerly, their faces alight with hope, but for all our excitement, we didn't forget to keep a sharp look-out for the *carabinieri*.

At last, we came in sight of the fief. It stretched out in front of us like a vast sea—I don't know how many hectares there were. Wherever we looked, there was only earth and sky. The few kilometres that separated us from it seemed endless, we felt as though we should never get there. Just before we reached our goal, we came to a knoll, and there we called a halt. It was quite possible that one or two *mafiosi* might be lurking about on the look-out for us, and we wondered which would be the wiser course: to occupy the land *en masse* or to break up into groups of four. But while we were discussing it, the local party leader made up his mind, and strode on to the fief. Anxious for his safety, we all followed.

Well, as I've told you already, the peasants instantly started to mark off their plots. The land was uncultivated, but to prevent it from being expropriated, the owner who knew what was in the wind had

had it ploughed up within the last few days. The *contadini* promptly began to break up the clods and fill in the furrows.

Presently, we broke off for a much-needed rest. Families clustered together and sat down to eat the bread they'd brought with them—a few had a little wine.

Earlier on, we'd caught sight of a man in the distance, dressed in Mafia style: riding-breeches, jacket, top boots and felt hat:

> *Silk hat, felt hat, you asked me here to meet you,*
> *I got your invitation and here I am to greet you!*

says the song, and I'd gone to meet *him*. He had a rifle on his shoulder. "What have you come for? What are you lot up to?" he asked. 'We're taking possession of the land under the Segni-Gullo law,'[5] I told him. I was careful to speak civilly, for I knew it was dangerous to cross him—anger this type of man, and he'll snipe at you under cover of a convenient fig-tree: ping! and you've had it! After I'd talked to this particular chap for a while, he took himself off.

Towards evening, there was a heavy downpour of rain. I found shelter in a nearby cottage, and waited there until my clothes had been dried off in the oven. The peasants called it a day, and started to walk back to the village; all but two of them who couldn't tear themselves away from the land. As soon as the rest had gone, the *carabinieri* who'd laid low while the whole crowd of them were there, came along and arrested the unfortunate pair.

I can't tell you what happened after that in Marineo, because that same evening I was ordered to go to Montelepre, and as I was arrested and imprisoned as a result of what took place there, I never learnt the rest of that particular story. The *contadini* of Montelepre, Cinisi, Carini, Partinico and Terrasini were agitating for the expropriation of the Piano degli Aranci fief, and my role was to find out exactly what the situation was in these villages. I was to have addressed an open-air meeting in the piazza at Carini, but as it was the local saint's day, and the celebrations were being staged there, it had to be held in the *Camera del Lavoro*[6] which was packed. Squads of *carabinieri* had

---

[5] Under this law, all uncultivated land was to be given to the peasants or the peasants' co-operatives. Signor Gullo, a Communist, and Signor Segni, a Christian Democrat, were in office for a term as Minister of Agriculture during the period 1946–50. *Trans. note.*

[6] Communist Trades Union—local HQ. *Trans. note.*

been posted outside the building and in all the nearby alleys; amongst them were militiamen of the C.F.R.B.[7] It was plain that the authorities were determined to do all they could to prevent us from occupying the fief. When the meeting was over, I left Carini, spent a short time in Terrasini and Partinico, and went on to Montelepre. I'd never seen so many radiant faces; the peasants were aglow at the thought that at long last their cherished dream was about to come true—that dream of an earthly paradise, a bit of land of their own. My own feelings at the sight of so many happy faces are indescribable —I can't put them into words.

At this particular time, the exploits of Giuliano[8] had made the little village of Montelepre the focus of world interest; here I was, in the very heart of the bandit country. The bandits held no terrors for me, but I confess that I couldn't help thinking from time to time about the thirty-six leaders of the Peasants Union who'd been murdered in different parts of Sicily, shot down by unseen assassins, literally riddled with lead. In spite of this, however, I often forsook caution. On one occasion, for instance, I had to go to Carini; a peasant from Montelepre came with me, and instead of sticking to the road, we took short cuts through the fields. I didn't follow the beaten track, either, when I walked to Partinico and back—I went across country, and ran the same risks. You know what risks I mean, I take it. I don't mind telling you that I was far more scared during those short walks than I had been at any time during the war. It's not so bad when you know where the enemy is, but the thought that a sniper may be lurking behind the cover of a fig-tree ready to pick you off is by no means pleasant.

One evening, I was addressing a meeting in the *Camera di Lavoro* in Montelepre when a *carabiniere* came in, said the sergeant wished to speak to me, and asked me to go along to the barracks. "Tell your sergeant I'll be there as soon as the meeting's over," I said. When we broke up, twenty peasants insisted on coming with me. The sergeant who was expecting me didn't seem at all perturbed. "I'm sorry to have put you to this trouble," he said, "but this is a danger zone on account

---

[7] C.F.R.B.—Comande Forze Repressione Banditismo—the special militia drafted to deal with the bandits. *Trans. note.*

[8] The most famous Sicilian bandit of the century. After a spectacular reign of seven years, he was killed by the police in 1950—he was then only twenty-seven. The full story of Giuliano is told in *God Protect Me From My Friends*, by Gavin Maxwell (Longmans). *Trans. note.*

of the bandits, and we have to have particulars of any strangers who come here; we want to know who they are and what they're doing in Montelepre. You, for instance—what's brought you to these parts? I've nothing against the *Camera di Lavoro*, I may say—I'm a working man myself. What's more, when I was in Turin, I made the acquaintance of Signora Togliatti—what do you think of that, eh?"

He kept me for some time, but when I left the barracks, all twenty of the peasants were still there, patiently waiting for me outside.

It was while I was in Montelepre that I realized that few of the *contadini* had any idea of the real purpose of their Union. They regarded it simply as an organization to which they could turn for help; hardly any of them grasped the fact that our struggle was not only economic but political—that it had to be both political and economic if we were to achieve our goal: that of setting up an entirely new form of government in Italy.

I went to Carini to make arrangements for the occupation of the fief. The entire district was swarming with *carabinieri*, and we had to try and think of how we could reach it without getting ourselves arrested. Plainly, we couldn't all go in a body, it would bring them down on us at once. For two hours on end, we leaders discussed ways and means in the *Camera di Lavoro*; I didn't know the locality but those who did suggested various side-roads and footpaths we might take to avoid being spotted immediately. At length, we decided to set out in groups of four or five, carrying hoes to make it seem that we were off to do a day's work in the fields. We were all to assemble at the Case Nuove; from there, with banners flying, we would make the stiff climb to Sagana, and from Sagana, we'd descend *en masse* to Piano degli Aranci and take possession of it.

Some of the leaders went off to the other villages to tell the *contadini* what we'd arranged. The rest of us spent the night in Carini, and as soon as it was beginning to get light, we dressed, and went from house to house, knocking at every door. "Wake up! We're going to start for the fief!" we called. "Land, land—who wants land?" In a very few minutes everyone was astir, and soon the first groups were on their way. We met a small detachment of *carabinieri*, but as we'd hoped, they took us for labourers off to do a day's hoeing. I suffered agonies scrambling up the rough paths—I was wounded in the leg during the war of liberation, and it gave me hell. Sometimes, I kept going by hanging on to the tail of a mule; once I just slid to the

ground, and had to rest there for a while before I could take another
step.

It was seven o'clock when those of us who'd started out first
reached the Case Nuove. One by one, the other groups arrived, and as
soon as we were all there, we hoisted our banners and began to ascend
to Sagana. We'd just reached the outskirts of the village when we saw
another band of peasants coming towards us with flags flying—it was
the contingent from Partinico.

We joined forces, hugged and embraced one another, and
marched on. But when we reached the tiny piazza, we saw it was
bristling with squads of *carabinieri* and C.F.R.B. An officer stepped
forward, and asked us why we had come. "We're going to occupy the
fief," we said straight out, and he immediately began to threaten us in
the hope we'd turn back. "It's against the law—do you want to land
yourselves in prison?" he blustered. Meanwhile, the sergeant had gone
up to a group of standard bearers, one of whom was carrying the Red
Flag. "Down with it! We're not Communists here!" he roared. It was
a very nasty moment; in Bisacquino, a refusal to lower the Red Flag
had ended up with shooting, and a number of villagers and *carabinieri*
had been wounded.

We were told to stack our banners against the wall; however, we
were allowed to leave them unfurled. If they thought the sight of
their machine-guns would scare us, they were wrong. The officer went
on talking to us—although we didn't know it, he was playing for time.
He told us that at that very minute the Prefect was in Montelepre
assuring the peasants that there was no need for them to occupy the
fief as it was to be expropriated immediately.

While we were waiting for our comrades from Montelepre to
arrive, we played cards to pass away the time. But after we'd waited
for I don't know how long, someone—I don't know who—said:
"Come on—don't let's hang round here any longer—let's go and
occupy the fief." We decided that the best thing to do was to send a
messenger to Montelepre to find out what was happening there; he'd
been gone a goodish while when we caught sight of figures in the
distance coming towards us. There were shouts of "The comrades!
Here they come!" but as they drew nearer, we saw the glitter of gold
braid and the glint of steel. Comrades! The advancing figures were
those of *carabinieri*, armed to the teeth!

Bandits—that's what we were to them and the C.F.R.B. Quite likely, the real bandits were watching the scene through fieldglasses from their mountain top eyrie, and splitting their sides at the joke!

The *carabinieri* rounded up us leaders and made us march into the great courtyard where the prison stood in the time of the Bourbons. The sergeant seated himself at a table, and ordered us to line up so that he could see which men came from which village. I stood apart from the rest. "You there—which village do you belong to?" he demanded. "I'm one of the Union leaders," I said. "I don't belong to any one village—I belong to them all." The sergeant then took down our surnames, our Christian names, our parents' names, and called us to attention. "Now, you lot, we know who you are. I warn you, we shall keep an eye on you in future, so I'd advise you to watch your step —if we catch you again, so much the worse for you." After this, we were marched out of the courtyard and into the piazza where we were ordered to halt outside the police-station: it was the turn of the officer in-charge to have his say: "You'd better be careful," he began. "If you break the law—" but we cut him short. "It's not your business to hold a meeting—stick to your job as a cop!" we yelled. The peasants had been told to disperse, but as the *carabinieri* were still holding us, their leaders, and were making no move to let us go, they stayed where they were. The *carabinieri* trained their machine-guns on the crowd. "Break it up!" they shouted, "Clear off—go home!" We wanted to avoid bloodshed at all costs, so we told them to obey. We leaders were hustled from the piazza to the road where a couple of lorries were drawn up. Just as we reached them, a car came along, and one of the *carabinieri* officers saluted smartly—the passenger inside it must have been the Prefect. We were then made to get into the lorries, and were driven off to the barracks.

In the meantime, however, the messenger we'd sent to Montelepre had got back to Sagana. He'd found the village surrounded by *carabinieri*—that was why our comrades hadn't been able to join us. He was a North Italian, a formidable type, who didn't care two hoots for the police. "Come on, all of you," he shouted. "Follow me. We'll occupy the fief, and to hell with the cops!"

When we arrived at the barracks, and the officer in charge learnt that, leaders or no leaders, the *contadini* had marched off to seize the land, we were immediately driven to Palermo, and consigned to the

Ucciardone, the prison where the bandit Pisciotta[9] was given a cup of poisoned coffee to drink and died in agonies. Here, we were formally charged with having incited the peasants to take unlawful possession of the fief.

Four of us were jammed into a cell barely large enough for two; there was hardly room for us to turn. What with the rancid soup they gave us and the pot which we had for a lavatory—well, you can imagine the stink. I made as much as I could of this "holiday," though, and spent the time teaching myself more about social problems. At the end of six months, I was released. I went back to Sagana where I helped some comrades to found a Communist cell, and we succeeded in getting a few more men to join the Party. I then returned to Palermo, and resumed my activities with the Agricultural Workers' Federation.

On the occasion of Eisenhower's visit of inspection to the Allied troops in Italy, the Sicilians organized a "Stop the War" demonstration. I was amongst the crowd in the Piazza Massimo when an incident occurred; I saw a woman struggling in the grip of the police who were hauling her into the van despite the protests of Deputy Colajanni, the representative of the Regional Assembly of Sicily. Those who couldn't see what was happening thought it was Colajanni who was being arrested. Shouts arose of "Long live Sicily! Long live the Sicilian Assembly!" and in a second, pandemonium broke loose. The *Celere*[10] instantly went into action, and one of them grabbed hold of me by the collar. "Let me go—can't you see I'm a disabled soldier?" I said, and tapped my badge. Actually, as I've been in prison I'm not allowed to wear it, but as I've a right to it, I pin it on just for the hell of the thing. I get a war pension from the State, but as I've done time, the Disabled Soldiers' Association won't give me a membership card. Quite likely, they'll have the gall to get my pension stopped for having told you this—we'll see. But to go back. I struggled to free myself but the *Celere* cracked me over the head with their rifle-butts, dragged me into the van and drove me off to the Faletta prison where they'd already taken a number of men and

[9] Giuliano's cousin. He was poisoned with strychnine. Eight more of Giuliano's company of bandits were poisoned in the Ucciardone—one died, the rest recovered. *Trans. note.*

[10] No English equivalent. The *Celere* are similar to the *Garde Mobile*—they are armed riot squads who are rushed up in jeeps to disperse crowds. The occasion when the Communists hold their annual rally is a field-day for the *Celere. Trans. note.*

women they'd arrested in the Piana dei Greci, which commemorates
the name of Damiono Lo Greco, a peasant who was shot and killed
while he, too, was demonstrating for peace. I spent eleven days in my
cell in the Faletta before I was brought before the Commission which
dealt with those who hadn't been previously convicted of a political
offence. It was then that I realized the value of *Unità*; although I was
shut away, it kept me in touch with everything that was happening
outside. In one issue, there was an article in the form of an open letter
signed by the leaders of the various party organizations and by several
deputies. To my great surprise, it was all about me. "Who is Gino
O.?" the letter began. Then followed the story of my life, the efforts
I'd made to lift myself out of the gutter, the success which had
crowned them, the way in which I'd redeemed myself by becoming
one of the leaders in the struggle for freedom and peace—it was all
there. If my comrades hadn't taken up my cause, helped and
supported me, I should undoubtedly have served a sentence of five
years.

When I was brought before the Commission, the Prefect asked me
what I'd been doing in the thick of the crowd, and deliberately flung
at me: "A good many wallets were stolen, you know." I felt
wretchedly ashamed and humiliated. The room I was in was richly
furnished—there was a couch covered in heavy velvet on which coats
had been strewn, and the air was redolent with the fragrance of
expensive cigarettes. The Prefect made a great deal of play over the
overcoat I was wearing. "Very smart, I must say—it must have
knocked you back a bit," he said sarcastically. It was American, of
course.[11]

I was put on probation for two years, which meant I had to report
regularly to the police and keep within certain limits, consequently I
couldn't carry on my political activities. I could hardly go to a police
sergeant and say: "Look here, I'm on probation, I'm not allowed to go
beyond such-and-such a street, but I'm off to the village of X. to hold
a political meeting," could I now?

Although I was quite useless for these two years, the Party allowed
me to retain my membership card. I'm sure this was a gesture of
comradeship and support, to prevent me from losing heart and going

[11] Bales of second-hand clothes were then being sent from the USA to Sicily, where
they were sold by weight. *Trans. note.*

to the bad. But the police—I had struggled with all my might to escape from my past, and now—they began to do their utmost to push me downhill. They were trying to make me, as they tried to make all those who had to report to them regularly, turn nark.

They continually found some pretext for summoning me to the station. On one of these occasions, the Inspector, using "tu" to me as though I were a kid, although I was already the father of five children, asked:

"Have you ever been in prison?"

"No," I said.

"In that case, we'll quash the probation order," he said, but a day or two later, he sent for me again. My dossier lay open on his desk.

"So you've never been in prison, eh?" he said.

"I thought you were asking me if I'd ever been imprisoned for a political offence, Your Excellency," I answered.

His manner changed, and he became quite paternal.

"Listen to me, my boy, keep your nose out of politics," he said. "Politics aren't your affair. Stick to your own line—find yourself a job."

"What sort of job, your Excellency?"

"Take out a hawker's licence, or—"

"But I can't take out a licence—you won't let me take one out as I've got a record."

"Well, really! You make me tired! Can you wonder at it that we have to keep chaps like you under special surveillance? Now, if you'd only try to live decently, and come along if you get to hear of anything interesting—come along to me personally, mind—not a word to anyone else," and he looked at me meaningly.

I understood, of course, but I'd have died rather than become a *cioccolattaro*, which is what we call a squealer, a nark, in Palermo.

The *cioccolattari* work in gangs of four or five; all of them have police records. They run a lottery which is a regular swindle. First, they buy about four hundred chocolates, then they make holes in some of them, and insert tiny slips of paper with numbers on them, the lowest being 10, the highest 5,000. The chocolates are then wrapped up, and the foil of those containing the high numbers is marked with minute dots so that the *cioccolattari* know them. The numbers represent lire—that's to say, if you buy a chocolate which happens to contain a slip with the figure 10, then they pay you 10 lire

The photograph of "the real Gino O" is included as a systematic shock to the reader, a shock inherent in all border-crossings.

The narrative component of photographs, drawings, paintings, sculpted friezes and capitals, stained-glass windows, panoramas, and what have you depends to a degree on the subdual of their self-interest, the creation of artificial space, by the modest aim of underlining particular moments in the artful time schemes of narration. Whether it is a picture of Gino O cutting hair in Palermo or of the figures generated out of Miss Fitzgerald's elliptical lines of force, the reader's knowledge of the stories and the conventions of iconography are solicited. If the greatest pleasures of space arts lie elsewhere, this scarcely occurred to artists before the twentieth century.

—they don't mind paying out small sums, but they take good care to see that the chocolates with the slips from 1,000 and upwards go to their confederates.

To attract a crowd, the *cioccolattari* clown about, deal one another resounding thwacks, and perform conjuring tricks: they produce an egg from a hat, etc. Then the member of the gang who gets the most applause starts selling the chocolates. If business is slow, he's quickly replaced by the expert amongst them whose patter soon warms up the onlookers. Very occasionally, he slips up, and the 5,000 lire chocolate goes to one of the crowd. The winner passes up his slip in great excitement, but does he get his prize? Not a bit of it. The *cioccolattaro* drops it into his hat which has a false bottom, "5,000—did I hear someone say he handed me a slip for 5,000?" he shouts. "I'm afraid he's made a mistake. If you don't believe me, ladies and gentlemen, see for yourselves—there's nothing inside my hat!" And of course, there isn't!

There are about two hundred *cioccolattari* in Palermo. If they weren't narks, they wouldn't be allowed to run this lottery which is nothing but an American style of swindle—all lotteries, even if they're straight, all games of chance are strictly illegal. The *cioccolattari* also work the three-card trick: "Spot the lady! Now you win and now you lose!"

It's sheer necessity that governs the relationship between poor and rich—between the poor devils who eat one day and starve the next and the gentry they depend on, the gentry who'll look after them provided they toe the line. Take, for instance, the hawkers who sell tripe and lights; tripe and lights are hard to come by, and consequently, they regard the merchant from whom they get their supplies as God Almighty. If he closes down on them, they've had it. He's a tin-pot tyrant whose word is law as far as they're concerned, who forces them to vote for certain candidates; generally speaking, they don't give a damn for politics, poor wretches, all they're voting for is their livelihood. The petty despots who compel them to sell themselves—for that's what it amounts to—are *mafiosi* acting on orders from higher up. Talking of the Mafia, let me tell you about one of its favourite rackets. The shop of a tradesman who's paid his protection money is broken into and looted; his "protectors" assure him they'll comb the various quarters and recover his goods for him. Well, in due course, the goods are found and restored to him, whereupon, he has to

show his gratitude by providing the lolly for a blow-out—quite a lot of
lolly, too, because the "thieves" who ransacked his place have to be
given their cut!

Although I'm still working as a barber, I no longer have a shop. I've
six children to keep, and as the Party's short of funds, it can't afford to
pay me. I attend to my regular customers at their own houses, but the
trouble is there aren't enough of them. However, I'm well known by
sight, particularly in the Capo, and chaps when they see me coming
along with my bag bring out their chairs and a bowl of hot water, and
I shave them on their own doorsteps. In that way, I manage to make
ends meet.

But what makes life such a frightful strain on me is that every
morning, when I set out, I know that I've simply got to make so
much. While I'm at X.'s house busy shaving him, I'm already
thinking of the 50 lire I'll get when I've finished, and which, as often
as not, I don't get. "I'll pay you tomorrow," he'll say, and that does
for me—it happens time and again. If a customer falls ill, the chances
I have of getting the money he owes me are practically nil. I've been
married for sixteen years, and we still haven't been able to buy half
the household stuff we need. We used to live on the third floor of a
tumbledown house in a room that was four metres long by two metres
wide; all eight of us were jamed into it—you can imagine what it was
like. A few days ago, the house began to fall to pieces in good earnest,
and we and seventeen other families were moved out. They put us
into this classroom, but when the school opens in five days' time, we'll
have to shift—what'll become of us then I've no idea.

I get my unemployment card renewed every month. For nine years,
my name's been down at the Labour Exchange, and I've never had
the offer of a single day's work. What makes it worse is the fact that
I'm an ex-serviceman in receipt of a State pension, and there's a law
which makes it obligatory that all men who come into this category
should be found employment. I went along yesterday to get my card
renewed—for the umpteenth time, I had to go through the same old
routine. I handed my card to the clerk who has to cope with the work
of five or six men—he doesn't know whether he's coming or going,
poor devil, it's no wonder he flies out at you for the least little thing—
you've only to look at him to see he's a mass of nerves. He has my
sympathy—even the cops have my sympathy nowadays. When I was

a kid, they treated me as a menace, chased me and persecuted me without mercy, all because they hadn't a clue. I've gradually come to see that they're not to blame for the things they do—they're just another lot of workers exploited by the State. When I was a nipper, the very sight of one of them heading towards me was enough to petrify me; I reacted just like a rabbit caught in the headlights of an oncoming car. But now when I meet them, I feel sorry for them. Their mentality hasn't altered a jot, they haven't take a single step forward. They're still without a clue.

Where was I? Oh yes, the Labour Exchange. As usual, the confusion there was frightful. Everyone jostled and pushed everyone else—you felt as though at any minute, you'd be trampled underfoot. Let me try and picture the scene for you. A voice suddenly makes itself heard above the din.

"Quiet, please!" Silence falls, and the official begins to reel off a list of names. "Mazzola—Ganci—Di Maggio—"

"Present!"

"Present!"

"Di Maggio—where's Di Maggio?"

"Di Maggio's not here."

A voice: "Get out of the way, you!"

Another voice: "Who are you shoving? I was here first!"

Then everyone starts grumbling loudly: "It's a scandal, that's what it is! Is this what they call keeping order?"

A voice: "There's only one way to clean up this place—chuck a bomb into it!"

Another (warningly): "Shut up, or you'll get yourself arrested as you did yesterday."

There are women in the crowd as well as men. A young chap takes advantage of the confusion to put his hand up several skirts. He keeps one hand in his trouser pocket and enjoys a free feel with the other.

It begins to rain; the crowd that's waiting outside surges forward trying to get under cover, and as fast as anyone forces his way in, those inside promptly chuck him out again. "Keep back—keep back, can't you?" yells the cop on duty at the door.

But they won't keep back. A disabled man tries to elbow his way through.

"Your papers!" shouts the cop. "Where do you think you're going?"

An official appears.

"Minasola! Minasola!"

He vanishes, and the door closes. Inside, uproar breaks out. "Has my name been called yet?" "Please—my card—" "Come back tomorrow—" "But I'm ill—" "Well, what do you expect *me* to do about it?"

It isn't a Labour Exchange, it's a Tower of Babel. . . .

Sometimes, I think: "Here I am, forty-two, and what have I got to show for all those years? Nothing . . ." But then I tell myself that I have at least spent some of them trying to help others so that they wouldn't have to go through all that I did. I carry on because I must —for the sake of my family, for the sake of the Party which made a new man of me. Before I leave home in the morning, I nearly always pause by the little bed where two of my children are lying asleep, and I bend down and kiss the baby. I've given him the love which I never had. "Even a chap like me isn't altogether useless," I think. But if I were to let myself slip back. . . .

All the kicks and knocks I've taken have left me unsure of myself; they've given me what's called an inferiority complex and I've never got rid of it. Although I've learnt to look at life very differently, it's still there, deep down inside me, and when I've had to stand up for a democratic principle within the Party, it's come to the surface more than once. I'll give you an example. It happened shortly after the last election but one, when I was responsible for the organization of the provincial *Amici dell' Unità*. One day, I went into my office, and was surprised to find that my table with all my papers on it was no longer there; it had been shifted into the passage, close to the lavatory. I couldn't think why it should have been moved there, and when I discovered that it had been done on the order of one of the heads, I was overcome with a wave of depression; I couldn't struggle out of this slough of despond, I was tormented by doubts, and I kept on asking myself: "Am I a worthwhile human being or am I just a nothing?" A bit later, I was transferred to another section, but my black mood persisted and my work went from bad to worse. Finally, I was summoned into the presence of Comrade B. Instead of finding fault with me, he talked to me in such a friendly and understanding way that I regained confidence in myself. The knowledge that he— my leader—still believed in me and valued my work, gave me the feeling that I'd been reborn.

If I had to keep on and on fighting, measuring my strength against the men who surround me, hemmed in by what I see happening on all sides, I'd often lose heart, but there's one thought that sustains me. If you shake a bottle containing vinegar and oil, the vinegar and oil will mix, but let it stand for a minute, and the oil floats to the top. To me, the oil stands for the truth—and the truth, by the very nature of things, can't be kept down for ever—sooner or later it's bound to come to the surface.

It's because I'm so certain of this that, while I'm struggling to support my family, I'm able to continue fighting side by side with my comrades for the good of the community. If any matter involving the interests of one particular quarter or one particular family happens to arise, I'm always ready to be called on, always ready to take up the cause. Here, read this letter I've just received from a comrade:

I'm writing to thank you and all the other comrades for your kindness to me during the months when I was doing my military service in Palermo. I can't tell you how much it meant to me. Thank you, too, for helping me understand a bit more about politics—I'll put my new knowledge to good use, I promise you—and still more thanks for the marvellous farewell dinner—I'll never forget it. Thanks a million for all your friendliness and hospitality to me and my army chums. I'll always remember you, and when I'm old and I take my grandchildren on my knee, instead of telling them fairy stories, I'll tell them about my heroic friends in Palermo who fought to make a better, more progressive Sicily, a Sicily freed from the exploiters and oppressors who sucked at her very life-blood. Be sure, too, that I'll tell them of the brotherly hand you held out, not only to me, but to all the comrades of far away Emilia . . .

TRANSLATED BY P. D. CUMMINS

A BORING STORY

(From an Old Man's Notebook)

Anton Chekhov

I

There is in Russia an eminent professor, Nikolai Stepanovich, a privy councillor, who has been awarded many decorations in his lifetime; indeed, he possesses so many Russian and foreign orders that whenever he has to put them all on the students call him "the iconostasis." He moves in most distinguished circles—at least during the last twenty-five or thirty years there has not been a single famous scholar or scientist in Russia with whom he has not been intimately acquainted. There is no one now with whom he could be on friendly terms but, so far as the past is concerned, the long list of his eminent friends would end with such names as Pirogov, Kavelin, and the poet Nekrasov, all of whom bestowed on him their warmest and most sincere friendship. He is an honorary Fellow of all the Russian and three foreign universities. Etcetera, etcetera. All this, and a great deal more, makes up what is known as my name.

This name of mine is well known. It is known to every educated person in Russia and abroad, it is mentioned by university lecturers with the addition of the adjectives "celebrated" and "esteemed." It is among those few fortunate names which it is considered bad taste to abuse or speak of disrespectfully in public or in print. And so it should be. For my name is closely associated with the idea of a man who is famous, richly endowed, and most certainly useful. I am as hardworking and as hardy as a camel, which is important, and I am talented, which is even more important. Besides I may as well add that I am a well brought up, modest, and honest fellow. I have never poked my nose into literature or politics, never sought popularity by engaging in polemics with ignoramuses, and never made speeches at dinners or at the graves of my colleagues. . . . There is in fact not a single blot on my name as a scientist, and I have no complaints to make. It is fortunate.

The bearer of this name, that is myself, is a man of sixty-two, with a bald head, false teeth, and an incurable tic. My name is as brilliant and attractive as I myself am dull and unprepossessing. My head and hands tremble from weakness; my neck, like that of one of Turgenev's heroines, resembles the finger-board of a double-bass; my chest is hollow and my back narrow. When I speak or lecture my mouth twists to one side; when I smile my whole face is covered with ghastly wrinkles. There is nothing impressive in my wretched figure; it is only perhaps when I suffer from the tic that I get a peculiar expression which in anyone who happens to look at me at the time provokes the stern and impressive thought: "That man will probably die soon."

I can still lecture quite well; as before, I can hold the attention of my audience for two hours. My passionate nature, the literary form of my exposition and my humour make the defects of my voice almost unnoticeable, though it is dry and harsh, and though its sing-song tone is that of a sanctimonious bigot. But I write badly. The small area of my brain which is in control of my writing abilities refuses to function. My memory has become weak; there is not enough consistency in my thoughts, and when I put them down on paper it always seems to me that I have lost the flair for giving them organic connexion, the construction is monotonous, the sentences barren and timid. Quite often I do not write what I mean to; when I write the end, I cannot remember the beginning. I often forget the most common words, and I always have to waste a great deal of energy to avoid superfluous phrases and unnecessary subordinate clauses in my writing, both of which, beyond a peradventure, prove the decline of my mental faculties. The remarkable thing is that the simpler the subject of my writing the more agonizing the strain. I feel much freer and much more intelligent when writing a scientific article than when writing a letter of congratulation or a report. One thing more: I find it much easier to write in German or English than in Russian.

As regards my present life, I must first of all mention the insomnia from which I have begun to suffer lately. If I were asked: "What is now the chief and fundamental fact of your existence?" I would reply: "Insomnia." As before, from force of habit, I undress and get into bed exactly at midnight. I fall asleep quite soon, but shortly after one o'clock I wake up with the feeling that I have not slept at all. I have to get out of bed and light the lamp. For an hour or two I pace up and down my room, gazing at the long pictures and photographs.

When I am tired of walking, I sit down by my desk. I sit there motionless, without thinking of anything and without feeling any desire for anything; if a book happens to lie in front of me, I draw it towards me mechanically and read without the slightest interest. Thus, quite recently I read mechanically a whole novel with the curious title *What the Swallow Sang Of*. To occupy my mind I sometimes make myself count to a thousand, or I call to mind the face of one of my colleagues and try to remember in what year and under what circumstances he joined the faculty. I like listening to sounds. Sometimes two doors away from me my daughter Lisa will say something rapidly in her sleep, or my wife will walk through the drawing-room with a candle and invariably drop a box of matches, or the warped wood of the wardrobe will creak, or the wick in the lamp will unexpectedly begin to hum—all these sounds for some reason excite me.

Not to sleep at night means to be conscious every minute that you are abnormal, and that is why I wait impatiently for the morning and the day, when I have the right not to sleep. Many wearisome hours pass before the cock crows in the yard. This is my first bringer of glad tidings. As soon as he has crowed, I know that an hour later the hall porter will wake up downstairs and will walk up the stairs for something or other, coughing irritably. And then it will gradually be getting lighter beyond the window, and the sound of voices will come from the street . . .

The day begins for me with the coming of my wife. She enters my room in her underskirt, with her hair undone, but having already had a wash and smelling of eau-de-Cologne. She looks as though she had come in by accident, and every time she says the same thing: "Sorry, I just looked in for a moment. You've slept badly again, haven't you?" Then she puts the lamp out, sits down at the table, and starts talking. I am no prophet, but I know beforehand what she will be talking about. Every morning the same thing. Usually, after anxious inquiries after my health, she suddenly remembers our officer son, who is serving in Warsaw. On the twentieth of each month we send him fifty roubles—which is usually the chief subject of our conversation.

"It's hard on us, of course," sighs my wife, "but until he can stand firmly on his own feet we must help him. The poor boy is in a strange country, his pay is small. Still, if you insist, we'll send him forty roubles next month instead of fifty. What do you think?"

Daily experience might have convinced my wife that expenses do not grow less by constantly talking about them; but my wife has no use for experience, and conscientiously every morning talks about our officer son and about bread being cheaper, thank God, while sugar has gone up two kopeks in price. And all this in a tone of voice as if she were telling me something new.

I listen to her, agreeing mechanically. And, probably because I have not slept all night, strange, inappropriate thoughts take hold of me. I look at my wife and wonder like a child. Bewildered, I ask myself: Is it possible that this very fat, clumsy old woman, whose dull expression is so full of petty cares and anxiety about a crust of bread, whose eyes are blurred with perpetual thoughts of debts and poverty, who can only talk of expenses and only smile when things get cheaper—is it possible that this woman was once that very slim Varya, whom I loved so passionately for her fine, clear intellect, her pure soul, her beauty, and—as Othello loved Desdemona—that she did pity me for the hardships of my scientific work? Is this woman really the same Varya, my wife, who once bore me a son?

I gaze intently at the face of this flabby, clumsy old woman, trying to discover my Varya in her, but nothing of the past remains about her except her anxiety about my health and her way of calling my salary *our* salary, and my hat *our* hat. It pains me to look at her, and to console her a little I let her talk about anything she pleases and don't say a word even when she is unfair to people or reproaches me for not taking up private practice and for not publishing textbooks.

Our conversation always ends in the same way. My wife suddenly remembers that I have not had my tea, and looks startled.

"What am I sitting here for?" she says, getting up. "The samovar has been on the table for hours and I sit chattering here. Good gracious, what an awful memory I have!"

She walks away quickly, but stops at the door to say:

"We owe Yegor five months' wages. You realize that, don't you? How many times have I told you that one should never let the servant's wages run on? It is much easier to pay ten roubles every month than fifty roubles for five months."

Outside the door she stops again.

"I'm not sorry for anyone as much as for our poor Lisa. The girl studies at the conservatoire, she's always in good society, and goes about in goodness only knows what. That fur coat of hers! Why, it's a disgrace to show herself in the street in it. If she were someone else it wouldn't matter so much, but everyone knows her father is a famous professor, a privy councillor!"

And having reproached me with my professional name and my rank, she goes away at last. Thus begins my day. It does not improve as it goes on.

While I am having breakfast, my daughter Lisa comes in, wearing her worn-out fur coat and hat and carrying her music, ready to go to the conservatoire. She is twenty-two. She looks even younger, pretty, a little like my wife when she was young. She kisses me tenderly on my temple and my hand.

"Good morning, Daddy. How are you?"

As a child she was very fond of ice-cream, and I often had to take her to the confectioner's. Ice-cream was the standard by which she judged all that was best. If she wanted to say something nice to me, she would say: "You're a plum ice, Daddy!" One of her fingers she called pistachio, another plum, still another raspberry, and so on. Usually, when she came to say good morning to me, I put her on my knees, kissed her fingers, and said:

"Plum . . . pistachio . . . raspberry . . ."

And now, too, from force of habit, I kiss Lisa's fingers, murmuring: "Pistachio . . . plum . . . lemon . . . ," but it is not the same thing. I am as cold as ice-cream and I feel ashamed. When my daughter comes in and touches my temple with her lips, I start as though I had been stung by a bee, smile constrainedly, and turn my face away. Ever since I began suffering from insomnia, one question keeps worrying me continually. My daughter often sees me, an old man, a famous scientist, blushing painfully because I owe our servant his wages; she sees how often the worry of small debts forces me to stop working and start pacing the room for hours on end thinking. Why then hasn't she come to me even once, without telling her mother, and whispered: "Father, here's my watch, my bracelets, my ear-rings, my dresses—pawn them, you need money . . ." Why, seeing how her mother and I, in an attempt to keep up appearances, try to hide our poverty from people, does she not give up the expensive pleasure of studying music? Anyway I should not have accepted her watch, the bracelets, or any sacrifice from her—God forbid!—I don't want that.

Incidentally, this reminds me of my son, the Warsaw army officer. He is an intelligent, honest, and sober fellow. But that is not enough for me. I can't help thinking that if I had an old father, and if I knew that there were moments when my father was ashamed of his poverty, I would have resigned my commission and taken a job as a labourer. Such thoughts about my children poison my existence. What good are they? Only a narrow-minded and embittered person can bear a grudge against ordinary people for not being heroes. But enough of that.

At a quarter to ten I have to go and give a lecture to my dear boys. I dress and walk along the road I have known for thirty years, a road which has a history of its own for me. Here is the large grey building with the chemist's shop; a small building stood on the site before, and it had a beer shop, in which I thought over my thesis and wrote my first love letter to Varya. I wrote it in pencil, on a sheet of paper with the printed heading *Historia Morbi*. And there is the grocer's shop; it used to belong to a little Jew who sold me cigarettes on credit, and later to a fat woman who was fond of students because "every one of them has a mother." Now it is owned by a red-headed tradesman who does not seem to take any interest in anything and who keeps drinking tea from a copper teapot. And here are the grim gates of the university, which have not been repaired for ages; a bored caretaker in a sheepskin, a broom, heaps of snow. . . . Such gates can hardly produce a wholesome impression on a lad fresh from the provinces who imagines that the temple of science really is a temple. On the whole, the dilapidated state of the university buildings, the gloom of its corridors, the dinginess of its walls, the lack of light, the dismal appearance of the stairs, the coat-hooks and the benches, occupy one of the foremost places in the history of Russian pessimism, they are part of the diathesis. . . . And here is our park. Since my student days it does not seem to have grown any worse or any better. I do not like it. It would be much more sensible if tall pine trees and sturdy oaks grew here instead of the consumptive lime trees, yellow acacias, and thin, clipped lilac bushes. A student, whose state of mind is largely dependent on his surroundings, should at every step see before him only what is grand and strong and elegant in the place where he studies. Heaven preserve him from gaunt trees, broken windows, drab walls, and doors covered with torn oilcloth.

As I approach the wing of the building in which I lecture, the door is flung open and I am met by my old associate, the hall porter, my namesake Nikolai, who is the same age as I. Having let me in, he clears his throat and says:

"It's frosty, sir."

Or, if my coat is wet:

"It's raining, sir."

Then he runs ahead of me and opens all the doors on my way. In my room he carefully helps me off with my coat and at the same time manages to tell me some university news. Because of the good understanding that exists between the university hall porters and caretakers, he knows everything that is going on in the four faculties, the registrar's office, the rector's room, and the library. What doesn't he know? When, for instance, the resignation of the rector or one of the deans is the subject of general discussion, I hear him telling the junior caretaker who the likely candidates are and explaining that so-and-so will not be approved by the minister and that so-and-so will himself refuse the post, and then going into fantastic details about some mysterious documents received in the registrar's office about some alleged secret conversation between the minister and the permanent head of the education department, and so on. Apart from these details, he almost always turns out to be right. The descriptions he gives of the personality of each character are highly original, but they also happen to be true. If you want to know in what year a certain person read his thesis, joined the staff, resigned, or died, you have only to consult the prodigious memory of this veteran and he will not only name you the year, month, and day but will supply you with all the details of this or any other event. Only he who loves can remember so much.

He is the guardian of the university traditions. From his predecessors he has inherited a great number of legends of university life, has added to this store a great deal of his own, procured during his years of service, and if you like he will tell you many stories, long and short. He can tell you of extraordinary sages who knew *everything*, of remarkable scholars who could go on working without sleep for weeks, of innumerable martyrs and victims of science; in his stories good always triumphs over evil, the weak always defeat the strong, the wise man the fool, the modest the proud, the young the old. . . . It is not necessary to take all these legends and cock-and-bull stories at their face value, but put them through a filter and something of real importance will remain: our excellent traditions and the names of true heroes acknowledged by all.

In our society all that is known about the world of science and learning is limited to stories of the extraordinary absentmindedness of old professors and a few witty sayings acribed to Gruber, Babukhim, and myself. For an educated society this is not enough. If we loved science, scientists, and students as Nikolai does, we would long ago have had a literature of epics, legends, and biographies—which unfortunately we have not got at present.

After he has told me the news, Nikolai's face assumes a stern expression and we embark on a business talk. If at the time an outsider could hear how freely Nikolai uses scientific terminology, he might be forgiven for thinking that he was a scholar disguised as an old soldier. By the way, the stories about the erudition of university porters are greatly exaggerated. It is true Nikolai knows more than a hundred Latin terms, can put a skeleton together and occasionally prepare a slide or amuse the students with some long, learned quotation, but so simple a theory as, for instance, the circulation of the blood is still as great a mystery to him as it was twenty years ago.

At the table in my room, bent low over a book or some slide or other, sits my dissector Peter Ignatyevich, an industrious, modest, but mediocre man of thirty-five, already bald and with a big paunch. He works from morning to night, reads a terrific lot, and remembers everything he has read, and in this respect he is worth his weight in gold; but in all other respects he is just a cart-horse, or in other words a learned blockhead. The characteristic cart-horse features which distinguish him from a man of talent are narrowness of outlook and sharply limited specialization. Apart from his special subject he is as naïve as a child. I remember one morning going into my room and saying:

"Have you heard the bad news? Skobelev is dead."

Nikolai crossed himself, but Peter Ignatyevich turned to me and asked:

"Who is Skobelev?"

Another time, a little earlier, I told him that Professor Petrov had died. Dear old Peter Ignatyevich asked:

"What was his subject?"

I suppose if Patti herself sang into his ear, if hordes of Chinese invaded Russia, if there were an earthquake, he would not turn a hair, but would go on looking into his microscope with one eye screwed up. In a word, "What's Hecuba to him?" I'd give a lot to see how that dry stick goes to bed with his wife.

Another trait: a fanatical belief in the infallibility of science and above all in everything the Germans write. He is sure of himself and his slides, he knows the purpose of life and is completely ignorant of the doubts and disappointments that turn talented men grey. A slavish worship of authority and a complete absence of independent thought. It is difficult to make him change his opinions and quite impossible to argue with him. How can you argue with a man who is firmly convinced that medicine is the best science, that doctors are the best people, and that medical traditions are the best traditions? The only thing that has survived from the bad past of medicine is the white tie doctors still wear; to a scholar, an educated man, there is really nothing but the general university tradition, without splitting up the faculties into medical, legal, and so on. Peter Ignatyevich finds it difficult to agree with this, and he is ready to argue with you about it till doomsday.

I can imagine his future quite plainly. In the course of his life he will make a few hundred slides, perfect in every respect, write a great number of dry but quite tolerably good papers, make a dozen conscientious translations; but he won't invent gunpowder. To invent gunpowder one needs imagination, inventiveness, and a capacity for divining things, and Peter Ignatyevich has nothing of the sort. To put it in a nutshell, so far as science is concerned, he is not a foreman but a labourer.

Peter Ignatyevich, Nikolai, and I lower our voices when we talk. We feel a little ill at ease. You get a strange feeling when you hear an audience roaring like a sea behind the door. In thirty years I have not grown accustomed to that feeling, and I experience it every morning. I button up my frock-coat nervously, ask Nikolai unnecessary questions, get cross. . . . It looks as though I were afraid; but it is not fear, it is something else which I cannot name or describe. I glance at my watch as though I did not know the right time.

"Well," I say, "it's time to go."

And we walk in procession, in the following order: Nikolai with the preparations or diagrams in front, myself after him; and after me, his head modestly bent, plods the cart-horse. Or, when necessary, a cadaver is carried in front on a stretcher, after the cadaver comes Nikolai, and so on. At my appearance the students get up, then sit down, and the roar of the sea suddenly dies down. A calm sets in.

I know what I am going to lecture about, but I do not know how I shall lecture, what I shall start and end with. There is not a single ready-made phrase in my head. But as soon as I glance at my audience, sitting round me in an amphitheatre, and utter the stereotyped "At our last lecture we stopped at—," the sentences roll out in a long succession and—I am off! I speak with irresistible rapidity and passion, and it seems that no power on earth could interrupt the flow of my speech. To lecture well, that is to say, without boring your listeners, and to benefit them, you must possess not only talent but also the right kind of skill as well as experience, you must also have a perfectly clear idea both of your own abilities and the subject of your address. In addition, you must never be thrown off your guard, never relax your attention, and never for a moment lose sight of your audience.

A good conductor, while conveying the ideas of the composer, performs a dozen things all at once: he reads the score, waves his baton, keeps an eye on the singer, motions to the drummer, the French horns, etc. It is the same with me when I am lecturing. In front of me are a hundred and fifty faces, all different from one another, and three hundred eyes staring straight into my face. My aim is to conquer this many-headed hydra. If I never allow their attention to slacken for a moment during the whole of my lecture, and at the same time never talk above their heads, then they are in my power. My other enemy is within me. This is the endless variety of forms, phenomena, and laws, and the great multitude of thoughts, my own and those of others, which arise from them. Every moment I must be able to extract from this enormous mass of material what is most important and necessary, and I must do it as quickly as I talk; moreover, I must convey my thought in the form that is accessible to the hydra's mind and is capable of exciting its attention. I must, besides, take good care to see that my thoughts are communicated not as they accumulate, but in the order required for the correct composition of the picture I intend to draw. Furthermore, I do my best to make sure that I try to invest my speech in a literary form, make my definitions brief and exact and the sentences as simple and elegant as possible. Every moment I must check myself and try to remember that I have only one hour and forty minutes at my disposal. In a word, I have plenty to do. At one and the same time I have to be a scientist, a teacher, and an orator; and it's a poor outlook for me if the orator gets the better of the teacher and scientist, or vice versa.

After lecturing for fifteen or thirty minutes, I suddenly notice that the students are beginning to stare at the ceiling or at Peter Ignatyevich; one of them is fumbling for his handkerchief, another trying to settle himself more comfortably, and a third smiling at his own thoughts. This means that their attention is beginning to slacken. I have to do something about it. I take advantage of the first opportunity to make a pun. All the hundred and fifty faces smile broadly, their eyes sparkle merrily, for a brief moment one can hear the roar of the sea. . . . I join in the laughter. Their attention is refreshed and I can go on.

No debate, no entertainment, no game has ever given me so much pleasure as giving a lecture. Only while lecturing have I been able to give myself up wholly to passion, and to understand that inspiration is not an invention of poets, but really exists. And I can't help thinking that Hercules, after the most sensational of his exploits, never had such an exquisite feeling of lassitude as I experienced every time after a lecture.

That was in the past. Now at lectures I experience nothing but torture. Scarcely half an hour passes before I begin to feel a terrible weakness in my legs and shoulders; I sit down, but I am not used to lecturing sitting down. A minute later I am on my feet again and lecture standing; then I sit down again. My mouth is dry, my voice hoarse, my head dizzy. . . . To conceal my condition from my audience, I take a drink of water now and then, cough and blow my nose as though I am suffering from a cold in the head, make inopportune puns, and at last announce an interval sooner than I ought to. But the worst of it is that I feel ashamed.

Conscience and reason tell me that the best thing I could do now is to deliver a farewell lecture to the boys, say my last word to them, give them my blessing, and give up my post to a younger and stronger man than myself. But—God be my judge—I have not the courage to act according to what my conscience tells me I ought to do.

Unfortunately, I am neither a philosopher nor a theologian. I know perfectly well I have no more than six months to live; it would therefore seem that I should be chiefly occupied with questions of the darkness beyond the grave and the visions that may visit my sleep in the grave. But for some reason my soul does not want to know anything about these questions; only my mind realizes their importance. Now that death is so near, all I am interested in is science, just as I was twenty or thirty years ago. Even while breathing my last I shall still believe that science is the most important, most beautiful, and most necessary thing in the life of man, that it always has been and will be the highest manifestation of love, and that it alone will enable man to conquer nature and himself. This belief is perhaps naïve and fundamentally unsound, but it is not my fault that I believe as I do and not otherwise; it is not in my power to overcome this belief of mine.

But that is not the point. All I ask is that allowance should be made for my weakness, and that it should be understood that to tear away from his university chair and his students a man who is more interested in the development of the bone-marrow than in the final goal of creation is tantamount to nailing him down in his coffin without waiting for him to die.

As a result of my insomnia and the struggle against my growing weakness, something strange is happening to me. In the middle of my lecture tears rise to my throat, my eyelids begin to itch, and I feel an hysterical, passionate desire to stretch out my hands and complain aloud. I feel like shouting in a loud voice that fate has sentenced me, a famous man, to death, that in six months' time another man will be in charge of this lecture room. I feèl like crying out that I have been poisoned, that new thoughts I did not know before have poisoned the last days of my life and keep stinging my brain like mosquitoes. At that moment my position seems so terrible to me that I should like all my students to be horrified, leap panic-stricken from their seats, and rush shrieking madly to the exit.

It is not easy to live through such moments.

II

After the lecture I work at home. I read periodicals and dissertations, prepare for my next lecture, and sometimes write something. My work is constantly interrupted, for I have to receive visitors.

The door bell rings. It is a colleague of mine who has come to talk over some business. He comes in with his hat and stick, and holding them out towards me says:

"I've just looked in for a moment. Don't get up, colleague. Only a couple of words."

First we try to show each other how extraordinarily polite we are and how glad we are to see each other. I make him sit down in an armchair, and he insists on my resuming my seat; at the same time we carefully stroke each other's waists, touching each other's buttons, and it looks as if we are feeling each other and are afraid of burning ourselves. We both laugh, though we have not said anything funny. Having sat down, we both bend our heads towards each other and start talking in an undertone. However well disposed we may be towards one another, we cannot help gilding our conversation with all sorts of Chinese civilities like "as you so justly observe" or "as I've already had the honour to tell you," or laughing heartily if either of us makes a pun, even though a bad one. Having finished our business, my colleague gets up abruptly and begins to take his leave, waving his hat towards my work. We again feel each other and laugh. I accompany him to the hall and help him on with his fur coat, while he does his best to decline so great an honour. Then, when Yegor opens the front door to him, he expresses his concern about my catching a cold, while I pretend to be ready to follow him even as far as the street. And when at last I am back in my study, my face is still wreathed in smiles, I suppose from inertia.

A little later, another ring. Someone comes into the hall, spends a long time taking off his coat and galoshes, and coughs. Yegor announces that one of my students wishes to see me. I say: "Show him in, please." A moment later a young man of pleasant appearance enters my study. For nearly a year our relationship has been rather strained: he gives me most abominable answers at examinations, and I give him the lowest marks. Every year I get about seven of these fine fellows whom I "persecute" or "plough," in the language of the students. Those of them who do not pass their examinations because of their incapacity or illness usually bear their cross with patience, and do not bargain with me; only those come to bargain with me at home who are optimists by nature, fellows of wide though not very profound interests, whose failure in examinations spoils their appetites and prevents them from going regularly to the opera. The former I make allowances for; the latter I "persecute" for a whole year.

"Sit down, please," I say to my visitor. "What can I do for you?"

"I am sorry to trouble you, sir," he begins, stammering and not looking me in the face. "I—er—shouldn't have taken the liberty of—er—troubling you sir, if—er. . . . You see, sir, I've sat for your examination five times and—er—have not passed. I beg you, sir, to be so kind as to give me a pass, because . . ."

The argument which all sluggards bring forward in their favour is always the same: they have passed in all the other subjects with distinction, but failed only in mine, which is all the more surprising because they have always studied my subject most diligently and know it thoroughly. They have failed because of some quite inexplicable misunderstanding.

"I am very sorry, my friend," I say to my visitor, "but I cannot give you a pass. Go and read through your lecture notes again, and then come to me. Then we shall see."

A pause. I cannot suppress a desire to torment the student a little for preferring beer and the opera to science and I say with a sigh:

"In my opinion, the best thing for you to do now is to give up medicine altogether. If a man of your ability is quite unable to pass the examination, then it is evident that you have neither the desire nor the vocation to be a doctor."

The optimistic fellow pulls a long face.

"I'm sorry, sir," he says with a laugh, "but that would certainly be a strange thing for me to do. To study for five years and then—give it up!"

"Yes, why not? After all, it's better to waste five years than to do something you do not like for the rest of your life."

But almost at once I feel sorry for him, and I hasten to say:

"However, just as you like. Read a little more, and then come to me."

"When?" the sluggard asks, dully.

"Any time you like. Tomorrow, even."

And I can read in his good-natured eyes: "I can come all right, but then you'll throw me out again, you dirty dog."

"Now, of course," I say, "you won't become a more learned person by sitting fifteen times for my examination, but it'll be good training for your character. That's something to be thankful for, too."

Silence. I rise, waiting for my visitor to go, but he stands there looking out of the window, fingering his little beard and thinking. The thing is becoming a bore.

The optimistic fellow has a pleasant, mellow voice, intelligent ironical eyes, and a complacent face that is somewhat crumpled by overdoses of beer and by lying about on sofas for hours. I expect he could tell me a great many interesting things about the opera, his love affairs, his fellow-students, among whom he is popular, but unfortunately it is not the thing to do. And yet I would gladly listen to him.

"I give you my word of honour, sir, that if you give me a pass, I—er . . ."

But as soon as it gets to "my word of honour," I wave my hands and sit down at my desk. The student thinks for another minute and then says gloomily:

"In that case, good-bye. . . . I'm sorry, sir."

"Good-bye, my friend. Good luck!"

He goes irresolutely out into the hall, slowly puts on his things, and, on going out into the street, no doubt meditates for a long time about his situation, but, unable to think of anything except calling me "an old devil," goes to a cheap restaurant to drink beer and dine, and then back home to sleep. Peace to your ashes, you honest hard-working fellow!

A third ring. In comes a young doctor in a new black suit, gold-rimmed spectacles, and of course a white tie. He introduces himself. I ask him to take a seat, and inquire after his business. The young priest of science begins telling me, not without agitation, that he has passed his doctor's examination this year and that now he has only to write his dissertation. He would like to work with me, under my guidance, and I would greatly oblige him by suggesting a subject for his dissertation.

"I should be delighted to be of use to you, colleague," I say, "but let's first of all see if we agree about what exactly a dissertation is supposed to be. This word is usually understood to mean a written composition which is the result of independent work. Isn't that so? A work written on a subject suggested by someone else and under the supervision of someone else has a different name."

The aspirant is silent. I lose my temper and jump out of my chair.

"Tell me why do you all come to me?" I shout angrily. "Do I keep a shop? I'm not a dealer in subjects for dissertations. For the hundredth time I ask you to leave me in peace. I'm sorry to be so outspoken, but I'm sick and tired of the whole thing!"

The aspirant is silent and only his face above his cheekbones colours slightly. His face shows a profound respect for my famous name and my erudition, but I can see from the expression in his eyes that he despises my voice, my pitiful figure, and my nervous gestures. In my anger, I strike him as an eccentric fellow.

"I don't keep a shop," I repeat angrily. "What an extraordinary business! Why don't you want to be independent? Why do you loathe freedom so much?"

I go on talking for a long time, but he keeps silent. In the end I gradually cool down and of course give in. The aspirant will receive a worthless subject from me and under my supervision write a dissertation which is of no earthly use to anyone, will defend it with dignity in a boring debate, and will get his useless doctorate of medicine.

The door bell can go on ringing for ever, but I will restrict myself to four. The bell rings for the fourth time and I hear familiar footsteps, the rustle of a dress, and the dear voice . . .

Eighteen years ago a colleague of mine, an eye specialist, died, leaving a seven-year-old daughter, Katya, and sixty thousand roubles. In his will he appointed me as her guardian. Katya lived in my family till she was ten, then she was sent to a boarding school and only lived with us during the summer holidays. I had no time to look after her education and no opportunity of keeping an eye on her except occasionally, and can therefore say very little about her childhood.

The first thing I remember, the memory which I treasure, is the extraordinary trustfulness with which she came into my home and allowed the doctors to treat her when she was ill, a trustfulness which always irradiated her sweet face. She might be sitting somewhere by herself with a bandage round her head, and would be sure to be watching something intently; whether she was watching me writing and turning over the pages of a book, or my wife bustling about, or the cook peeling potatoes in the kitchen, or the dog playing about, her eyes invariably expressed the same thing: "Everything that is going on in this world is wise and wonderful." She was inquisitive and liked to talk to me very much. She would sit facing me at the table, watching my movements and asking questions. She was interested to know what I was reading, what I did at the university, whether I was not afraid of the cadavers, and what I did with my salary.

"Do the students fight at the university?" she would ask.

"Yes, they do, my dear."

"And do you make them go down on their knees?"

"I do."

And it seemed so funny to her that the students fought and I made them go down on their knees that she burst out laughing. She was a gentle, patient, and good child. I often happened to see how something was taken away from her, or how she was unjustly punished, or her curiosity was not satisfied; at such moments sadness would be added to her usual expression of trustfulness, but that was all. I did not know how to stick up for her and it was only when I saw her looking sad that I was overcome by a desire to draw her close to me and tell her how sorry I was for her in the words of an old nurse: "You poor little orphan!"

I remember too that she was very fond of dressing up and sprinkling herself with scent. In this respect she was like me. I too like good clothes and fine scent.

I regret that I had neither the time nor the inclination to watch the beginning and the growth of the passion which took hold of Katya when she was fourteen or fifteen. I am talking of her passionate love for the theatre. When she came from her boarding school to live with us for the summer, there was nothing she spoke about with such pleasure and enthusiasm as plays and actors. She used to tire us with her constant talk about the theatre. My wife and children would not listen to her. I alone had not the courage to refuse her my attention. Whenever she felt like sharing her raptures, she would come to my study and say in an imploring voice:

"Do let me talk to you about the theatre."

I used to show her my watch and say:

"I give you half an hour from—now!"

Later she began bringing home dozens of portraits of actors and actresses she worshipped; then she tried a few times to take part in amateur theatricals, and at last, when she left school, she told me that she was born to be an actress.

I never shared Katya's theatrical enthusiasms. In my opinion, if a play is good there is no need to trouble the actors for it to produce the desired impression: all you have to do is to read it. On the other hand, if the play is bad no acting will make it good.

When I was young I often went to the theatre, and now too my family takes a box twice a year and takes me there for "an airing." This, of course, is not enough to give me the right to express an opinion on the theatre, but I will say just a few words about it. In my opinion, the theatre has not improved in the last thirty or forty years. I am still unable to get a glass of clean water in the corridors or the foyer. I am still being fined twenty kopeks for my fur coat by the cloakroom attendants, although there is nothing reprehensible in wearing warm clothes in winter. Music is still quite unnecessarily being played in the intervals, adding something new and completely uncalled for to the impression received from the play. Men still go to the bar for a drink during the intervals. Since there is no progress in little things, it would be a waste of time to look for it in bigger things. When an actor, entangled from head to foot in theatrical traditions and prejudices, tries to give us a simple, ordinary monologue like "To be or not to be" not at all simply, but for some reason always with hissings and convulsions, or when he tries to convince me at all costs that Chatsky, who is always talking with fools and is in love with a fool of a girl, is a very clever man and *The Misfortune of Being Clever* is not a boring play, then what I get from the stage is a whiff of the same old routine which I found so boring forty years ago when I was regaled with classical howlings and beatings of the breast. And every time I come out of the theatre I am a more confirmed conservative than when I entered it.

It is not difficult to persuade a sentimental and credulous crowd that the theatre in its present state is a school. But anyone who knows the real meaning of a school will not swallow this sort of bait. I do not know what it will be like in fifty or a hundred years, but under present conditions the theatre can serve only as a place of entertainment. But this place of entertainment is too expensive to be worth while. It deprives the state of thousands of young, healthy, and talented men and women, who if they were not dedicated to the theatre could have become good doctors, farmers, schoolmistresses, or army officers; it deprives the public of their evening hours—the best time for intellectual work and friendly conversations. Not to mention the waste of money and the moral injury suffered by the spectators when they see murder, adultery, and slander wrongly treated on the stage.

Katya, however, was of quite another opinion. She assured me that the theatre, even in its present state, was far superior to lectures, far superior to books, far superior to anything in the world. The theatre was a force, uniting in itself all the arts, and the actors were missionaries. No particular art or science was able to exert such a

strong and beneficial influence on the human soul as the stage, and
that was the real reason why even the mediocre actor enjoyed greater
popularity in the country than the greatest scientist or artist. Indeed,
no public activity could give such satisfaction and enjoyment as
acting.

So one fine day Katya joined a theatrical company and went away, I
believe, to Ufa, taking with her a great deal of money, thousands of
rainbow-coloured hopes and grandiose views on the business of the
theatre.

Her first letters, written during the journey, were wonderful. I read
them, and was simply amazed that these small sheets of paper could
contain so much youthful enthusiasm, purity of soul, divine naïveté,
and at the same time so many subtle and sensible views, which would
have done honour to a first-class masculine intelligence. The Volga,
the countryside, the towns she visited, her fellow-actors, her successess
and failures, she did not so much describe as glorify in song; every line
breathed the trustfulness which I was used to seeing on her face—and
with all this a mass of grammatical mistakes and an almost total
absence of punctuation marks.

Six months had scarcely passed when I received a highly poetic and
rapturous letter beginning with the words: "I have fallen in love." She
enclosed a photograph of a young man with a clean-shaven face, in a
wide-brimmed hat and a plaid thrown over one shoulder. The next
letters were just as wonderful, but now punctuation marks began to
make an appearance, there were no more grammatical mistakes, and
they exuded a strong masculine odour. Katya began to write how
splendid it would be to build a big theatre somewhere on the Volga,
make it into a limited company, and get the rich businessmen and
shipowners to join it as shareholders. There would be plenty of
money, the box-office receipts would be enormous and the actors
would work on a partnership basis. . . . This might be a good thing,
for all I know, but it seemed to me that such ideas could only come
from a man's head.

Be that as it may, for a year or two everything was apparently all
right: Katya was in love, had faith in her work, and was happy; but
later on I began to be conscious of unmistakable signs of despondency
in her letters. At first Katya began to complain to me about her
fellow-actors—this was the first and most ominous sign. If a young
scientist or writer begins his career by complaining bitterly about

scientists or writers, it means that he is already worn out and no longer fit for his work. Katya wrote that her fellow-actors did not go to rehearsals and did not know their parts; that they showed an utter contempt for the public by their production of ridiculous plays and by the way they behaved on the stage; in the interests of the box-office receipts, which was the only topic of conversation among them, actresses of the legitimate stage degraded themselves by singing music-hall songs, while tragic actors sang similar songs in which they made fun of deceived husbands and the pregnancy of unfaithful wives, and so on. In fact, it was quite amazing that provincial theatres still existed and that they could carry on in so meagre and bad an art form.

In reply I sent Katya a long and, I am afraid, rather boring letter. Among other things, I wrote: "I have often had the chance of talking with old actors, most honourable men, who have been good enough to be amiable to me. From talking to them I realized that their activities are guided not so much by reason and freedom of choice as by the prevalent social mood and fashion; the best of them have at one time or another had to act in tragedies, operettas, Parisian farces, and pantomimes, and they always considered that in every case they were following the right path and were of benefit to society. So, you see, the source of the evil must be sought not in the actors, but deeper down, in the art itself and in the attitude of society towards it." This letter of mine only exasperated Katya. She wrote in reply: "We are talking about different things. I did not write to you about those honourable men who have been good enough to like you, but of a gang of rogues who have no idea of honour. They are a horde of savages, who found themselves on the stage only because they wouldn't have been given a job anywhere else, and who call themselves actors out of sheer arrogance. Not a single talented person among them, but any number of mediocrities, drunkards, schemers, and scandalmongers. I can't tell you how bitter I feel that the art I love so much should have fallen into the hands of people I detest; it hurts me that the best men should only see evil from a distance and refuse to go nearer, and instead of doing something about it write platitudes in a ponderous style and dispense moral judgements nobody cares a rap about. . . ." And so on in the same vein.

A little later I received the following letter:

"I have been cruelly deceived. I can't go on living any more. Make use of my money as you think fit. I have loved you as a father and as my only friend. Forgive me."

So it seemed that *he* belonged to "the horde of savages," too. Afterwards I gathered from certain hints that there had been an attempt at suicide. Katya, it seems, tried to poison herself. I think she must have been seriously ill afterwards, for the next letter from her I received from Yalta, where the doctors had probably sent her. Her last letter to me contained a request to send her a thousand roubles to Yalta as quickly as possible, and concluded with the words: "I am sorry my letter is so gloomy. Yesterday I buried my child." After spending about a year in the Crimea, she came back home.

She had been away for about four years, and I must confess that during the whole of that time I played a rather strange and unenviable part so far as she was concerned. When at the very beginning she told me that she was going on the stage and when later she wrote to me about her love, when every now and then she succumbed to fits of extravagance so that I had to send her one or two thousand roubles at her request, when she wrote to me of her intention to take her life and then of the death of her child, I was at a loss what to do every time, and all I did to help her was to think a lot about her and write her long boring letters which I need not have written at all. And yet I took the place of a father to her and I loved her like my own daughter.

At present Katya lives within half a mile of me. She has taken a five-roomed flat and furnished it very comfortably, with the good taste that is part of her nature. If anyone were to try to describe her way of life, then the predominant mood would have to be its indolence. Soft couches and soft chairs for her indolent body, thick carpets for her indolent feet, faded, dim, or soft colours for her indolent eyes; for her indolent soul, plenty of cheap fans on the walls, as well as small pictures in which originality of execution predominates over content; and an over-abundance of little tables and shelves, full of useless and worthless things, shapeless scraps of material in place of curtains. . . . All this, combined with a horror of bright colours, symmetry, and space, shows a perversion of natural taste, too, quite apart from spiritual indolence. Katya lies on a couch for days, reading books, mostly novels and short stories. She goes out only once a day, in the afternoon, to come and see me.

I am working, and Katya sits not far away from me on a sofa. She is

silent and keeps wrapping herself in her shawl as though she were
cold. Either because I like her, or because I got used to her frequent
visits when she was still a little girl, her presence does not prevent me
from concentrating. Occasionally I ask her something, without thinking, and she gives me a curt answer; or, for a moment's relaxation, I
turn round and look at her as, lost in thought, she browses through a
medical journal or a newspaper. It is then that I notice the absence of
her former look of trustfulness. Her expression is now cold, indifferent, abstracted, like that of passengers who have to wait a long time
for their train. She dresses as before, well and simply, but negligently;
it is quite evident that her dress and hair suffer not inconsiderably
from the couches and rocking-chairs on which she lies all day and
every day. Neither is she as inquisitive as she used to be. She no longer
asks me any questions, just as though she had experienced everything
in life and did not expect to hear anything new.

At about five o'clock, people can be heard moving about in the
large drawing-room and the sitting-room. It is Lisa, who has come
back from the conservatoire and brought some of her friends with her.
You can hear them playing the piano, trying out their voices, and
laughing loudly. Yegor is laying the table in the dining-room, rattling
the plates and dishes.

"Good-bye," says Katya. "I won't go in to see your people today.
They must excuse me. I haven't time. Come and see me."

When I see her to the front door, she looks me up and down
sternly and says in a vexed tone of voice:

"You get thinner and thinner. Why don't you look after yourself?
You ought to consult a doctor. I'll go to Sergey Fyodorovich and ask
him to come and see you. Let him examine you."

"No, Katya."

"I can't understand why your family doesn't do anything about it.
A fine family you've got!"

She puts on her coat furiously, and one or two hairpins invariably
fall on the floor from her negligently done hair. She is too lazy and in
too much of a hurry to tidy her hair; she pushes the straggling curls
perfunctorily under her hat and goes away.

When I enter the dining-room, my wife asks me:

"Has Katya been with you? Why didn't she come to see us? It's
really extraordinary . . ."

"Mother," Lisa says to her reproachfully, "if she doesn't want to come, she needn't. We're not going to go down on our knees to her, are we?"

"Say what you like, it's downright rude! To sit for hours in your father's study and forget all about us! Still, she can do as she likes, I suppose."

Varya and Lisa both hate Katya. Their hatred is quite incomprehensible to me, but I expect that to understand it one must be a woman. I'm ready to bet anything you like that of the one hundred and fifty young students whom I see almost daily in my lecture room, and of the hundred or so middle-aged and elderly men I see every week, not one would be able to understand their hatred and their feeling of disgust for Katya's past, that is to say, for the fact that she has been pregnant without being married and has had an illegitimate child; at the same time I cannot think of a single woman or girl of my acquaintance who does not consciously or unconsciously entertain such feelings. And this is not because a woman is more virtuous or purer than a man: for virtue and purity, if they are not free from feelings of malice, differ very little from vice. I explain it simply by the backwardness of women. The uneasy feeling of compassion and the pricks of conscience a modern man experiences at the sight of unhappiness speak much more of culture and moral development than do hatred and disgust. A modern woman is as coarse at heart and as liable to burst into tears as a woman in the Middle Ages. In my opinion, those who advise her to get the same education as a man are very sensible.

My wife also dislikes Katya for having been an actress, for her ingratitude, her pride, her eccentricity, and for all those innumerable vices one woman can always discover in another.

Besides myself and my family, we have two or three of my daughter's girl friends to dinner, as well as Alexander Adolfovich Gnekker, Lisa's admirer and suitor. He is a fair young man of about thirty, of medium height, very stout, broad shouldered, with reddish whiskers round his ears and a dyed moustache which gives his chubby, smooth face a doll-like look. He wears a very short jacket, a fancy waistcoat, large check trousers very wide at the top and very narrow at the bottom, and yellow, flat-heeled boots. He has bulging lobster-like eyes, his tie is like a lobster's tail, and in fact this young man seems to exude the smell of lobster soup. He visits us every day, but no one in the family knows where he comes from, where he was educated, or what he lives on. He does not play any musical instruments, nor does he sing, but he seems to have some connexion with music and singing, sells pianos somewhere, is often to be seen at the conservatoire, knows all the celebrities, and organizes concerts; he gives his opinion on music with the air of an authority, and I have noticed that everybody readily agrees with him.

Rich people always have hangers-on about them, and so have the arts and sciences. I believe there is no science or art in the world which is free from the presence of such "foreign bodies" as this Mr. Gnekker. I am no musician, and I may be wrong about Gnekker, whom I do not know very well, besides. But his authoritative air as well as the air of dignity he assumes when standing beside a grand piano and listening to the singing or playing, strikes me as a little suspicious.

You may be a man of excellent breeding and a privy councillor a hundred times over, but if you have a daughter you can never be absolutely secure against the petty middle class atmosphere which is so often introduced into your house and your state of mind by courtships, engagements, and weddings. For instance, I can never reconcile myself to the solemn expression on my wife's face every time Gnekker pays us a visit, or to the bottles of Lafitte, port, and sherry which are on the table solely on his account, so that he shall see with his own eyes how grandly and sumptuously we live. Nor can I stand Lisa's laughter and her manner of screwing up her eyes when men come to our house. Above all, I simply cannot understand why a person utterly alien to my habits and the whole tenor of my life, a person who is quite unlike the people I am fond of, should come to visit me every day and have dinner with me. My wife and the servants whisper mysteriously that he is the "fiancé," but I still can't understand why he is here. His presence bewilders me, just as much as though a Zulu were put next to me at table. I find it strange, too, that my daughter, whom I still look upon as a child, should love that tie, those eyes, those chubby cheeks . . .

Before, I either enjoyed my dinner or was indifferent to it, but now it rouses in me nothing but boredom and irritation. Ever since I became a privy councillor and served my term as head of the faculty, my family has for some reason considered it necessary to make a thorough change in our menu and our arrangements at dinner. Instead of the plain dishes I was used to as a student and doctor, I am now fed on thick soup with some sort of white bits of something resembling icicles floating about in it, and kidneys in Madeira sauce. My high rank and fame have deprived me for ever of cabbage soup, delicious pies, goose and apple sauce, and bream with buckwheat. They have also deprived me of my maidservant Agasha, a talkative and amusing old woman, instead of whom Yegor, a stupid and supercilious fellow, now serves at dinner, with a white cotton glove on his right hand. The intervals between the courses are brief, but they seem terribly long, because there is nothing to fill them. Gone are the old gaiety, the unconstrained conversations, the jokes, the laughter, the mutual endearments, and the feeling of happiness which thrilled the children, my wife, and myself when we used to meet round the dinner table.

To a busy man like myself, dinner meant a time of rest in the family circle, and to my wife and children it was a festive occasion, brief, it is true, but bright and joyful, for they knew that for half an hour I belonged not to science, not to my students, but to them alone and no one else. No more getting tipsy on one glass of wine, no more Agasha, no more bream with buckwheat, no more of the gay uproar at table following slightly unconventional incidents such as a fight between the cat and the dog under the table or Katya's bandage falling off her cheek into her soup.

Our present dinner is as unappetizing to describe as it is to eat. There's my wife's solemn face, with its assumed air of gravity and habitual worried expression as she nervously examines our plates.

"I see you don't like the roast meat," she says, addressing Gnekker. "You don't really, do you? Tell me, please."

"Don't worry, my dear," I feel obliged to say. "The meat's delicious."

"You always take my part, Nikolai," she says. "You never tell the truth. Why does Mr. Gnekker eat so little?"

And this goes on all through the meal.

Lisa laughs her abrupt, staccato laugh and screws up her eyes. I look at both of them, and it is only now, at dinner, that I see quite clearly that their inner life has long ago escaped me completely. I have a feeling as though I had once—a long time ago—lived at home with a real family, but that now I am dining out with a woman who is not really my wife and looking at a girl who is not really my daughter Lisa. A great change has taken place in both of them, and I have failed to notice the long process that has led up to the change, so it's no wonder I'm unable to understand it now. Why did this change take place? I don't know. Perhaps the whole trouble is that the Lord has not given my wife and daughter the strength He gave me. From my childhood I have grown accustomed to resisting outside influences, and I have steeled myself properly to do so; such vicissitudes of life as fame, high rank, transition from comfort to living beyond my means, acquaintance with the aristocracy, and so on, have had no particular influence on me, and I have remained safe and sound; but on the weak, on my wife and Lisa, unsteeled as they were, all this has fallen like an avalanche and crushed them.

The young ladies and Gnekker talk of fugues, counterpoint, singers and pianists, Bach and Brahms; and my wife, afraid of being suspected to be an ignoramus in music, smiles as though she knows all about it and murmurs: "Splendid, splendid. . . . Really. . . . No?" Gnekker eats sedately, jokes sedately, and listens condescendingly to the remarks of the young ladies. Occasionally he cannot resist his impulse to talk bad French, and then for some unknown reason he finds it necessary to address me grandly as *"Votre Excellence."*

And I am morose. Evidently I embarrass them, and they embarrass me. I have never before been aware of possessing any class antagonisms, but now I am worried by something of the kind. I try to find only bad traits in Gnekker, find them in no time at all, and am tormented by the thought that a man who does not belong to my social circle should have usurped the place of my daughter's fiancé. His presence has a bad effect on me in another way, too. As a rule, when I am left alone or find myself among people I am fond of, it never occurs to me to think of my own achievements, and if I do think of them they seem so trivial to me, as though I had become a scientist only yesterday; but in the company of people like Gnekker my achievements seem to tower like a cloud-capped mountain, at the foot of which the swarming Gnekkers are hardly visible to the eye.

After dinner I retire to my study and light my pipe, one for the whole day, the only survivor of my bad old habit of smoking from morning till night. While I am smoking, my wife comes in and sits down to talk to me. Just as in the morning, I know beforehand what our talk will be about.

"I must have a serious talk to you, Nikolai," she begins. "About Lisa, I mean. Why don't you pay any attention?"

"Oh? To what?"

"You pretend not to notice anything. It's not good enough. You can't just ignore everything. Gnekker will probably propose to Lisa. What do you say to that?"

"Well, I can't very well say he's a bad man because I don't know him well enough; but I've told you a thousand times that I don't like him."

"But," she says, getting up and pacing the room agitatedly, "you can't take up such an attitude towards a serious step like that! You can't. When it concerns the happiness of your daughter, we must abandon all personal considerations. I know you don't like him. All right. But if we refuse him now, if we break it off, how can you be sure that Lisa won't bear a grudge against us all her life? There aren't many eligible young men nowadays, and it is quite likely that she won't get another chance. He is very much in love with Lisa, and I think she likes him. Of course, he has no definite position of any kind, but we can't do anything about it, can we? Let's hope that one day he will get some permanent job. He comes from a good family and is well off."

"How do you know that?"

"He said so. His father has a big house in Kharkov and an estate nearby. I'm afraid, Nikolai, you'll have to go to Kharkov."

"Why?"

"You'll be able to find out there. You know some of the professors there, and they'll help you. I'd go there myself, but I'm a woman. I can't . . ."

"I won't go to Kharkov," I say sullenly.

My wife looks frightened and an expression of agonizing pain appears on her face.

"For God's sake, Nikolai!" she implores me with a whimper. "For God's sake, take this burden off my shoulders. I'm suffering!"

It hurts me to look at her.

"Oh, very well, Varya," I say, tenderly. "I'll go to Kharkov if you want me to. I'll do anything you want."

She presses her handkerchief to her eyes and goes to her room to cry. I am left alone.

A little later a lamp is brought in. Familiar shadows I've long since come to dislike fall on the walls from the chairs and the lampshade, and when I look at them it seems to me that it is already night and my damned insomnia is about to begin. I lie down on my bed, then get up again and pace the room, and lie down again. . . . As a rule, my nervous tension reaches its climax after dinner, before the evening. I begin to cry for no apparent reason and hide my head under the pillow. At those moments I'm afraid someone may come in. I'm afraid of sudden death. I'm ashamed of my tears, and altogether something awful is going on inside me. I feel that I can't bear to look any longer at my lamp, my books, the shadows on the floor, that I can no longer bear to hear the voices in the drawing-room. A kind of invisible and incomprehensible force pushes me violently out of the house. I jump up, put on my hat and coat hurriedly, and go cautiously out into the street, taking every care not to be seen by anyone in the house. Where am I to go?

The answer to this question has long been in my head—to Katya.

III

As usual, she is lying on the ottoman or on a couch, reading a book. Seeing me, she raises her head indolently, sits up, and stretches out her hand to me.

"You're always lying down," I say after a short pause for rest. "It's not good for you. You ought to find something to do."

"Oh?"

"Yes, you ought to find something to do."

"What? A woman can become either a domestic servant or an actress."

"Very well then. If you don't want to do domestic work, why not go on the stage?"

She makes no answer.

"You ought to get married," I say, half in jest.

"There's no one I'd like to marry. Besides, I don't want to marry."

"But you can't live like that."

"Without a husband? What does that matter? There are lots of men, if that were what I wanted."

"That's not nice, Katya."

"What's not nice?"

"Why, what you just said."

Noticing that I am upset and wishing to gloss over the bad impression, Katya says:

"Come, I'll show you something. This way."

She takes me to a small and very cosy little room, points to the writing desk, and says:

"There it is. I got it ready for you. You will work here. Come every day, and bring your work with you. At home they only interfere with you. Will you work here? Would you like to?"

Not to hurt her feelings by a refusal, I tell her I will and that I like her room very much. Then we both sit down in the cosy little room and begin to talk.

Warm comfortable surroundings and the presence of an understanding companion arouse in me not a feeling of pleasure as before but a strong desire to complain and grumble. For some reason it seems to me that if I complained and grumbled I'd feel better.

"Things are bad, my dear," I begin with a sigh. "Very bad."

"What's the matter?"

"You see, my dear, the highest and most sacred prerogative of kings is the right to pardon. I have always felt myself a king, for I have availed myself of that prerogative again and again. I have never judged, I have always made allowances, I have gladly granted free pardons right and left to everybody. Where others have protested and been indignant, I have only advised and persuaded. All my life I have tried my best to make my company tolerable to my family, my students, my colleagues, and my servants. And this attitude of mine towards people has, I know, had a salutary effect on everyone who has had anything to do with me. But now I am a king no longer. What is going on inside me now is something tolerable only in a slave: day and night evil thoughts fill my head, and feelings I never knew before have built a nest in my heart. I hate, I despise, I am filled with indignation, I am exasperated, and I am afraid. I have become quite excessively strict, demanding, irritable, rude, suspicious. Even the things which formerly used to make me perpetrate a pun, and laugh good-humouredly, merely make me feel sick at heart now. My sense of logic, too, has undergone a change: before, it was only money I despised, but what I loathe now is not money but the rich, as if they were to blame; before, I hated violence and tyranny, but now I hate the people who use violence, as though they alone were to blame, and not all of us who do not know how to educate one another. What does it mean? If my new thoughts and my new feelings are the result of a change in my convictions, how can this change have arisen? Has the world become worse? Have I become better? Or have I been blind and indifferent till now? If this change has arisen from a general decline in my mental and physical faculties—for I am sick, you see, I lose weight every day—then my position is pitiful indeed. For it can only mean that my new thoughts are morbid and abnormal, and that I ought to be ashamed of them and regard them as contemptible."

"Sickness has nothing to do with it," Katya interrupts me. "It is simply that your eyes have been opened. That's all. You see things now which for some reason you did not want to notice before. In my opinion, you must first of all make a final break with your family and leave them."

"You're talking nonsense."

"You don't love them any more, do you? Then why be hypocritical about it? What sort of a family is it, anyhow? Nonentities! If they were to die today, by tomorrow no one would notice their absence."

Katya despises my wife and daughter as much as they hate her. It is almost impossible nowadays to speak of people being entitled to despise one another. But if one accepts Katya's point of view and admits that they are entitled to, one has to admit that she is just as much entitled to despise my wife and daughter as they are to hate her.

"Nonentities," she repeats. "Did you have any dinner today? They didn't forget to call you to have your dinner? They still remember that you exist?"

"Katya," I say severely, "please don't talk like that."

"Why, do you think I enjoy talking about them? I'd be glad not to know them at all! Listen to me, dear. Leave everything and go away. Go abroad. The sooner the better."

"What nonsense! And the university?"

"And the university, too. What do you want it for? What's the use of it, anyway? You've been lecturing for thirty years, and where are your pupils? Are there many famous scientists among them? Count them! And to multiply the doctors who exploit ignorance and make fortunes you don't need to be a good and talented man. You're not wanted."

"Dear me, how severe you are!" I exclaim, horrified. "How severe!

Not another word, or I'll go. I don't know what to reply to these bitter things you say."

The maid comes in to tell us that tea is served. At the tea table our conversation, thank God, takes a different turn. Having uttered my complaints, I cannot resist giving way to another weakness of old age —reminiscences. I tell Katya about my past, and to my own great surprise expatiate on incidents I never suspected I remembered so well. She listens to me with deep emotion, with pride, with bated breath. I particularly like to tell her how I once studied at a theological college and how I dreamed of entering a university.

"I used to walk about in the grounds of the seminary," I tell her, "and whenever the wind brought the strains of a concertina and a song from some far-away country pub, or a *troika* dashed past the seminary fence with a jingle of bells, it was enough for a feeling of happiness to flood not only my breast, but also my belly, legs, and hands. . . . I would listen to the strains of the concertina or to the sounds of the harness bells dying away in the distance, and imagine myself a doctor, and paint all sorts of pictures—each one more thrilling than the next. And, as you see, my dreams came true. I have got more than I dared to dream of. For thirty years I have been a popular professor, have had excellent colleagues, enjoyed an honourable reputation. I loved, I married for passionate love, I had children. In short, looking back, the whole of my life seems a beautiful and ably made composition. All that remains for me to do now is not to spoil the ending. This makes it necessary that I should die like a man. If death is really a danger, then it must be met in a way worthy of a teacher, a scientist, and a citizen of a Christian state: boldly and in a calm spirit. But I'm afraid I am spoiling the ending. I am drowning, and I am calling to you for help, and you say: 'Drown! That's how it should be!' "

At that moment the front door bell rings. Katya and I both recognize the ring and say:

"That must be Mikhail Fyodorovich!"

And indeed a minute later Mikhail Fyodorovich, a university colleague of mine, a philologist, comes in. He is a tall, well-built man of fifty, clean-shaven, with thick grey hair and black eyebrows. He is a good man and an excellent friend. He belongs to an old aristocratic family, rather fortunate and gifted, which has played an outstanding part in the history of our literature and education. He is himself clever, gifted, and highly educated, but not without certain oddities of character. To a certain extent all of us are a bit odd, all of us are eccentrics, but his oddities are rather exceptional and not without danger to his friends. Among the latter I know quite a few who are unable to see his many good points because of these oddities of his.

As he comes in, he slowly removes his gloves and says in his velvety bass:

"Good evening. Having tea? Excellent! It's hellishly cold."

Then he sits down at the table, takes a glass of tea, and immediately starts talking. The most characteristic thing about his conversation is its invariably jocular tone, a sort of blend of philosophy and buffoonery, like Shakespeare's grave-diggers. He always talks about serious things, but never seriously. His opinions are always harsh and abusive, but his gentle, smooth, and jocular tone somehow prevents his harshness and abusiveness from grating on the ears, and you soon get used to them. Every evening he brings half a dozen stories of university life, and he usually starts with them when he sits down at the table.

"Oh dear," he sighs, twitching his black eyebrows sardonically, "what comical fellows there are in the world!"

"Why?" asks Katya.

"I was coming from my lecture today and who should I meet on the stairs but that silly old fool N. There he was, his horsy chin thrust out as usual, looking for someone to complain to about his headaches, his wife, and the students who won't go to his lectures. Good Lord, I thought, he's seen me and I'm in for it now, no escape . . ."

And so on in the same vein. Or he would begin like this:

"I was at our Z's public lecture yesterday. I am amazed how our *alma mater* (may she forgive me for mentioning her at this witching hour of night) dares to show the public such imbeciles and patent idiots as that Z fellow. Why, he's known all over Europe as a born fool. Good Lord, you wouldn't find another like him in the whole of Europe, not even if you went looking for him with a torch in daylight! He lectures—believe it or not—just as if he were sucking sweets, with a sort of lisp. Gets frightened, can't read his own writing, his insipid thoughts hardly moving at all, like a bishop riding a bicycle, and worst of all you can't make out what he's trying to say. You could die of boredom, which can only be compared to the boredom in the assembly hall at the annual conferment of degrees, when the traditional graduation speech—damn it—is made."

And immediately an abrupt change of subject.

"About three years ago—Nikolai Stepanych here will remember—it was my turn to make that speech. Hot, close, my uniform tight under my arms—frightful! I spoke for half an hour, an hour, an hour and a half, two hours. . . . Well, I thought to myself, thank God I've only ten more pages left. Actually I counted on leaving out the last four pages, for they were quite superfluous. So, I said to myself, that leaves only six pages. At that moment I happened to look up and there in the front row I saw a general with a ribbon round his neck, and a bishop, sitting side by side. The poor fellows, stiff with boredom, were staring open-eyed to keep themselves from falling asleep, but trying to look as if they were following my speech closely, as if they understood it and liked it. Well, I thought, if you really like it, you shall have the whole damn lot! Just to teach you a lesson. So I read through all the last four pages!"

When he talks, only his eyes and eyebrows smile, as is the case with all sardonic people. There is neither hatred nor malice in his eyes at such moments, but a great deal of wit, and the sort of fox-like cunning which can only be seen in the faces of very observant people. Talking of his eyes, I have noticed another peculiarity about them. When he takes a glass from Katya, or listens to her remarks, or follows her with his eyes when she goes out of the room for a little while, I catch a look in his eyes of something gentle, beseeching, pure . . .

The maid takes the samovar away and places on the table a big piece of cheese, fruit, and a bottle of Crimean champagne, a rather bad wine which Katya had got to like while living in the Crimea. Mikhail Fyodorovich takes two packs of cards from the bookcase and begins to lay out a game of patience. He assures us that some games of patience demand great concentration and attention, but he goes on talking nevertheless while laying out the cards. Katya keeps an attentive eye on his cards and helps him, more by dumb show than words. During the whole of the evening she drinks no more than two glasses of wine; I drink only a quarter of a glass; the rest falls to the lot of Mikhail Fyodorovich, who can drink any amount without getting drunk.

Over the game of patience we solve all sorts of problems, mostly of the lofty order, and most of our sharpest criticism is directed against our dearest love—science.

"Science, thank heavens, has had its day," says Mikhail Fyodorovich. "Its goose is cooked. Yes, sir. Mankind is beginning to feel the need of putting something else in its place. It grew up in the soil of prejudice, it was nourished on prejudice and is now itself the quintessence of prejudice, like its defunct grandmothers' alchemy, metaphysics, and philosophy. And, really, what has science given to man? The difference between the learned Europeans and the Chinese, who get along without science, is trifling, purely external. The Chinese have no knowledge of science, and what have they lost?"

"Flies have no knowledge of science, either," I say, "but what does it prove?"

"You needn't get angry, Nikolai Stepanych. I'm only saying it between ourselves. I'm much more careful than you think. I wouldn't dream of saying so in public. The great majority of people still cherish the prejudice that the arts and sciences are superior to agriculture and commerce, superior to industry. Our sect makes a living out of that prejudice, and I'm the last man in the world to destroy it. God forbid!"

During the game of patience the younger generation, too, gets it in the neck.

"Our student audiences, too, are degenerating rapidly," Mikhail Fyodorovich declares with a sigh. "I'm not speaking of ideals and so on—if only they knew how to work and think properly. Yes, indeed, 'Sadly I behold our younger generation,' as the poet said."

"Yes, they're terribly degenerate," agrees Katya. "Tell me, has there been even one outstanding personality among your students during the last five or ten years?"

"I don't know about the other professors, but I can't think of anyone among my own students."

"I've met many students and young scholars in my time, as well as a great number of actors, and, well, I don't think I've ever been fortunate enough to come across a single interesting person among them, let alone demigods or men of real talent."

All this talk about degeneracy always makes me feel as if I had accidentally overheard some unpleasant remark about my daughter. What I find so offensive is that these accusations are utterly unfounded and are based on such hackneyed commonplaces and such scarifying phantoms as degeneracy, lack of ideals, or references to the glorious past. Any accusation, even if made in the presence of ladies, should be formulated with the utmost definitiveness, otherwise it is no accusation but mere gossip, unworthy of decent people.

I am an old man; I've been a university teacher for thirty years and I have not noticed any degeneration or lack of ideals, and I don't find that things are worse now than before. My caretaker Nikolai, whose experience in this case is not without value, maintains that students today are neither better nor worse than those of former times.

If I were asked what it was I did not like about my present students, I should not give an immediate answer or say much, but whatever I said would be sufficiently definite. I know their shortcomings, and I need not therefore resort to some hazy commonplaces. What I don't like about them is that they smoke and drink too much and get married too late, that they are feckless, and often so callous that they do not seem to notice that some of their fellow-students are starving, and that they don't pay their debts to the Students' Aid Society. They are ignorant of modern languages and express themselves incorrectly in Russian; only yesterday, my colleague the professor of hygenics complained to me that he had to give twice as many lectures because of their unsatisfactory knowledge of physics and complete ignorance of meteorology. They are readily influenced by the latest writers, even those who are not the best, but are completely indifferent to classics like Shakespeare, Marcus Aurelius, Epictetus, and Pascal, and their lack of experience of everyday life is perhaps best seen in this inability to distinguish between the great and the small. All the difficult questions of a more or less social character (for instance, the question of land settlement in distant provinces) they solve by subscription lists, and not by scientific investigation and experiment, though that is at their disposal and corresponds entirely with their vocation. They readily become house physicians, assistant lecturers, laboratory assistants, non-resident physicians, and they are quite willing to occupy these posts till they are forty, though independence, a sense of freedom, and personal initiative are not less necessary in science than they are, for instance, in art or commerce. I have pupils and students, but no assistants and successors, and that is why I love them and feel for them but am not proud of them. Etc., etc. . . . .

But such shortcomings, however numerous, can give rise to pessimistic or abusive moods only in a timid and pusillanimous man. They are all of an accidental and transitory nature, and depend entirely on circumstances; in ten or so years they will most probably disappear or give way to other and fresh shortcomings, which are inevitable and which will in turn frighten the faint-hearted. The sins of students often annoy me, but this annoyance is nothing compared to the joy I have felt these thirty years when talking to my students, lecturing to them, watching their relationships, and comparing them to people who do not belong to their social group.

Mikhail Fyodorovich goes on with his disparaging talk, Katya listens to him, and neither of them notices the deep abyss into which such a seemingly innocent pastime as talking ill of their neighbours is leading them. They do not seem to realize how an ordinary conversation can gradually turn into mockery and derision, and how both of them even stoop to defamation and slander.

"You certainly come across some queer types," says Mikhail Fyodorovich. "I went to see Yegor Petrovich yesterday and found one of your medicos there. A third-year student, I believe. A curious face. Reminded me of Dobrolyubov: a stamp of profound thought on his brow. We started talking. 'Wonders will never cease, young man,' I said to him. 'I've just read that some German—I forget his name—has extracted a new alkaloid from the human brain—idiotine.' And what do you think? He really believed me—there was an expression of reverential awe on his face: 'See what our scientists can do!' And the other day I went to the theatre. I took my seat. In front of me two students were sitting, one apparently a law student, one of the 'comrades,' and the other, a hirsute fellow, a medical student. The medical student was as drunk as a cobbler. He just sat there dozing and nodding. But as soon as an actor began to recite some soliloquy in a loud voice or simply raised his voice, our medico gave a start, nudged his neighbour, and asked: 'What did he say! Was it noble?' 'Yes, very noble,' our 'comrade' replied. 'Bravo!' roared the medical student. 'Noble! Bravo!' You see, the drunken sot didn't go to the theatre for the sake of art, but for noble sentiments. It's noble sentiments he wants."

Katya listens and laughs. Her laughter is rather strange: inhalation followed rapidly and rhythmically by exhalation. It is as though she were playing a mouth-organ, and in her face only her nostrils seem to laugh. I lose heart and don't know what to say. I flare up, jump up from my seat, and shout:

"Shut up, will you? What are you sitting there like a couple of toads for, poisoning the air with your breath? Enough!"

And without waiting for them to stop their slanderous talk, I get up to go home. It is time, anyway—eleven o'clock.

"I'll stay a little longer," says Mikhail Fyodorovich. "You don't mind, do you, Yekaterina Vladimirovna?"

"Not in the least," replies Katya.

"*Bene.* In that case, let's have another bottle."

They see me off to the hall, with candles in their hands, and while I am putting on my fur coat Mikhail Fyodorovich says:

"You're looking awfully thin and old today, Nikolai Stepanych. What's the matter? Are you ill?"

"Yes, a little."

"He won't see a doctor," Katya puts in gloomily.

"Why don't you? You can't go on like this. The Lord helps those who help themselves, my dear chap. Give my regards to your wife and daughter and my apologies for not coming to see them. I shall be going abroad shortly and I'll come to say good-bye before I leave. I shan't forget. I'm leaving next week."

I come away from Katya's feeling irritated, frightened by the talk of my illness, and dissatisfied with myself. I ask myself why really I don't consult one of my colleagues. But immediately I can see my colleague, after examining me, going silently over to the window, standing there for a while thinking, then turning round to me and saying casually, trying to prevent me from reading the truth on his face: "I don't see anything special so far. But all the same, my dear colleague, I'd advise you to give up your work." And that will deprive me of my last hope.

Which of us doesn't have hopes? Now, when I diagnose and treat myself, I sometimes hope that my ignorance deceives me, that I am mistaken about the albumen and sugar I find in my urine, about my heart, and about the oedematose swellings which I have already noticed in the morning; when, with the eagerness of a hypochondriac, I again read through the text-books on therapy and change my medicine every day, it always seems to me that I shall come across something comforting. The triviality of it all!

Whether the sky is covered with clouds or the moon and stars shine in it, on returning home I always look up at it and think that I shall soon be dead. It would seem that at such moments my thoughts ought to be as deep as the sky, bright and striking. . . . But no! I think about myself, my wife, Lisa, Gnekker, the students, and about people in general; my thoughts are mean and trivial. I try to deceive myself, and my view on life might be expressed in the words of the famous Arakcheyev, who wrote in one of his private letters: "No good thing in the world can be without some evil, and there is always more bad than good." In other words, everything is disgusting, there is nothing to live for, and the sixty-two years of my life must be regarded as wasted. I catch myself in these thoughts and try to convince myself that they are accidental and transient and not deeply rooted in me, but immediately I think:

"If that is so, then why do I long to go to those two toads every evening?"

And I vow never to go and see Katya again, though I know very well that I will go to her again the next day.

As I pull my front-door bell and then go upstairs, I feel that I have no family and have no desire to get it back. It is clear that these new Arakcheyev thoughts of mine are neither accidental nor transient, but have taken possession of all my being. With a sick conscience, dejected, languid, scarcely able to move my limbs, as though carrying an enormous weight on my shoulders, I go to bed and soon fall asleep.

And then—insomnia.

IV

Summer comes and life changes.

One fine morning Lisa comes into my room and says in a jesting tone:

"Come on, your excellency! Everything's ready."

My excellency is led out into the street, put into a cab, and driven away. Having nothing to do, I read the signboards backwards as I am being driven past. The word for "tavern," *Traktir*, becomes Ritkart. That would make a very good name for a German nobleman's family —Baroness von Ritkart. Further on I drive across open country, past a cemetary, which makes no impression on me whatsoever, although I shall be lying there soon. Then we are driven through a wood and once more through open country. Nothing interesting. After two hours' drive my excellency is taken to the ground floor of a country cottage and placed in a small but very cheerful room with blue wallpaper.

At night insomnia again, but in the morning I do not keep awake and do not listen to my wife, but stay in bed. I am not asleep. I am in that somnolent state when one is hardly conscious of one's surroundings, and when one knows that one is not asleep and yet has dreams. At noon I get up and sit down at my desk from force of habit, though I don't work but amuse myself with yellow French paperbacks sent by Katya. No doubt it would be more patriotic to read Russian authors, but to tell the truth I am not particularly fond of them. With the exception of one or two classics, the whole of our modern literature strikes me not as literature but as a kind of home industry which only exists because of being encouraged and whose products are only reluctantly purchased. The best of these home products can hardly be described as in any way remarkable, and one cannot praise them sincerely without a qualifying "but"; the same can be said about all the literary novelties I have read during the last ten or fifteen years. Clever, noble, but not talented; talented, noble, but not clever; or finally, talented, clever, but not noble.

I cannot honestly say that French books are talented, clever, and noble, and they do not really satisfy me; but they are not as boring as Russian books, and it is not rare to find in them the most important element of creative art—the sense of personal freedom, which Russian authors do not possess. I cannot remember a single new book in which the author does not do his best from the very first page to entangle himself in all sorts of conventionalities and compromises with his conscience. One writer is afraid to speak of the naked body, another has bound himself hand and foot by psychological analysis, a third must have "a warm attitude towards his fellow-men," a fourth purposely fills his pages with descriptive passages so as not to be suspected of tendentiousness. . . . One is absolutely set on appearing in his works as a member of the middle classes, another as a nobleman; and so on. Deliberateness, cautiousness, craftiness, but no freedom, no courage to write as one likes, and therefore no creative art.

All this refers to works of fiction.

As for serious articles by Russian writers, on sociology, for instance, on art, and so on, I don't read them, out of mere timidity. As a boy and a young man I was for some reason afraid of hall porters and theatre attendants, and that fear has remained with me to this day. I am still afraid of them. People say that it is very difficult to understand why hall porters and theatre attendants look so self-important, so haughty, so grandly impolite. When I read serious articles I feel the same kind of vague apprehension. Their extraordinary self-importance, their magisterial playfulness, the familiarity with which they treat foreign authors, the pompous way in which they utter their clichés—all this I find utterly incomprehensible and frightening, and quite unlike the modesty and the calm gentlemanly tone to which I am used when reading our writers on medicine and the natural sciences. It is not only articles. I find it as hard to read even the translations made or edited by serious Russian writers. The arrogantly self-assured and complacent tone of the prefaces, the multitude of footnotes by the translator which prevent me from concentrating, the question marks and parenthetical "sics" scattered by the generous translator throughout the book or articles, seem to me an unwarranted intrusion both on the author's independence and on my own as a reader.

I was once invited in my capacity as an expert to the assize court; during a break in the proceedings, one of the other experts called my attention to the rude way in which the public prosecutor treated the defendants, among whom were two educated women. I don't think I exaggerated at all when I replied that this rudeness was no worse than the way authors of serious articles treat one another. Indeed, they treat one another so rudely that one can only speak of it with pain. They treat each other or the writers they criticize either with excessive respect, without regard to their own dignity, or on the other hand with less reserve that I have treated my future son-in-law Gnekker in these notes and in my thoughts. Accusations of irresponsibility, of ulterior motives, and even of all sorts of crimes are the usual embellishments of serious articles. And that is, as young doctors like to say in their papers, quite *ultima ratio*. Such an attitude cannot but have an effect on the morals of the younger generation of writers, and I am therefore not at all surprised to find that in the new novels added to our literature during the last ten or fifteen years the heroes drink a great deal of vodka and the heroines are anything but chaste.

I read French novels and keep glancing through the open window. I can see the toothed palings of the fence of my front garden, a couple of gaunt trees, and beyond the fence the road, a field, then a wide strip of pine forest. I am often amused to watch a boy and a girl, both ragged and almost white-haired, climbing the fence and laughing at my bald pate. In their sparkling eyes I can read: "Come on, baldy!" These are almost the only human beings who do not seem to care a damn about my reputation or my high rank.

I don't have visitors every day now. I will mention only the visits of Nikolai and Peter Ignatyevich. Nikolai usually comes to see me on holidays, apparently on business but actually because he likes to see me. When he arrives, he is more than a bit tight, which never happens to him in the winter.

"Well, how are things?" I ask, coming out into the hall.

"Sir," he says, pressing his hand to his heart and looking at me with the rapture of a lover, "may the Lord strike me dead where I stand! May I drop dead! *Gaudeamus igitur juvenestus* . . ."

And he kisses me eagerly on the shoulders, the sleeves, the buttons.

"Is everything all right over there?" I ask.

"Sir, as before God . . ."

He never stops invoking the deity, without rhyme or reason, and I soon get bored with him and send him off to the kitchen, where he is given dinner. Peter Ignatyevich also comes on holidays specially to see me and share his thoughts with me. He usually sits down near the table, modest, clean, sensible, not daring to cross his legs or lean on the table. And all the time he goes on talking to me in his quiet, even, thin voice about what he considers the highly interesting and piquant items he has gleaned from periodicals and books. These are alike and follow the same pattern: a Frenchman has made a discovery, someone else—a German—has shown him up, proving that the discovery was made as long ago as 1870 by some American, and a third, also a German, has outwitted them both, showing that they have made fools of themselves by mistaking air bubbles under a microscope for a dark pigment. Even when he wants to amuse me, Peter Ignatyevich tells his stories at great length and in detail, as though he were defending a thesis, with a most detailed enumeration of the bibliographical sources he has used, taking particular care not to make mistakes in his dates, the number of the journal, or names, never saying Petit but always Jean-Jacques Petit. If he happens to stay to dinner, he tells the same piquant stories all through the meal, boring us all to death. If Gnekker and Lisa start talking in his presence about fugues, counterpoint, Bach, or Brahms, he lowers his head modestly and looks embarrassed: he feels ashamed that people should be talking of such trivial things in the presence of such serious people as myself and him.

In my present mood, five minutes are enough to bore me as much as though I had been seeing and listening to him for an eternity. I hate the poor wretch. His quiet even voice and his pedantic language make me wilt, and his stories dull my senses. He cherishes the most kindly feelings towards me, and talks to me only to give me pleasure; and I repay him by staring fixedly at him as though I wanted to hypnotize him, and keep saying to myself: "Go, go, go! . . ." But he is proof against suggestion and sits, sits, sits . . .

While he is with me I cannot get rid of the thought that when I die, he will most probably be appointed in my place, and my poor lecture-room appears to me like an oasis in which the well-spring has dried up; and I am uncivil, silent, morose with Peter Ignatyevich, as though it were his fault and not mine that I am having such thoughts. When, as is his wont, he starts extolling the German scientists, I no longer answer him jokingly, but mutter glumly:

"Your Germans are donkeys . . ."

This reminds me of the late Professor Nikita Krylov, who, when bathing in Reval with Pirogov, got angry with the the water, which was very cold, and swore: "Bloody Germans!" I behave badly to Peter Ignatyevich, and it is only when he is gone and I catch a glimpse of his grey hat on the other side of the fence that I feel like calling him back and saying: "I'm sorry, my dear fellow!"

Dinner is much more boring than in the winter. The same Gnekker, whom I now hate and despise, dines with us almost every day. Before, I used to put up with his presence in silence, but now I direct all sorts of uncomplimentary remarks at him, which make my wife and Lisa blush. Carried away by malicious feeling. I often say silly things, and I don't know why I say them. Thus, one day, after looking at Gnekker contemptuously for a long time, I blurted out for no reason at all:

> Eagles may often lower than chickens fly
> But never will chickens fly up to the sky . . .

And what's so annoying is that the chicken Gnekker turns out to be

much more intelligent than the eagle professor. Knowing that my
wife and daughter are on his side, he employs the following tactics:
replies to my uncomplimentary remarks with a condescending silence
(the old man has gone off his head, what's the use of talking to
him?), or keeps pulling my leg goodhumouredly. It really is amazing
how petty a man may become. During the whole of the meal I am
capable of imagining that Gnekker will turn out to be an adventurer,
that my wife and daughter will realize their mistake, that I will tease
them—and similar ridiculous fantasies, when I have one foot in the
grave!

There are misunderstandings now, too, which I was previously
aware of only by hearsay. Greatly as I am ashamed of it, I will
describe one of them, which occurred after dinner the other day.

I was sitting in my room, smoking my pipe. My wife came in as
usual and began telling me how nice it would be if I went to Kharkov,
now that it was so warm and I was free, and made inquiries about
Gnekker.

"All right," I said, "I'll go."

My wife, looking pleased with me, got up and went to the door, but
turned back at once.

"Incidentally," she said, "there's something I want to talk to you
about. I'm sorry, but you see all our friends and neighbours have been
remarking on the way you see Katya every day. Now I agree she's a
clever and well-educated girl, and I daresay you find it agreeable to be
with her, but don't you think that for a man of your age and your
position it's a bit odd to take pleasure in her company? Besides, her
reputation, you know . . ."

All my blood suddenly rushed from my brain, my eyes flashed, I
jumped to my feet, and clutching at my head and stamping, I
screamed in a frenzy:

"Leave me alone! Leave me alone! Leave me!"

I expect my face must have looked terribly distorted, and my voice
must have sounded very strange, for my wife turned pale and also
uttered a kind of frenzied desperate scream. At our cries, Lisa and
Gnekker came rushing in, followed by Yegor.

"Leave me!" I kept shouting. "Get out! Leave me!"

My feet grew numb, as if they did not exist. I felt myself falling
into somebody's arms, for a few moments I heard someone sobbing,
then I sank into a faint which lasted for two or three hours.

Now about Katya. She comes to see me every day, which of course our friends and neighbours could not help noticing. She comes in for a few minutes and then takes me out for a drive. She has her own horse and a new carriage she bought this summer. Altogether she lives in grand style. She has rented an expensive country residence with a large garden and moved her furniture into it, keeps two maids and a coachman . . .

"What will you live on, Katya, after you've squandered all the money your father left you?"

"I'll worry about it when it happens," she replies.

"That money, my dear, deserves to be treated with more respect. It was earned by a good man and by honest labour."

"You've told me that before. I know."

At first we drive through open country, then through the pine wood I can see from my window. The countryside looks as beautiful to me as ever, though the devil does whisper in my ear that all those pines and firs, those birds and white clouds, will not notice my absence in three or four months after I am dead. Katya likes taking the reins, she enjoys the fine weather and my sitting beside her. She's in a good mood and does not say disagreeable things.

"You're a very good man, Nikolai," she says. "You're a rare specimen, and there's no actor who could represent you on the stage. Even a bad actor could manage me or Mikhail Fyodorovich, but no one could do you. And I envy you. I envy you terribly. But what do I represent? What?"

She thinks for a moment, then asks me:

"Tell me, I am a negative phenomenon, aren't I?"

"Yes," I reply.

"I see. So what am I to do?"

What answer can I give her? It is easy to say "work" or "give your property to the poor" or "know thyself," and because it is so easy to say that, I don't know what answer to give.

My therapeutist colleagues, when teaching, tell their students "to individualize each separate case." One has only to take this advice to realize that the remedies recommended in textbooks as the best, and entirely suitable as a standard rule, are quite unsuitable in individual cases. The same applies to moral ailments.

But I have to give her an answer, so I say:

"You've too much time on your hands, my dear. You ought to find some occupation. Why shouldn't you go on the stage again, if that's your vocation?"

"I can't."

"You talk and look as if you'd been hard done by. I don't like it, my dear. It's all your own fault. Remember you began by getting angry with people and things, but you did nothing to improve the one or the other. You didn't struggle against evil, you got tired, and you're the victim of your own weakness, not of the struggle. I realize, of course, that you were young and inexperienced then. Now everything can be different. Go back to the stage—do! You will work, serve the sacred cause of art . . ."

"Don't try to pull the wool over my eyes, my dear sir," Katya interrupts me. "Let's agree once and for all to talk about actors, actresses, and writers, and let's leave art out of it. You're a rare and excellent person, but I don't think your knowledge of art is so thorough as to justify you in calling it sacred with a clear conscience. You have neither the ear nor the flair for art. You have been busy all your life, and haven't had the time for acquiring the flair. And as a matter of fact I don't like all this talk about art," she goes on nervously. "I don't like it. Art has been vulgarized enough already, thank you very much!"

"Who vulgarized it?"

"The actors by drunkenness, the papers by their over-familiar treatment, clever people by philosophy."

"Philosophy has nothing to do with it."

"Besides, anyone who philosophizes shows that he understands nothing."

To prevent our conversation from turning into an interchange of sharp words, I hasten to change the subject, and then I am silent for a long time. It is only when we emerge from the woods and approach Katya's house that I return to our former subject of conversation.

"You didn't answer me," I say. "Why don't you want to go back to the stage? Or do you?"

"My dear sir, that really is cruel!" she cries, and suddenly blushes all over. "Do you want me to tell you the truth? By all means if that's —if that's what you want. I have no talent, you see. I have no talent and . . . and lots of vanity! That's all there is to it."

Having made this admission, she turns her face away from me, and to conceal her trembling hands tugs at the reins violently.

As we drive up to her house, from a distance we can see Mikhail

Fyodorovich walking about near the gate waiting for us impatiently.

"There's that Mikhail Fyodorovich again!" says Katya in vexation. "Take him away from me, please. I'm sick and tired of him. He's played out. To hell with him!"

Mikhail Fyodorovich should have gone abroad long ago, but he keeps putting off his departure every week. A change has come over him lately: his face looks pinched; he has begun to be affected by drink, something that has never happened to him before, and his black eyebrows have begun to go grey. When our carriage draws up at the gate he cannot conceal his joy and impatience. He fussily helps Katya and myself to get out, he is in a hurry, laughs, rubs his hands; and the gentle, beseeching, pure expression which I noticed before only in his eyes is now spread all over his face. He is happy and at the same time ashamed of his happiness, ashamed of his habit of coming to see Katya every evening, and he finds it necessary to explain his visit by some such obvious absurdity as: "I was passing on business and I thought to myself why not drop in for a minute."

The three of us go into the house. At first we have tea, then the long-familiar two packs of cards appear on the table, followed by a big piece of cheese, fruit, and a bottle of Crimean champagne. The subjects of our conversation are not new, but the same as they were in the winter. The university, the students, literature, and the theatre all come in for their share of abuse; the air grows thick and close with spiteful gossip, and it is poisoned not as in the winter by the breath of two toads, but of three. In addition to the deep velvety laugh and the high-pitched reedy laughter that reminds one of a mouth-organ, the maid who waits on us hears the unpleasant jarring laugh of comic generals in stage farces: Heh—heh—heh . . .

V

There are terrible nights with thunder, lightning, rain, and high winds, which the peasants call "sparrow" or "equinoctial" nights. There was one such equinoctial night in my private life too.

I woke up after midnight and suddenly leapt out of my bed. It seemed to me for some reason that I was about to die suddenly. Why? There was not a single sensation in my body which pointed to a rapid end, but my heart was seized with a feeling of horror just as though I had suddenly seen a vast ominous glow in the sky.

I lighted my lamp hastily, took a sip of water straight from the decanter, and then rushed over to the open window. It was a magnificent night. There was the scent of new-mown hay in the air, and some other delicious smell. I could see the serrated tops of the fence, the sleepy gaunt trees near the window, the road, and the dark strip of woods; a bright calm moon in the sky, and not a single cloud. Perfect stillness, not a leaf stirred. It seemed to me as if the whole world was looking at me, listening, intent on hearing how I was going to die.

I felt terrified. I shut the window and rushed back to my bed. I felt my pulse and, unable to find it in my wrist, began feeling for it in my temples, my chin, and again in my wrist, and all the time I was bathed in a cold sweat and everything I touched was cold and clammy. My breathing grew more and more rapid, my body trembled, everything inside me was in motion, and my face and bald head felt as though they were covered by a cobweb.

What was I to do? Call my family? No, I mustn't do that. I did not see what my wife and daughter could do if they came in.

I hid my head under the pillow, shut my eyes, and waited, waited. . . . My back was cold, and it seemed almost as if it were drawn inwards. I had a curious feeling that death was quite certain to approach me from behind, very quietly . . .

"Kee-wee! Kee-wee!" A loud squeak suddenly resounded in the stillness of the night, and I could not tell whether it was coming from my chest or from outside.

"Kee-wee!"

God, how awful! I wanted to have another drink of water, but I was too terrified to open my eyes, afraid to raise my head. It was an unaccountable animal terror, and I was absolutely at a loss to understand what I was so afraid of: was it because I wanted to live, or that some new pain, never before experienced, awaited me?

In the room upstairs someone was groaning or laughing. . . . I listened. A little later there was the sound of footsteps on the stairs. Someone was coming down quickly, then running up again. A minute later footsteps could be heard again coming down; someone stopped outside my door and listened.

"Who's there?" I shouted.

The door opened; I opened my eyes boldly and saw my wife. Her face was pale and her eyes blotchy with crying.

"You're not asleep?" she asked.

"What do you want?"

"For God's sake, go and see Lisa Something's terribly wrong with her."

"Very well . . . gladly . . ." I muttered, pleased not to be alone. "Very well. . . . One moment . . ."

I followed my wife, listened to what she told me, but I was too agitated to understand a word of what she said. Bright spots of light danced on the stairs from her candle, our long shadows trembled, my feet got entangled in the long skirt of my dressing gown. I was out of breath, and I felt as if someone were chasing me and trying to seize me from behind. "Any moment now I shall die here on the stairs. . . . Now, now! . . ." But the stairs were behind us; we were walking along a dark corridor with an Italian window at the end, and at last entered Lisa's room. Lisa was sitting moaning on the bed in her chemise, her bare feet hanging down.

"Oh dear, oh dear," she was muttering, screwing up her eyes because of our candle. "I can't, I can't . . ."

"Lisa, my child," I said, "what's the matter with you?"

Seeing me, she uttered a cry and flung her arms round my neck.

"Daddy, darling Daddy," she sobbed, "dear, dear Daddy. . . . Oh, darling, I don't know what's the matter with me. . . . I feel so awful!"

She was embracing me, kissing me, murmuring the endearing names I used to hear from her when she was still a child.

"Come, come, my child, calm yourself," I said. "Don't cry, I don't feel so well myself."

I tried to cover her, my wife gave her something to drink, and both of us jostled about confusedly round the bed; my shoulder brushed against hers, and I remembered how we used to bath our children together.

"Do something for her, do something," my wife implored me.

But what could I do? There was nothing I could do. There was some heavy load on the poor girl's heart, but I understood nothing, knew nothing, and could only murmur: "It's nothing, nothing. It'll pass. Go to sleep, go to sleep . . ."

As though on purpose, a dog suddenly began howling in our yard just then, at first quietly and irresolutely, then loudly, in two voices. I had never before attached any significance to such omens as the howling of dogs or the hooting of owls, but at that moment my heart contracted painfully, and I hastened to explain the reason for that howling.

"It's a lot of nonsense," I thought. "The influence of one organism on another. My violent nervous tension communicated itself to my wife, to Lisa, to the dog, that's all. . . . Transmissions like that explain premonitions, previsions . . ."

When a little later I returned to my room to write out a prescription for Lisa, I no longer thought that I would die soon. I simply felt so sick at heart and so wretched that I was even sorry I had not died suddenly. I stood for a long time motionless in the middle of the room, thinking what to prescribe for Lisa, but the moans upstairs ceased and I decided not to prescribe anything. But I still remained standing there . . .

There was a dead silence, the sort of silence which, as some writer put it, seemed to ring in the ears. Time passed slowly, the shafts of moonlight on the window-sill did not change their position, just as if they were frozen. . . . It was still a long time till dawn.

Suddenly the garden gate creaked; someone was stealing towards the house and, breaking a twig from one of the gaunt trees, began tapping cautiously on the window.

"Nikolai Stepanych," I heard someone whisper, "Nikolai Stepa-nych!"

I opened the window and thought I was dreaming: under the window, clinging close to the wall, stood a woman in a black dress, brightly lit by the moon, looking at me with wide-open eyes. Her face was pale, austere, and looked unreal in the moonlight, like marble.

"It's me," she said. "Me—Katya."

In moonlight all women's eyes look big and black, everyone looks taller and paler, and that was probably why I did not recognize her at first.

"What's the matter?"

"I'm sorry," she said, "but I suddenly felt so unbearably wretched. I couldn't stand it any longer and drove over here. There was a light in your window and—I decided to knock. . . . I'm awfully sorry. . . . Oh, if you knew how sick at heart I felt! What are you doing now?"

"Nothing. . . . Insomnia . . ."

"I had a kind of premonition. Still, it's all nonsense . . ."

Her eyebrows lifted, her eyes gleamed with tears, and her whole face glowed as thought with light, with the familiar expression of trustfulness I had not seen on it for such a long time.

"Nikolai Stepanych," she said in a beseeching voice, holding out both hands to me, "my dear, I beg you . . . if you don't scorn my friendship and my respect for you, please do what I ask."

"What is it?"

"Take my money."

"What will you be thinking of next! What do I want your money for?"

"You could go away for treatment somewhere. You must get good medical treatment. Will you take it? Will you? Darling, will you?"

She looked eagerly into my face and repeated:

"Will you? Will you take it?"

"No, my dear friend, I won't take it," I said. "Thanks all the same."

She turned her back on me and lowered her head. I must have refused in a tone of voice that did not admit of any further talk about money.

"Go back to bed," I said. "I'll see you tomorrow."

"So you don't consider me your friend?" she asked despondently.

"I didn't say that. But your money is no use to me now."

"I'm sorry," she said, lowering her voice to a whole octave. "I understand. To be beholden to a person like me . . . a retired actress. . . . Oh well. Good-bye."

And she went away so quickly that I had no time even to say good-bye to her.

VI

I am in Kharkov.

Since it would be useless, besides being beyond my strength, to fight against my present state of mind, I have decided that the last days of my life shall be irreproachable—outwardly, at any rate; if I have been unfair towards my family, as I realize very well, I shall do my best to do what they want. If I am to go to Kharkov, to Kharkov I shall go. Besides, of late I have become so indifferent to everything that it is absolutely all the same to me where I go—to Kharkov, to Paris, or to Berdichev.

I arrived here at noon and put up at a hotel not far from the cathedral. I felt sick in the train, chilled through and through by draughts, and now I sit on the bed, holding my head between my hands and waiting for the tic. I ought really to have paid a visit to the local professors, I know, but I have neither the will nor the strength.

The old hotel waiter comes in to ask whether I have brought my own bed linen. I keep him for about five minutes and question him about Gnekker, on whose account I have come here. The waiter turns out to be a native of Kharkov; he knows the town like the back of his hand but cannot recall a family by the name of Gnekker. I ask him about estates, and get the same answer.

The clock in the corridor strikes one, then two, then three. . . . The last months of my life, while I wait for death, seem much longer than the whole of my life to me. Never before, though, have I been able to submit with a good grace to the slow passage of time, as I do now. Before, when waiting at the station for a train or invigilating at an examination, a quarter of an hour would seem an eternity to me, but now I can sit motionless on my bed all night, thinking with complete indifference that tomorrow and the day after tomorrow the nights will be just as long and as ghastly . . .

The clock in the corridor strikes five, six, seven. . . . It is getting dark.

I feel a dull pain in my cheek—the beginning of the tic. To distract myself by thinking of something, I try to adopt the point of view I used to hold when I was not indifferent to everything, and I ask myself why I, a famous man, a privy councillor, am sitting in this small hotel room, on this bed covered by a strange grey blanket. Why am I looking at that cheap tin washstand and listening to the jarring chimes of the wretched clock in the corridor? Is this worthy of my fame and my high position in society? And I reply to these questions with an ironical smile. The naïveté with which in my youth I exaggerated the importance of fame and the exceptional position famous men apparently occupy seems ridiculous to me now. I am famous, my name is spoken with reverence, my portrait has appeared in the illustrated weekly *Niva* and in the *Universal Illustrated Monthly*, I have even read my biography in a German journal—and what does it all amount to? Here I am all alone in a strange town, on a strange bed, rubbing my aching cheek with my hand. . . . Family troubles, the callousness of creditors, the rudeness of railway guards, the inconvenience of the passport system, the expensive and unwholesome food in the refreshment rooms, the general ignorance and coarseness of the people—all this, and a great deal more that would take too long to enumerate, concerns me no less than it does any tradesman who is known only in his own little street. In what way is my position so exceptional? Suppose I were a thousand times more famous, suppose I were a hero of whom my country is proud, all the papers publishing bulletins of my illness, every post already bringing me letters of sympathy from my colleagues, my students, and the public; yet all that would not prevent me from dying in a strange bed, in misery and total loneliness. . . . No one can be blamed for this, of course; but, miserable sinner that I am, I do not like my popular name. I feel that it has deceived me.

At about ten I fall asleep, and in spite of my tic sleep soundly and would have slept a long time if I had not been wakened. Soon after one o'clock there is a sudden knock at my door.

"Who's there?"

"A telegram, sir."

"You could have waited till tomorrow," I mutter angrily, as I take the telegram from the night porter. "I shan't fall asleep again now."

"Very sorry, sir. There was a light in your room, so I thought you were awake."

I open the telegram and first of all look at the signature. It's from my wife. What does she want?

"Gnekker and Lisa were married secretly yesterday stop come back."

I read the telegram, but my alarm does not last long. It is not so much what Gnekker and Lisa have done that frightens me as the fact that I am so completely indifferent to the news of their marriage. Philosophers and sages are said to be indifferent. It isn't true. Indifference is paralysis of the soul, premature death.

I go back to bed and try to think of some ideas to occupy my mind. What am I to think about? It seems to me that everything has already been thought of and there is nothing new that is capable of arousing my thoughts.

Daybreak finds me sitting on the bed, clasping my knees and trying, having nothing better to do, to know myself. "Know thyself" is most excellent and useful advice; the pity is the ancients did not think it necessary to show us the way to avail ourselves of this advice.

When I felt like trying to understand someone or myself before, I used to take into consideration desires and not actions, about which everything is conditional. Tell me what you want and I will tell you what you are.

And now, too, I examine myself: what do I want?

I want our wives, our children, our friends, our students to love not our name, our firm, our label, but ourselves, ordinary human beings.

What else? I should like to have assistants and successors. What else? I should like to wake in a hundred years and take a look, even if only with one eye, at what has happened to science. I should like to live another ten years. . . . What more?

Nothing more. I think and think, and cannot think of anything. And however much I were to think and however far I were to scatter my thoughts, it is clear to me that the main thing, something very important, is lacking in my desires. In my partiality for science, in my desire to live, in my sitting here on a strange bed and in my longing to know myself, in all my thoughts, feelings, and concepts about everything, there is no common link, there is nothing that might bind it together in one whole. Each thought and each feeling lives in me separately, and the most skilful analyst could not discover what is known as a ruling idea or what might be called the god of the living man in all my opinions of science, the theatre, literature, students, and all the pictures my imagination conjures up.

And if that is not there, nothing is there.

In view of such poverty, any serious illness, the fear of death, the influence of circumstances and people, is quite sufficient to turn upside down and smash into smithereens everything which I have hitherto regarded as my view of things and in which I have seen the meaning and joy of life. There is nothing surprising, therefore, in my having darkened the last months of my life by thoughts and feelings worthy of a slave and a barbarian, in my being indifferent now and not noticing the dawn. When a man lacks the things that are higher and stronger than all external influences, a bad cold in the head is enough to upset his equilibrium and make him see an owl in every bird and hear a dog's howl in every sound. And all his pessimism or optimism, all his thoughts, great or small, are in this case merely a symptom and nothing more.

I am beaten. If that is so, there is no point in going on thinking, no point in going on talking. I shall sit and wait in silence for what is to come.

In the morning the porter brings me tea and a copy of the local newspaper. I read mechanically through the advertisements on the first page, the editorial, the extracts from other newspapers and periodicals, the news items. Among the news items I find the following piece of information: "Yesterday our famous scientist, Professor Nikolai Stepanovich so-and-so, arrived by express train and is staying at the—Hotel."

Big names are evidently created to live by themselves, apart from those who bear them. Now my name is walking unworried all over Kharkov, and in three months' time it will shine in golden letters on a tombstone as bright as the sun itself—and that's when I myself will be covered with earth . . .

A light knock at the door. Someone still wants me, it seems.

"Who's there? Come in."

The door opens, and I step back in astonishment and quickly draw my dressing-gown more tightly round me. Katya stands before me.

"Good morning," she says, out of breath with walking up the stairs. "You didn't expect me, did you? I—I've come here too."

She sits down and goes on, stammering and not looking at me.

"Why don't you ask me how I am? I—I came here too—today. I found out you were at this hotel and I came to see you."

"I'm delighted to see you," I say, shrugging my shoulders, "but I must say I am surprised. You seem to have dropped from the sky. What are you doing here?"

"Me? Oh, I just came, you know . . ."

Silence. Suddenly she gets up impulsively and walks up to me.

"Nikolai Stepanych," she says, turning pale and pressing her hands to her breast, "I can't go on living like this. I can't! I can't! For God's sake tell me quickly, this minute, what am I to do? Tell me, what am I to do?"

"What can I tell you?" I say, looking bewildered at her. "I can't tell you anything."

"Say something, I implore you," she goes on, gasping for breath and trembling all over. "I swear I can't go on like this any more! It's more than I can bear."

She collapses on a chair and starts sobbing. She throws her head back, wrings her hands, stamps her feet; her hat falls off and dangles by its elastic band, her hair comes undone.

"Help me! Help me!" she implores. "I can't go on like this any more!"

She takes a handkerchief out of her bag and pulls out a few letters, which fall from her knees on to the floor. I pick them up, and on one of them I recognize Mikhail Fyodorovich's handwriting and accidentally read part of a word, "passionate . . ."

"I'm sorry, I can't tell you anything, Katya," I say.

"Help me!" she cries, sobbing. And catching me by the hand, she begins to kiss it. "Why, you're my father, my only friend! You're clever, you're well educated, you've lived so long. You've been a teacher. Tell me—what am I to do?"

"Honestly, Katya, I don't know . . ."

I am at a loss, embarrassed, touched by her sobs, and can hardly stand on my feet.

"Come, Katya, let's have breakfast," I say, with a strained smile. "Do stop crying."

"Just one word, only one word," she says, crying and holding out her hands to me. "What shall I do?"

"What a strange girl you are," I murmur. "So intelligent, and suddenly tears, if you please!"

A pause. Katya puts her hair to rights, puts on her hat, then crumples the letters and puts them back in her bag. She does it all in silence and without hurry. Her face, her bosom, and her gloves are wet with tears, but her face already looks cold and severe. I look at her, and feel ashamed that I am happier than she. The absence in myself of what my philosopher colleagues call a ruling idea I noticed only shortly before my death, in the evening of my life; and the soul of this poor girl has never known and will not find a place of refuge all her life—all her life.

"Come, Katya, let's have breakfast," I say.

"No, thanks," she replies coldly.

Another minute passes in silence.

"I don't like Kharkov," I say. "Too dull. A dull sort of town."

"I suppose so. Ugly. I'm not staying here long. Just passing through. Leaving today."

"Where are you going?"

"To the Crimea. I mean the Caucasus."

"I see. For long?"

"Don't know."

Katya gets up and holds out her hand to me, smiling coldly and not looking at me.

I want to ask her: "So you won't be at my funeral?" But she does not look at me; her hand is cold, like the hand of a stranger. I accompany her to the door in silence. She goes out of my room and walks along the long passage without looking back. She knows I am following her with my eyes, and I expect she will look round when she gets to the turning.

No, she does not look round. I catch a glimpse of her black dress for the last time, the sound of her footsteps dies away. . . . Good-bye, my treasure.

TRANSLATED BY DAVID MAGARSHACK

. .
. .
. .

Modern fiction, the fiction of motive rather than event, has grown up cheek by jowl with the secular confession. "Gino O" is a tape-recorded autobiography edited by a social scientist in the interests of constructing a picture of a community or manner of living. The editing requires a sensitivity groomed by the sort of selectivity, variation in mood and scene, sense of place, occasion, and detail characteristic of modern fiction. Yet "Gino O" also harks back to pre-Rousseau autobiography; like Augustine's, it is at least partially presented as propaganda: "Except for the Party (Church or what have you) my life might have gone down the drain."

Compared with another retrospective confession, that of Chekhov's professor, Gino's account seems an almost haphazard string of events, as full of holes as a net.

MADEMOISELLE DE PLÉMEUR
Champion of the "Three hundred metres"

Henry de Montherlant

Unlike most athletes and most spectators (it is curious to see how cruelly and unfairly female athletes are made fun of by the very people who extravagantly over-estimate the social role of women), I maintain that sports as practised by women—running, jumping and throwing the javelin—can provide the keenest enjoyment, both athletic and aesthetic. No doubt it is more difficult for a woman than for a man to be a satisfactory, average athlete, but at almost any female athletic meeting, you will find a handful of women who show themselves to be perfectly accomplished and whose performances, from the technical point of view, are no less interesting than those of the men. This is true for France and, still more so, for other countries.

The new contribution made by women to athletics is not technical, but aesthetic and moral.

Aesthetic. We see women as they could be if the duplicity, viciousness and bad taste of the male did not force them into disastrous courses of action: the distortion of the body by corsets, tight shoes[1] and high heels and of the figure by clothes; not to mention make-up. Morphologically, the only difference between men and women is in the chest and the pelvis, which are both more pronounced in the female for utilitarian reasons: gestation and suckling. If the female pelvis is too broad, it is ugly; it makes the silhouette clumsy, by appearing top-heavy above the shortened and

---

[1] The male tries to make the female "doll-like" or even frankly ridiculous, to maintain his advantage over her. The female connives in this through stupidity. Do women realize, for instance, that their superstitious belief in the prettiness of small feet is only a survival of the masculine idea: "With small feet, she will be handicapped and will be easier to keep under control"? The Chinese admit that this is their intention in crippling their women's feet. The Phoenicians put their girls' feet in fetters so that they should not be "loose," in any sense.

rather bandy legs. The breasts, even when prominent, are beautiful, if they remain firm. The muscles, in a woman as in a man, are always beautiful provided they are not too pronounced; there is no beauty, nor even gracefulness, where there is no suggestion of inner strength, the "discrete strength" that Aristotle asked for (just as the soul can have no valid feeling if it is without strength). Even a young child cannot be beautiful unless he displays a certain latent vigour; stature has nothing to do with the matter.

All that was enunciated in the Greek canon of the Golden Age, which is perfect both for men and women. To depart from it ever so slightly is to fall into error.

Up to the age of twenty-three, I was disconcerted by the paradox that nature makes us burn with desire for bodies which are ugly, and which we know to be ugly. The female bodies depicted by the painters and sculptors of the day, the bodies I had seen undressed, although they belonged to "pretty women," and even professional models, were horrible, yet opinion was unanimous in proclaiming that the rolls of fat, drooping dugs and bulging behinds of these saddle-backed, blown-out, shapeless creatures, were the most sublime, and indeed the only, expression of Beauty with a capital B. Never having come across, in real life, any female bodies resembling Greek statuary or the women in certain old masterpieces, I concluded that they were idealized inventions. But in 1919, I saw young girls practising on sports grounds, and others who had been trained according to George Hébert's "natural method," and I read Hébert's indispensable book, L'Education physique féminine. What a revelation! It was as if I had discovered another sex. I suddenly realized that the female body could be beautiful, if it were exercised. For six years or more, I was literally unable to take an interest in any women other than athletes. I could hold my head high and approve of the feeling which drew me to them, whereas until then I had been ashamed of being attracted in spite of myself by bodies that satisfied neither my reason nor my taste. At last I had found women with whom I could be on an equal footing.

As for the moral effect of female athletics, I don't know whether it has been important for many men, but it certainly was for me. It was in Sports clubs that I was able to experience the strange and charming feeling of pure comradeship between men and women—all of them lightly clad. There were two quite distinct categories: the body and the flesh. The body of a woman member of the club was merely an object of beauty and of athletic prowess. If she aroused other feelings in me, they were kept on a short lead and released only outside the club; and even then I considered them as being a due that had to be paid to nature. I approved of them, of course, but on their own level; and I accepted the rule that the flesh must take second place, when this rule was formulated by athletics, whereas it seemed ridiculous to me when it was put forward by religious and moral codes. Sometimes, the flesh even seemed a corrupting influence! The story of the young man and the girl in *Le Songe* is based on this conception.

Later, I adopted a different philosophy of life: I came to believe that nothing mattered. But even now, if I happen to meet women athletes, the mewings and crowings of the male suddenly seem very vulgar; I may add that I have observed this reaction, which was characteristic of Peyrony in 1920, in a number of young Frenchmen in 1938. And I remained convinced that my conduct with regard to girl athletes between 1919 and 1925 stood rather high in the scale of refinement. There was some affectation in it, but only a little and that little was of good quality.

However, it was a relationship that was always to some extent *sui generis*. On the sports field women arouse no more emotion than do men or boys, but the emotion is different. The sounds of their lax Ionian harp, or erratic Phrygian flute, which upset the severe Laconian functioning of male athletics, can be heard in the story of Mademoiselle de Plémeur.

. . . It was one July, during an Atlantic crossing. I can still see her leaning against the rail beside me, erect, serious, smiling towards the horizon, with her smile gleaming from the highest point of her person as a peal of bells rings out from the highest point in the sky. Her arms were naked under their transparent blue covering and in the sun they had the muted light of the sun during a time of eclipse, and when the shadow of a sail fell across them they took on the appearance of tawny sand glimpsed through a liquid dream. I moved to one side a little to get a better view of her and the wind brought me the wholesome scent of her hair.

Without turning her head, she said: "I saw your name written on the waters."

I have found, among female athletes, a number of girls who represent the last, extreme flowering of those aristocratic Breton families in which an independent, rebellious spirit has been perpetuated throughout the centuries. They were girls who had gone in for athletics as their brothers engaged in Left-Wing politics. They threw all the rich qualities, all the better humours of their ancient blood into what was, for them, a misdemeanour.

When I first got to know Mlle de Plémeur, she was the pride of her club: champion of the three hundred metres and, in her day, unbeatable in France over that distance. She was, moreover, very much the artistic type in athletics—uneven, capricious, easily discouraged and easily elated, and so outlandish in behaviour that, but for her ability, she would have been expelled from the club as being "impossible."

She was twenty-four, which, for a girl, is late autumn. Her long and shapely limbs passed more or less unnoticed, perhaps because she lacked the piquancy that Frenchmen prefer above everything else; also, perhaps, because she was always impossibly dressed. Her face was not worth looking at (but how insignificant a face is compared to a body!). As an athlete in action, she was transfigured, and escaped into a form of human perfection.

Her brother was in the camel corps in Africa, after getting himself involved in some unsavoury affair; old M. de Plémeur had come to the police-station and sobbed, while the inspector left his titled catch to cool off on the bench where they usually put the pimps; and the policemen had kept looking round and sniggering: "Just think of it. A Viscount!" She, we understood, through a sudden whim or intolerable boredom, had left her noble father who, hidden away in his filthy ancestral home at Morlaix, was drowning in drink the anguish of gradually having to admit that he would soon be a pauper. She detested "society" and lived in a little boarding-house, steering back—so it was said—to her ancestral home, all those who feather their nests with the plumes of decadent aristocrats. And sometimes, when physical exercise was no longer giving her face the sublime expression of a virgin-maenad, I thought I could discern there the sadness I notice every day, and always with the same pity, on faces I pass in the streets: "Perhaps I shall never get married."

Am I mistaken? But athletics, like religion, can sometimes be a substitute activity. I have known young men and women look upon the mastery of their bodies as a means of recovering self-confidence, of compensating for some weakness or failure in their everyday lives. A fresh idol and a fresh illusion.

One day, to everybody's surprise, Mlle de Plémeur was soundly beaten in the three hundred metres through proving unable to put on a final "spurt." She accepted defeat in that sporting spirit which is so praiseworthy when it occurs in a female temperament. But, without saying good-bye to anyone, she stopped coming to the sports ground, gave no sign of life and it was only by chance that we learned, after an interval, that she had gone back to Morlaix.

Three months later, there was a ring at my door. It was Mlle de Plémeur, dripping with rain, who had come all the way out to Neuilly. In the sitting-room, as soon as she had taken her hat off and shaken her head like a little girl to loosen and fluff out her Breton hair, which would suffer no parting, she declared without any preamble:

"I gave it all up. I'm getting too old, aren't I? I could see the fat coming back and my muscles getting stiffer. And then, a month ago . . . You know, the last spurt of flame just before the fire goes out . . . I can feel in my body that I've got my old form back; it's unbelievable. No good trying to understand. Form is still half a mystery to us; it comes and goes, like a snake or a will o' the wisp. Now that I've lost my sprint I've been practising longer distances on my own. And I'm sure—do you hear?—absolutely certain I can break the women's record for the thousand metres, which is three minutes sixteen seconds. Only I must make the attempt straight away; I may lose my form from one day to the next. That's why I've come here. All the officials are away at the club. So I thought of you. Tomorrow, if possible, you must come and time me . . . I'll only come back to the club and take up the good old life again where I left off if I can do it with you to testify that I've broken the record . . . You must . . ."

There was no need to beg. She had convinced me. No doubt there wasn't much point in her desire to break the record, because even if she succeeded, her performance would not be officially recognized, not having been properly checked. But what did that matter? I would be making her happy and doing no one any harm. When people have only desires of this kind, should we not make haste to grant them without fuss the trifle that will satisfy? It is so soon too late.

However, rather mischievously, I let her run on, as pressing, over-eloquent and absorbed in her subject as Emma Bovary must have been when she was begging cash from M. Guillaumin. Sitting opposite her, I realized with curiosity that in three months I had forgotten many of her facial expressions, whereas I remembered tiny particularities of her body, as if she had belonged to me. From childhood, I have always attached more importance to bodies than to faces, and a sweet little face on a teratological body—the typical Parisian product —has never given me the same emotion as indifferent features above a beautifully shaped figure.

"You will put an end to love-making!" groan the opponents of female athletics, who consider that for a young woman to show a bare leg anywhere except behind the footlights is to endanger the future of the race. "*Let women retain her mystery!*" Whichever way I twist this egregious injunction, I cannot get it to mean anything other than: "Hide three-quarters of a woman's body from view if we want her to appear beautiful. For the love of the fair sex, leave the coverings in place and don't look too closely." This strange defence amounts to an insult; what are we to think of women who approve of such honeyed caddishness! How can one fail to be struck by the lack of self-confidence betrayed by their age-old frenzy for disguise! It makes one think of the poet's fine phrase: "Is there any better mark of a legitimate and authentic power than that it should not be exercised behind a veil?" (Valéry) In Mlle de Plémeur's case, I realized with sadness that she had done herself harm, socially, through not taking advantage of her "mystery." Her very straightforwardness and accessibility had classed her, once and for all, as an eternal comrade, and no one, apparently, had ever expected her to be anything more. To a certain extent, she was paying for her healthiness by not being happy.

We decided to go to the club ground next morning at eight. Mlle de Plémeur took her leave. After getting half-way through the door, she came back into the entrance hall:

"G. (this was the director of the club) has written to tell me that Serrurier (one of the other women athletes) has resigned suddenly because one of the younger girls gave her a horribly mocking look once when she made a clumsy mistake during practice. He says that, from now on, to prevent the young girls making fun of the older ones, he has put them in separate groups and is training them at different times. To think that we've had to come to that! It's a battlefield, isn't it?"

"No, just a chicken-run, with the hens pecking each other slowly to death."

"You can guess, can't you, why G. wrote to tell me?"

"No . . ."

"Why, don't you understand? He's implying: 'If you went off for the same reason as Serrurier, you have nothing to fear; you can come back now, the old ones are in a separate pen.' "

"No," I said, taking pity on her, "that isn't the way I understand his letter at all."

She gave a wry, forced little smile, a pathetic little twist that hardly moved her lips:

"Well, we'll see where I stand tomorrow morning."

I much prefer, to the official grounds of famous clubs where the fine ladies along the touch-line burst out laughing if you sprawl on the turf with the ball, those patchy suburban sports fields, where you play on a litter of old tins, to an audience of thirty shivering citizens, between factories which, with their tall chimneys, are like huge steamships that have come to rest in port. And I like the Paris suburbs, with their splendid, infinitely evocative place names—*La Plaine, Le Point du Jour* . . . In a book I wrote when I was twenty, *La Relève du matin*, I referred to the "delicious working-class suburbs." When, next morning, I walked on to the misty, sodden and deserted field overlooked by the fortifications, my heart was that of a man who is going to act as second at a duel. Mlle de Plémeur came towards me impatiently, as if I were late; I held out my watch, which said five to; she took this as a personal affront. When I saw how far her three months in Brittany had brought her down from that lofty plane of dignity and reason to which athletics had once raised her, I sensed what a collapse was in store for her if her attempt failed.

She began her preparations, running on the spot in little bursts and nervously rolling the lower hem of her shorts; she unwound the bandages from her feet which were already black with cinder dust from the track, and I saw again her rather thick ankles, which were of the kind that I both approve of mentally and find very much to my taste. The skin on the front of her legs bore no trace of the scratches that had often been left on them, in her active periods, by the track shoes of some (well-intentioned?) opponent she had been closely following during a race. I particularly recall the moment when she sat down on the grass and the masseur massaged her legs (downy calves and smooth thighs). And while the sensitive hands climbed tremblingly like flames, higher and higher, until they went under the wide openings of her shorts, I watched her face with intense, stealthy attention, to discover some imperceptible sign which might enlighten me about the fundamental meaning of the moment. But her upright posture, the lift of her head, which was like a bird of prey's, her gaze which remained fixed in the distance, her pinched lips in her blanched face and the suggestion of rigidity which petrified her whole being, expressed only the choking tenseness of anxiety. And I was so uncomfortable myself that I called out: "Come on!" to speed up the start.

She had been walking; now she was running. It was as if a spoken sentence had ended in song. Like a singer, a dancer or an evoker of harmonies, she had become a link between the sublime and ourselves. Oh, woman, instrument of the ineffable, we humbly salute you for your great virtues! Why did I mention your mistakes, your shortcomings, your pettiness? You are now wholly justified.

She covered the first lap in three seconds more than the French record time. This was good going, and I called it out to her as she went past. Then her features stiffened: Joan of Arc, leading her men into battle, must have had that grave, sealed countenance; Joan of Arc, or perhaps Mlle de Plémeur's ancestor, the regicide member of the *Convention*, when he cast his vote in favor of Capet's death? On she ran, the light-footed maiden, and her lithe leg movements, so marvellously delicate and piercing that I imagined them leaving on the cinder track a pointed trace like the marks of goats' feet, were replaced by a more vigorous stride which brought even her neck muscles into play. Even so, when she came round again she had lost two seconds more. I thought that the wiser course was to call out: "Equal time!"

She began on the third of the four laps.

If I close my eyes, it all comes to life again, the early morning with its faint, pricking drizzle, the loneliness, the silence and the girl, no longer in the first flush of youth, running in the bleak open air. There were only the two of us, she and I; and her whole achievement was a waste. She was running with a beauty there was no one to witness to accomplish an aim no one was interested in; she was running, perhaps for the last time, and surpassing herself, perhaps for the last time; she was running in a state of sacred horror, as if fiercely pursued by age and sad time. Two centuries ago, wearing a hair shirt and crazed by the Cross, Mlle de Plémeur would have trudged with bleeding feet along the roads. On that suburban running-track, I saw re-enacted the eternal effort of all those who once believed that, to hear the Oracle, they had only to make the offering of a moment's noble madness.

She passed me again, with her head on one side, and her face already expressing fatigue, suffering, a deeper self that I had not known before, a further reason why she should be loved. How many young women athletes have I seen display, for the benefit of the curious and while their mothers were looking on, the final secret released by a contorted face, that spasm of pain that formerly only the husband had the right to wallow in, since he was its creator and its master! She had lost three more seconds, making a total of eight. The situation was irretrievable. I shouted: "You've lost four seconds."

How long did the harsh sentence take to travel from her mind to her body? I could take a stone and mark the exact spot on the track where her strength flagged and jibbed. From then on, it was only a question of will-power, character and anger; it was no longer the body which ran but the soul—a naked soul, a breath of life, which followed the track as a will o' the wisp follows the course of a river.

For my part, pressing her emotion against my own, I would have liked to rush to meet her, to catch her by her beautiful, darling wrists and say to her: "Poor little thing, my poor little old thing, stop all this at once! What are we doing here? It's true that I'm younger than you are, but don't you see that I'm your father now talking to you and that you are my wandering child? I have said, I have even proclaimed, that only victory could inspire me with love, and yet I love you more in your hour of distress than I did in all your triumphs, and I am going back on my word and I shall do so again, thirty, forty, fifty times because it pleases me to do so and I can do anything I wish. But, I beg of you, don't be unhappy to so little purpose. Don't waste your aptitude for suffering; you should keep it in your most secret heart for the man who is perhaps waiting for you and who will unleash it with equivocal pride." What happens to all those words that come to our lips but are never uttered, and yet are always the kindest words? If an angel records them somewhere and a day comes when they are made known, how completely exonerated we shall be when we awake!

The reader will excuse me if I don't go into the details of the finish.

When she appeared in the straight, I was as worked up as she was. By a brave effort, she had managed not to lose any more time; nevertheless she was still eight seconds over the record. Should I tell her? Should I kill her last hope and bar her from the possibility of greatness? Ought I not to assure her that she had been successful?

She threw herself on to the tape with a contorted corpse's mouth, snapping and sucking at the air as if she were dying and trying to bite at life.

The record was three minutes sixteen seconds. I stopped the watch, and read off the time:

"Twenty-four."

When I looked up, she was walking off to the dressing-rooms. I followed her and pushed on ahead a little so as to see not her but the clear, comforting space in front; her legs had been white with talcum powder but the cinder dust from the track had stuck to the sweat and blackened them up to the knees; her face was pale, but a rather disquieting band of sharp pink ran across her forehead and round her temples, near the roots of her hair. We covered some thirty yards or more in this order. Suddenly I heard a noise, understood what it meant and swung round. She had collapsed; her chest and face were in the mud and she was shaking with sobs.

I looked at her for a moment, then turning my back towards her, I walked up and down as we do when we are waiting for someone who happens to be late. For the first time, I felt really in love with her, more in love than I could have been, had she been sobbing because of me. However, the illusion lasted only a moment.

Soon she got on to her feet again and, using the flat of her hand, squashed her tears on to the rings under her eyes, which were as blue and shimmering as aponeuroses. We went on towards the dressing-rooms without uttering a word.

When she was dressed again, she began to make jokes, laughing that grating sort of female laugh which is only bearable if we feel the urge to stop it with a kiss. She asked me for a cigarette. She had never been in the habit of smoking, because she had always been in training. This gave me a glimpse of her internal collapse and of the sad depths above which there was now nothing left to hold her.

When we parted, she thanked me for having proved, by refusing either to deceive her or pity her, that I did not despise her.

She was never seen at the club again. Athletics were Mlle de

Plémeur's only support, her backbone, her nunnery. What can have become of her, since, into the bargain, she hadn't a penny? The young men of my generation only marry their mistresses. Has Mlle de Plémeur at last "understood"?

TRANSLATED BY JOHN WEIGHTMAN

A CADDY'S DIARY

Ring Lardner

Wed. Apr. 12.

I am 16 of age and am a caddy at the Pleasant View Golf Club but only temporary as I expect to soon land a job some wheres as asst pro as my game is good enough now to be a pro but to young looking. My pal Joe Bean also says I have not got enough swell head to make a good pro but suppose that will come in time, Joe is a wise cracker.

But first will put down how I come to be writeing this diary, we have got a member name Mr Colby who writes articles in the newspapers and I hope for his sakes that he is a better writer then he plays golf but any way I cadded for him a good many times last yr and today he was out for the first time this yr and I cadded for him and we got talking about this in that and something was mentioned in regards to the golf articles by Alex Laird that comes out every Sun in the paper Mr Colby writes his articles for so I asked Mr Colby did he know how much Laird got paid for the articles and he said he did not know but supposed that Laird had to split 50-50 with who ever wrote the articles for him. So I said don't he write the articles himself and Mr Colby said why no he guessed not. Laird may be a master mind in regards to golf he said, but that is no sign he can write about it as very few men can write decent let alone a pro. Writeing is a nag.

How do you learn it I asked him.

Well he said read what other people writes and study them and write things yourself, and maybe you will get on to the nag and maybe you wont.

Well Mr Colby I said do you think I could get on to it?

Why he said smileing I did not know that was your ambition to be a writer.

Not exactly was my reply, but I am going to be a golf pro myself and maybe some day I will get good enough so as the papers will want

I should write them articles and if I can learn to write them myself why I will not have to hire another writer and split with them.

Well said Mr Colby smileing you have certainly got the right temperament for a pro, they are all big hearted fellows.

But listen Mr Colby I said if I want to learn it would not do me no good to copy down what other writers have wrote, what I would have to do would be write things out of my own head.

That is true said Mr. Colby.

Well I said what could I write about?

Well said Mr Colby why don't you keep a diary and every night after your supper set down and write what happened that day and write who you cadded for and what they done only leave me out of it. And you can write down what people say and what you think and etc., it will be the best kind of practice for you, and once in a wile you can bring me your writeings and I will tell you the truth if they are good or rotten.

So that is how I come to be writeing this diary is so as I can get some practice writeing and maybe if I keep at it long enough I can get on to the nag.

Friday, Apr. 14.

We been haveing Apr. showers for a couple days and nobody out on the course so they has been nothing happen that I could write down in my diary but dont want to leave it go to long or will never learn the trick so will try and write a few lines about a caddys life and some of our members and etc.

Well I and Joe Bean is the 2 oldest caddys in the club and I been cadding now for 5 yrs and quit school 3 yrs ago tho my mother did not like it for me to quit but my father said he can read and write and figure so what is the use in keeping him there any longer as greek and latin dont get you no credit at the grocer, so they lied about my age to the trunce officer and I been cadding every yr from March till Nov and the rest of the winter I work around Heismans store in the village.

Dureing the time I am cadding I generally always manage to play at lease 9 holes a day myself on wk days and some times 18 and am never more than 2 or 3 over par figures on our course but it is a cinch.

I played the engineers course 1 day last summer in 75 which is some golf and some of our members who has been playing 20 yrs would give their right eye to play as good as myself.

I use to play around with our pro Jack Andrews till I got so as I could beat him pretty near every time we played and now he wont play with me no more, he is not a very good player for a pro but they claim he is a good teacher. Personly I think golf teachers is a joke tho I am glad people is suckers enough to fall for it as I expect to make my liveing that way. We have got a member Mr Dunham who must of took 500 lessons in the past 3 yrs and when he starts to shoot he trys to remember all the junk Andrews has learned him and he gets dizzy and they is no telling where the ball will go and about the safest place to stand when he is shooting is between he and the hole.

I dont beleive the club pays Andrews much salery but of course he makes pretty fair money giveing lessons but his best graft is a 3 some which he plays 2 and 3 times a wk with Mr Perdue and Mr Lewis and he gives Mr Lewis a stroke a hole and they genally break some wheres near even but Mr Perdue made a 83 one time so he thinks that is his game so he insists on playing Jack even, well they always play for $5.00 a hole and Andrews makes $20.00 to $30.00 per round and if he wanted to cut loose and play his best he could make $50.00 to $60.00 per round but a couple of wallops like that and Mr Perdue might get cured so Jack figures a small stedy income is safer.

I have got a pal name Joe Bean and we pal around together as he is about my age and he says some comical things and some times will wisper some thing comical to me wile we are cadding and it is all I can do to help from laughing out loud, that is one of the first things a caddy has got to learn is never laugh out loud only when a member makes a joke. How ever on the days when theys ladies on the course I dont get a chance to caddy with Joe because for some reason another the woman folks dont like Joe to caddy for them wile on the other hand they are always after me tho I am no Othello for looks or do I seek their flavors, in fact it is just the opp and I try to keep in the back ground when the fair sex appears on the seen as cadding for ladies means you will get just so much money and no more as theys no chance of them loosning up. As Joe says the rule against tipping is the only rule the woman folks keeps.

Theys one lady how ever who I like to caddy for as she looks like Lillian Gish and it is a pleasure to just look at her and I would caddy for her for nothing tho it is hard to keep your eye on the ball when you are cadding for this lady, her name is Mrs Doane.

Sat. Apr. 15.

This was a long day and am pretty well wore out but must not get behind in my writeing practice. I and Joe carried all day for Mr Thomas and Mr Blake. Mr Thomas is the vice president of one of the big banks down town and he always slips you a $1.oo extra per round but beleive me you earn it cadding for Mr Thomas, there is just 16 clubs in his bag includeing 5 wood clubs tho he has not used the wood in 3 yrs but says he has got to have them along in case his irons goes wrong on him. I dont know how bad his irons will have to get before he will think they have went wrong on him but personly if I made some of the tee shots he made today I would certainly considder some kind of a change of weppons.

Mr Thomas is one of the kind of players that when it has took him more than 6 shots to get on the green he will turn to you and say how many have I had caddy and then you are suppose to pretend like you was thinking a minute and then say 4, then he will say to the man he is playing with well I did not know if I had shot 4 or 5 but the caddy says it is 4. You see in this way it is not him that is cheating but the caddy but he makes it up to the caddy afterwards with a $1.oo tip.

Mr Blake gives Mr Thomas a stroke a hole and they play a $10.oo nassua and neither one of them wins much money from the other one but even if they did why $10.oo is chickens food to men like they. But the way they crab and squak about different things you would think their last $1.oo was at stake. Mr Thomas started out this A.M. with a 8 and a 7 and of course that spoilt the day for him and me to. Theys lots of men that if they dont make a good score on the first 2 holes they will founder all the rest of the way around and raze H with their caddy and if I was laying out a golf course I would make the first 2 holes so darn easy that you could not help from getting a 4 or better on them and in that way everybody would start off good natured and it would be a few holes at lease before they begun to turn sour.

Mr Thomas was beat both in the A.M. and P.M. in spite of my help as Mr Blake is a pretty fair counter himself and I heard him say he got a 88 in the P.M. which is about a 94 but any way it was good enough to win. Mr Blakes regular game is about a 90 takeing his own figures

A Caddy's Diary
Ring Lardner

and he is one of these cocky guys that takes his own game serious and snears at men that cant break 100 and if you was to ask him if he had ever been over 100 himself he would say not since the first yr he begun to play. Well I have watched a lot of those guys like he and I will tell you how they keep from going over 100 namely by doing just what he done this A.M. when he come to the 13th hole. Well he missed his tee shot and dubbed along and finely he got in a trap on his 4th shot and I seen him take 6 wallops in the trap and when he had took the 6th one his ball was worse off then when he started so he picked it up and marked a X down on his score card. Well if he had of played out the hole why the best he could of got was a 11 by holeing his next niblick shot but he would of probly got about a 20 which would of made him around 108 as he admitted takeing a 88 for the other 17 holes. But I bet if you was to ask him what score he had made he would say O I was terrible and I picked up on one hole but if I had of played them all out I guess I would of had about a 92.

These is the kind of men that laughs themselfs horse when they hear of some dub takeing 10 strokes for a hole but if they was made to play out every hole and mark down their real score their card would be decorated with many a big casino.

Well as I say I had a hard day and was pretty sore along towards the finish but still I had to laugh at Joe Bean on the 15th hole which is a par 3 and you can get there with a fair drive and personly I am genally hole high with a midiron, but Mr Thomas topped his tee shot and dubbed a couple with his mashie and was still quiet a ways off the green and he stood studing the situation a minute and said to Mr Blake well I wonder what I better take here. So Joe Bean was standing by me and he said under his breath take my advice and quit you old rascal.

Mon. Apr. 17.

Yesterday was Sun and I was to wore out last night to write as I cadded 45 holes. I cadded for Mr Colby in the A.M. and Mr Langley in the P.M. Mr Thomas thinks golf is wrong on the sabath tho as Joe Bean says it is wrong any day the way he plays it.

This A.M. they was nobody on the course and I played 18 holes by myself and had a 5 for a 76 on the 18th hole but the wind got a hold of my drive and it went out of bounds. This P.M. they was 3 of us had a game of rummy started but Miss Rennie and Mrs Thomas come out to play and asked for me to caddy for them, they are both terrible.

Mrs Thomas is Mr Thomas wife and she is big and fat and shakes like jell and she always says she plays golf just to make her skinny and she dont care how rotten she plays as long as she is getting the exercise, well maybe so but when we find her ball in a bad lie she aint never sure it is hers till she picks it up and smells it and when she puts it back beleive me she don't cram it down no gopher hole.

Miss Rennie is a good looker and young and they say she is engaged to Chas Crane, he is one of our members and is the best player in the club and dont cheat hardly at all and he has got a job in the bank where Mr Thomas is the vice president. Well I have cadded for Miss Rennie when she was playing with Mr Crane and I have cadded for her when she was playing alone or with another lady and I often think if Mr Crane could hear her talk when he was not around he would not be so stuck on her. You would be surprised at some of the words that falls from those fare lips.

Well the 2 ladies played for 2 bits a hole and Miss Rennie was haveing a terrible time wile Mrs Thomas was shot with luck on the greens and sunk 3 or 4 putts that was murder. Well Miss Rennie used some expressions which was best not repeated but towards the last the luck changed around and it was Miss Rennie that was sinking the long ones and when they got to the 18th tee Mrs Thomas was only 1 up.

Well we had started pretty late and when we left the 17th green Miss Rennie made the remark that we would have to hurry to get the last hole played, well it was her honor and she got the best drive she made all day about 120 yds down the fair way. Well Mrs Thomas got nervous and looked up and missed her ball a ft and then done the same thing right over and when she finely hit it she only knocked it about 20 yds and this made her lay 3. Well her 4th went wild and lit over in the rough in the apple trees. It was a cinch Miss Rennie would win the hole unless she dropped dead.

Well we all went over to hunt for Mrs Thomas ball but we would of been lucky to find it even in day light but now you could not hardly see under the trees, so Miss Rennie said drop another ball and we will not count no penalty. Well it is some job any time to make a woman give up hunting for a lost ball and all the more so when it is going to cost her 2 bits to play the hole out so there we stayed for at lease 10 minutes till it was so dark we could not see each other let alone a lost ball and finely Mrs Thomas said well it looks like we could not finish, how do we stand? Just like she did not know how they stood.

You had me one down up to this hole said Miss Rennie.

Well that is finishing pretty close said Mrs Thomas.

I will have to give Miss Rennie credit that what ever word she thought of for this occasion she did not say it out loud but when she was paying me she said I might of give you a quarter tip only I have to give Mrs Thomas a quarter she dont deserve so you dont get it.

Fat chance I would of had any way.

Thurs. Apr. 20

Well we been haveing some more bad weather but today the weather was all right but that was the only thing that was all right. This P.M. I cadded double for Mr Thomas and Chas Crane the club champion who is stuck on Miss Rennie. It was a 4 some with he and Mr Thomas against Mr Blake and Jack Andrews the pro, they was only playing best ball so it was really just a match between Mr Crane and Jack Andrews and Mr Crane win by 1 up. Joe Bean cadded for Jack and Mr Blake. Mr Thomas was terrible and I put in a swell P.M. lugging that heavy bag of his besides Mr Cranes bag.

Mr Thomas did not go off of the course as much as usual but he kept hitting behind the ball and he run me ragged replaceing his divots but still I had to laugh when we was playing the 4th hole which you have to drive over a ravine and every time Mr Thomas misses his tee shot on this hole why he makes a squak about the ravine and says it ought not to be there and etc.

Today he had a terrible time getting over it and afterwards he said to Jack Andrews this is a joke hole and ought to be changed. So Joe Bean wispered to me that if Mr Thomas kept on playing like he was the whole course would be changed.

Then a little wile later when we come to the long 9th hole Mr Thomas got a fair tee shot but then he whiffed twice missing the ball by a ft and the 3d time he hit it but it only went a little ways and Joe Bean said that is 3 trys and no gain, he will have to punt.

But I must write down about my tough luck, well we finely got through the 18 holes and Mr Thomas reached down in his pocket for the money to pay me and he generally pays for Mr Crane to when they play together as Mr Crane is just a employ in the bank and dont have much money but this time all Mr Thomas had was a $20.00 bill so he said to Mr Crane I guess you will have to pay the boy Charley so Charley dug down and got the money to pay me and he paid just what it was and not a dime over, where if Mr Thomas had of had the change I would of got a $1.00 extra at lease and maybe I was not sore and Joe Bean to because of course Andrews never gives you nothing and Mr Blake dont tip his caddy unless he wins.

They are a fine bunch of tight wads said Joe and I said well Crane is all right only he just has not got no money.

He aint all right no more than the rest of them said Joe.

Well at lease he dont cheat on his score I said.

And you know why that is said Joe, neither does Jack Andrews cheat on his score but that is because they play to good. Players like Crane and Andrews that goes around in 80 or better cant cheat on their score because they make the most of the holes in around 4 strokes and the 4 strokes includes their tee shot and a couple of putts which everybody is right there to watch them when they make them and count them right along with them. So if they make a 4 and claim a 3 why people would just laugh in their face and say how did the ball get from the fair way on to the green, did it fly? But the boys that takes 7 and 8 strokes to a hole can shave their score and you know they are shaveing it but you have to let them get away with it because you cant prove nothing. But that is one of the penaltys for being a good player, you cant cheat.

To hear Joe tell it pretty near everybody are born crooks, well maybe he is right.

Wed. Apr. 26.

Today Mrs Doane was out for the first time this yr and asked for me to caddy for her and you bet I was on the job. Well how are you Dick she said, she always calls me by name. She asked me what had I been doing all winter and was I glad to see her and etc.

She said she had been down south all winter and played golf pretty near every day and would I watch her and notice how much she had improved.

Well to tell the truth she was no better than last yr and wont never be no better and I guess she is just to pretty to be a golf player but of course when she asked me did I think her game was improved I had to reply yes indeed as I would not hurt her feelings and she laughed like my reply pleased her. She played with Mr and Mrs Carter and I carried the 2 ladies bags wile Joe Bean cadded for Mr Carter. Mrs Carter is a ugly dame with things on her face and it must make Mr Carter feel sore when he looks at Mrs Doane to think he married Mrs Carter but I suppose they could not all marry the same one and besides Mrs Doane would not be a sucker enough to marry a man like he who drinks all the time and is pretty near always stood, tho Mr Doane who she did marry aint such a H of a man himself tho dirty with money.

They all gave me the laugh on the 3d hole when Mrs Doane was makeing her 2d shot and the ball was in the fair way but laid kind of bad and she just ticked it and then she asked me if winter rules was in force and I said yes so we teed her ball up so as she could get a good shot at it and they gave me the laugh for saying winter rules was in force.

You have got the caddys bribed Mr Carter said to her.

But she just smiled and put her hand on my sholder and said Dick is my pal. That is enough of a bribe to just have her touch you and I would caddy all day for her and never ask for a cent only to have her smile at me and call me her pal.

Sat. Apr. 29.

Today they had the first club tournament of the yr and they have a monthly tournament every month and today was the first one, it is a handicap tournament and everybody plays in it and they have prizes for low net score and low gross score and etc. I cadded for Mr Thomas today and will tell what happened.

They played a 4 some and besides Mr Thomas we had Mr Blake and Mr Carter and Mr Dunham. Mr Dunham is the worst man player in the club and the other men would not play with him a specialy on a Saturday only him and Mr Blake is partners together in business. Mr Dunham has got the highest handicap in the club which is 50 but it would have to be 150 for him to win a prize. Mr Blake and Mr Carter has got a handicap of about 15 a piece I think and Mr Thomas is 30, the first prize for the low net score for the day was a dozen golf balls and the second low score a ½ dozen golf balls and etc.

Well we had a great battle and Mr Colby ought to been along to write it up or some good writer. Mr Carter and Mr Dunham played partners against Mr Thomas and Mr Blake which ment that Mr Carter was playing Thomas and Blakes best ball, well Mr Dunham took the honor and the first ball he hit went strate off to the right and over the fence outside of the grounds, well he done the same thing 3 times. Well when he finely did hit one in the course why Mr Carter said why not let us not count them 3 first shots of Mr Dunham as they was just practice. Like H we wont count them said Mr Thomas we must count every shot and keep our scores correct for the tournament.

All right said Mr. Carter.

Well we got down to the green and Mr Dunham had about 11 and Mr Carter sunk a long put for a par 5, Mr Blake all ready had 5 strokes and so did Mr Thomas and when Mr Carter sunk his putt why Mr Thomas picked his ball up and said Carter wins the hole and I and Blake will take 6s. Like H you will said Mr Carter, this is a tournament and we must play every hole out and keep our scores correct. So Mr Dunham putted and went down in 13 and Mr Blake got a 6 and Mr Thomas missed 2 easy putts and took a 8 and maybe he was not boiling.

Well it was still their honor and Mr Dunham had one of his dizzy spells on the 2d tee and he missed the ball twice before he hit it and then Mr Carter drove the green which is only a midiron shot and then Mr Thomas stepped up and missed the ball just like Mr Dunham. He was wild and yelled at Mr Dunham no man could play golf playing with a man like you, you would spoil anybodys game.

Your game was all ready spoiled said Mr Dunham, it turned sour on the 1st green.

You would turn anybody sour said Mr Thomas.

Well Mr Thomas finely took a 8 for the hole which is a par 3 and it certainly looked bad for him winning a prize when he started out with 2 8s, and he and Mr Dunham had another terrible time on No 3 and wile they was messing things up a 2 some come up behind us and hollered fore and we left them go through tho it was Mr Clayton and Mr Joyce and as Joe Bean said they was probly dissapointed when we left them go through as they are the kind that feels like the day is lost if they cant write to some committee and preffer charges.

Well Mr Thomas got a 7 on the 3d and he said well it is no wonder I am off of my game today as I was up ½ the night with my teeth.

Well said Mr Carter if I had your money why on the night before a big tournament like this I would hire somebody else to set up with my teeth.

Well I wished I could remember all that was said and done but any way Mr Thomas kept getting sore and sore and we got to the 7th tee and he had not made a decent tee shot all day so Mr Blake said to him why dont you try the wood as you cant do no worse?

By Geo I beleive I will said Mr Thomas and took his driver out of the bag which he had not used it for 3 yrs.

Well he swang and zowie away went the ball pretty near 8 inchs distants wile the head of the club broke off clean and saled 50 yds down the course. Well I have got a hold on myself so as I dont never laugh out loud and I beleive the other men was scarred to laugh or he would of killed them so we all stood there in silents waiting for what would happen.

Well without saying a word he come to where I was standing and took his other 4 wood clubs out of the bag and took them to a tree which stands a little ways from the tee box and one by one he swang them with all his strength against the trunk of the tree and smashed them to H and gone, all right gentlemen that is over he said.

Well to cut it short Mr Thomas score for the first 9 was a even 60 and then we started out on the 2d 9 and you would not think it was the same man playing, on the first 3 holes he made 2 4s and a 5 and beat Mr Carter even and followed up with a 6 and a 5 and that is how he kept going up to the 17th hole.

What has got in to you Thomas said Mr Carter.

Nothing said Mr Thomas only I broke my hoodoo when I broke them 5 wood clubs.

Yes I said to myself and if you had broke them 5 wood clubs 3 yrs ago I would not of broke my back lugging them around.

Well we come to the 18th tee and Mr Thomas had a 39 which give him a 99 for 17 holes, well everybody drove off and as we was following along why Mr Klabor come walking down the course from the club house on his way to the 17th green to join some friends and Mr Thomas asked him what had he made and he said he had turned in a 93 but his handicap is only 12 so that give him a 81.

That wont get me no wheres he said as Charley Crane made a 75.

Well said Mr Thomas I can tie Crane for low net if I get a 6 on this hole.

Well it come his turn to make his 2d and zowie he hit the ball pretty good but they was a hook on it and away she went in to the woods on the left, the ball laid in behind a tree so as they was only one thing to do and that was waste a shot getting it back on the fair so that is what Mr Thomas done and it took him 2 more to reach the green.

How many have you had Thomas said Mr Carter when we was all on the green.

Let me see said Mr Thomas and then turned to me, how many have I had caddy?

I dont know I said.

Well it is either 4 or 5 said Mr Thomas.

I think it is 5 said Mr Carter.

I think it is 4 said Mr Thomas and turned to me again and said how many have I had caddy?

So I said 4.

Well said Mr Thomas personly I was not sure myself but my caddy says 4 and I guess he is right.

Well the other men looked at each other and I and Joe Bean looked at each other but Mr Thomas went ahead and putted and was down in 2 putts.

Well he said I certainly come to life on them last 9 holes.

So he turned in his score as 105 and with his handicap of 30 why that give him a net of 75 which was the same as Mr Crane so instead of Mr Crane getting 1 dozen golf balls and Mr Thomas getting ½ a dozen golf balls why they will split the 1st and 2d prize makeing 9 golf balls a piece.

Tues. May 2.

This was the first ladies day of the season and even Joe Bean had to carry for the fair sex. We cadded for a 4 some which was Miss Rennie and Mrs Thomas against Mrs Doane and Mrs Carter. I guess if they had of kept their score right the total for the 4 of them would of ran well over a 1000.

Our course has a great many trees and they seemed to have a traction for our 4 ladies today and we was in amongst the trees more than we was on the fair way.

Well said Joe Bean theys one thing about cadding for these dames, it keeps you out of the hot sun.

And another time he said he felt like a boy scout studing wood craft.

These dames is always up against a stump he said.

And another time he said that it was not fair to charge these dames regular ladies dues in the club as they hardly ever used the course.

Well it seems like they was a party in the village last night and of course the ladies was talking about it and Mrs Doane said what a lovely dress Miss Rennie wore to the party and Miss Rennie said she did not care for the dress herself.

Well said Mrs Doane if you want to get rid of it just hand it over to me.

I wont give it to you said Miss Rennie but I will sell it to you at ½ what it cost me and it was a bargain at that as it only cost me a $100.00 and I will sell it to you for $50.00.

I have not got $50.00 just now to spend said Mrs Doane and besides I dont know would it fit me.

Sure it would fit you said Miss Rennie, you and I are exactly the same size and figure, I tell you what I will do with you I will play you golf for it and if you beat me you can have the gown for nothing and if I beat you why you will give me $50.00 for it.

All right but if I loose you may have to wait for your money said Mrs Doane.

So this was on the 4th hole and they started from there to play for the dress and they was both terrible and worse then usual on acct of being nervous as this was the biggest stakes they had either of them ever played for tho the Doanes has got a bbl of money and $50.00 is chickens food.

Well we was on the 16th hole and Mrs Doane was 1 up and Miss Rennie sliced her tee shot off in the rough and Mrs Doane landed in some rough over on the left so they was clear across the course from each other. Well I and Mrs Doane went over to her ball and as luck would have it it had come to rest in a kind of a groove where a good player could not hardly make a good shot of it let alone Mrs Doane. Well Mrs Thomas was out in the middle of the course for once in her life and the other 2 ladies was over on the right side and Joe Bean with them so they was nobody near Mrs Doane and I.

Do I have to play it from there she said. I guess you do was my reply.

Why Dick have you went back on me she said and give me one of her looks.

Well I looked to see if the others was looking and then I kind of give the ball a shove with my toe and it come out of the groove and laid where she could get a swipe at it.

This was the 16th hole and Mrs Doane win it by 11 strokes to 10 and that made her 2 up and 2 to go. Miss Rennie win the 17th but they both took a 10 for the 18th and that give Mrs Doane the match.

Well I wont never have a chance to see her in Miss Rennies dress but if I did I aint sure that I would like it on her.

Fri. May 5.

Well I never thought we would have so much excitement in the club and so much to write down in my diary but I guess I better get the excitement broke loose and I was getting ready to play around busy writeing it down as here it is Friday and it was Wed. A.M. when when Harry Lear the caddy master come running out with the paper in his hand and showed it to me on the first page.

It told how Chas Crane our club champion had went south with $8000 which he had stole out of Mr Thomas bank and a swell looking dame that was a stenographer in the bank had elloped with him and they had her picture in the paper and I will say she is a pip but who would of thought a nice quiet young man like Mr Crane was going to prove himself a gay Romeo and a specialy as he was engaged to Miss Rennie tho she now says she broke their engagement a month ago but any way the whole affair has certainly give everybody something to talk about and one of the caddys Lou Crowell busted Fat Brunner in the nose because Fat claimed to of been the last one that cadded for Crane. Lou was really the last one and cadded for him last Sunday which was the last time Crane was at the club.

Well everybody was thinking how sore Mr Thomas would be and they would better not mention the affair around him and etc. but who should show up to play yesterday but Mr Thomas himself and he played with Mr Blake and all they talked about the whole P.M. was Crane and what he had pulled.

Well Thomas said Mr Blake I am curious to know if the thing

come as a surprise to you or if you ever had a hunch that he was libel to do a thing like this.

Well Blake said Mr Thomas I will admit that the whole thing come as a complete surprise to me as Crane was all most like my son you might say and I was going to see that he got along all right and that is what makes me sore is not only that he has proved himself dishonest but that he could be such a sucker as to give up a bright future for a sum of money like $8000 and a doll face girl that cant be no good or she would not of let him do it. When you think how young he was and the career he might of had why it certainly seems like he sold his soul pretty cheap.

That is what Mr Thomas had to say or at lease part of it as I cant remember a ½ of all he said but any way this P.M. I cadded for Mrs Thomas and Mrs Doane and that is all they talked about to, and Mrs Thomas talked along the same lines like her husband and said she had always thought Crane was to smart a young man to pull a thing like that and ruin his whole future.

He was geting $4000 a yr said Mrs Thomas and everybody liked him and said he was bound to get ahead so that is what makes it such a silly thing for him to of done, sell his soul for $8000 and a pretty face.

Yes indeed said Mrs Doane.

Well all the time I was listening to Mr Thomas and Mr Blake and Mrs Thomas and Mrs Doane why I was thinking about something which I wanted to say to them but it would of ment me looseing my job so I kept it to myself but I sprung it on my pal Joe Bean on the way home tonight.

Joe I said what do these people mean when they talk about Crane selling his soul?

Why you know what they mean said Joe, they mean that a person that does something dishonest for a bunch of money or a gal or any kind of a reward why the person that does it is selling his soul.

All right I said and it dont make no differents does it if the reward is big or little?

Why no said Joe only the bigger it is the less of a sucker the person is that goes after it.

Well I said here is Mr Thomas who is vice president of a big bank and worth a bbl of money and it is just a few days ago when he lied about his golf score in order so as he would win 9 golf balls instead of a ½ a dozen.

Sure said Joe.

And how about his wife Mrs Thomas I said, who plays for 2 bits a hole and when her ball dont lie good why she picks it up and pretends to look at it to see if it is hers and then puts it back in a good lie where she can sock it.

And how about my friend Mrs Doane that made me move her ball out of a rut to help her beat Miss Rennie out of a party dress.

Well said Joe what of it?

Well I said it seems to me like these people have got a lot of nerve to pan Mr Crane and call him a sucker for doing what he done, it seems to me like $8000 and a swell dame is a pretty fair reward compared with what some of these other people sells their soul for, and I would like to tell them about it.

Well said Joe go ahead and tell them but maybe they will tell you something right back.

What will they tell me?

Well said Joe they might tell you this, that when Mr Thomas asks you how many shots he has had and you say 4 when you know he has had 5, why you are selling your soul for a $1.00 tip. And when you move Mrs Doane ball out of a rut and give it a good lie, what are you selling your soul for? Just a smile.

O keep your mouth shut I said to him.

I am going to said Joe and would advice you to do the same.

MY RELATION TO "HER"

Søren Kierkegaard

August 24, 1849. Infandum me jubes, Regina, renovare dolorem[1]

Regina Olsen—I saw her first at the Rørdams. I really saw her there before, at a time when I did not know her family . . .

Even before my father died I had decided upon her. He died (Aug. 9, 1838). I read for my examination. During the whole of that time I let her being penetrate mine.

In the summer of 1840 I took my theological examination.

Without further ceremony I thereupon called at their house. I went to Jutland and perhaps even at that time I was fishing for her, e.g., by lending them books in my absence and by suggesting that they should read certain passages.

In August I returned. The period from August 9 till the beginning of September I used in the strict sense to approach her.

On September 8 I left my house with the firm purpose of deciding the matter. We met each other in the street outside their house. She said there was nobody at home. I was foolhardly enough to look upon that as an invitation, just the opportunity I wanted. I went in with her. We stood alone in the living room. She was a little uneasy. I asked her to play me something as she usually did. She did so; but that did not help me. Then suddenly I took the music away and closed it, not without a certain violence, threw it down on the piano and said: "Oh, what do I care about music now! It is you I am searching for, it is you whom I have sought after for two years." She

---

This account was sent to Regina Olsen on S. K.'s death, together with all the papers relating to their engagement. They were edited under her supervision, but not published until after her death, by Raphael Meyer in 1904 under the title *Kierkegaardske Papirer: Forlovelsen.*

[1] "Thou biddest me, Regina, renew the unspeakable grief."

was silent. I did nothing else to make an impression upon her; I even warned her against myself, against my melancholy. When, however, she spoke about Schlegel[2] I said, "Let that relationship be a parenthesis; after all the priority is mine." (N.B. It was only on the 10th that she spoke of Schlegel; on the 8th she did not say a word.)

She remained quite silent. At last I left, for I was anxious lest someone should come and find both of us, and she so disturbed. I went immediately to Etatsraad Olsen.[3] I know that I was terribly concerned that I had made too great an impression upon her. I also feared that my visit might lead to a misunderstanding and even hurt her reputation.

Her father said neither yes nor no, but he was willing enough, as I could see. I asked for a meeting: it was granted to me for the afternoon of the 10th. I did not say a single word to persuade her. She said, Yes.

I immediately assumed a relation to the whole family, and turned all my virtuosity upon her father whom, moreover, I have always loved.

But inwardly, the next day I saw that I had made a false step. A penitent such as I was, my *vita ante acta*, my melancholy, that was enough.

I suffered unspeakably at that time.

She seemed to notice nothing. On the contrary her spirits were so high that once she said she had accepted me out of pity. In short, I have never known such high spirits.

In one sense that was the danger. If she does not take it more to heart, I thought, than her own words betray: "if she thought I only came from force of habit she would break off the engagement at once"; if she does not take it more to heart, then I am saved. I pulled myself together again. In another sense I must admit my weakness, that for a moment she vexed me.

Then I sent my whole strength to work—she seriously gave way and precisely the opposite happened, she gave herself unreservedly to me, she worshiped me. To a certain extent I myself bear the guilt of that. While I perceived the difficulty of the position only too clearly, and recognized that I must use the maximum of strength in order if possible to burst through my melancholy, I had said to her: "Surrender to me; your pride makes everything easier for me." A perfectly

---

[2] The man Regina eventually married.

My Relation to "Her"
Søren Kierkegaard

true word; honest towards her, melancholy and treacherous towards myself.[3]

And now of course my melancholy awoke once more. Her devotion once again put the whole "responsibility" upon me on a tremendous scale, whereas her pride had almost made me free from "responsibility." My opinion is, and my thought was, that it was God's punishment upon me.

I cannot decide clearly what purely emotional impression she made upon me. One thing is certain: that she gave herself to me, almost worshiping me, asking me to love her, which moved me to such an extent that I was willing to risk all for her. How much I loved her is shown by the fact that I always tried to hide from myself how much she had moved me, which however really has no relation to the passions. If I had not been a penitent, had not had my *vita ante acta*, had not been melancholy, my union with her would have made me happier than I had ever dreamed of being. But insofar as I was what, alas, I was, I had to say that I could be happier in my unhappiness without her than with her; she had moved me and I would have liked, more than liked, to have done everything.

But there was a divine protest, that is how I understood it. The wedding. I had to hide such a tremendous amount from her, had to base the whole thing upon something untrue.

I wrote to her and sent her back the ring. The letter is to be found word for word in the "psychological experiment."[4] With all my strength I allowed that to become purely historical; for I spoke to no one of it, not to a single man; I who am more silent than the grave. Should the book come into her hands I wanted her to be reminded of it.

What did she do? In her womanly despair she overstepped the boundary. She evidently knew that I was melancholy; she intended that anxiety should drive me to extremes. The reverse happened. She certainly brought me to the point at which anxiety drove me to extremes; but then with gigantic strength I constrained my whole nature so as to repel her. There was only one thing to do and that was to repel her with all my powers.

[3] To some extent she suspected my condition, for she often answered: "You are never happy; and so it is all one to you whether I remain with you or not." She also once said to me that she would never ask me about anything if only she might remain with me. (K)

[4] A part of the *Stages* by Frater Taciturnitus.

During those two months of deceit I observed a careful caution in what I said directly to her from time to time: "Give in, let me go; you cannot bear it." Thereupon she answered passionately that she would bear anything rather than let me go.

I also suggested giving the appearance that it was she who broke off the engagement, so that she might be spared all offense. That she would not have. She answered: if she could bear the other she could bear this too. And not unsocratically she said: In her presence no one would let anything be noticed and what people said in her absence remained a matter of indifference.

It was a time of terrible suffering: to have to be so cruel and at the same time to love as I did. She fought like a tigress. If I had not believed that God had lodged a veto she would have been victorious.

And so about two months later it broke. She grew desperate. For the first time in my life I scolded. It was the only thing to do.

When I left her I went immediately to the Theater because I wanted to meet Emil Boesen. (That gave rise to what was then said in Copenhagen, that I had looked at my watch and said to the family that if they had anything more in their minds would they please hurry up as I had to go to the theater.) The act was finished. As I left the stalls Etatsraad Olsen came up to me and said, "May I speak to you?" We went together to his house. "It will be her death, she is in absolute despair." I said, "I shall calm her down; but everything is settled." He said, "I am a proud man and I find it difficult to say, but I beg you, do not break with her." He was indeed a noble-hearted man; I was deeply moved. But I did not let myself be persuaded. I remained with the family to dinner. I spoke to her as I left. The following morning I received a letter from him saying she had not slept all night, and asking me to go and see her. I went and tried to persuade her. She asked me: "Are you never going to marry?" I answered, "Yes, perhaps in ten years' time when I have sown my wild oats; then I shall need some young blood to rejuvenate me." That was a necessary cruelty. Then she said, "Forgive me for the pain I have caused you." I answered: "It is for me to ask forgiveness." She said: "Promise to think of me." I did so. "Kiss me," she said. I did so, but without passion. Merciful God!

And so we parted. I spent the whole night crying on my bed. But the next day I behaved as usual, wittier and in better spirits than ever.

That was necessary. My brother told me he wanted to go to the family and show them that I was not a scoundrel. "If you do, I will put a bullet through your head," which is the best proof of how deeply concerned I was. I went to Berlin. I suffered greatly. I thought of her every day. Until now I have kept my promise and have prayed for her at least once and often twice a day, in addition to the other times I might think about her.

When the bonds were broken my thoughts were these: either you throw yourself into the wildest kind of life—or else become absolutely religious, but it will be different from the parson's mixture . . .

TRANSLATED BY ALEXANDER DRU

JOYCE ON JOYCE

James Joyce

To Harriet Shaw Weaver
24 June 1921   71 *rue du Cardinal Lemoine, Paris* V

Dear Miss Weaver: . . . A nice collection could be made of legends about me. Here are some. My family in Dublin believe that I enriched myself in Switzerland during the war by espionage work for one or both combatants. Triestines, seeing me emerge from my relative's house occupied by my furniture for about twenty minutes every day and walk to the same point, the G.P.O., and back (I was writing *Nausikaa* and *The Oxen of the Sun* in a dreadful atmosphere) circulated the rumour, now firmly believed, that I am a cocaine victim. The general rumour in Dublin was (till the prospectus of *Ulysses* stopped it) that I could write no more, had broken down and was dying in New York. A man from Liverpool told me he had heard that I was the owner of several cinema theatres all over Switzerland. In America there appear to be or have been two versions: one that I was an austere mixture of the Dalai Lama and sir Rabindranath Tagore. Mr Pound described me as a dour Aberdeen minister. Mr Lewis told me he was told that I was a crazy fellow who always carried four watches and rarely spoke except to ask my neighbour what o'clock it was. Mr Yeats seemed to have described me to Mr Pound as a kind of Dick Swiveller. What the numerous (and useless) people to whom I have been introduced here think I don't know. My habit of addressing people I have just met for the first time as "Monsieur" earned for me the reputation of a *tout petit bourgeois* while others consider what I intend for politeness as most offensive. . . . One woman here originated the rumour that I am extremely lazy and will never do or finish anything. (I calculate that I must have spent nearly 20,000 hours in writing *Ulysses*.) A batch of people in Zurich persuaded themselves that I was gradually going mad and actually endeavoured to induce me to enter a sanatorium where a certain Doctor Jung (the Swiss Tweedledum who is not to be confused with the Viennese Tweedledee, Dr Freud) amuses himself at the expense (in every sense of the word) of ladies and gentlemen who are troubled with bees in their bonnets.

I mention all these views not to speak about myself but to show you how conflicting they all are. The truth probably is that I am a quite commonplace person undeserving of so much imaginative painting. There is a further opinion that I am a crafty simulating and dissimulating Ulysses-like type, a "jejune jesuit," selfish and cynical. There is some truth in this, I suppose: but it is by no means all of me (nor was it of Ulysses) and it has been my habit to apply this alleged quality to safeguard my poor creations . . .

The director of *L'Oeuvre* theatre who was so enthusiastic about *Exiles* and bombarded me with telegrams has just written a most insolent letter in slang to say that he was not such a fool as to put on the piece and lose 15,000 francs. My consolation is that I win a box of preserved apricots—a bet I made with Mr Pound (who was optimistic) after a cursory inspection of the director aforesaid. I signed a letter giving him *carte blanche* to do what he liked with the play, adapt it, put it on, take it off, lock it up etc knowing that if I refused to sign in a week it would have been said that I was an impossible person, that I was introduced to the great actor Lugné-Poë and given a great opportunity and would not take it. I have been a year in Paris and in that time not a word about me has appeared in any French periodical. Six or seven people are supposed to be translating *Dubliners* in different parts of France. The novel is translated and presented but I can get no reply from the publishers (?) about it though I have written four times asking even for the return of the typescript. I never go to any of the various weekly reunions as it is a waste of time for me at present to be cooped up in overcrowded rooms listening to gossip about absent artists and replying to enthusiastic expressions about my (unread) masterpiece with a polite amused reflective smile. The only person who knows anything worth mentioning about the book is Mr Valery Larbaud. He is now in England. Would you like him to visit you before he returns? . . .

Mr Lewis was very agreeable, in spite of my deplorable ignorance of his art, even offering to instruct me in the art of the Chinese of which I know as much as the man in the moon. He told me he finds life in

London very depressing. There is a curious kind of honour-code
among men which obliges them to assist one another and not hinder
the free action of one another and remain together for mutual
protection with the result that very often they wake up the next
morning sitting in the same ditch.

This letter begins to remind me of a preface by Mr George Bernard
Shaw. It does not seem to be a reply to your letter after all . . . You
have already one proof of my intense stupidity. Here now is an
example of my emptiness. I have not read a work of literature for
several years. My head is full of pebbles and rubbish and broken
matches and lots of glass picked up "most everywhere." The task I set
myself technically in writing a book from eighteen different points of
view and in as many styles, all apparently unknown or undiscovered by
my fellow tradesmen, that and the nature of the legend chosen would
be enough to upset anyone's mental balance. I want to finish the book
and try to settle my entangled material affairs definitely one way or
the other (somebody here said of me: "They call him a poet. He
appears to be interested chiefly in mattresses"). And, in fact, I was.
After that I want a good long rest in which to forget *Ulysses*
completely.

I forgot to tell you another thing. I don't even know Greek though
I am spoken of as erudite. My father wanted me to take Greek as
third language, my mother German and my friends Irish. Result, I
took Italian. I spoke or used to speak modern Greek not too badly (I
speak four or five languages fluently enough) and have spent a great
deal of time with Greeks of all kinds from noblemen down to
onionsellers, chiefly the latter. I am superstitious about them. They
bring me luck.

I now end this long rambling shambling speech, having said
nothing of the darker aspects of my detestable character. I suppose
the law should now take its course with me because it must now seem
to you a waste of rope to accomplish the dissolution of a person who
has now dissolved visibly and possesses scarcely as much "pendibility"
as an uninhabited dressinggown.

OF THE DISADVANTAGE OF GREATNESS

Michel de Montaigne

Since we cannot attain it, let us take our revenge by speaking ill of it. Yet it is not absolutely speaking ill of something to find some defects in it; there are some in all things, however beautiful and desirable they may be. In general greatness has this evident advantage, that it can step down whenever it pleases, and that it almost has the choice of both conditions. For one does not fall from every height; there are more from which one can descend without falling.

It does indeed seem to me that we overvalue it, and overvalue too the resolution of people we have either seen or heard of who despised it or laid it down of their own accord. Its essence is not so obviously advantageous that it cannot be refused except by a miracle.

I find the effort to bear ills a very hard one; but as for being content with a mediocre measure of fortune, and eschewing greatness, I find very little difficulty in that. To eschew greatness is a virtue, it seems to me, which I, who am only a gosling, could attain without great striving. What may not be done by those who would also put in consideration the glory that goes with this refusal, in which there may lurk more ambition than in the very desire and enjoyment of greatness, inasmuch as ambition never follows its own bent better than by some out-of-the-way and unused path?

I sharpen my courage toward endurance, I weaken it toward desire. I have as much to wish for as another, and I allow my wishes and inclinations as much freedom and indiscretion; yet it has never occurred to me to wish for empire or royalty, or for the eminence of those high and commanding fortunes. I do not aim in that direction, I love myself too well. When I think of growing, it is in a lowly way, with a constrained and cowardly growth, strictly for myself: in resolution, wisdom, health, beauty, and even riches. But that prestige, all that powerful authority, oppresses my imagination. And quite in contrast to that other, I would perhaps prefer to be second or third in Périgueux rather than first in Paris; at least, without prevarication, rather the third in Paris than the first in responsibility. I want neither to be a wretched unknown, wrangling with a doorkeeper, nor to make the crowds where I pass split in adoration. I am trained to a middle station, by my taste as well as by my lot. And I have shown, in the conduct of my life and of my enterprises, that I have rather avoided than otherwise stepping above the degree of fortune in which God placed me at birth. Every natural arrangement is equally just and easy.

My soul is so craven that I do not measure good fortune by its height; I measure it by its facility.

But if my heart is not great enough, it is compensatingly open, and it orders me boldly to publish its weakness. If I were asked to compare the life of L. Thorius Balbus, a gentleman, handsome, learned, healthy, intelligent, abounding in all sorts of advantages and pleasures, leading a tranquil life all his own, his soul well prepared against death, superstition, pain, and the other encumbrances of human necessity, at last dying in battle, arms in hand, for the defense of his country, on the one hand; and on the other hand the life of M. Regulus, great and lofty as every man knows it to be, and his admirable end; the one without a name, without distinction, the other marvelously exemplary and glorious: I would certainly say what Cicero says, if I could speak as well as he. But if I had to apply their lives to mine, I would also say that the first is as much according to my reach—and according to my desire, which I accommodate to my reach—as the second is far beyond it; that I can attain the latter only by veneration, but that I could readily attain the other in practice. Let us return to our temporal greatness, from which we started.

I have a distaste for mastery, both active and passive. Otanes, one of the seven who had some right to aspire to the throne of Persia, took a course that I would gladly have taken. He abandoned to his competitors his chance of attaining it either by election or by lot, provided that he and his family might live in that empire free of all subjection and mastery save that of the ancient laws, and have every freedom that would not be prejudicial to these; balking at either commanding or being commanded.

The toughest and most difficult occupation in the world, in my opinion, is to play the part of a king worthily. I excuse more of their faults than people commonly do, in consideration of the dreadful weight of their burden, which dazes me. It is difficult for a power so immoderate to observe moderation. And yet even for men of a less excellent nature, it is a singular incitement to virtue to be lodged in a place where you can do no good that is not put in the record and account, where the slightest good action affects so many people, and where your ability, like that of preachers, is principally addressed to the populace, an inexact judge, easy to dupe, easy to satisfy.

There are few things on which we can give a sincere judgment, because there are few in which we have not in some way a private interest. Superiority and inferiority of position, mastery and subjection, are forced into a natural envy and contention; they must pillage one another perpetually. I do not believe either one about the rights of the other; let us give the floor to reason, which is inflexible and impassive, when we can dispose of it.

Less than a month ago I was leafing through two Scottish books debating this subject. The democrat makes the king's situation worse than a carter's; the monarchist lodges him a few fathoms above God in power and sovereignty.

Now the disadvantage of greatness, which I have chosen to comment on here because of an occasion that has just called my attention to it, is this. There is perhaps nothing more pleasant in association with men than the trials of strength we have with one another, in rivalry of honor and worth, whether in exercises of the body or of the mind; and in these sovereigns have no real share. In truth, it has often seemed to me that by force of respect princes are treated disdainfully and insultingly in these matters. For what used to offend me immeasureably in my childhood, that those who exercised with me would not take it seriously, considering me unworthy of their making an effort, is what we see happen to princes every day, since everyone considers himself too base to make an effort against them. If people recognize that princes have the slightest desire for victory, there is no one who will not labor to give it to them and who will not rather betray his own glory than offend theirs; everyone exerts only as much effort as is needed to serve their honor.

What share do they have in the melee in which everyone is on their side? I seem to see those paladins of times past going into jousts and combats with enchanted bodies and weapons.

Brisson, in a race against Alexander, only pretended to run his best; Alexander scolded him for it, but he should have had him whipped.

In consideration of this, Carneades used to say that the sons of princes learned nothing rightly but how to manage horses, since in every other exercise everyone gives way to them and lets them win; but a horse, who is neither a flatterer nor a courtier, will throw the son of a king just as he would the son of a porter.

Homer was constrained to consent that Venus, so sweet and delicate a saint, should be wounded in the battle of Troy, so as to endow her with courage and boldness, qualities not found in those who are exempt from danger. The gods are made to be angry, to fear, to flee, to be jealous, sorrowful, and passionate, in order to honor them with virtues which among us are built of these imperfections. He who does not share the risk and difficult can claim no involvement in the honor and pleasure that follow hazardous actions. It is a pity to have so much power that everything gives way to you. Your fortune repeals society and companionship too far from you; it plants you too far apart. That ease and slack facility of making everything bow beneath you is the enemy of every kind of pleasure. That is sliding, not walking; sleeping, not living. Imagine man accompanied by omnipotence: he is sunk; he must ask you for hindrance and resistance, as an alms; his being and his welfare are in indigence.

Their good qualities are dead and wasted, for these are felt only by comparison, and they are out of comparison. They have little knowledge of true praise, being battered with such continual and uniform approbation. Are they dealing with the stupidest of their subjects? They have no way of getting the advantage over him. If he says: "It is because he is my king," it seems to him he has said clearly enough that he lent a hand to his own defeat.

Their royal status stifles and consumes their other real and essential qualities; these are sunk in royalty; and it leaves them nothing to recommend themselves by but those actions that directly concern and serve it, the duties of their office. It takes so much to be a king that he exists only as such. That extraneous glare that surrounds him hides him and conceals him from us; our sight breaks and is dissipated by it, being filled and arrested by this strong light. The Senate decreed the prize for eloquence to Tiberius; he refused it, thinking that from a judgment so far from free, even if it had been honest, he could have no satisfaction.

As we yield to them all the advantages of honor, so we confirm and authorize the defects and vices they have, not only by approbation but also by imitation. Every one of the followers of Alexander carried his head on one side, as he did; and the flatterers of Dionysius bumped into one another in his presence, stumbled upon and knocked over what was at their feet, to signify that they were as shortsighted as he. Even hernias have sometimes served as a recommendation and favor. I have seen men affect deafness. And because the master hated his wife, Plutarch saw courtiers repudiate theirs, whom they loved.

What is more, lechery has been seen in fashion among them, and every sort of dissoluteness; as also disloyalty, blasphemy, cruelty; as also heresy; also superstition, irreligion, laxity, and worse, if worse there be: an example even more dangerous than that of the flatterers of Mithridates, who, because their master was envious of the honor of being a good doctor, brought him their limbs to be incised and cauterized. For those others allow their soul to be cauterized, a nobler and more delicate part.

But, to end where I began, when the Emperor Hadrian was arguing with the philosopher Favorinus about the interpretation of some word, Favorinus soon yielded him the victory. When his friends complained to him, he said: "You are jesting; would you want him to be less learned than I, he who commands thirty legions?" Augustus wrote some verses against Asinius Pollio. "And I," said Pollio, "am keeping quiet; it is not wise to be a scribe against a man who can proscribe." And they were right. For Dionysius, because he could not match Philoxenus in poetry, and Plato in prose, condemned the one to the quarries and sent the other to be sold as a slave on the island of Aegina.

TRANSLATED BY DONALD M. FRAME

INTO MISSISSIPPI

John Howard Griffin

My money was running low so I decided to cash some travelers checks before leaving. The banks were closed, since it was past noon on Saturday, but I felt I would have no difficulty with travelers checks in any of the larger stores, especially those on Dryades where I had traded and was known as a customer.

I took the bus to Dryades and walked down it, stopping at the dime store where I'd made most of my purchases. The young white girl came forward to wait on me.

"I need to cash a travelers check," I said smiling.

"We don't cash any checks of any kind," she said firmly.

"But a travelers check is perfectly safe," I said.

"We just don't cash checks," she said and turned away.

"Look, you know me. You've waited on me. I need some money."

"You should have gone to the bank."

"I didn't know I needed the money until after the banks closed," I said.

I knew I was making a pest of myself, but I could scarcely believe this nice young lady could be so unsympathetic, so insolent when she discovered I did not come in to buy something.

"I'll be glad to buy a few things," I said.

She called up to the bookkeeping department on an open mezzanine. "Hey! Do we cash travelers ch—"

"No!" the white woman shouted back.

"Thank you for your kindness," I said and walked out.

I went into one store after the other along Dryades and Rampart streets. In every store their smiles turned to grimaces when they saw I meant not to buy but to cash a check. It was not their refusal—I could understand that; it was the bad manners they displayed. I began to feel desperate and resentful. They would have cashed a travelers check without hesitation for a white man. Each time they refused me, they implied clearly that I had probably come by these checks dishonestly and they wanted nothing to do with them or me.

Finally, after I gave up hope and decided I must remain in New Orleans without funds until the banks opened on Monday, I walked toward town. Small gold-lettering on the window of a store caught my attention: CATHOLIC BOOK STORE. Knowing the Catholic stand on racism, I wondered if this shop might cash a Negro's check. With some hesitation, I opened the door and entered. I was prepared to be disappointed.

"Would you cash a twenty-dollar travelers check for me?" I asked the proprietress.

"Of course," she said without hesitation, as though nothing could be more natural. She did not even study me.

I was so grateful I bought a number of paperback books—works of Maritain, Aquinas and Christopher Dawson. With these in my jacket, I hurried toward the Greyhound bus station.

In the bus station lobby, I looked for signs indicating a colored waiting room, but saw none. I walked up to the ticket counter. When the lady ticket-seller saw me, her otherwise attractive face turned sour, violently so. This look was so unexpected and so unprovoked I was taken aback.

"What do you want?" she snapped.

Taking care to pitch my voice to politeness, I asked about the next bus to Hattiesburg.

She answered rudely and glared at me with such loathing I knew I was receiving what the Negroes call "the hate stare." It was my first experience with it. It is far more than the look of disapproval one occasionally gets. This was so exaggeratedly hateful I would have been amused if I had not been so surprised.

I framed the words in my mind: "Pardon me, but have I done something to offend you?" But I realized I had done nothing—my color offended her.

"I'd like a one-way ticket to Hattiesburg, please," I said and placed a ten-dollar bill on the counter.

"I can't change that big a bill," she said abruptly and turned away, as though the matter were closed. I remained at the window, feeling strangely abandoned but not knowing what else to do. In a while she flew back at me, her face flushed, and fairly shouted: "I *told* you—I can't change that big a bill."

"Surely," I said stiffly, "in the entire Greyhound system there must be some means of changing a ten-dollar bill. Perhaps the manager—

She jerked the bill furiously from my hand and stepped away from the window. In a moment she reappeared to hurl my change and the ticket on the counter with such force most of it fell on the floor at my feet. I was truly dumfounded by this deep fury that possessed her whenever she looked at me. Her performance was so venomous, I felt sorry for her. It must have shown in my expression, for her face congested to high pink. She undoubtedly considered it a supreme insolence for a Negro to dare to feel sorry for her.

I stooped to pick up my change and ticket from the floor. I wondered how she would feel if she learned that the Negro before whom she had behaved in such an unlady-like manner was habitually a white man.

With almost an hour before bus departure, I turned away and looked for a place to sit. The large, handsome room was almost empty. No other Negro was there, and I dared not take a seat unless I saw some other Negro also seated.

Once again a "hate stare" drew my attention like a magnet. It came from a middle-aged, heavy-set, well-dressed white man. He sat a few yards away, fixing his eyes on me. Nothing can describe the withering horror of this. You feel lost, sick at heart before such unmasked hatred, not so much because it threatens you as because it shows humans in such an inhuman light. You see a kind of insanity, something so obscene the very obscenity of it (rather than its threat) terrifies you. It was so new I could not take my eyes from the man's face. I felt like saying: "What in God's name are you doing to yourself?"

A Negro porter sidled over to me. I glimpsed his white coat and turned to him. His glance met mine and communicated the sorrow, the understanding.

"Where am I supposed to go?" I asked him.

He touched my arm in that mute and reassuring way of men who share a moment of crisis. "Go outside and around the corner of the building. You'll find the room."

The white man continued to stare, his mouth twisted with loathing as he turned his head to watch me move away.

In the colored waiting room, which was not labeled as such, but rather as COLORED CAFÉ, presumably because of interstate travel regulations, I took the last empty seat. The room was crowded with glum faces, faces dead to all enthusiasm, faces of people waiting.

The books I had bought from the Catholic Book Store weighed heavily in my pocket. I pulled one of them out and, without looking at the title, let it fall open in my lap. I read:

" . . . *it is by justice that we can authentically measure man's value or his nullity . . . the absence of justice is the absence of what makes him man.*" Plato.

I have heard it said another way, as a dictum: "*He who is less than just is less than man.*"

I copied the passage in a little pocket notebook. A Negro woman, her face expressionless, flat, highlighted with sweat, watched me write. When I turned in my seat to put the notebook in my hip pocket, I detected the faintest smile at the corners of her mouth.

They called the bus. We filed out into the high-roofed garage and stood in line, the Negroes to the rear, the whites to the front. Buses idled their motors, filling the air with a stifling odor of exhaust fumes. An army officer hurried to get at the rear of the white line. I stepped back to let him get in front. He refused and went to the end of the colored portion of the line. Every Negro craned his head to look at the phenomenon. I have learned that men in uniform, particularly officers, rarely descend to show discrimination, perhaps because of the integration of the armed forces.

We sweated through our clothes and I was ready to leave and try for a later bus when they allowed us to board. Though nominally segregation is not permitted on interstate buses, no Negro would be fool enough to try to sit anywhere except at the rear on one going into Mississippi. I occupied a seat to myself not far from the back. Muffled conversations sprang up around me.

"Well, here we go into Mississippi—the most lied-about state in the union—that's what they claim," a man behind me said.

"It's the truth, too," another said. "Only it's Mississippi that does all the lying."

We drove through New Orleans under an overcast sky. Air conditioning in the bus cooled us comfortably. As we crossed the bridge, the water of Lake Pontchartrain reflected the sky's gray tone, with whitecaps on its disturbed surface.

The bus stopped at the outskirts of town to take on more

passengers. Among them was a striking Negro man, tall, slender, elegantly dressed—the "Valentino" type. He wore a mustache and a neatly trimmed Van Dyke beard. He walked toward the rear, giving the whites a fawning, almost tender look. His expression twisted to a sneer when he reached the back and surveyed the Negroes.

He sat sidewise in an empty seat across the aisle from me and began to harangue two brothers behind him. "This place stinks. Damned punk niggers. Look at all of them—bunch of dirty punks—don't know how to dress. You don't deserve anything better. *Mein Kampf!* Do you speak German? No. You're ignorant. You make me sick."

He proceeded to denounce his race venomously. He spoke fragments of French, Spanish and Japanese.

I averted my head to the window and watched the country fly past as we traveled through an area of sunlight. I did not want to become involved in any discussion with this strange man. He was soon in violent argument with one of the brothers. They quarreled to the point of rage over whether Juárez was in Old Mexico or New Mexico.

The elegant one shouted, "You can't lie to Christophe. Christophe's got brains. No ignorant punk like you can fool him. You never been to Juárez!"

He jumped abruptly to his feet. Fearing violence, I turned toward him. He stood poised, ready to strike the other, his eyes narrowed to slits of hatred.

"If you hit me, you'll just be hitting me in the wrong," the poorly dressed Negro said, looking calmly up at Christophe. His seat companion added with a gentle smile, "He's my brother. I'd have to take his part."

"You threatening me?" Christophe whispered.

"No, now look," the brother placated. "Why don't you two agree just not to talk."

"He won't say another word to me? You promise?" Christophe said. He lowered his fist, but his face did not relax.

"No, he won't—will you?"

The poorly dressed one shrugged his shoulders pleasantly. "I guess——"

"Don't speak! Don't speak!" Christophe shouted into his face.

"Okay . . . Okay . . ." he said, glancing toward me as though to say the elegant Christophe must be insane.

Christophe glared at him for some time before moving over into the seat next to me. His presence set my nerves on edge. He was cunning and apparently vicious and I did not know what kind of scene he might start. I stared out the window, turning so far he could see only the back of my head.

He slouched far down in the seat and, working his hands wildly in the air as though he were playing a guitar, he began to sing the blues, softly, mournfully, lowering his voice at the obscene words. A strange sweetish odor detached from him. I supposed it to be marijuana, but it was only a guess.

I felt his elbow dig into my ribs. "How you like that, pappy?"

I nodded, trying to be both polite and noncommittal. He had pulled his hat down over his eyes. He lighted a cigarette and let it dangle from his lips. I turned back to the window, hoping he would leave me alone.

He nudged me again and I looked around. He bent his head far back to gaze at me under his lowered hat brim. "You don't dig the blues, do you, daddy?"

"I don't know," I said.

He studied me with narrowed eyes. Then, as though he had found some answer, he flashed me a magnificent smile, learned hard against me and whispered. "I bet you dig this, daddy."

He punched his hat back, concentrated, stiffened his hands, palms upward, in a supplicating gesture and began softly to chant *Tantum ergo sacramentum, Veneremur cernui* in as beautiful Latin as I have ever heard. I stared at him dumfounded as he chanted the Gregorian version of this famous text.

He glanced at me tenderly, his face soft as though he were on the verge of tears. "That got you, didn't it, dad?"

"Yes," I said.

He made a huge sign of the cross, lowered his head and recited, again with perfect Latin diction, the *Confiteor*. When it was over, he remained still, in profound introspection. Above the hum of the bus's wheels on the pavement, silence surrounded us. No one spoke. Doubtless those nearest us who had witnessed the strange scene were perplexed.

"You were an altar boy, I guess," I said.

"I was," he said, not raising his head. "I wanted to be a priest." His mobile face revealed every emotion. His eyes darkened with regret.

The man across the aisle grinned and said: "Better not believe anything he tells you."

Christophe's handsome face congealed instantly to hatred.

"I told you not to talk to me!

The man's brother intervened. "He just forgot." Then to the poorly dressed one, "Don't say *anything* to him. He can't stand you."

"I was talking to the other fellow, the one in the dark glasses," he said.

"Shut up!" Christophe shouted. "You were talking *about* me—and I don't even want you to do that."

"Just be quiet," the man's brother said. "He's going to be mad at you anything you say."

"Goddamn, it's a free sonofabitching country," the other said feebly, the smile remaining unchanged on his face. "I'm not afraid of him."

"Well, just hush—no need in you talking to him," his brother pleaded.

"You keep him quiet—or else," Christophe said haughtily.

My stomach contracted with uneasiness, certain there would be a fight. I was astonished to see Christophe cut his eyes around to me and wink, as though secretly he were amused. He glared his "enemy" down for some time before turning back to me. "I came to sit by you because you're the only one here that looks like he's got enough sense to carry on an intelligent conversation."

"Thank you," I said.

"I'm not pure Negro," he said proudly. "My mother was French, my father Indian."

"I see . . ."

"She was Portuguese, my mother—a lovely woman," Christophe sighed.

"I see . . ."

The man across the aisle smiled broadly at the obvious admission of a lie from Christophe. I gave him a warning glance and he did not challenge our friend's French-Portuguese-Indian background.

"Let's see," Christophe said, eying me speculatively. "What blood have you got? Give me a minute. Christophe never makes a mistake. I can always tell what kind of blood a man's got in him." He took my face between his hands and examined me closely. I waited, certain this strange man would expose me. Finally, he nodded grave to indicate he had deciphered my blood background. "I have it now." His eyes glowed and he hesitated before making his dramatic announcement to the world. I cringed, preparing explanations, and then decided to try to stop him from exposing me.

"Wait—let me——"

"Florida Navaho," he interrupted triumphantly. "Your mother was part Florida Navaho, wasn't she?"

I felt like laughing, first with relief and then at the thought of my Dutch-Irish mother being anything so exotic as Florida Navaho. At the same time, I felt vaguely disappointed to find Christophe no brighter than the rest of us.

He waited for my answer.

"You're pretty sharp," I said.

"Ha! I never miss." Instantly, his expression degenerated to viciousness. "I hate us, Father."

"I'm not a Father."

"Ah, you can't fool Christophe. I know you're a priest even if you are dressed in civilian clothes. Look at these punks, Father. Dumb, ignorant bastards. They don't know the score. I'm getting out of this country."

His anger vanished. He leaned to whisper in my ear, his voice suddenly abject. "I'll tell you the truth, Father. I'm just out of the pen—four years. I'm on my way to see my wife. She's waiting with a new car for me in Slidell. And God . . . what a reunion we're going to have!"

His face crumpled and his head fell against my chest. Silently he wept.

"Don't cry," I whispered. "It's all right. Don't cry."

He raised his head and rolled his eyes upward in agony. His face bathed in tears, all of his arrogant defenses gone, he said: "Sometime, Father, when you say Mass, will you take the white Host for Christophe?"

"You're wrong to believe I'm a priest," I said. "But I'll remember you the next time I go to Mass."

"Ah, that's the only peace," he sighed. "That's the peace my soul longs for. I wish I could come back home to it, but I can't—I haven't been inside a church in seventeen years."

"You can always go back."

"Nah," he snorted. "I've got to shoot up a couple of guys."

My surprise must have shown. A smile of glee lighted his face. "Don't worry, Daddy. I'm going to watch out. Why don't you get off with me and let's shoot up this town together."

I told him I could not. The bus slowed into Slidell. Christophe got to his feet, straightened his tie, stared furiously at the man across the aisle for a moment, bowed to me and got off. We were relieved to have him gone, though I could not help wondering what his life might be were he not torn with the frustrations of his Negro-ness.

At Slidell we changed into another Greyhound bus with a new driver—a middle-aged man, large-bellied with a heavy, jowled face filigreed with tiny red blood vessels near the surface of his cheeks.

A stockily built young Negro, who introduced himself as Bill Williams, asked if I minded having him sit beside me.

Now that Christophe was gone, the tensions disappeared in our Negro section. Everyone knew, from having heard our conversation, that I was a stranger in the area. Talk flowed easily and they surrounded me with warmth.

"People come down here and say Mississippi is the worst place in the world," Bill said. "But we can't all live in the North."

"Of course not. And it looks like beautiful country," I said, glancing out at giant pine trees.

Seeing that I was friendly, he offered advice. "If you're not used to things in Mississippi, you'll have to watch yourself pretty close till you catch on," he said.

The others, hearing, nodded agreement.

I told him I did not know what to watch out for.

"Well, you know you don't want to even look at a white woman. In fact, you look down at the ground or the other way."

A large, pleasant Negro woman smiled at me across the aisle. "They're awful touchy on that here. You may not even know you're looking in a white woman's direction, but they'll try to make something out of it," she said.

"If you pass by a picture show, and they've got women on the posters outside, don't look at them either."

"Is it that bad?"

He assured me it was. Another man said: "Somebody's sure to say, 'Hey, boy—what are you looking at that white gal like *that* for?'"

I remembered the woman on the bus in New Orleans using almost the same expression.

"And you dress pretty well," Bill continued, his heavy black face frowning in concentration. "If you walk past an alley, walk out in the middle of the street. Plenty of people here, white and colored, would knock you in the head if they thought you had money on you. If white boys holler at you, just keep walking. Don't let them stop you and start asking you questions."

I told him I appreciated his warning.

"Can you all think of anything else?" he asked the others.

"That about covers it," one of them said.

I thanked him for telling me these things.

"Well, if I was to come to your part of the country, I'd want somebody to tell me," Bill said.

He told me he was a truck driver, working out of Hattiesburg. He had taken a load to New Orleans, where he had left his truck for repairs and caught the bus back to Hattiesburg. He asked if I had made arrangements for a place to stay. I told him no. He said the best thing would be for me to contact a certain important person who would put me in touch with someone reliable who would find me a decent and safe place.

It was late dusk when the bus pulled into some little town for a stop. "We get about ten minutes here," Bill said. "Let's get off and stretch our legs. They've got a men's room here if you need to go."

The driver stood up and faced the passengers. "Ten-minute rest stop," he announced.

The whites rose and ambled off. Bill and I led the Negroes toward the door. As soon as he saw us, the driver blocked our way. Bill slipped under his arm and walked toward the dim-lit shed building.

"Hey, boy, where you going?" the driver shouted to Bill while he stretched his arms across the opening to prevent my stepping down. "Hey, you, boy, I'm talking to you." Bill's footsteps crunched unhurriedly across the gravel.

I stood on the bottom step, waiting. The driver turned back to me.

"Where do you think you're going?" he asked, his heavy cheeks quivering with each word.

"I'd like to go to the rest room." I smiled and moved to step down.

He tightened his grip on the door facings and shouldered in close to block me. "Does your ticket say for you to get off here?" he asked.

"No sir, but the others——"

"Then you get your ass back in your seat and don't you move till we get to Hattiesburg," he commanded.

"You mean I can't go to the——"

"I mean get your ass back there like I told you," he said, his voice rising. "I can't be bothered rounding up all you people when we get ready to go."

"You announced a rest stop. The whites all got off," I said, unable to believe he really meant to deprive us of rest-room privileges.

He stood on his toes and put his face up close to mine. His nose flared. Footlights caught silver glints from the hairs that curled out of his nostrils. He spoke slowly, threateningly: "Are you arguing with me?"

"No sir . . ." I sighed.

"Then you do like I say."

We turned like a small herd of cattle and drifted back to our seats. The others grumbled about how unfair it was. The larger woman was apologetic, as though it embarrassed her for a stranger to see Mississippi's dirty linen.

"There's no call for him to act like that," she said. "They usually let us off."

I sat in the monochrome gloom of dusk, scarcely believing that in this year of freedom any man could deprive another of anything so basic as the need to quench thirst or use the rest room. There was nothing of the feel of America here. It was rather some strange country suspended in ugliness. Tension hung in the air, a continual threat, even though you could not put your finger on it.

"Well," I heard a man behind me say softly but firmly, "if I can't go in there, then I'm going in here. I'm not going to sit here and bust."

I glanced back and saw it was the same poorly dressed man who had so outraged Christophe. He walked in a half crouch to a place behind the last seat, where he urinated loudly on the floor. Indistinguishable sounds of approval rose around me—quiet laughter, clearing throats, whispers.

"Let's all do it," a man said.

"Yeah, flood this bus and end all this damned foolishness."

Bitterness dissolved in our delight to give the bus driver and the bus as good as they deserved.

The move was on, but it was quelled by another voice: "No, let's don't. It'll just given them something else to hold against us," an older man said. A women agreed. All of us could see the picture. The whites would start claiming that we were unfit, that Negroes did not even known enough to go to the rest room—they just did it in the back of the bus; never mentioning, of course, that the driver would not let us off.

The driver's bullish voice attracted our attention.

"Didn't you hear me call you?" he asked as Bill climbed the steps.

"I sure didn't," Bill said pleasantly.

"You deaf?"

"No sir."

"You mean to stand there and say you didn't hear me call you?"

"Oh, were you calling me?" Bill asked innocently. "I heard you yelling 'Boy,' but that's not my name, so I didn't know you meant me."

CANTO LXXXIII

Ezra Pound

ὕδωρ
HUDOR et Pax
Gemisto stemmed all from Neptune
      hence the Rimini bas reliefs
Sd Mr Yeats (W. B.) "Nothing affects these people
        Except our conversation"
lux enim
      ignis est accidens   and,
wrote the prete in his edition of Scotus:
Hilaritas   the virtue *hilaritas*

the queen stitched King Carolus' shirts or whatever
while Erigena put greek tags in his excellent verses
      in fact an excellent poet, Paris
        toujours Pari'
           (Charles le Chauve)

      and you might find a bit of enamel
      a bit of true blue enamel
        on a metal pyx or whatever
    omnia, quae sunt, lumina sunt, or whatever

so they dug up his bones in the time of De Montfort
    (Simone)

        Le Paradis n'est pas artificiel
and Uncle William dawdling around Notre Dame
in search of whatever
        paused to admire the symbol
with Notre Dame standing inside it

Whereas in St Etienne
           or why not Dei Miracoli:
mermaids, that carving,

    in the drenched tent there is quiet
           sered eyes are at rest

    the rain beat as with colour of feldspar
    blue as the flying fish off Zoagli
pax, ὕδωρ   "ΥΔΩΡ
      the sage
delighteth in water
    the humane man has amity with the hills

as the grass grows by the weirs
         thought Uncle William   *consiros*
as the grass on the roof of St What's his name
   near "Cane e Gatto"
     soll deine Liebe sein
it would be about a-level the windows
     the grass would, or I dare say above that
     when they bless the wax for the Palio

Olim de Malatestis
      with Maria's face there in the fresco
    painted two centuries sooner,
   at least that
before she wore it
    As Montino's
in that family group of about 1820
   not wholly Hardy's material

      OΙ πάντα 'ρει

as he was standing below the altars
     of the spirits of rain
   "When every hollow is full
     it moves forward"
   to the phantom mountain above the cloud
But in the caged panther's eyes:

"Nothing. Nothing that you can do . . ."
green pool, under green of the jungle,
caged: "Nothing, nothing that you can do."

Δρυάς, your eyes are like clouds

Nor can who has passed a month in the death cells
        believe in capital punishment
No man who has passed a month in the death cells
        believes in cages for beasts

Δρυάς, your eyes are like the clouds over Taishan
        When some of the rain has fallen
        and half remains yet to fall

The roots go down to the river's edge
        and the hidden city moves upward
            white ivory under the bark

With clouds over Taishan-Chocorura
        when the blackberry ripens
and now the new moon faces Taishan
one must count by the dawn star
        Dryad, thy peace is like water
There is September sun on the pools

Plura diafana
        Heliads lift the mist from the young willows
there is no base seen under Taishan
        but the brightness of 'udor   ὔδωρ
the poplar tips float in brightness
only the stockade posts stand

And now the ants seem to stagger
            as the dawn sun has trapped their shadows,
this breath wholly covers the mountains
            it shines and divides
it nourishes by its rectitude
does no injury
overstanding the earth it fills the nine fields
                    to heaven

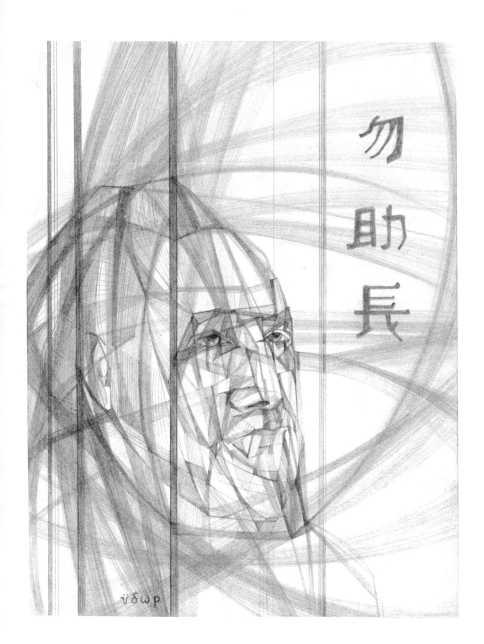

CANTO LXXXIII
Ezra Pound

Boon companion to equity
    it joins with the process
        lacking it, there is inanition

When the equities are gathered together
as birds alighting
it springeth up vital

If deeds be not ensheaved and garnered in the heart
there is inanition

      (have I perchance a debt to a man named Clower)

that he eat of the barley corn
and move with the seed's breath

the sun as a golden eye
      between dark cloud and the mountain

"non combaattere" said Giovanna
       meaning, as before stated, don't work so hard
don't

     as it stands in the Kung-Sun Chow.
San Gregorio, San Trovaso
Old Ziovan raced at seventy after his glories
       and came in long last
and the family eyes stayed the same Adriatic
       for three generations (San Vio)
and was, I suppose, last month the Redentore as usual

Will I ever see the Giudecca again?
      or the lights against it, Ca' Foscari, Ca' Giustinian
or the Ca', as they say, of Desdemona
or the two towers where are the cypress no more
      or the boats moored off le Zattere
or the north quai of the Sensaria DAKRUŌN ΔΑΚΡΥΩΝ

      and Brother Wasp is building a very neat house
      of four rooms, one shaped like a squat indian bottle
      La vespa, *la* vespa, mud, swallow system
so that dreaming of Bracelonde and of Perugia
and the great fountain in the Piazza
or of old Bulagaio's cat that with a well timed leap
      could turn the lever-shaped door handle
It comes over me that Mr. Walls must be a ten-strike
with the signorinas
and in the warmth after chill sunrise
an infant, green as new grass,
has stuck its head or tip
out of Madame La Vespa's bottle

mint springs up again
      in spite of Jones' rodents
as had the clover by the gorilla cage
      with a four-leaf

When the mind swings by a grass-blade
      an ant's forefoot shall save you
the clover leaf smells and tastes as its flower

      The infant has descended,
      from mud on the tent roof to Tellus,
like to like colour he goes amid grass-blades
      greeting them that dwell under XTHONOS ΧΘΟΝΟΣ
ΟΙ ΧΘΟΝΙΟΙ;   to carry our news
         εἰς χθονίους   to them that dwell under the earth,
begotten of air, that shall sing in the bower
      of Kore,   Περσεφόνεια
and have speech with Tiresias, Thebae

Cristo Re, Dio Sole

in about ½ a day she has made her adobe
(la vespa) the tiny mud-flask

    and that day I wrote no further

There is fatigue deep as the grave.
The Kakemono grows in flat land out of mist
    sun rises lop-sided over the mountain
      so that I recalled the noise in the chimney
as it were the wind in the chimney
    but was in reality Uncle William
downstairs composing
that had made a great Peeeeacock
    in the proide ov his oiye
    had made a great peeeeeeecock in the . . .
made a great peacock
    in the proide of his oyyee

proide ov his oy-ee
as indeed he had, and perdurable

a great peacock aere perennius
    or as in the advice to the young man to
breed and get married (or not)
      as you choose to regard it

at Stone Cottage in Sussex by the waste moor
(or whatever) and the holly bush
    who would not eat ham for dinner
because peasants eat ham for dinner
    despite the excellent quality
and the pleasure of having it hot

well those days are gone forever
    and the traveling rug with the coon-skin tabs
and his hearing nearly all Wordsworth
    for the sake of his conscience but
preferring Ennemosor on Witches

did we ever get to the end of Doughty:
       The Dawn in Britain?
                      perhaps not
     Summons withdrawn, sir.)
(bein' aliens in prohibited area)
clouds lift their small mountains
       before the elder hills

A fat moon rises lop-sided over the mountain
the eyes, this time my world,
     But pass and look *from* mine
        between my lids
          sea, sky, and pool
          alternate
          pool, sky, sea,

morning moon against sunrise
like a bit of the best antient greek coinage

     und

Mir sagen
Die Damen
Du bist Greis,
     Anacreon

And that a Madonna novecento

cd/be as a Madonna quattrocento
This I learned in the Tirol
       and as perfect
where they paint the houses outside with figures
and the deep inner courts run back triple

    "Das heis' Walterplatz"
    heard in Bozen (Bolzano)
and in my mother's time it was respectable,
it was social, apparently,
              to sit in the Senate gallery

or even in that of the House
    to hear the fire-works of the senators
(and possibly representatives)
as was still done in Westminster in my time
and a very poor show from the once I saw it)

but if Senator Edwards cd/ speak
and have his tropes stay in the memory 40 years, 60 years?
in short/the descent
has not been of advantage either
    to the Senate or to "society"
                    or to the people
   The States have passed thru a
              dam'd supercilious era
Down, Derry-down/
    Oh let an old man rest.

. .
. .
. .

Nothing in the collection is further from narrative than this Canto from Pound's epic poem, but perhaps the distance itself will account for some of the morphologist's pleasure. For there is a narrative here, subordinate though it may be to the depiction of the transient, the recurrent, and the permanent, the tripod of the immense work. The narrative element is the old man in the detention camp outside Pisa whose "mind swings by a grass blade." Trying to hold himself together, he thinks of some fructifying elements or conditions, water first, because his tent is drenched, and in Greek, because of Thales for whom it was the basic form of matter. The difficulties of the Canto largely disappear in a careful reading of the whole poem, but readers whose pleasure is sullied by looking things up may yet delight in the clarity of particulars, their juxtapositions—which have little to do with psychological association—and, above all, in the radiant force of the narrative center, the reflective old man holding on to what he knows and sees for dear life.

VOLTAIRE

Jacques Casanova de Seingalt

"M. de Voltaire," said I, "this is the happiest moment of my life. I have been your pupil for twenty years and my heart is full of joy to see my master."

"Honour me with your attendance on my course for twenty years more and promise me that you will bring me my fees at the end of that time."

"Certainly, if you promise to wait for me."

This Voltairean sally made all present laugh, as was to be expected, for those who laugh keep one party in countenance at the other's expense, and the side which has the laughter is sure to win; this is the rule of good society.

I was not taken by surprise; I had expected this and hoped to have my revenge.

Just then two Englishmen came in and were presented to him.

"These gentlemen are English," said Voltaire. "I wish I were."

I thought the compliment false and out of place; for the gentlemen were obliged to reply out of politeness that they wished they had been French or, if they did not care to tell a lie, they would be embarrassed to tell the truth. I believe every man of honour should put his own nation first.

A moment after Voltaire turned to me again and said that, as I was a Venetian, I must know Count Algarotti.

"I know him, but not because I am a Venetian, as seven-eights of my dear countrymen are not even aware of his existence."

"I should have said, 'as a man of letters.' "

"I know him from having spent two months with him in Padua seven years ago, and what particularly attracted my attention was the admiration he professed for M. de Voltaire."

"That is flattering for me, but he has no need of admiring anyone."

"If Algarotti had not begun by admiring others, he would never

150

have made a name for himself. As an admirer of Newton, he endeavoured to teach the ladies to discuss the theory of light."

"Did he succeed?"

"Not as well as M. de Fontenelle in his *Plurality of Worlds*; however, one may say he has succeeded."

"True. If you see him in Bologna, tell him I am expecting to hear from him about Russia. He can address the letters to my banker, Bianchi, in Milan, and they will be sent on to me."

"I will not fail to do so if I see him."

"I have heard that the Italians do not care for his style."

"No; all that he writes is full of French idioms; his style is wretched."

"But do not these French turns increase the beauty of your language?"

"They make it insufferable, as French would be, mixed with Italian or German, even though it were written by M. de Voltaire."

"You are right; every language should preserve its purity. Livy has been criticised on this account; his Latin is said to be tainted with patavinity."

"When I began to learn Latin, the Abbé Lazzarini told me he preferred Livy to Sallust."

"The Abbé Lazzarini, author of the tragedy, *Ulisse il giovine?* You must have been very young; I wish I had known him. But I knew the Abbé Conti well; the same that was Newton's friend and whose four tragedies contain the whole of Roman history."

"I also knew and admired him. I was young, but congratulated myself on being admitted into the society of these great men. It seems as if it were yesterday, though it is many years ago; and now in your presence my inferiority does not humiliate me. I wish to be the younger son of all humanity."

"Better so that to be the chief and eldest. May I ask you to what branch of literature you have devoted yourself?"

"To none; but that, perhaps, will come later. In the meanwhile I read as much as I can and try to study character on my travels."

"That is the way to become learned, but the book of humanity is too vast. Reading a history is the easier way."

"Yes, if history did not lie. One is not sure of the truth of the facts. It is tiring, while the study of the world is amusing. Horace, whom I know by heart, is my guidebook."

"Algarotti, too, has all Horace in his head. Of course you are fond of poetry?"

"It is my passion."

"Have you composed many sonnets?"

"Ten or twelve I like and two or three thousand which in all probability I have not read twice."

"The Italians are mad after sonnets."

"Yes; if one can call it a madness to desire to put thought into measured harmony. The sonnet is difficult because the thought has to be fitted exactly into the fourteen lines."

"It is Procrustes' bed and that's the reason you have so few good sonnets. As for us, we have not one; but that is the fault of our language."

"And of the French genius, which considers that a thought, when extended, loses all its force."

"And you do not think so?"

"Pardon me, it depends on the kind of thought. A witty saying, for example, will not make a sonnet; in French or Italian it belongs to the domain of epigram."

"What Italian poet do you like best?"

"Ariosto; but I cannot say I love him better than the others, for he is my only love."

"You know the others, though?"

"I think I have read them all, but all their lights pale before Ariosto's. Fifteen years ago I read all you had written against him, and I said that you would retract when you had read his works."

"I am obliged to you for thinking that I had not read them. As a matter of fact I had done so, but I was young. I knew Italian very imperfectly and, being prejudiced by the learned Italians who adore Tasso, I was unfortunate enough to publish a criticism on Ariosto which I thought my own, while it was only the echo of those who had prejudiced me. I adore your Ariosto."

"Ah! M. de Voltaire, I breathe again. But be good enough to have the work excommunicated in which you turned this great man into ridicule."

"What use would that be? All my books are excommunicated; but I will give you a good proof of my retraction."

I was astonished! The great man began to recite the two fine passages from the thirty-fourth and thirty-fifth cantos in which the divine poet speaks of the conversation of Astolpho with St. John, and he did it without missing a single line or committing the slightest fault against the laws of prosody. He then pointed out the beauties of the passages with his natural insight and with a great man's genius. I could not have had anything better from the lips of the most skilled commentators in Italy. I listened to him with the greatest attention, hardly daring to breathe and waiting for him to make a mistake, but I had my trouble for nothing. I turned to the company, crying that I was more than astonished and that all Italy should know what I had seen. "And I, sir," said the great man, "will let all Europe know of the amends I owe to the greatest genius our continent has produced."

Greedy of the praise which he deserved so well, Voltaire gave me the next day his translation of the stanza which Ariosto begins thus:

> *Quindi avvien che tra principi e signori.*

The lines were as follows:

> *Les papes, les Césars, apaisant leur querelle*
> *Jurent sur l'Evangile une paix éternelle;*
> *Vous les voyez l'un de l'autre ennemis;*
> *C'était pour se tromper qu'ils s'étaient réunis;*
> *Nul serment n'est gardé, nul accord n'est sincère;*
> *Quand la bouche a parlé, le cœur dit le contraire.*
> *Du ciel qu'ils attestaient, ils bravaient le courroux;*
> *L'intérêt est le dieu qui les gouverne tous.*

At the end of the recitation, which gained the applause of all who heard it, although not one of them knew Italian, Madame Denis, his niece, asked me if I thought the passage her uncle had just recited one of the finest the poet had written.

"Yes, but not the finest."

"It ought to be, for, but for it, Signor Lodovico would not have gained his apotheosis."

"He has been canonized then? I was not aware of that."

At these words the laugh, headed by Voltaire, was for Madame Denis. Everybody laughed except myself, and I continued to look perfectly serious.

Voltaire was vexed at not seeing me laugh like the rest and asked me the reason.

"Are you thinking," said he, "of some more than human passage?"

"Yes," I answered.

"What passage is that?"

"The last thirty-six stanzas of the twenty-third canto, where the poet describes in detail how Roland became mad. Since the world has existed, no one has discovered the springs of madness unless Ariosto himself, who became mad in his old age. These stanzas inspire honour, M. de Voltaire, and I am sure they must have made you tremble."

"Yes, I remember they render love dreadful. I long to read them again."

"Perhaps the gentleman will be good enough to recite them," said Madame Denis, with a side glance at her uncle.

"Willingly," said I, "if you will have the goodness to listen to me."

"You have learnt them by heart, then, have you?" said Voltaire.

"Yes, it was a pleasure and no trouble. Since I was sixteen, I have read over Ariosto two or three times every year; it is my passion and the lines have naturally become linked in my memory without my having given myself any pains to learn them. I know it all, except his long genealogies and his historical tirades, which fatigue the mind and do not touch the heart. It is only Horace that I know throughout, in spite of the often prosaic style of his epistles, which are certainly far from equalling Boileau's."

"Boileau is often too lengthy; I admire Horace but, as for Ariosto, with his forty long cantos, there is too much of him."

"It is fifty-one cantos, M. de Voltaire."

The great man was silent, but Madame Denis was equal to the occasion.

"Come, come," said she, "let us hear the thirty-six stanzas which earned the author the title of 'divine' and which are to make us tremble."

I then began, in an assured voice, but not in that monotonous tone adopted by the Italians with which the French so justly reproach us. The French would be the best reciters if they were not constrained by the rhyme, for they say what they feel better than any other people. They have neither the passionate, monotonous tone of my fellow countrymen nor the sentimentality of the Germans nor the fatiguing mannerisms of the English; to every period they give its proper expression, but the recurrence of the same sounds partly spoils their recitation. I recited the five verses of Ariosto as if it had been rhythmic prose, animating it by the sound of my voice and the movements of my eyes and by modulating my intonation according to the sentiments with which I wished to inspire my audience. They saw how hardly I could restrain my tears, and every eye was wet; but when I came to the stanza:

> Poichè allargare il freno al dolar puote,
> Che resta sola senza altrui rispetto,
> Giù dagli occhi rigando per le gote
> Sparge un fiume de lacrime sul petto,

the tears coursed down my cheeks to such an extent that everyone began to sob. M. de Voltaire and Madame Denis threw their arms round my neck; but their embraces could not stop me, for Roland, to become mad, had to notice that he was in the same bed in which Angelica had lately been found in the arms of the too fortunate Medor, and I had to reach the next stanza. For my voice of sorrow and wailing I substituted the expression of that terror which arose naturally from the contemplation of this fury, which was in its effects like a tempest, a volcano or an earthquake.

When I had finished, I received with a sad air the congratulations of the audience. Voltaire cried:

"I always said so; the secret of drawing tears is to weep oneself, but they must be real tears and, to shed them, the heart must be stirred to its depths. I am obliged to you, sir," he added, embracing me, "and I promise to recite the same stanzas myself to-morrow and to weep like you."

He kept his word.

"It is astonishing," said Madame Denis, "that intolerant Rome should not have condemned *The Song of Roland*."

"Far from it," said Voltaire, "Leo X excommunicated whoever should dare to condemn it. The two great families of Este and Medici interested themselves in the poet's favour. Without that protection, it is probable that the one line on the donation of Rome by Constantine to Silvester, where the poet speaks of *puzza forte*, would have sufficed to put the whole poem under an interdict."

"I believe," said I, "that the line which has excited the most talk is that in which Ariosto throws doubt on the general resurrection. Ariosto," I added, "in speaking of the hermit who would have hindered Rhodomonte from getting possession of Isabella, widow of Zerbin, paints the African who, wearied of the hermit's sermons, seizes him and throws him so far that he dashes him against a rock, against which he remains in a dead swoon, so that *al novissimo di forse fia desto.*"

This *forse* which may possibly have been placed there only as a flower of rhetoric or as a word to complete the verse, raised a great uproar, which would doubtless have greatly amused the poet if he had had time!

"It is a pity," said Madame Denis, "that Ariosto was not more careful in these hyperbolical expressions."

"Be quiet, niece; they are full of wit. They are all golden grains, which are dispersed throughout the work in the best taste."

The conversation was then directed towards various topics, and at last we got to *L'Ecossaise*, which we had played at Soleure.

They knew all about it.

M. de Voltaire said that, if I liked to play it at his house, he would write to M. de Chavigni to send me Lindane and he himself would play Montrose. I excused myself by saying that Madame M—— was at Bâle and that I should be obliged to go on my journey the next day. At this he exclaimed loudly, aroused the whole company against me and said at last that he should consider my visit as an insult unless I spared him a week, at least, of my society.

"Sir," said I, "I came to Geneva only to have the honour of seeing you and, now that I have obtained that favour, I have nothing more to do."

"Did you come to speak to me or for me to speak to you?"

"In a measure, of course, to speak to you, but much more for you to speak to me."

"Then stay here three days at least; come to dinner every day and we will have some conversation."

The invitation was so flattering and pressing that I could not refuse it with a good grace. I therefore accepted and I then left to go and write.

I had not been back for a quarter of an hour when a syndic of the town, an amiable man, whom I had seen at M. de Voltaire's and whose name I shall not mention, came and asked to be permitted to

VOLTAIRE
Jacques Casanova de Seingalt

sup with me. "I was present," said he, "at your argument with the great man and, though I did not open my mouth, I should much like to have an hour's talk with you." By way of reply I embraced him, begging him to excuse my dressing-gown and telling him that I should be glad if he would spend the whole night with me.

The worthy man spent two hours with me without saying a word on the subject of literature, but to please me he had no need to talk of books, for he was a disciple of Epicurus and Socrates and the evening was spent in telling little stories, in bursts of laughter and in accounts of the various kinds of pleasure obtainable in Geneva. Before leaving me, he asked me to come and sup with him on the following evening, promising that boredom should not be of the party.

"I shall wait upon you," said I.

"Very good, but don't tell anyone of the party."

I promised to follow his instructions.

Next morning young Fox came to see me with the two Englishmen I had seen at M. de Voltaire's. They proposed a game of quinze, which I accepted, and, after losing fifty louis I left off, and we walked about the town till dinner-time.

We found the Duc de Villars at Les Délices; he had come there to consult Dr. Tronchin, who had kept him alive for the last ten years.

I was silent during the repast, but at dessert M. de Voltaire, knowing that I had reasons for not liking the Venetian government, introduced the subject; but I disappointed him, as I maintained that in no country could a man enjoy more perfect liberty than in Venice.

"Yes," said he, "provided he resigns himself to play the part of a dumb man."

Seeing that I did not care for the subject, he took me by the arm to his garden, of which he said he was the creator. The principal walk led to a pretty running stream.

" 'Tis the Rhône," said he, "which I send into France."

"It does not cost you much in carriage, at all events," said I.

He smiled pleasantly and pointed out the principal street of Geneva and Mont Blanc, which is the highest point of the Alps.

Bringing back the conversation to Italian literature, he began to talk nonsense with much wit and learning, but always concluding with a false judgment. I let him talk on. He spoke of Homer, Dante and Petrarch and everybody knows what he thought of those great geniuses, but he did himself wrong in writing what he thought. I contented myself with saying that, if those great men did not merit the esteem of those who studied them, it would at all events be a long time before they had to come down from the high place in which the praise of centuries had placed them.

The Duc de Villars and the famous Tronchin came and joined us. The doctor, a tall, fine man, polite, eloquent without being a conversationalist, a learned physican, a man of wit, a favourite pupil of Boerhaave, without scientific jargon or charlatanism or self-sufficiency, enchanted me. His system of medicine was based on regimen and, to apply it, he had to be a man of profound science. I had been assured, but can scarcely believe it, that he cured a consumptive patient of a secret disease by means of the milk of an ass, which he had submitted to thirty strong frictions of mercury by four sturdy porters.

As to Villars, he also attracted my attention but in a way quite different than did Tronchin. On examining his face and manner, I thought I saw before me a woman of seventy dressed as a man, thin and emaciated but still proud of her looks and with claims to past beauty. His cheeks and lips were painted, his eyebrows blackened and his teeth false; he wore a huge wig, which exhaled amber, and at his buttonhole was an enormous bunch of flowers which touched his chin. He affected a gracious manner and spoke so softly that it was often impossible to hear what he said. He was excessively polite and affable and his manners were those of the Regency. His whole appearance was supremely ridiculous. I was told that in his youth he was a lover of the fair sex but, now that he was no longer good for anything, he had modestly made himself into a woman and had four pretty pets in his employ, who took turns in the disgusting duty of warming his old carcass at night.

Villars was governor of Provence and had his back eaten up with cancer. In the course of nature he should have been buried ten years before, but Tronchin kept him alive with his regimen and by feeding the wounds on slices of veal. But for this, the cancer would have killed him. His life might well be called an artificial one.

I accompanied M. de Voltaire to his bedroom, where he changed his wig and put on another cap, for he always wore one on account of the rheumatism to which he was subject. I saw on the table the *Summa* of St. Thomas and, among other Italian poets, the *Secchia Rapita* of Tassoni.

"This," said Voltarie, "is the only tragi-comic poem Italy has. Tassoni was a monk, a wit and a genius, as well as a poet."

"I will grant his poetical ability but not his learning, for he ridiculed the system of Copernicus and said that, if his theories were followed, astronomers would not be able to calculate lunations or eclipses."

"Where does he make that ridiculous remark?"

"In his academical discourses."

"I have not read them, but I will get them."

He took a pen and noted the name down and said. "But Tassoni criticised Petrarch very ingeniously."

"Yes, but he dishonoured his taste and literature thereby, as did Muratori."

"Here he is. You must allow that his learning is immense."

"*Est ubi peccat.*"

Voltaire opened a door and I saw a hundred great files full of papers.

"That's my correspondence," said he. "You see before you nearly fifty thousand letters, to which I have replied."

"Have you a copy of your answers?"

"Of a good many of them. That's the business of a servant of mine who has nothing else to do."

"I know plenty of booksellers who would give a good deal to get hold of your answers."

"Yes; but look out for the booksellers when you publish anything, if you have not yet begun; they are greater robbers than Barabbas."

"I shall not have anything to do with these gentlemen till I am an old man."

"Then they will be the scourge of your old age."

Thereupon I quoted a macaronic verse by Merlin Coccaius.

"Where's that from?"

"It's a line from a celebrated poem in twenty-four cantos."

"Celebrated?"

"Yes, and, what is more, worthy of being celebrated; but, to appreciate it, one must understand the Mantuan dialect."

"I could make it out if you could get me a copy."

"I shall have the honour of presenting you with one to-morrow."

"You will oblige me extremely."

We had to leave his room and spend two hours in the company, talking over all sorts of things. Voltaire displayed all the resources of his brilliant and fertile wit and charmed everyone in spite of his sarcastic observations, which did not even spare those present, but he had an inimitable manner of lancing a sarcasm without wounding a person's feelings. When the great man accompanied his witticisms with a graceful smile, he could always get a laugh.

He kept up a notable establishment and an excellent table, a rare circumstance with his poetic brothers, who are rarely favourites of Plutus as he was. He was then sixty years old and had a hundred and twenty thousand francs a year. It has been said maliciously that this great man enriched himself by cheating his publishers, whereas the fact was that he fared no better than any other author and, instead of duping them, was often their dupe. The Cramers must be excepted, whose fortune he made. Voltaire had other ways of making money than by his pen; and, as he was greedy of fame, he often gave his works away on the sole condition that they were to be printed and published. During the short time I was with him, I was a witness of such a generous action; he made a present to his bookseller of *The Princess of Babylon*, a charming story which he had written in three days.

My Epicurean syndic was exact to his appointment and took me to a house at a little distance, where he introduced me to three young ladies who, without being precisely beautiful, were certainly charming. Two of them were sisters. I had an easy and pleasant welcome and from their intellectual appearance and gay manners I anticipated a delightful evening, and I was not disappointed. The half hour before supper was passed in conversation, decent but without restraint, and during supper, from the hints the syndic gave me, I guessed what would happen after dessert.

It was a hot evening and, on the pretext of cooling ourselves, we undressed so as to be almost in a state of nature. What an orgy we had! I am sorry I am obliged to draw a veil over the most exciting details. In the midst of our licentious gaiety, whilst we were heated by love, champagne and a discourse of an exciting nature, I proposed to recite Grécourt's *Y Grec*. When I had finished the voluptuous poem, worthy of an abbé's pen, I saw that the eyes of the three beauties were all aflame, and said, "Ladies, if you like, I will show you all three, one after the other, why the sentence, *Gaudeant bene nati*, was uttered."

And, without waiting for their reply, I took them one after the other and . . . succeeded in making them happy. The syndic was radiant, he was pleased at having given me a present entirely to my taste, and I fancied that the entertainment was not displeasing to the three Graces, who were kept low by the Sybarite, as his power was chiefly limited to desiring. The girls lavished their thanks on me, while I endeavoured to assure them of my gratitude; but they leapt for joy when they heard the syndic asking me to come next day.

As he was taking me back to my inn, I told him how great a pleasure he had given me, and he said he had brought up the three jewels himself.

"You," he added, "are the only man they know besides myself. You shall see them again, but I beg you will take care not to leave anything behind you, for in this town of prejudices that would be a great misfortune for them and for me."

"You are always moderate in your enjoyment, then?" I said to him.

"Unfortunately that is no merit as far as I am concerned. I was born for the service of love and Venus has punished me for worshipping her when I was too young."

After a good night's sleep I awoke in an active mood and began to write a letter to Voltaire in blank verse, which cost me four times the pains that rhyme verses would have done. I sent it to him with the poem of Teofilo Folengo, but I made a mistake in doing so, as I might have known he would not care for it; one cannot appreciate what one does not understand. I then went to Mr. Fox, where I found the two Englishmen, who offered me my revenge. I lost a hundred louis and was glad to see them set out for Lausanne.

The syndic had told me that the three young ladies belonged to respectable families but were not rich. I puzzled my head to think of some useful present I might make them without offending them and at last hit on a plan of the most ridiculous nature, as the reader will see. I went to a jeweller and told him to make me three golden balls, each of two ounces in weight.

At noon I went to M. de Voltaire's. He was not to be seen, but Madame Denis consoled me for his absence. She had wit, learning without pretension, taste and a great hatred for the King of Prussia, whom she called a "villain." She asked about my beautiful house-keeper and congratulated me on having married her to a respectable man. Although I feel now that she was quite right, I was far from thinking so then; the impression was too fresh on my mind. Madame Denis begged me to tell her how I had escaped from The Leads, but, as the story was rather a long one, I promised to satisfy her another time.

M. de Voltaire did not dine with us; he appeared, however, at five o'clock, holding a letter in his hand.

"Do you know," said he, "the Marquis Albergati Capacelli, senator of Bologna, and Count Paradisi?"

"I do not know Paradisi, but I know Albergati by sight and by reputation; he is not a senator, but one of the Forty, who at Bologna are fifty."

"Dear me! That seems rather a riddle!"

"Do you know him?"

"No, but he has sent me Goldoni's plays, the translation of my *Tancred* and some Bologna sausages and he says he will come and see me."

"He will not come; he is not such a fool."

"How a fool? Would there be anything foolish in coming to see me?"

"Certainly not, as far as you are concerned; but very much so for his own sake."

"Would you mind telling me why?"

"He knows what he would lose; for he enjoys the idea you seem to have of him and, if he came, you would see his nothingness, and goodbye to the illusion. He is a worthy man, with six thousand sequins a year and a craze for the theatre. He is a rather good actor and has written several comedies in prose, but they are fit neither for the study nor for the stage."

"You certainly give him a coat which does not make him look any bigger."

"I assure you it is not quite small enough."

"But tell me how it is with this "Forty" and this "fifty" of Bologna?"

"Just as at Bâle noon is at eleven."

"I understand; just as your Council of Ten is composed of seventeen members."

"Exactly; but the cursed Forty of Bologna are men of another kind."

"Why 'cursed'?"

"Because they are not subject to the fisc and are thus enabled to commit whatever crimes they like with perfect impunity; all they have got to do is to live outside the state borders on their revenues."

"That is a blessing and not a curse; but let me return to our subject. I suppose the Marquis Albergati is a man of letters?"

"He writes well enough, but he is fond of the sound of his own voice, his style is prolix and I don't think he has much brains."

"He is an actor, I think you said?"

"Yes, and a very good one, especially when he plays the lover's part in one of his own plays."

"Is he a handsome man?"

"Yes, on the stage, but not elsewhere; his face lacks expression."

"But his plays give satisfaction?"

"Not to persons who understand play-writing; they would be hissed if they were intelligible."

"And what do you think of Goldoni?"

"I have the highest opinion of him. Goldoni is the Italian Molière."

"Why does he call himself 'poet to the Duke of Parma'?"

"No doubt to prove that a wit as well as a fool has his weak points; in all probability the duke knows nothing about it. He also calls himself a barrister, though he is such only in his own imagination. Goldoni is a good play-writer and nothing more. Everybody in Venice knows me for his friend and I can therefore speak of him with authority. He does not shine in society and, in spite of the keen satire in his works, he is of an extremely gentle disposition."

"So I have been told. He is poor and wants to leave Venice. The managers of the theatres where they play his pieces will not like that."

"People talked about getting him a pension, but the project has been relegated to the Greek Kalends, as they said that, if he had a pension, he would write no more."

"Cumæ refused to give a pension to Homer, for fear that all the blind men would ask for a pension."

We spent a pleasant day and he thanked me heartily for the copy of the *Macaronicon*, which he promised to read. He introduced me to a Jesuit he had in his household who was called Adam, and he added, after telling me his name, "not the first Adam." I was told afterwards that Voltaire used to play backgammon with him and, when he lost, he would throw the dice and the box at his head. If Jesuits were treated like that all the world over, perhaps we should have none but inoffensive Jesuits at last, but that happy time is still far off.

I had scarcely got to my inn in the evening when I received my three golden balls and, as soon as the syndic came, we set off to renew our voluptuous orgy. On the way he talked about modesty and said:

"That feeling which prevents our showing those parts which we have been taught to cover from our childhood may often proceed from virtue, but it is weaker than the force of education, as it cannot resist an attack when the attacking party knows what he is about. I think the easiest way to vanquish modesty is to ignore its presence, to turn it into ridicule, to carry it by storm. Victory is certain. The hardihood of the assailer subdues the assailed, who usually only wishes to be conquered and nearly always thanks you for your victory.

"Clement of Alexandria, a learned man and a philosopher, has remarked that the modesty which appears so deeply rooted in women's hearts really goes no farther than the clothes they wear and that, when these are plucked off, no trace of it remains."

We found the three girls lightly clad and sitting on a large sofa, and we sat down opposite to them. Pleasant talk and a thousand amorous kisses occupied the half hour just before supper and our combat did not begin till we had eaten a delicious repast, washed down with plenty of champagne.

When it was time to part, these girls, who had up till then led a life of privation, threw their arms round my neck, overwhelmed me with caresses and declared how much they owed me. The syndic told them I was going in two days and suggested they should make me stay a day longer in Geneva, and I made this sacrifice joyfully. The worthy syndic had an engagement on the following day and I sorely needed a holiday myself. He took me back to my inn, thanking me almost as heartily as his charming nymphs.

After a calm and refreshing sleep of ten hours, I felt myself able to enjoy and appreciate the delightful society of M. de Voltaire. I went to his house but was disappointed in my hopes, as it pleased the great man to be in a fault-finding and sarcastic mood the whole day. He knew I had to leave on the morrow.

He began by thanking me at table for my present of Merlin Coccaius.

"You certainly gave it me with good intentions," said he, "but I owe you no thanks for praising it so highly, as you made me waste four hours in reading nonsense."

I felt my hair stand on end but mastered my emotions and told him quietly enough that one day, perhaps, he would find himself obliged to praise the poem more highly than I had done. I quoted several instances of the insufficiency of a first perusal.

"That's true," said he, "but, as for your Merlin, I will read him no more. I have put him beside Chapelain's *Pucelle*."

"Which pleases all the critics, in spite of its bad versification, for it is a good poem and Chapelain was a real poet, though he wrote bad verses. I cannot overlook his genius."

My frankness must have shocked him, and I might have guessed it when he told me he had put the *Macaronicon* beside the *Pucelle*. I knew that there was a poem of the same title in circulation which passed for Voltaire's, but I also knew that he disavowed it, and I thought that would make him conceal the vexation my explanation must have caused him. It was not so, however; he contradicted me sharply and I closed with him.

"Chapelain," said I, "has the merit of having rendered his subject matter agreeable without pandering to the tastes of his readers by saying things shocking to modesty and piety. So thinks my master Crébillon."

"Crébillon! You cite a weighty authority. But how is my friend Crébillon your master, may I ask?"

"He taught me to speak French in less than two years and, as a mark of my gratitude, I translated his *Rhadamiste* into Italian Alexandrines. I am the first Italian who has dared to use this metre in our language."

"The first? I beg your pardon, as that honour belongs to my friend Pierre-Jacques Martelli."

"I am sorry to be obliged to tell you that you are making a mistake."

"Why, I have his works, printed at Bologna, in my room!"

"I don't deny that; I am only talking about the metre used by Martelli. What you are thinking of must be verses of fourteen syllables without alternative masculine and feminine rhymes. However, I confess that he thinks he has imitated the French Alexandrines and his preface made me explode with laughter. Have you read it?"

"Read it? I always read prefaces, and Martelli proves there that his verses have the same effect in Italian as our Alexandrine verses have in French."

"Exactly, that's what's so amusing. The worthy man is quite mistaken and I only ask you to listen to what I have to say on the subject. Your masculine verse has only twelve poetic syllables, and the feminine, thirteen. All Martelli's lines have fourteen syllables, except those that finish with a long vowel, which at the end of a line always counts as two syllables. You will observe that the first hemistich in Martelli always consists of seven syllables, while in French it has only six. Your friend Pierre-Jacques was either stone deaf or very hard of hearing."

"Then you have followed our theory of versification rigorously."

"Just so, in spite of the difficulty, as nearly all our words end with a short syllable."

"What reception was accorded to your innovation?"

"It was not found pleasing, because nobody knows how to recite my verses; but I hope to triumph when I deliver them myself before our literary clubs."

"Do you remember any of your version of the *Rhadamiste?*"

"I remember it all."

"You have a wonderful memory; I should be glad to hear it."

I began to recite the same scene that I had recited to Crébillon ten years before, and I thought M. de Voltaire listened with pleasure.

"It doesn't strike one as at all harsh," said he.

This was the highest praise he would give me. In his turn the great man recited a passage from *Tancred*, which had not as yet been published and which was afterwards considered, and rightly, as a masterpiece.

We should have got on very well if we had kept to that, but, on my quoting a line of Horace to praise one of his pieces, he said that Horace was a great master who had given precepts which would never be out of date. Thereupon I answered that he himeslf had violated one of them, but that he had violated it grandly.

"Which is that?"

"You do not write *contentus paucis lectoribus.*"

"If Horace had had to combat the hydra-headed monster of

superstition, he would have written as I have written—for all the world."

"It seems to me that you might spare yourself the trouble of combating what you will never destroy."

"That which I cannot finish others will and I shall always have the glory of having been the first in the field."

"Very good; but supposing you succeed in destroying superstitution. what are you going to put in its place?"

"I like that. If I deliver the race of man from a wild beast which is devouring it, am I to be asked what I intend to put in its place?"

"It is not devouring it; on the contrary, it is necessary to its existence."

"Necessary to its existence! That is a horrible blasphemy, the falsity of which will be seen in the future. I love the human race; I would fain see men free and happy, like myself, and superstition and freedom cannot go together. Where do you find an enslaved and yet a happy people?"

"You wish, then, to see the people sovereign?"

"God forbid! There must be a sovereign to govern the masses."

"In that case you must have superstition, for without it the masses will never obey a mere man decked with the name of monarch."

"I will have no monarch; the word expresses despotism, which I hate as I do slavery."

"What do you mean, then? If you wish to put the government in the hands of one man, such a man, I maintain, will be a monarch."

"I would have a sovereign ruler of a free people, of which he is the chief by an agreement which binds them both, which would prevent him from becoming a tyrant."

"Addison will tell you that such a sovereign is a sheer impossibility. I agree with Hobbes—of two evils choose the lesser. A nation without superstition would be a nation of philosophers, and philosophers would never obey. The people will be happy only when they are crushed and downtrodden and bound in chains."

"This is horrible; and you are of the people yourself. If you have read my works, you must have seen how I show that superstition is the enemy of kings."

"Read your works? I have read and re-read them, especially in places where I have differed from you. Your ruling passion is the love of humanity. *Est ubi peccas.* This blinds you. Love humanity, but love it as it is. It is not fit to receive the blessings you would lavish on it and which would only make it more wretched and perverse. Leave men their devouring monster; it is dear to them. I have never laughed so heartily as at Don Quixote assailed by the galley slaves whom his generosity had set free."

"I am sorry that you have such a bad opinion of your fellow creatures. And, by the way, tell me whether there is freedom in Venice."

"As much as can be expected under an aristocracy. Our liberty is not so great as that which the English enjoy, but we are content."

"Even under The Leads?"

"My imprisonment was certainly despotic; but, as I had knowingly abused my liberty, I am satisfied that the government was within its right in shutting me up without the usual formalities."

"All the same, you made your escape."

"I used my rights, as they used theirs."

"Very good! But, as far as I can see, no one in Venice is really free."

"That may be; but you must agree that the essence of freedom consists in thinking you have it."

"I shall not agree to that so easily. You and I see liberty from very different points of view. The aristocrats, the members of the government even, are not free in Venice; for example, they cannot travel without permission."

"True, but that is a restriction of their own making, to preserve their power. Would you say that a Bernese is not free because he is subject to the sumptuary laws, which he himself has made?"

"Well, well, I wish the people made the laws everywhere."

After this lively answer he abruptly asked me what part I came from.

"From Roche," said I. "I should have been very sorry to leave Switzerland without seeing the famous Haller. In my travels I render homage to my learned contemporaries and you come the last and best."

"You must have liked Haller."

"I spent three of the happiest days of my life with him."

"I congratulate you. He is a great man and worthy of all honour."

"I think as you do and I am glad to hear you doing him justice; I am sorry he was not so just towards you."

"Well, you see we may be both of us mistaken."

At this reply, the quickness of which constituted its chief merit, everybody present began to laugh and applaud.

No more was said of literature and I became a silent actor till M. de Voltaire retired, when I approached Madame Denis and asked if she had any commands for me in Rome. I went home well pleased at having, as I foolishly believed at the time, compelled the giant of intellect to listen to reason, but there was a rankling feeling left in my heart against him which made me for the next ten years criticise all that he wrote.

I am sorry now for having done so, though, on reading my censures over again, I find that in many places I was right. I would have done better, however, to have kept silence, respected his genius and suspected my own opinions. I should have considered that, if it had not been for those quips and cranks which made me hate him on the third day, I should have thought him wholly sublime. This thought alone should have silenced me, but an angry man always thinks himself right. Posterity, on reading my attack, will rank me among the Zoiluses and the humble apology I now make to the great man's shades may not be read.

If we meet in the halls of Pluto, the more peccant parts of our mortal nature purged away, all will be made up; he will receive my heartiest apologies; he will be my friend and I, his sincere admirer.

I spent part of the night and the whole of the following day in writing down my conversations with Voltaire, and they amounted to nearly a volume, of which I have given only a mere abridgment. Towards the evening my Epicurean syndic called on me and we went to sup with the three nymphs and for five hours indulged in every species of wantonness, in which I had a somewhat fertile imagination. On leaving I promised to call on them again on my return from Rome and I kept my word. I set out the next day, after dining with the syndic, who accompanied me as far as Annecy, where I spent the night. Next day I dined at Aix-in-Savoy, with the intention of lying at Chambéry, but my destiny ordered otherwise.

Aix is a villainous hole to which the mineral waters attract people of fashion towards the end of the summer, a circumstance of which I

was then ignorant. I dined hastily, wishing to set out immediately for
Chambéry, when in the middle of my repast a crowd of fashionable
people burst into the room. I looked at them without stirring,
replying with a nod to be bows which some of them made me. I soon
discovered from their conversation that they had all come to take the
waters. A gentleman of fine presence came up to me and asked if I
were going to Turin; I answered that my way was to Marseilles.

Their dinner was served and everybody sat down. Among them I
noticed several pleasant-looking ladies, with gentlemen who were
either their husbands or their lovers. I concluded that I might find
some amusement with them, as they all spoke French with that easy
tone of good society which is so attractive, and I felt that I should be
inclined to stay without much pressing, for that day at all events.

I finished my dinner before the company had come to the end of
their first course and, as my coach could not go for another hour, I
went up to a pretty woman and complimented her on the good the
waters of Aix seemed to have done her, saying that her appetite made
all who looked at her feel hungry.

"I challenge you to prove that you are speaking the truth," said she,
with a smile. I sat down next to her and she gave me a nice piece of
the roast, which I ate as if I had been fasting.

While I was talking with the lady and eating the morsels she gave
me, I heard a voice saying that I was in the abbé's place and another
voice replying that the abbé had been gone for half an hour.

"Why has he gone?" asked a third. "He said he was going to stay
here for another week." At this there was some whispering, but the
departure of an abbé had nothing interesting in it for me and I
continued eating and talking. I told Le Duc, who was standing
behind my chair, to get me some champagne. I offered the lady some,
she accepted and everyone began to call for champagne. Seeing my
neighbour's spirits rising, I proceeded to make love to her and asked
her if she were always as ready to defy those who paid their court to
her.

"So many of them," she answered, "are not worth the trouble."

She was pretty and quick-witted, and I took a fancy to her and
wished for some pretext on which I could put off my departure, when
chance came to my aid.

"The place next to you was conveniently empty," said a lady to my
neighbour, who was drinking with me.

"Very conveniently, for my neighbour wearied me."

"Had he no appetite?" said I.

"Gamesters have an appetite only for money."

"Usually, but your power is extraordinary, for never before have I partaken of two dinners in one day."

"Only out of pride, as I am sure you will eat no supper."

"Let us make a bet on it."

"We will; we will bet the supper."

"All right."

All the guests began to clap and my fair neighbour blushed with pleasure. I ordered Le Duc to tell my coachman that I should not be going till the next day.

"It is my business," said the lady, "to order the supper."

"Yes, you are right; for he who pays orders. My part will be to hold my own with you and, if I eat as much as you, I shall be the winner."

"Very good."

At the end of the dinner, the individual who had addressed me before called for cards and made a small bank of faro. He put down twenty-five Piedmontese pistoles and some silver money to amuse the ladies—altogether it amounted to nearly forty louis. I remained a spectator during the first deal and convinced myself that the banker played very honourably.

Whilst he was getting ready for the second deal, the lady asked me why I did not play. I whispered to her that she had made me lose my appetite for money. She repaid this compliment with a charming smile.

After this declaration, feeling myself entitled to play, I put down forty louis and lost them in two deals. I got up and, on the banker saying very politely that he was sorry for my loss, I replied that it was a mere nothing, but that I always made it a rule never to risk a sum of money larger than the bank. Somebody then asked me if I knew a certain Abbé Gilbert.

"I knew a man of that name in Paris," said I. "He came from Lyons and owes me a pair of ears, which I mean to cut off his head when I meet him."

My questioner made no reply to this and everybody remained silent, as if nothing has been said. From this I concluded that the abbé aforesaid must be the same whose place I had occupied at dinner. He had doubtless seen me on my arrival and had taken himself off. This abbé was a rascal who has visited me at Little Poland, to whom I had entrusted a ring which had cost me five thousand florins in Holland; next day the scoundrel had disappeared.

When everybody had left the table, I asked Le Duc if I were well lodged.

"No," said he. "Would you like to see your room?"

He took me to a large room, a hundred paces from the inn, whose sole furniture consisted of its four walls, all the other rooms being occupied. I complained vainly to the inn-keeper, who said, "It's all I can offer you, but I will have a good bed, a table and chairs taken there."

I had to content myself with it, as there was no choice.

"You will sleep in my room," said I to Le Duc. "Take care to provide yourself with a bed and bring my baggage in."

"What do you think of Gilbert, sir?" said my Spaniard. "I did not recognise him till he was going, and I had a lively desire to take him by the back of his neck."

"You would have done well to have satisfied that desire."

"I will when I see him again."

As I was leaving my big room, I was accosted politely by a man who said he was glad to be my neighbour, and offered to take me to the fountain if I were going there. I accepted his offer. He was a tall, fair man, about fifty years old; he must once have been handsome, but his excessive politeness should have made me suspect him; however, I wanted somebody to talk to and to give me the various pieces of information I required. On the way he informed me of the social standing of the people I had seen, and I learnt that none of them had come to Aix for the sake of the waters.

"I am the only one," said he, "who takes the waters from necessity. I am consumptive; I am getting thinner every day and, if the waters don't do me any good, I shall not last much longer."

"So all the others have come here only for amusement's sake?"

"And to game, sir, for they are all professional gamesters."

"Are they French?"

"They are all from Piedmont or Savoy; I am the only Frenchman here."

"What part of France do you come from?"

"From Lorraine; my father, who is eighty years old, is the Marquis Désarmoises. He keeps on living only to spite me, for, as I married against his wishes, he has disinherited me. However, as I am his only son, I shall inherit his property after his death, in spite of him. My house is at Lyons, but I never go there, as I have the misfortune to be in love with my eldest daughter and my wife watches us so closely as to make my courtship hopeless."

"That is very fine; otherwise, I suppose, your daughter would take pity on her amorous papa?"

"I daresay, for she is very fond of me and has an excellent heart."

TRANSLATED BY ARTHUR MACHEN

FILIAL SENTIMENTS OF A PARRICIDE

Marcel Proust

When M. van Blarenberghe the elder died several months ago, I remembered that my mother had known his wife very well. Since the death of my parents I am (in a sense which it would be irrelevant to describe here) less myself, more their son. Without giving up my own friends, I turn more readily to theirs. And the letters I write now are for the most part ones I think they would have written, ones they can write no longer, letters of congratulation or condolence to friends of theirs whom I often scarcely know. So when Mme. van Blarenberghe lost her husband, I wished to tell her of the grief my parents would have felt. I recalled that some years earlier I had occasionally dined with her son at the houses of mutual friends. To him I wrote, speaking more for my late parents than for myself. I got in reply the following beautiful letter, conspicuous for great filial love. I think that this document should be made public because of the meaning given it by the drama that followed so shortly, especially the meaning it gives to the drama. Here is the letter:

Les Timbrieux, par Josselin (Morbihan)
September 24, 1906

I deeply regret, dear sir, that I was unable to thank you sooner for the sympathy you showed me in my sorrow. But my grief has been so great that on the advice of doctors I have been traveling for the past four months. I am only now, and with painful effort, beginning to take up my regular life again. Surely you will forgive me.

I wish to tell you, however belatedly, that I was much moved by your remembering our old and excellent relations and profoundly touched by the sentiment that inspired you to write me and my mother in the name of your parents, who left us so prematurely. I did not have the honor of knowing them well, but I remember how much my father appreciated your father and what a pleasure it was for my mother to see Mme. Proust.

It was most considerate of you to send us their message from beyond the grave. I will soon return to Paris and if I succeed at all in overcoming the need for isolation which I have felt since the death of him who absorbed my every interest and inspired my every joy, I would be very happy to meet you and talk with you of the past.

Very affectionately,

H. VAN BLARENBERGHE

This letter touched me very much. I pitied one who suffered so, I pitied him, yet I envied him: he still had his mother. In consoling her he would console himself. I could not agree to his suggestion of a meeting, only because I was prevented by practical details. But above all the letter wrought a favorable change in my memory of him. The good relations to which he alluded were really of the most banal social kind. At the tables where we sometimes dined, I had scarcely had a chance to talk with him, but the great intellectual distinction of our hosts on those occasions remained for me, and still remains, a guaranty that Henri van Blarenberghe, under his rather conventional exterior—the index, perhaps, of his surroundings rather than of his real personality—hid an original and lively nature. Besides, among those strange flashes of the memory which our brain, so small and yet so vast, stores in prodigious number, if I seek those which represent Henri van Blarenberghe, the flash which always remains most vivid to me is of a face smiling in a way that was particularly fine, the lips still parted after having thrown off some witty remark. Pleasant and rather distinguished, so I "resaw" him, as one might say. Our eyes have more part than we can believe in this active exploration of the past which we call memory. If you look at someone while his mind is intent upon bringing back something from the past, restoring it to life for an instant, you will see that his eyes go suddenly blind to the surrounding objects which they reflected an instant before. "Your eyes are blank, you are somewhere else," we say; however, we see only the external signs of the phenomenon that takes place in the mind. At such a moment the most beautiful eyes in the world no longer touch us with their beauty; they are, to change the meaning of a phrase of Well's, no more than "machines to explore time," the telescopes of the invisible, which become at best measures to gauge one's advancing age. One feels indeed, when one sees the unsteady gaze of old men, the gaze worn out with endless adaptation to a time so different, often so distant from their own, blindfold itself in order to recall the past, one feels indeed that the curve of their gaze, crossing "the shadow of the days" they have lived, comes to rest several feet before them, so it seems, but in reality fifty or sixty years behind. I remember how the enchanting eyes of Princess Mathilde were transformed when they fixed themselves on images of the great men and magnificent scenes of the beginning of the century. Such images, emanating from her memories, she saw and we shall never see. At the moments when my eyes met hers, I had a sense of the supernatural; her gaze, by some feat of resurrection, firmly and mysteriously joined the present to the past.

Pleasant and rather distinguished, I said, and it is thus that, in one of the more vivid images my memory had stored of him, I resaw Henri van Blarenberghe. But after receiving this letter, I retouched the image in the depths of my memory by interpreting, in terms of a profounder sensibility, a mind less mundane, certain details of his glance and bearing which could, indeed, permit of a more sympathetic and arresting meaning than I had at first allowed. Then, recently, at the request of a friend, I asked him for information concerning an employee of the Chemins de fer de l'Est (M. van Blarenberghe was president of the Board of Directors). Because he had ignored my change of address, his reply, written on the twelfth of last January, did not reach me until the seventeenth, not fifteen days ago, less than eight days before the drama.

48, RUE DE LA BIENFAISANCE
January 12, 1907

DEAR SIR,

I have asked the Compagnie de l'Est for the whereabouts of X, but they have no record of him. Are you right about the name?—if so, the man has disappeared from the company without a trace; he must have had a very provisional and minor connection.

I am distressed at the news of your health since the sad and untimely death of your parents. If it is any consolation to you, I have suffered many physical and moral ailments in attempting to recover from the shock of my father's death. One must always hope . . . I do not know what the year 1907 holds for me, but let us pray that it may bring some improvement to us both, and that in several months we shall be able to see each other.

Please accept, I beg you, my deepest sympathy.

H. VAN BLARENBERGHE

Five or six days after getting this letter, I recalled, on waking up in the morning, that I had meant to answer it. The day had brought one of those unexpected cold spells which, like high tides of the air, wash over the dykes raised between ourselves and nature by great towns, and battering our closed windows, reaching into our very rooms, make our chilly shoulders feel, through a quickening touch, the furious return of the elements. Days troubled by brusque barometric changes, by shocks even more grave. No joy, after all, in so much violence. We weep for the snow which is about to fall and, as in the lovely verse of André Rivoire, things have the air of "waiting for the snow." Scarcely does "a depression move towards the Balearics," as the newspapers say, or Jamaica begin to quake, when at the same instant in Paris the sufferers from migraine, rheumatism, asthma, no doubt the insane too, reach their crises; the nerves of so many people are united with the farthest points of the universe by bonds which the victims often wish less tight. If the influence of the stars on at least some of them shall one day be recognized (Framery, Pelletan, quoted by M. Brissaud), to whom does the poet's line apply better than to such nervous ones?—

Et de longs fils soyeux l'unissent aux étoiles.

On getting up I prepared to answer Henri van Blarenberghe. But before writing him I wanted to glance at *Figaro*, to proceed to that abominable and voluptuous act called "reading the newspapers," thanks to which all the world's misfortunes and cataclysms of the last twenty-four hours, the battles costing fifty thousand lives, the crimes, the strikes, the bankruptcies, the fires, the poisonings, the suicides, the divorces, the crude emotions of statesman and actor, transmuted for our personal consumption, make for us, who are not involved, a fine little morning treat, an exciting and tonic accompaniment to the sipping of *café au lait*. The fragile thread of *Figaro*, soon enough broken by an indolent gesture, alone divides us from all the world's misery. From the first sensational news of so many people's grief, news we shall soon enjoy relating to friends who have not yet read the paper, we are brought briskly back to the existence which, at the first moment of waking, we had felt it futile to recapture. And if at moments we melt into tears, it is at a phrase like this one: "An impressive silence gripped all hearts, drums sounded on the field, the troops presented arms, a tremendous cry rose up: 'Three cheers for

Fallières!' " For this we weep, as we refuse to weep for misfortunes closer to our hearts. Base hypocrites who weep only for the anguish of Hercules or the travels of a President of the Republic! Nevertheless, that morning I did not enjoy reading *Figaro*. I had just skimmed with delight through the volcanic eruptions, the ministerial crises, the duels of *apaches*, and I was calmly beginning to read a column whose title, "A Drama of Madness," was peculiarly adapted to quicken my morning energies, when suddenly I saw that the victim was Mme. van Blarenberghe; that the murderer, who had presently killed himself, was her son, Henri van Blarenberghe, whose letter lay near me waiting to be answered: *"One must always hope. . . . I do not know what* 1907 *holds for me, but let us pray it will bring improvement,"* etc. One must always hope! I do not know what 1907 holds for me! Life had not been long in answering him. 1907 had not cast off her first month before she brought him her present: musket, revolver, and dagger, and a veil for his mind such as Athena fitted on that of Ajax so that he would slaughter the shepherds and flocks in the Greek camp without knowing what he did. "I it was who put the false images in his eyes. And he rushed upon them, striking here and there, thinking that with his own hand he killed the Atrides, hurling himself now on the sheep, now on the shepherds. I made him the prey of raging madness; I forced him into the snares. He came back, his head dripping with sweat and his hands red with blood." As long as the mad strike they know nothing; then, the fit having passed, what anguish! Tekmessa, Ajax's wife, described it: "His madness is over, his frenzy has fallen like the breath of Motos. But, having recovered his wits, he is now tormented by a new affliction; for to contemplate his own evil deeds when he alone has caused them bitterly increases his anguish. Once he knows what has happened, he cries out in lamentation, he who used to say that a man was ignoble to weep. He sits immobile, shrieking, plotting, no doubt, some dark design against himself." But when the madness is over for Henri van Blarenberghe, it is not butchered sheep and shepherds he has before him. The anguish does not lie at once since he himself is not yet dead when he sees his murdered mother before him; since he himself is not yet dead when he hears his dying mother say to him, like Prince Andrey's wife in Tolstoy: "Henri, what have you done to me! What have you done to me!" "When they reached the landing between the first and second floors," says *Le Matin*, "the servants saw Mme. van Blarenberghe, her face distorted by terror, descend two or three steps, crying: 'Henri! Henri! what have you done!' Then the poor woman, covered with blood, threw her arms in the air and fell on her face. . . . The horrified servants went out to get help. A little later, four policemen whom one of them had found forced open the murderer's door. Besides slashing himself with a dagger, he had ripped open the whole left side of his face with a bullet. *His eye lay on the pillow*." Here I no longer think of Ajax. In that eye "which lay on the pillow" I recognize the eye of the miserable Oedipus, torn out in the most terrible act in the history of human suffering! "Oedipus bursts in with loud cries, goes, comes, demands a sword. . . . With a dread shriek he throws himself against the double doors, pulls the boards from the hinges, rushes into the room where he sees Jocasta hanging by the cord which had strangled her. Seeing her thus, the wretch trembles with horror, looses the cord; his mother's body falls to the ground. He rips the gold brooches from Jocasta's garments, with them he tears his wide-open eyes, saying that they shall no longer see the evil he has suffered and the disaster he has caused, and, shouting curses, again he strikes his eyes, the lids open, and from his bloody eyeballs a rain, a hail of black blood flows down his cheeks. He cries that the parricide must be shown to all the Cadmeans. He wants to be driven from the land. Ah, their old felicity was a true felicity; but from this day on they shall know all the evils that have a name. Lamentations, ruin, death, disgrace." And in thinking of Henri van Blarenberghe's pain when he saw his dead mother, I think of another mad man, of Lear clasping the body of his daughter Cordelia. "Oh! she's gone forever! She's as dead as earth. No, no, no life! Why should a dog, a horse, a rat, have life, and thou no breath at all? Thou'lt come no more, never, never, never, never, never! Look on her, look, her lips, look there, look there!"

In spite of his horrible wounds Henri van Blarenberghe did not die at once. And I cannot help finding very harsh (although perhaps necessary; can one be sure what really constituted the drama? Remember the brothers Karamazov) the act of the superintendent of police. "The unfortunate man was not dead. The superintendent took him by the shoulders and said: 'Do you hear me? Answer.' The murderer opened his one eye, blinked for an instant and fell back in a coma." To this cruel superintendent I want to speak the words used by Kent in the scene from *King Lear* which I quoted just now to stop

Edgar from arousing the already fainting Lear: "Vex not his ghost: O! let him pass; he hates him that would upon the rack of this tough world stretch him out longer."

If I have insisted on repeating these great tragic names, especially those of Ajax and Oedipus, the reader should understand why, and also why I have published these letters and written this page. I wished to show in what a pure and religious atmosphere of moral beauty, bespattered but not defiled, occurred this explosion of madness and blood. I wished to open the room of crime to the air of heaven, to show that this commonplace event was exactly one of those Greek dramas, the presentation of which was almost a religious ceremony and that the poor parricide was not a criminal brute, a being outside humanity, but a noble example of humanity, a man of enlightened soul, a tender and dutiful son whom the most ineluctable fatality—let us say pathological fatality, as the world would say—has thrown, most unfortunate of mortals, into a crime and an expiation worthy of fame.

"I do not easily believe in death," says Michelet in an admirable passage. It is true that he says it of a sea nettle, whose death, so little different from its life, is scarcely notable; and one might also wonder whether Michelet's phrase may not be simply one of those "basic recipes" which great writers soon acquire, thanks to which they are sure of being able to serve up to their clientele at a moment's notice the particular feast which it demands of them. Although I believe without difficulty in the death of a sea nettle, I cannot easily believe in the death of a person, even in the simple eclipse, the simple decay of his reason. Our sense of the soul's continuity is very strong. What! this spirit which, a moment ago, controlled life by its views, controlled death, inspired in us so much respect, there it is, controlled by life, by death, weaker than our own spirit which, however much it may desire, can no longer bow before what has so quickly become little more than a nonentity! It is with madness as with the impairment of faculties in the old, as with death. What? The man who yesterday wrote the letter quoted above, so noble, so intelligent, this man today . . . ? And also, for the smallest details are important here, the man who was attached so wisely to the small things of life, who answered a letter so elegantly, who met an overture so correctly, who respected the opinion of others, who desired to appear to them, if not influential, at least amiable, who conducted his game on the

social exchequer with such finesse and integrity! . . . I say that all
this is very important, and if I have quoted the whole first part of the
second letter which, to tell the truth, may seem interesting to no one
but myself, it is because that practical good sense seems still more
remote from what has happened than the beautiful and profound
sadness of the last lines. Often, in a ravaged spirit, it is the main
branches, the crown, which survive the longest, after disease has
already cleared away all the lower branches. Here, the spiritual plant
is intact. And just now, as I was copying these letters, I would have
liked to be able to communicate the extreme delicacy, and more, the
incredible preciseness of the hand which had written so clearly and
neatly.

"What have you done to me! What have you done to me!" If we
think of it, perhaps there is no truly loving mother who would not be
able, on her last day and often long before, to reproach her son with
these words. At bottom, we make old, we kill all those who love us, by
the anxiety we cause them, by that kind of uneasy tenderness we
inspire and ceaselessly put in a state of alarm. If we can see in a
beloved body the slow work of destruction side by side with the
painful fondness which rouses it, see the faded eyes, the hair long
rebelliously black at last vanquished like the rest and growing white,
the arteries hardened, the kidneys choked up, the heart strained,
courage gone before life, the walk slackened and heavy, the spirit
knowing it can hope for nothing yet unwearingly rebounding with
invincible hopes, the gaiety even, innate and seemingly immortal,
which made such a pleasant companion for sadness, now finally
exhausted, perhaps the one who can see this, in that tardy moment of
lucidity which even lives most bewitched by idle fancies may have, for
even Don Quixote had such a moment, perhaps that one, like Henri
van Blarenberghe when he had dispatched his mother with a blow
of the dagger, would shrink from the horror of his life and rush for
a revolver so that he might die at once. In most men a vision so
painful (supposing that they are able to rise to it) blots out immediately the slightest rays of the joy of living. But what joy, what
reason for living, what life can withstand this vision? Which, the
vision or the joy of living, is true, which is "the Truth"?

TRANSLATED BY BARBARA ANDERSON

GUY DE MAUPASSANT

Isaac Babel

In the winter of 1916 I found myself in St. Petersburg with a forged passport and not a cent to my name. Alexei Kazantsev, a teacher of Russian literature, took me into his house.

He lived on a yellow, frozen, evil-smelling street in the Peski district. The miserable salary he received was padded out a bit by doing translations from the Spanish; Blasco Ibanez was just becoming famous at that time.

Kazantsev had never so much as passed through Spain but his love for that country filled his whole being. He knew every castle, every garden and every river in Spain. There were many other people huddling around Kazantsev, all of them, like myself, flung out of the round of ordinary life. We were half-starved. From time to time the yellow press would publish, in the smallest print, unimportant news items written by us.

I spent my mornings hanging around the morgues and police stations.

Kazantsev was happier than any of us, for he had a country of his own—Spain.

In November I was given the chance to become a clerk at the Obukhov Mills. It was a rather good position and would have exempted me from military service.

I refused to become a clerk.

Even in those days, when I was twenty years old, I had told myself: better to starve, go to jail, or become a bum than spend ten hours every day in an office behind a desk.

There was nothing particularly laudable in my resolve, but I have never broken it and I never will. The wisdom of my ancestors was firmly lodged in my head: we are born to enjoy our work, our fights, and our love; we are born for that and for nothing else.

Listening to my bragging Kazantsev ruffled the short yellow fluff on the top of his head. The horror in his stare was mixed with admiration.

At Christmas-time we had luck. Benderski, the lawyer, who owned a publishing house called "Halcyon," decided to publish a new edition of Maupassant's works. His wife, Raissa, tried to do the translation but nothing came of her lofty ambition.

Kazantsev, who was known as a translator of Spanish, had been asked whether he could recommend someone to assist Raissa Mikhailovna. He told them of me.

The next day, in someone else's coat, I managed to carry myself to Benderski's. They lived at the corner of Nevsky and Moika, in a house of Finland granite, adorned with pink columns, cornices and coats-of-arms made of stone.

Bankers without a history and catapulted out of nowhere, converted Jews who had become rich selling materials to the army, put up these pretentious mansions in St. Petersburg before the war.

There was a red carpet on the stairs. On the landings, upon their hind legs, stood plush bears. Crystal lamps burned in their open mouths.

The Benderskis lived on the third floor. A high-breasted maid, with a white cap on her head, opened the door. She led me into a drawing room decorated in the old Slav style. Blue paintings by Roerich depicting prehistoric stones and monsters hung on the walls.

The high-breasted maid moved smoothly and majestically. She had an excellent figure, was near-sighted and rather haughty. In her open gray eyes one saw a petrified lewdness. She moved slowly. I thought— when she makes love she must move with unheard-of agility. The brocade portiere over the doorway suddenly rustled. A black-haired woman with pink eyes and a wide bosom entered the room. It was easy to recognize in Raissa Benderski one of those charming Jewesses who have come to us from Kiev and Poltava, from the opulent steppe towns full of chestnut trees and acacias. The money made by their clever husbands is transformed by these women into a pink layer of fat on the belly, the back of the neck, and the well-rounded shoulders. Their sleepy and subtle smiles drive officers from the local garrisons crazy.

"Maupassant," Raissa said to me, "is the only passion of my life."

Trying to restrain the sway of her big hips, she left the room and returned with a translation of "Miss Harriet." In her translation not even a trace was left of Maupassant's free flowing sentences, with their fragrance of passion. Raissa Benderski took pains to write correctly and precisely, and all that resulted was something lifeless and slightly distorted, as Jews wrote Russian in the old days.

I took the manuscript with me and in Kazantsev's attic, among my sleeping friends, I spent the night cutting my way like a woodsman through the tangled undergrowth of her prose. It is not such dull work as it might seem. A phrase is born into the world both good and bad at the same time. The secret lies in a slight, almost invisible twist. The lever should rest in your hand, getting warm, and you can only turn it once, not twice.

Next morning I brought back the corrected manuscript. Raissa wasn't lying when she told me that Maupassant was her sole passion. She sat motionless, her hands clasped together, as I read it to her. Her silky hands drooped to the floor, her forehead paled, and the lace between her crushed breasts danced and heaved.

"How did you do it?"

I began to speak of style, of the army of words, of the army in which all kinds of weapons may come into play. No iron can stab the human heart with such force as a period put just at the right place. She listened with her head down and her painted lips half open. In her hair, pressed smooth, divided by a part, and looking like patent leather, shone a dark gleam. Her legs in tight-fitting stockings, with strong, soft calves, were planted wide-apart on the carpet.

The maid, glancing to the side with her petrified wanton eyes, brought in the breakfast on a tray.

The glassy rays of the Petersburg sun lay on the pale and uneven carpet. Twenty-nine volumes of Maupassant stood on a shelf above the desk. The sun with its fingers of melting dissolution touched the morocco backs of the books—the magnificent grave of a human heart.

Coffee in blue cups was served and we began translating "Idyl." Everyone remembers the story of the youthful, hungry carpenter who sucked the breast of the stout nursing mother to relieve her of the milk with which she was over-laden. It happened in a train going from Nice to Marseilles, at noon on a very hot day, in the land of roses, the birthplace of roses, where beds of flowers flow down to the seashore.

I left the Benderski's with a twenty-five rouble advance. That night our crowd at Peski got drunk as a flock of drugged geese. Between drinks we spooned up the best caviar, and then changed over to liver sausage. Half-soused, I began to berate Tolstoi.

"He turned yellow, your Count, he was afraid. His religion was all fear. . . . He was frightened by the cold, by old age, by death, and he made himself a warm coat out of his faith . . ."

"Go on, go on," Kazantsev urged, swaying his bird-like head.

We fell asleep on the floor beside our beds. I dreamed of Katya, a forty-year-old washerwoman who lived a floor below us. We went to her every morning for our boiling water. I had never seen her face distinctly, but in my dream we did god-awful things together. We almost destroyed each other with kisses. The very next morning I couldn't restrain myself from going to her for boiling water.

I saw a wan woman, a shawl across her chest, with ash-grey hair and labor-worn, withered hands.

From then on I took my breakfast at the Benderski's every day. A new stove, herrings and chocolates appeared in our attic. Twice Raissa took me out in her carriage for drives to the islands. I couldn't prevent myself from telling her all about my childhood. To my amazement the story turned out to be very sordid. From under her moleskin cowl her gleaming, frightened eyes stared at me. The rusty fringe of her eyelashes quivered with pity.

I met Raissa's husband, a yellow-faced Jew with a bald skull and a flat, powerful body that seemed always poised obliquely, ready for flight.

There were rumors about his being close to Rasputin. The enormous profits he made from war supplies drove him almost crazy, giving him the expression of a person with a fixed hallucination. His eyes never remained still; it seemed that reality was lost to him forever. Raissa was embarrassed whenever she had to introduce him to new acquaintances. Because of my youth I noticed this a full week later than I should have.

After the New Year Raissa's two sisters arrived from Kiev. One day I brought the manuscript of "L'aveux" and, not finding Raissa at home, came back that evening. They were at dinner. Silvery, neighing laughter and excited male voices came from the dining room. In rich houses without tradition dinners are always noisy. It was a Jewish

noise, rolling and tripping and ending up on a melodious, singsong
note. Raissa came out to me in evening dress, her back bare. Her feet
stepped awkwardly in wobbling, patent leather slippers.

"I'm drunk, darling," she said, and held out her hands, loaded with
chains of platinum and emerald stars.

Her body swayed like a snake's dancing to music. She tossed about
her marcelled hair, and suddenly, with a tinkle of rings, slumped into
a chair with ancient Russian carvings. Scars glowed on her powdered
back.

Women's laughter again came from the dining room. Raissa's
sisters, with delicate moustaches and as full-bosomed and round-
bodied as Raissa herself, entered the room. Their busts jutted forward
and rose to a point and their black hair shimmered in the air. Both of
them had their own Benderskis for husbands. The room was filled
with disjointed, chaotic feminine merriment, the merriment of ripe
women. The husbands wrapped the sisters into their sealskin furs and
Orenburg shawls, and shod them in black boots. From the snowy
peaks of their shawls only painted, glowing cheeks, marble noses and
eyes with their Jewish glitter could be seen. After having made some
more happy noise, they left for the theater, where "Judith" was being
sung by Chaliapin.

"I want to work," Raissa lisped, stretching her bare arms to me,
"we've skipped a whole week."

She brought a bottle and two glasses from the dining room. Her
breasts swung free beneath the sack-like gown; the nipples rose under
the clinging silk.

"It's very valuable," said Raissa, pouring out the wine, "Muscatel
'83. My husband will kill me when he finds out."

I had never drunk Muscatel of 1883 and tossed off three glasses one
after the other without thinking. They carried me swiftly away into
alleys where an orange flame danced and sounds of music could be
heard.

"I'm drunk, darling. . . . What do we do today?"

"Today it's 'L'aveu.' . . . The sun is the hero of this story, *le soleil
de France*. Molten drops of it pattering on the red-haired Celeste
changed into freckles. The sun's direct rays and wine and apple cider
burnished the face of the coachman Polyte. Twice a week Celeste
drove into town to sell cream, eggs and chickens. She gave Polyte ten
sous for herself and four for her basket. And every time Polyte would

wink at red-haired Celeste and ask: 'When are we going to have a bit of fun, *ma belle?*' 'What do you mean. Monsieur Polyte?' Jogging up and down on the box, the coachman explained, 'To have a bit of fun means . . . why, what the hell, to have a bit of fun. . . . A lad with a lass, no music necessary . . .'

" 'I do not care for such jokes, M'sieur Polyte,' replied Celeste, moving farther away the skirts that hung over her mighty calves in red stockings.

"But that devil Polyte kept right on guffawing and coughing: 'Ah, but one day we shall have our bit of fun, *ma belle,*' while tears of delight rolled down a face the color of brick-red wine and blood."

I downed another glass of the rare muscatel. Raissa touched glasses with me. The maid with the stony eyes crossed the room and disappeared.

"*Ce diable de Polyte.* . . . In the course of two years Celeste had paid him forty-eight francs, that is, two francs short of fifty francs! At the end of the second year, when they were alone in the carriage, Polyte, who had had some cider before setting out, asked her his usual question: 'What about having some fun today, M'amselle Celeste?' And she replied, lowering her eyes, 'I am at your disposal, M'sieur Polyte.' "

Raissa flung herself down on the table, laughing. "*Ce diable de Polyte . . .*"

"A white, spavined mare was harnessed to the carriage. The white hack, lips pink with age, went forward at a walking pace. The gay sun of France poured down on the ancient coach, screened off from the world by a weather-beaten hood. . . . A lad with a lass, no music necessary . . ."

Raissa held out a glass to me. It was the fifth.

"*Mon vieux,* to Maupassant."

"And what about having some fun today, *ma belle.*"

I reached over to Raissa and kissed her on the lips. They quivered and swelled.

"You're funny," she mumbled through her teeth, recoiling.

She pressed herself against the wall, stretching out her bare arms. Spots began to glow on her arms and shoulders. Of all gods ever put on the crucifix, this was the most ravishing one.

"Be so kind as to sit down, M'sieur Polyte."

She pointed to an oblique blue armchair, done in Slavonic style. Its back was constructed of carved interlacing bands with colorful pendants. I groped my way to it, stumbling as I went.

Night had blocked the path of my famished youth with a bottle of '83 Muscatel and twenty-nine books, twenty-nine bombs stuffed with pity, genius and passion. . . . I sprang up, knocking over the chair and banging against the shelf. The twenty-nine volumes crashed onto the floor, their pages flew open, they fell on their edges . . . and the white mare of my fate went on at a walking pace.

"You are funny," growled Raissa.

I left the granite house on the Moika at twelve o'clock, before the sisters and the husband returned from the theater. I was sober and could have walked a chalk-line, but it was pleasanter to stagger, so I swayed from side to side, singing in a language I had just invented. Through the tunnels of the streets bounded by lines of street lights, the steamy fog billowed. A monster roared behind the boiling walls of the buildings. The roads amputated the legs of those walking on them.

Kazantsev was asleep when I got home. He slept sitting up, his thin legs extended in their felt boots. The canary fluff rose on his head. He had fallen asleep by the stove bending over a volume of *Don Quixote*, edition 1624. On the fly-leaf of the book was a dedication to the Duc de Broglio. I got into bed quietly, so as not to wake Kazantsev, moved the lamp close to me and began to read a book by Edouard de Menial on "The Life and Work of Guy de Maupassant."

That night I learned from Edouard de Menial that Maupassant was born in 1850, a child of a Normandy gentleman and Laure Lepoitevin, Flaubert's cousin. He was twenty-five when he was first attacked by hereditary syphilis. His productivity and joy of life withstood the development of the disease. At first he suffered from headaches and spasms of hypochondria. Then the spectre of blindness arose before him. His sight weakened. He became suspicious of everyone, unsociable and quarrelsome in a petty way. He struggled furiously, dashed about the Mediterranean in a yacht, fled to Tunis, Morocco, Central Africa . . . and wrote ceaselessly. He attained fame, and at forty years of age cut his own throat, lost a great deal of blood yet lived through it. He was then put away in a mad-house. There he crawled about on his hands and knees and devoured his own excrement. The last line inscribed on his hospital report read: *Monsieur de Maupassant va s'animaliser.*

I read the book to the end and got up from bed. The fog came close to the window and the world was hidden away. My heart contracted as the foreboding of some essential truth touched me with light fingers.

TRANSLATED BY RAYMOND ROSENTHAL AND WACLAW SOLSKI

. .
.   .
. .

Seekers after touchstones might preserve the three hundred and fifty words beginning "The next day, in someone else's coat" and ending " 'is the passion of my life.' " The mixture of furniture and flesh, summary and scene, the scarcely explicit but powerful pressure of "I's" desires, the line of dialogue cracking against the mass of comic sensuousness, the precision and—even in translation—the beauty of varied sentences in brilliant assemblage, these will serve as character witnesses for the art and power of modern fiction. Behind them lie a hundred and fifty years of great fiction-writers forming and subtilizing the conventions of their art in Russian, French, and English.

DER DOPPELGÄNGER

Heinrich Heine / Franz Schubert

Translation of Der Doppelgänger:
The night's still, the backstreets quiet; in this house, my sweetheart lived; she's been gone a long time, yet there, in the same square, stands the house. There's also a man standing there, staring up, wringing his hands in misery. I'm terrified. When I see his face, the moon shows me my own. You, Double, you pale companion, why are you aping the misery of love which terrified me in this square so many nights, so long ago? (R.S.)

. .
.   .
. .

Schubert's is not so much a setting of Heine's rapid little ghost poem as an assault on it; consider the treatment of diesem, Haus, mein, and dieselben in the first few bars. A new scheme for the evocation of tension has been constructed outside of the text. Occasionally, as on eigene, a poetic climax is reinforced—set—by the music, but on the whole, Schubert's use of the poem, like Heine's of the narrative element in his lyric form, is to extend an illusory temptation that narrative will account for the major excitement of the piece, whereas, in each case, the dominant art works not to augment the excitement or refinement of narrative revelation but to offer its special reaction to a type of event.

DER DOPPELGÄNGER
Heinrich Heine/Franz Schubert

A WAYSIDE COMEDY

Rudyard Kipling

Because to every purpose there is time and judgment, therefore the misery of man is great upon him. —*Eccles*. viii. 6.

Fate and the Government of India have turned the Station of Kashima into a prison; and, because there is no help for the poor souls who are now lying there in torment, I write this story, praying that the Government of India may be moved to scatter the European population to the four winds.

Kashima is bounded on all sides by the rock-tipped circle of the Dosehri hills. In Spring, it is ablaze with roses; in Summer, the roses die and the hot winds blow from the hills; in Autumn, the white mists from the *jhils* cover the place as with water, and in Winter the frosts nip everything young and tender to earth-level. There is but one view in Kashima—a stretch of perfectly flat pasture and plough-land, running up to the gray-blue scrub of the Dosehri hills.

There are no amusements, except snipe and tiger shooting; but the tigers have been long since hunted from their lairs in the rock-caves, and the snipe only come once a year. Narkarra—one hundred and forty-three miles by road—is the nearest station to Kashima. But Kashima never goes to Narkarra, where there are at least twelve English people. It stays within the circle of the Dosehri hills.

All Kashima acquits Mrs. Vansuythen of any intention to do harm; but all Kashima knows that she, and she alone, brought about their pain.

Boulte, the Engineer, Mrs. Boulte, and Captain Kurrell know this. They are the English population of Kashima, if we except Major Vansuythen, who is of no importance whatever, and Mrs. Vansuythen, who is the most important of all.

You must remember, though you will not understand, that all laws weaken in a small and hidden community where there is no public opinion. When a man is absolutely alone in a Station he runs a certain rish of falling into evil ways. This risk is multiplied by every addition to the population up to twelve—the Jury-number. After that, fear and consequent restraint begin, and human action becomes less grotesquely jerky.

There was deep peace in Kashima till Mrs. Vansuythen arrived. She was a charming woman, every one said so everywhere; and she charmed every one. In spite of this, or, perhaps, because of this, since Fate is so perverse, she cared only for one man, and he was Major Vansuythen. Had she been plain or stupid, this matter would have been intelligible to Kashima. But she was a fair woman, with very still gray eyes, the colour of a lake just before the light of the sun touches it. No man who had seen those eyes could, later on, explain what fashion of woman she was to look upon. The eyes dazzled him. Her own sex said that she was "not bad looking, but spoilt by pretending to be so grave." And yet her gravity was natural. It was not her habit to smile. She merely went through life, looking at those who passed; and the women objected while the men fell down and worshipped.

She knows and is deeply sorry for the evil she has done to Kashima; but Major Vansuythen cannot understand why Mrs. Boulte does not drop in to afternoon tea at least three times a week. "When there are only two women in one Station, they ought to see a great deal of each other," says Major Vansuythen.

Long and long before ever Mrs. Vansuythen came out of those far-away places where there is society and amusement, Kurrell had discovered that Mrs. Boulte was the one woman in the world for him and—you dare not blame them. Kashima was as out of the world as Heaven or the Other Place, and the Dosehri hills kept their secret well. Boulte had no concern in the matter. He was in camp for a fortnight at a time. He was a hard, heavy man, and neither Mrs. Boulte nor Kurrell pitied him. They had all Kashima and each other for their very, very own; and Kashima was the Garden of Eden in those days. When Boulte returned from his wanderings he would slap Kurrell between the shoulders and call him "old fellow," and the three would dine together. Kashima was happy then when the judgment of God seemed almost as distant as Narkarra or the railway that ran down to the sea. But the Government sent Major Vansuythen to Kashima, and with him came his wife.

The etiquette of Kashima is much the same as that of a desert island. When a stranger is cast away there, all hands go down to the shore to make him welcome. Kashima assembled at the masonry platform close to the Narkarra Road, and spread tea for the Vansuythens. That ceremony was reckoned a formal call, and made them free of the Station, its rights and privileges. When the Vansuythens were settled down, they gave a tiny house-warming to all Kashima; and that made Kashima free of their house, according to the immemorial usage of the Station.

Then the Rains came, when no one could go into camp, and the Narkarra Road was washed away by the Kasun River, and in the cup-like pastures of Kashima the cattle waded knee-deep. The clouds dropped down from the Dosehri hills and covered everything.

At the end of the Rains, Boulte's manners towards his wife changed and became demonstratively affectionate. They had been married twelve years, and the change startled Mrs. Boulte, who hated her husband with the hate of a woman who has met with nothing but kindness from her mate, and, in the teeth of this kindness, has done him a great wrong. Moreover, she had her own trouble to fight with— her watch to keep over her own property, Kurrell. For two months the Rains had hidden the Dosehri hills and many other things besides; but, when they lifted, they showed Mrs. Boulte that her man among men, her Ted—for she called him Ted in the old days when Boulte was out of earshot—was slipping the links of the allegiance.

"The Vansuythen Woman has taken him," Mrs. Boulte said to herself; and when Boulte was away, wept over her belief, in the face of the overvehement blandishments of Ted. Sorrow in Kashima is as fortunate as Love, because there is nothing to weaken it save the flight of Time. Mrs. Boulte had never breathed her suspicion to Kurrell because she was not certain; and her nature led her to be very certain before she took steps in any direction. That is why she behaved as she did.

Boulte came into the house one evening, and leaned against the door-posts of the drawing-room, chewing his moustache. Mrs. Boulte was putting some flowers into a vase. There is a pretense of civilisation even in Kashima.

"Little woman," said Boulte quietly, "do you care for me?"

"Immensely," said she, with a laugh. "Can you ask it?"

"But I'm serious," said Boulte. "Do you care for me?"

Mrs. Boulte dropped the flowers, and turned round quickly. "Do you want an honest answer?"

"Ye-es, I've asked for it."

Mrs. Boulte spoke in a low, even voice for five minutes, very distinctly, that there might be no misunderstanding her meaning. When Samson broke the pillars of Gaza, he did a little thing, and one not to be compared to the deliberate pulling down of a woman's homestead about her own ears. There was no wise female friend to advise Mrs. Boulte, the singularly cautious wife, to hold her hand. She struck at Boulte's heart, because her own was sick with suspicion of Kurrell, and worn out with the long strain of watching alone through the Rains. There was no plan or purpose in her speaking. The sentences made themselves; and Boulte listened, leaning against the door-post with his hands in his pockets. When all was over, and Mrs. Boulte began to breathe through her nose before breaking out into tears, he laughed and stared straight in front of him at the Dosehri hills.

"Is that all?" he said. "Thanks, I only wanted to know, you know."

"What are you going to do?" said the woman, between her sobs.

"Do! Nothing. What should I do? Kill Kurrell or send you Home, or apply for leave to get a divorce? It's two days' dâk into Narkarra." He laughed again and went on: "I tell you what *you* can do. You can ask Kurrell to dinner to-morrow—no, on Thursday, that will allow you time to pack—and you can bolt with him. I give you my word I won't follow."

He took up his helmet and went out of the room, and Mrs. Boulte sat till the moonlight streaked the floor, thinking and thinking and thinking. She had done her best upon the spur of the moment to pull the house down; but it would not fall. Moreover, she could not understand her husband, and she was afraid. Then the folly of her useless truthfulness struck her, and she was ashamed to write to Kurrell, saying: "I have gone mad and told everything. My husband says that I am free to elope with you. Get a dâk for Thursday, and we will fly after dinner." There was a cold-bloodedness about that procedure which did not appeal to her. So she sat still in her own house and thought.

At dinner-time Boulte came back from his walk, white and worn and haggard, and the woman was touched at his distress. As the evening wore on, she muttered some expression of sorrow, something approaching to contrition. Boulte came out of a brown study and said, "Oh, *that!* I wasn't thinking about that. By the way, what does Kurrell say to the elopement?"

"I haven't seen him," said Mrs. Boulte. "Good God! is that all?"

But Bolte was not listening, and her sentence ended in a gulp.

The next day brought no comfort to Mrs. Boulte, for Kurrell did not appear, and the new life that she, in the five minutes' madness of the previous evening, had hoped to build out of the ruins of the old, seemed to be no nearer.

Boulte ate his breakfast, advised her to see her Arab pony fed in the verandah, and went out. The morning wore through, and at midday the tension became unendurable. Mrs. Boulte could not cry. She had finished her crying in the night, and now she did not want to be left alone. Perhaps the Vansuythen Woman would talk to her; and, since talking opens the heart, perhaps there might be some comfort to be found in her company. She was the only other woman in the Station.

In Kashima there are no regular calling-hours. Every one can drop in upon every one else at pleasure. Mrs. Boulte put on a big *terai* hat, and walked across to the Vansuythen's house to borrow last week's "Queen." The two compounds touched, and instead of going up the drive, she crossed through the gap in the cactus-hedge, entering the house from the back. As she passed through the dining-room, she heard, behind the *purdah* that cloaked the drawing-room door, her husband's voice, saying—

"But on my Honour! On my Soul and Honour, I tell you she doesn't care for me. She told me so last night. I would have told you then if Vansuythen hadn't been with you. If it is for *her* sake that you'll have nothing to say to me, you can make your mind easy. It's Kurrell—"

"What?" said Mrs. Vansuythen, with an hysterical little laugh. "Kurrell! Oh, it can't be! You two must have made some horrible mistake. Perhaps you—you lost your temper, or misunderstood, or something. Things *can't* be as wrong as you say."

Mrs. Vansuythen had shifted her defence to avoid the man's pleading, and was desperately trying to keep him to a side-issue.

"There must be some mistake," she insisted, "and it can be all put right again."

Boulte laughed grimly.

"It can't be Captain Kurrell! He told me that he had never taken the least—the least interest in your wife, Mr. Boulte. Oh, *do* listen! He said he had not. He swore he had not," said Mrs. Vansuythen.

The *purdah* rustled, and the speech was cut short by the entry of a

little, thin woman, with big rings round her eyes. Mrs. Vansuythen
stood up with a gasp.

"What was that you said?" asked Mrs. Boulte. "Never mind that
man. What did Ted say to you? What did he say to you? What did
he say to you?"

Mrs. Vansuythen sat down helplessly on the sofa, overborne by the
trouble of her questioner.

"He said—I can't remember exactly what he said—but I understood him to say—that is—But, really, Mrs. Boulte, isn't it rather a
strange question?"

"*Will* you tell me what he said?" repeated Mrs. Boulte. Even a
tiger will fly before a bear robbed of her whelps, and Mrs. Vansuythen
was only an ordinarily good woman. She began in a sort of despera-
tion: "Well, he said that he never cared for you at all, and, of course,
there was not the least reason why he should have, and—and—that
was all."

"You said he *swore* he had not cared for me. Was that true?"

"Yes," said Mrs. Vansuythen very softly.

Mrs. Boulte wavered for an instant where she stood, and then fell
forward fainting.

"What did I tell you?" said Bolte, as though the conversation had
been unbroken. "You can see for yourself. She cares for *him*." The
light began to break into his dull mind, and he went on—"And he—
what was he saying to you?"

But Mrs. Vansuythen, with no heart for explanations or impas-
sioned protestations, was kneeling over Mrs. Boulte.

"Oh, you brute!" she cried. "Are *all* men like this? Help me to get
her into my room—and her face is cut against the table. Oh, *will* you
be quiet, and help me to carry her? I hate you, and I hate Captain
Kurrell. Lift her up carefully and now—go! Go away!"

Boulte carried his wife into Mrs. Vansuythen's bedroom, and
departed before the storm of that lady's wrath and disgust, impeni-
tent and burning with jealousy. Kurrell had been making love to Mrs.
Vansuythen—would do Vansuythen as great a wrong as he had done
Boulte, who caught himself considering whether Mrs. Vansuythen
would faint if she discovered that the man she loved had forsworn
her.

In the middle of these meditations, Kurrell came cantering along
the road and pulled up with a cheery, "Good-mornin'. 'Been mashing

Mrs. Vansuythen as usual, eh? Bad thing for a sober, married man, that. What will Mrs. Boulte say?"

Boulte raised his head and said slowly, "Oh, you liar!" Kurrell's face changed. "What's that?" he asked quickly.

"Nothing much," said Boulte. "Has my wife told you that you two are free to go off whenever you please? She has been good enough to explain the situation to me. You've been a true friend to me, Kurrell—old man—haven't you?"

Kurrell groaned, and tried to frame some sort of idiotic sentence about being willing to give "satisfaction." But his interest in the woman was dead, had died out in the Rains, and, mentally, he was abusing her for her amazing indiscretion. It would have been so easy to have broken off the thing gently and by degrees, and now he was saddled with—Boulte's voice recalled him.

"I don't think I should get any satisfaction from killing you, and I'm pretty sure you'd get none from killing me."

Then in a querulous tone, ludicrously disproportioned to his wrongs, Boulte added—

"'Seems rather a pity that you haven't the decency to keep to the woman, now you've got her. You've been a true friend to *her* too, haven't you?"

Kurrell stared long and gravely. The situation was getting beyond him.

"What do you mean?" he said.

Boulte answered, more to himself than to the questioner: "My wife came over to Mrs. Vansuythen's just now; and it seems you'd been telling Mrs. Vansuythen that you'd never cared for Emma. I suppose you lied, as usual. What had Mrs. Vansuythen to do with you, or you with her? Try to speak the truth for once in a way."

Kurrell took the double insult without wincing, and replied by another question: "Go on. What happened?"

"Emma fainted," said Boulte simply. "But, look here, what had you been saying to Mrs. Vansuythen?"

Kurrell laughed. Mrs. Boulte had, with unbridled tongue, made havoc of his plans; and he could at least retaliate by hurting the man in whose eyes he was humiliated and shown dishonourable.

"Said to her? What *does* a man tell a lie like that for? I suppose I said pretty much what you've said, unless I'm a good deal mistaken."

"I spoke the truth," said Boulte, again more to himself than to Kurrell. "Emma told me she hated me. She has no right in me."

"No! I suppose not. You're only her husband, y'know. And what did Mrs. Vansuythen say after you had laid your disengaged heart at her feet?"

Kurrell felt almost virtuous as he put the question.

"I don't think that matters," Boulte replied; "and it doesn't concern you."

"But it does! I tell you it does—" began Kurrell shamelessly.

The sentence was cut by a roar of laughter from Boulte's lips. Kurrell was silent for an instant, and then he, too, laughed—laughed long and loudly, rocking in his saddle. It was an unpleasant sound— the mirthless mirth of these men on the long, white line of the Narkarra Road. There were no stranger in Kashima, or they might have thought that captivity within the Dosehri hills had driven half the European population mad. The laughter ended abruptly, and Kurrell was the first to speak.

"Well, what are you going to do?"

Boulte looked up the road, and at the hills. "Nothing," said he quietly; "what's the use? It's too ghastly for anything. We must let the old life go on. I can only call you a hound and a liar, and I can't go on calling you names for ever. Besides which, I don't feel that I'm much better. We can't get out of this place. What *is* there to do?"

Kurrell looked round the rat-pit of Kashima and made no reply. The injured husband took up the wondrous tale.

"Ride on, and speak to Emma if you want to. God knows I don't care what you do."

He walked forward, and left Kurrell gazing blankly after him. Kurrell did not ride on either to see Mrs. Boulte or Mrs. Vansuythen. He sat in his saddle and thought, while his pony grazed by the roadside.

The whir of approaching wheels roused him. Mrs Vansuythen was driving home Mrs. Boulte, white and wan, with a cut on her forehead.

"Stop, please," said Mrs. Boulte, "I want to speak to Ted."

Mrs. Vansuythen obeyed, but as Mrs. Boulte leaned forward, putting her hand upon the splashboard of the dog-cart, Kurrell spoke.

"I've seen your husband, Mrs. Boulte."

There was no necessity for any further explanation. The man's eyes were fixed, not upon Mrs. Boulte, but her companion. Mrs. Boulte saw the look.

"Speak to him!" she pleaded, turning to the woman at her side. "Oh, speak to him! Tell him what you told me just now. Tell him you hate him. Tell him you hate him!"

She bent forward and wept bitterly, while the *sais*, impassive, went forward to hold the horse. Mrs. Vansuythen turned scarlet and dropped the reins. She wished to be no party to such unholy explanations.

"I've nothing to do with it," she began coldly; but Mrs. Boulte's sobs overcame her, and she addressed herself to the man. "I don't know what I am to say, Captain Kurrell. I don't know what I can call you. I think you've—you've behaved abominably, and she has cut her forehead terribly against the table."

"It doesn't hurt. It isn't anything," said Mrs. Boulte feebly. "*That* doesn't matter. Tell him what you told me. Say you don't care for him. Oh, Ted, *won't* you believe her?"

"Mrs. Boulte has made me understand that you were—that you were fond of her once upon a time," went on Mrs. Vansuythen.

"Well!" said Kurrell brutally. "It seems to me that Mrs. Boulte had better be fond of her own husband first."

"Stop!" said Mrs. Vansuythen. "Hear me first. I don't care—I don't want to know anything about you and Mrs. Boulte; but I want *you* to know that I hate you, that I think you are a cur, and that I'll never, *nev*er speak to you again. Oh, I don't care to say what I think of you, you—man!"

"I want to speak to Ted," moaned Mrs. Boulte, but the dog-cart rattled on, and Kurrell was left on the road, shamed, and boiling with wrath against Mrs. Boulte.

He waited till Mrs. Vansuythen was driving back to her own house, and, she being freed from the embarrassment of Mrs. Boulte's presence, learned for the second time her opinion of himself and his actions.

In the evenings it was the wont of all Kashima to meet at the platform on the Nakarra Road, to drink tea and discuss the trivialities of the day. Major Vansuythen and his wife found themselves alone at the gathering-place for almost the first time in their remembrance; and the cheery Major, in the teeth of his wife's remarkably reasonable suggestion that the rest of the Station might be sick, insisted upon driving round to the two bungalows and unearthing the population.

"Sitting in the twilight!" said he, with great indignation, to the Boultes. "That'll never do! Hang it all, we're one family here! You *must* come out, and so must Kurrell. I'll make him bring his banjo."

So great is the power of honest simplicity and a good digestion over guilty consciences that all Kashima did turn out, even down to the banjo; and the Major embraced the company in one expensive grin. As he grinned, Mrs. Vansuythen raised her eyes for an instant and looked at all Kashima. Her meaning was clear. Major Vansuythen would never know anything. He was to be the outsider in that happy family whose cage was the Dosehri hills.

"You're singing villainously out of tune, Kurrell," said the Major truthfully. "Pass me that banjo."

And he sang in excruciating-wise till the stars came out and all Kashima went to dinner.

That was the beginning of the New Life of Kashima—the life that Mrs. Boulte made when her tongue was loosened in the twilight.

Mrs. Vansuythen has never told the Major; and since he insists upon keeping up a burdensome geniality, she has been compelled to break her vow of not speaking to Kurrell. This speech, which must of necessity preserve the semblance of politeness and interest, serves admirably to keep alight the flame of jealousy and dull hatred in Boulte's bosom, as it awakens the same passions in his wife's heart. Mrs. Boulte hates Mrs. Vansuythen because she has taken Ted from her, and, in some curious fashion, hates her because Mrs. Vansuythen —and here the wife's eyes see far more clearly than the husband's— detests Ted. And Ted—that gallant captain and honourable man— knows now that it is possible to hate a woman once loved, to the verge of wishing to silence her forever with blows. Above all, is he shocked that Mrs. Boulte cannot see the error of her ways.

Boulte and he go out tiger-shooting together in all friendship. Boulte has put their relationship on a most satisfactory footing.

"You're a blackguard," he says to Kurrell, "And I've lost any self-respect I may ever have had; but when you're with me, I can feel certain that you are not with Mrs. Vansuythen, or making Emma miserable."

Kurrell endures anything that Boulte may say to him. Sometimes they are away for three days together, and then the Major insists upon his wife going over to sit with Mrs. Boulte, although Mrs. Vansuythen has repeatedly declared that she prefers her husband's company to any in the world. From the way in which she clings to him, she would certainly seem to be speaking the truth.

But of course, as the Major says, "in a little Station we must all be friendly."

THE SAINTED BREECHES OF FRA NICOLO

Masuccio Salernitano

Catania, as we know well, is reckoned a noble and illustrious place among the famous cities of the island of Sicily. There, not long past, resided a doctor of medicine, Maestro Rogero Campisciano by name, and this man, although he was full of years, took to wife a young girl called Agata, of a very honorable family of the city before-named, who in the general opinion was the fairest and most graceful lady at that time living in all the island. On this account her husband loved her dearly as his own life.

Now because it very rarely or never happens that love escapes long from the plague of jealousy, this doctor in a very short time became so jealous of his wife, without any other reason, that he forbade her to socialize, not only with strangers but even with friends and relations. And although he had very close relations with the friars minor in the city, being the keeper of their funds, the procurator of the order, and intimately acquainted with their affairs, nevertheless, for the better safeguarding of his lady, he commanded and laid a charge upon her that she should keep from all traffic with the friars, just as if they had been dissolute laymen.

It chanced, however, in the course of time, that there arrived in Catania a minor friar called Fra Nicolo da Narni, who, though he put on the air of a bigot and walked clattering along with a pair of wooden sandals like prison shackles, with a leather patch on the breast of his frock, and bent neck, full of hypocrisy, was nevertheless a fresh-colored, handsome, young fellow. And besides this, he had studied at Perugia, had gained considerable knowledge of the doctrine there taught, was a far-famed preacher, and was enrolled in the confraternity of Saint Bernard—a fact he never failed to make known. He declared, moreover, that he had certain relics of this saint, by virtue of which God had already shown and continued to show many miracles. On account of this, and of the devout name enjoyed by his order, he drew to his preaching a marvelous great crowd.

In this way it happened that on a certain morning when he was preaching, he espied among the crowd of women in the church the afore-named Madonna Agata, who seemed to him a carbuncle in the midst of many of the whitest pearls, and letting fall upon her many glances from the tail of his eye without in any way interrupting his sermon, he said to himself over and over again that the man worthy to enjoy the love of such a beautiful young woman might reckon himself most fortunate.

Agata, as was the wont of all those who came to hear the preaching, kept her eyes steadily fixed on the preacher in admiration, and, since he appeared to her to be handsome beyond ordinary, she wished to herself (without thoughts of undisciplined lust) that her husband were more like this handsome friar, and at the same time she began to think and to deliberate that she would like to make confession to Fra Nicolo.

And thus, holding fast to this idea of hers, as soon as she saw him come down from the pulpit she went to meet him and besought him to hear her. The friar was inwardly overjoyed, but not to allow the corruption of his mind to show itself on his face, answered that it was not part of his duty to hear confessions. The lady replied: "But may not I, for the sake of Maestro Rogero, my husband, enjoy some privilege with you?" To this the friar answered: "Ah, then you are the wife of our procurator? For the respect I bear him I will willingly listen to your confession."

And when they had withdrawn themselves aside, and the friar had taken up his position in the place where they were accustomed to hear confessions, and the lady had gone down on her knees before him, she began to confess herself according to the accustomed rule. After she had confessed some of her sins, telling the friar of the inordinate jealousy of her husband, she asked him of his kindness if there were any means within his power thoroughly to clear out of her husband's head all such delusions, believing perhaps that such ailments might be healed by herbs and plasters as her husband healed his patients.

The friar set gladly to work to consider a proposition such as this, for it seemed to him that his good fortune was about to open for him the door to the path he so keenly desired to tread; wherefore, after he had given Madonna Agata consolation in many words he thus answered her: "My daughter, it is no marvel that your husband should be so jealous of you; indeed, otherwise he would be held by me, and by every other man as well, to be something less than the prudent gentleman he is. Nor ought he to be blamed for this, since it arises solely from the working of Nature, who, having produced you with so great and angelic loveliness, has rendered it impossible to possess you without the sharpest pangs of jealousy."

The lady, smiling at these words, saw that the time had now come to return to the attendants who were awaiting her; so after certain other soft words, she begged the friar to give her absolution. He heaved a deep sigh, turned towards her with a pitiful countenance, and thus answered: "My daughter, no one who is himself bound can give release to another, and since you in so short space of time have made me a slave, I can neither absolve you nor myself, without aid from you."

The courteous lady, who was by birth a Sicilian, quickly understood this ambiguous speech, remarking besides what a good-looking young fellow he was, and feeling no small gratification that he seemed to be so mightily taken by her. Still she was somewhat surprised to find that friars took thought of such matters, because, on account of her youth and the careful guard kept over her by her husband, she had not only been kept from all dealing with religious persons of every sort, but had been firmly persuaded that the making of men into friars did not differ from the making of cocks into capons.

However, she saw clearly enough that Fra Nicolo was more of a cock than a capon, and with a longing such as she had never before known, and with the firm resolve to give him her love at all hazard, she thus answered him: "My father, leave the grief to me, since I, coming here free, now return home the slave of you and of love." To this the friar replied, with the greatest joy he had ever known: "Since then our wills conform, can you not devise some way by which we both of us, breaking forth at the same moment from this cruel prison, may taste the full joy our flowering youth permits?"

She answered that she would willingly agree to this, if she could, adding these words: "At this moment I am reminded of a plan whereby, in spite of all the jealousy of my husband, we may be able to carry out our intention. For, almost every month I am wont to be afflicted with a very grave distemper of the heart, so severe that it robs me of all power of sensation, nor up to the present time have I been able in the least degree to remedy this condition by any device of the physicians. Indeed, certain old women have declared that my ailment proceeds from the womb, because I am young and fit to bear children, but by reason of the age of my husband I am not able to do so. I have thought that on one of these days when my husband goes on his practice in the country, I might feign to be taken ill with one of my accustomed attacks. Then, sending for you in haste, I might beg you to lend me certain relics of San Griffone, and you, on your part, must be prepared to come with them to me secretly; and by the aid of a very trusty maid of mine, we can be together to our pleasure."

To this the friar, overjoyed, replied: "My daughter, may you be blessed by God for the excellent plan you have devised. It seems to me that we are in duty bound to carry it out, and I will bring with me a good friend of mine, who by compassion will not let your trusty waiting-woman be neglected." Then, having come to these conclusions, they parted with many warm and amorous sighs. As soon as she had returned home, the lady made known to her maid the plan devised with the friar for their common gratification and pleasure. The maid, who was mightily pleased at the news, answered that she was fully ready for everything her mistress might command.

Fortune was very kind to them, for the very next morning Maestro Rogero betook himself to visit his patients outside the city, according to the prescient surmise of his wife, who at once, in order to let no delay interfere with the course of the affair, began to call upon San Griffone to come to her aid, feigning to be afflicted with an attack of her customary distemper. Then the maid said to her, by way of counsel: "Why do you not send for those sacred relics of the saint which are reputed miraculous by all men?"

Then the lady, according to the plan they had arranged between themselves, making believe that she could speak only with great difficulty, turned towards the maid, and said: "I beseech you to send for them," and the woman, as if she were filled with pity, replied: "I will go myself for them." So, having set forth at the top of her speed and found the friar and given him the message which had been arranged, Fra Nicolo, together with a companion of his, a sprightly young fellow and one well fitted for the business in hand, at once set forth.

When they were come into the chamber, and when Fra Nicolo, with a very devout look upon his face, had drawn near the bed upon which the lady was lying alone, she, who was tenderly awaiting him, received him with the greatest humility, and said: "O father, pray to God and to glorious San Griffone on my behalf." To this the friar replied: "May the Creator make you worthy of what you ask; but you on your part must give evidence of devout behavior, and if you wish to receive His grace through the virtue of the holy relics I have with me, it is right that first we should resort with contrition to holy confession, so that the soul being cleansed, the body may with ease be brought back to health." The lady answering, said: "I have not thought or wished for anything else; I beg this grace most earnestly at your hands."

When they had said this, they gave courteous dismissal to all persons in the chamber, so that there remained no one else except the maid and the companion who had come with the friar. Then, having securely locked themselves in, so that they might be in no danger of interruption, each lecherously took to his lady. Fra Nicolo got upon the bed, and counting on perfect security, took off his breeches to free his legs and flung them on the head of the bed. Then, having folded the lovely young woman in a close embrace, they began the sweet, desired hunt, and having held his well-trained hound on the leash a long time, he fiercely caught two hares in the same den. The hound was recalled to search for a third, when they became aware that Maestro Rogero on horseback was down below, having come back sooner than they had anticipated.

The friar in great haste flung himself off the bed, overcome with fear and vexation, and forgetting entirely the breeches which he had laid at the bed's head, while the waiting-woman, not at all pleased with the interruption, unfastened the door of the chamber, and having called to the people who were waiting in the hall without, bade them come in at their pleasure, adding that, by the grace of God, her lady was now almost entirely healed, and praising God and San Griffone.

The matter stood thus when Maestro Rogero came into the chamber, and as soon as he realized that something strange had happened, he was no less disturbed at finding that friars had begun to frequent his house than at the fresh indisposition of his beloved spouse; but she, observing at a glance that his humor was mightily changed, cried out: "Oh husband, truly I should have been a dead women by this time if our preacher had not come to my aid with the relics of the most blessed San Griffone. These, as soon as he brought them near to my heart, took away all the pain and agony I suffered, just as a flood of water quenches a little fire."

The credulous husband, when he heard how a remedy had at last been found for an ailment hitherto deemed incurable, fell a-thanking God and San Griffone with no small satisfaction, and at last, turning to the friar, gave him unbounded thanks for the great benefit he had wrought, and thus, after certain other devout and saintly speeches, the friar and his companion took their leave in the most seemly manner.

Now, as they were walking along, Fra Nicolo began to feel somewhat free about the breech, and then it came into his mind how he had left behind him at the head of the bed the garment he usually wore; whereupon, overcome beyond measure with grief and confusion, he turned to his companion and told him of the accident which had befallen him. His friend consoled him as best he could and bade him cease from disquieting himself, forasmuch as the maid, who would be the first to find the breeches, would assuredly hide them, and, laughing as he spoke, added these words: "My master, it is quite clear that you are not used to put up with inconvenience of any sort, since it seems that you must, wherever you may be, allow your hound free leash. But perhaps you follow the example of the Dominican friars, who always take their dogs about with them unconfined by leash of any sort, and, although they often get fine game, it is nevertheless a fact that hounds that are leashed are always keener and more tenacious of their prey."

To this the friar replied: "What you say is true enough, but would to God that no scandal may arise on account of the fault I have committed; and, tell me, how did you fare with the prey I let fall into your clutches? For my own part, I know that my hawk managed to capture a brace of partridges, and just as I was trying for a third, Messer Rogero came back." "May he first have broken his neck," his friend answered; "I am no smith myself, but I managed to make two nails out of one heating of the furnace, and had got one finished complete and the other only lacking the head, when the girl, cursing the hour she was born, cried out, 'Here is the maestro at the door.' And thus the work which you had put in my way was left incomplete."

Said the friar: "May God grant me leave to go back to the hunt I was forced to give over, and then you too, if you should still be in the mood, may turn out your nails by the hundred." To this the friend replied: "You will not find me wanting, but I believe the feathers of those two partridges you took are worth more than all the nails they make in Milan." At this speech the friar laughed heartily, and with many other witty words concerning their late adventure, they went on, joking between themselves.

As soon as the friars had left the chamber, Maestro Rogero, going up to his wife's side and caressing her neck and her bosom, asked her whether the pain had caused her great suffering. In the course of their conversation over this and other matters, Maestro Rogero stretched out his hand to compose the pillows under his wife's head and caught hold of the laces of the breeches which the friar had left there.

When he had drawn them forth and observed at once they were of the sort commonly worn by friars, he cried out with a face totally changed: "What the devil is this, O Agata? What are these friar's breeches doing here?" But the young wife, who was very wary and prudent (and love, moreover, had recently aroused yet more her intelligence), answered without delaying a moment: "And what is the long story I have just told you, my husband, if these be not the miraculous breeches which formerly belonged to the glorious San Griffone, and which our good father, the preaching friar, brought hither this morning as one of the most famous relics of the saint? Wherefore Almighty God, by the virtue of these, has already shown me great favor, and though I was fully assured of being entirely freed from my trouble, yet for greater security, and for piety's sake as well, I besought Fra Nicolo, when he was about to take it away, that he would leave it with me until the time of vespers, at which hour he or some other should send for it."

The husband, when he heard this answer so ready and so well fitted for the occasion, either believed it or made as if he believed it; but, as is the nature of the jealous, his brain was buffeted about without ceasing by the two contrary winds which this accident had stirred up; nevertheless, without giving any farther answer to the remarks of his wife, he held his peace.

The wily young woman, being well assured that her husband was still somewhat disturbed in his mind, now began to scheme how she might by a new ruse clear out entirely from his breast all the suspicious thoughts he nursed there; so turning towards her maid, she said: "Go now at once to the convent, and as soon as you shall have found the friar preacher, tell him to send for the relics which he left with me, for by God's mercy I have had no occasion to use them more."

The discreet waiting-woman, comprehending fully what the lady in truth wanted, went with all speed to the convent and bade them quickly summon the friar preacher, who came to the door, and thinking perhaps that she had come to bring back the keepsake which he had left behind him, he put on a smiling face and asked her, "What news?" "No good news," she answered with a very ill grace, "thanks to your carelessness, and it would have been worse but for the prudence of my mistress." "What's up?" cried the friar, and the girl related to him, point by point, all that had happened, adding that it seemed to her that they should send to fetch the aforesaid relics with some show of ceremony without delay.

Then the friar said, "Keep your mind at ease," and having taken leave of her and bidden her to hope that all things ill done would be repaired, he sought out the superior, and spoke to him in these words: "Good father, I have just committed a most grievous sin, one for which in due time you can punish me as I deserve, but just now I beseech you to give me instant help, as the needs of the case demand, and in the quickest way possible." Then Fra Nicolo set forth the whole story.

The superior, perturbed in no small measure over the affair, took the friar sharply to task for his imprudence, and thus addressed him: "See now what comes of working miracles! A clever fellow you are. You fancied, indeed, that you could go safely to work; if you must needs take off your breeches, could you not think of some other way of hiding them, either in the sleeves or in the breast of your gown, or some other place about your person? You, accustomed as you are to be mixed up in such scandals, did not think of the great burden of conscience and obloquy of the world with which we of your order shall have to battle. Truly, I know not why I should not forthwith send you to prison as you richly deserve. Nevertheless, seeing that at the present moment it is more important to mend matters than to inflict punishment, and that the affair concerns to the highest degree the honor of the order, we will postpone your chastisement to some future time."

Then, having set ringing the bell of the chapter house and assembled all the friars, the superior told them how, in the house of

Maestro Rogero the physician, God had that very day wrought a most evident miracle by the virtue of the breeches which formerly belonged to San Griffone. Having told them the story in the fewest possible words, he persuaded them that it behooved them to go at once to the house of the aforesaid physician and bring back the holy relic with high solemnities and a procession, to give honor and glory to God and enhance the miracles of the saint.

The friars were duly mustered and ranged two by two, and took their way towards the house with the cross at the head of the procession. The superior, clad in a sumptuous cope, bore the tabernacle of the altar on his arm, and marching along in silence they came to the physician's house.

When Maestro Rogero became aware of their presence, he went out to meet the superior and demanded of him the cause of this unwonted visit, whereupon the latter, with a joyous face, made answer to him in terms he had before arranged: "Well-beloved Maestro, the rules of our order require that we should carry in secret the relics of our saint to the house of anyone who may wish to have them, and in like manner if it should happen that the sick person, through any failing of his own, should receive no benefit from the ministration, that we should secretly fetch them home again in order that the fame of miracles should not be diminished. But where God, through the relics, wills to exhibit evident miracles, it is our duty to fetch the holy relic back to our church with all the ceremony and solemnity possible, thus proclaiming the miracle and recording it in public form. And for the reason that your wife (as you already know) has been freed from the dangerous disease which afflicted her through the working of our relic, we are now come in this solemn fashion to bear it back to our house."

The physician, when he saw the whole congregation of friars with so great a show of devotion, at once settled in his mind that these holy men would never have gathered themselves together to any ill purpose; so, accepting as gospel truth the fictitious reasons of the superior, and driving away entirely all suspicious thoughts from his mind, he said: "You are all right welcome." And taking the friar preacher by the hand, he led him into the chamber where Madonna Agata still was.

She, who had in no wise gone to sleep during such business, had now the breeches all ready and wrapped in a white and perfumed linen cloth. The superior, when they were displayed to him, kissed them with the deepest reverence, and made the physician and the lady do the same, and all those who were in the room kissed them likewise. Next, they placed the breeches in the tabernacle which they had brought with them for that purpose, and after a sign had been given to the company, they all began to sing in harmony *Veni Creator Spiritus*, and in this order, traversing the city accompanied by a huge crowd, they bore the relic back to their church and there placed it above the high altar, letting it remain several days in order that all those who had already heard of the miraculous occurrence might pay their devotions to it.

Maestro Rogero, being very set on increasing the reverence of the people towards the order, let pass no opportunity of telling to whatever gatherings of men he chanced to encounter as he went about his practice, both within and without the city, the solemn miracle which God had wrought in his house through the power of the breeches of San Griffone.

And while he occupied himself in this office, Fra Nicolo and his friend did not neglect to resume that rich hunt which they had once begun, to the great delight both of the mistress and of the maid. Madonna Agata, independent of any sensual delight she might enjoy, came to the conclusion that this operation was in truth the only one of any service to cure her attacks, for it brought relief to the very seat of her distemper. Besides this, being the wife of a physician, she had often heard tell of that text of Avicenna in which he lays down the dictum, "that partial remedies give relief, but continuous ones cure." Having tasted both the one sort and the other with much delight, she was duly conscious that, through the opportune ministrations of the holy friar, she had been entirely freed of the incurable mother-sickness which had plagued her so long.

THE WORDS UPON THE WINDOW PANE

William Butler Yeats

A lodging house room, an armchair, a little table in front of it, chairs on either side. A fireplace and window. A kettle on the hob and some tea-things on a dresser. A door at back and towards the right. Through the door one can see an entrance hall. The sound of a knocker. Miss Mackenna passed the door, returns bringing with her John Corbet, a man of twenty two or twenty three, and Doctor Trench, a man of between sixty and seventy.

DOCTOR TRENCH   (*in hall*) May I introduce John Corbet, one of the Corbets of Ballymoney, but at present a Cambridge student? This is Miss Mackenna our enthusiastic secretary. (*They come into room, and take off their coats.*)

MISS MACKENNA   I thought it better to let you in myself. This country is still sufficiently medieval to make spiritualism an undesirable theme for gossip. Give me your coats and hats, I will put them in my own room. It is just across the hall. Better sit down, your watches must be fast. Mrs. Henderson is lying down, as she always does before a séance. We won't begin for ten minutes yet. (*She goes out with hats and coats.*)

DOCTOR TRENCH   Miss Mackenna does all the real work of the Dublin Spiritualists Association. She did all the correspondence with Mrs. Henderson and persuaded the landlady to let her this big room and a small room upstairs. We are a poor society and could not guarantee anything in advance. Mrs. Henderson has come from London at her own risk. She was born in Dublin and wants to spread the movement here. She lives very economically and does not expect a great deal. We all give what we can. A poor woman with the soul of an apostle.

JOHN CORBET   Have there been many séances?

DOCTOR TRENCH   Only three so far.

JOHN CORBET I hope she will not mind my scepticism. I have looked into Myers' "Human Personality" and a wild book by Conan Doyle, but am unconvinced.

DOCTOR TRENCH We all have to find the truth for ourselves. Lord Dunraven, then Lord Adare, introduced my father to the famous David Home. My father often told me that he saw David Home floating in the air in broad daylight, but I did not believe a word of it. I had to investigate for myself, and I was very hard to convince. Mrs. Piper, an American trance medium, not unlike Mrs. Henderson, convinced me.

JOHN CORBET A state of somnambulism and voices coming through her lips that purport to be those of dead persons?

DOCTOR TRENCH Exactly: quite the best kind of mediumship if you want to establish the identity of a spirit. But do not expect too much. There has been a hostile influence.

JOHN CORBET You mean an evil spirit?

DOCTOR TRENCH The poet Blake said that he never knew a bad man that had not something very good about him. I say a hostile influence, an influence that disturbed the last séance very seriously. I cannot tell you what happened, for I have not been at any of Mrs. Henderson's séances. Trance mediumship has nothing new to show me. I told the young people when they made me their President that I would probably stay at home, that I could get more out of Emanuel Swedenborg than out of any séance. (*A knock.*) That is probably old Cornelius Patterson; he thinks they race horses and whippets in the other world and is, so they tell me, so anxious to find out if he is right that he is always punctual. Miss Mackenna will keep him to herself for some minutes. He gives her tips for Harold's Cross.

(*Miss Mackenna crosses to hall door and admits Cornelius Patterson. She brings him to her room across the hall.*)

JOHN CORBET (*who has been wandering about*) This is a wonderful room for a lodging house.

DOCTOR TRENCH It was a private house until about fifty years ago. It was not so near the town in those days and there are large stables at the back. Quite a number of notable people lived here. Grattan was born upstairs, no, not Grattan, Curran perhaps—I forget—but I do know that this house in the early part of the eighteenth century belonged to friends of Jonathan Swift, or rather of Stella. Swift chaffed her in the *Journal to Stella* because of certain small sums of money she lost at cards probably in this very room. That was before Vanessa appeared upon the scene. It was a country house in those days surrounded by trees and gardens. Somebody cut some lines from a poem of hers upon the windowpane—tradition says Stella herself. (*A knock.*) Here they are but you will hardly make them out in this light. (*They stand in the window. Corbet stoops down to see better. Miss Mackenna and Abraham Johnson enter and stand near door.*)

ABRAHAM JOHNSON   Where is Mrs. Henderson?

MISS MACKENNA   She is upstairs, she always rests before a séance.

ABRAHAM JOHNSON   I must see her before the séance. I know exactly what to do to get rid of this evil influence.

MISS MACKENNA   If you go up to see her there will be no séance at all. She says it is dangerous even to think, much less to speak, of an evil influence.

ABRAHAM JOHNSON   Then I shall speak to the President.

MISS MACKENNA   Better talk the whole thing over first in my room. Mrs. Henderson says that there must be perfect harmony.

ABRAHAM JOHNSON   Something must be done. The last séance was completely spoilt. (*A knock.*)

MISS MACKENNA   That may be Mrs. Mallet, she is a very experienced spiritualist. Come to my room, old Patterson and some others are there already. (*She brings him to the other room and later crosses to hall-door to admit Mrs. Mallet.*)

JOHN CORBET   I know these lines well—they are part of a poem Stella wrote for Swift's fifty-fourth birthday. Only three poems of hers —and some lines she added to a poem of Swift's—have come down to us, but they are enough to prove her a better poet than Swift. Even those few words on the window make me think of a seventeenth century poet, Donne or Crashaw (*he quotes*):

> You taught how I might youth prolong
> By knowing what is right and wrong,
> How from the heart to bring supplies
> Of lustre to my fading eyes.

How strange that a celibate scholar, well on in life, should keep the love of two such women. He met Vanessa in London at the height of his political power. She followed him to Dublin. She loved him for nine years, perhaps died of love; but Stella loved him all her life.

THE WORDS UPON THE WINDOW PANE
William Butler Yeats

DOCTOR TRENCH   I have shown that writing to several persons and you are the first who has recognised the lines.

JOHN CORBET   I am writing an essay on Swift and Stella for my doctorate at Cambridge. I hope to prove that in Swift's day men of intellect reached the height of their power—the greatest position they ever attained in Society and the State—that everything great in Ireland and in our character, in what remains of our architecture, comes from that day; that we have kept its seal longer than England.

DOCTOR TRENCH   A tragic life, Ormonde, Harley, Bolingbroke, all those great Ministers that were his friends, banished and broken.

JOHN CORBET   I do not think you can explain him in that way— his tragedy had deeper foundations. His ideal order was the Roman Senate, his ideal men Brutus and Cato; such an order and such men had seemed possible once more; but the movement passed and he foresaw the ruin to come, Democracy, Rousseau, the French Revolution, that is why he hated the common run of men,—"I hate lawyers, I hate doctors" he said "though I love Doctor So-and-so and Judge So-and so,"— that is why he wrote Gulliver, that is why he wore out his brain, that is why he felt *saevo indignatio*, that is why he sleeps under the greatest epitaph in history. You remember how it goes? It is almost finer in English than in Latin:—"He has gone where fierce indignation can lacerate his heart no more."

(*Abraham Johnson comes in, followed by Mrs. Mallet and Cornelius Patterson.*)

ABRAHAM JOHNSON   Something must be done, Doctor Trench, to drive away the influence that has destroyed our séances. I have come here week after week at considerable expense. I am from Belfast. I am by profession a minister of the Gospel, I do a great deal of work among the poor and ignorant. I produce considerable effect by singing and preaching, but I know that my effect should be much greater than it is. My hope is that I shall be able to communicate with the great Evangelist Sankey. I want to ask him to stand invisible beside me when I speak or sing, and lay his hands upon my head and give me such a portion of his power that my work may be blessed as the work of Moody and Sankey was blessed.

MRS. MALLET   What Mr. Johnson says about the hostile influence is quite true. The last two séances were completely spoilt. I am thinking of starting a teashop in Folkestone. I followed Mrs. Henderson to Dublin to get my husband's advice, but two spirits kept talking and would not let any other spirit say a word.

DOCTOR TRENCH   Did the spirits say the same thing and go through the same drama at both séances?

MRS. MALLET   Yes—just as if they were characters in some kind of horrible play.

DOCTOR TRENCH   That is what I was afraid of.

MRS. MALLET   My husband was drowned at sea ten years ago but constantly speaks to me through Mrs. Henderson as if he were still alive. He advises me about everything I do, and I am utterly lost if I cannot question him.

CORNELIUS PATTERSON   I never did like the Heaven they talk about in churches, but when somebody told me that Mrs. Mallet's husband ate and drank and went about with his favourite dog, I said to myself, "That is the place for Corney Patterson." I came here to find out if it was true and I declare to God I have not heard one word about it.

ABRAHAM JOHNSON   I ask you, Doctor Trench, as President of the Dublin Spiritualist Association, to permit me to read the ritual of exorcism appointed for such occasions. After the last séance I copied it out of an old book in the library of Belfast University. I have it here. (*He takes paper out of his pocket.*)

DOCTOR TRENCH   The spirits are people like ourselves, we treat them as our guests and protect them from discourtesy and violence, and every exorcism is a curse or a threatened curse. We do not admit that there are evil spirits. Some spirits are earth-bound—they think they are still living and go over and over some action of their past lives, just as we go over and over some painful thought, except that where they are thought is reality. For instance, when a spirit which has died a violent death comes to a medium for the first time, it relives all the pains of death.

MRS. MALLET   When my husband came for the first time the medium gasped and struggled as if she was drowning. It was terrible to watch.

DOCTOR TRENCH   Sometimes a spirit relives not the pain of death but some passionate or tragic moment of life. Swedenborg describes this and gives the reason for it. There is an incident of the kind in the *Odessey*, and many in Eastern literature; the murderer repeats his murder, the robber his robbery, the lover his serenade, the soldier hears the trumpet once again. If I were a Catholic I would say that such spirits were in Purgatory. In vain do we write *requiescat in pace* upon the tomb, for they must suffer, and we in our turn must suffer until God gives peace. Such spirits do not often come to séances unless those séances are held in houses where those spirits lived, or where the event took place. This spirit which speaks those incomprehensible words, and does not answer when spoken to, is of such a nature. The more patient we are, the more quickly will it pass out of its passion and its remorse.

ABRAHAM JOHNSON   I am still convinced that the spirit which disturbed the last séance is evil. If I may not exorcise it I will certainly pray for protection.

DOCTOR TRENCH   Mrs. Henderson's control, Lulu, is able and experienced and can protect both medium and sitters, but it may help Lulu if you pray that the spirit find rest.

(*Abraham Johnson sits down and prays silently moving his lips. Mrs. Henderson comes in with Miss Mackenna and others. Miss Mackenna shuts the door.*)

DOCTOR TRENCH   Mrs. Henderson, may I introduce to you Mr. Corbet, a young man from Cambridge and a sceptic, who hopes that you will be able to convince him.

MRS. HENDERSON   We were all sceptics once. He must not expect too much from a first séance. He must persevere. (*She sits in the armchair, and the others begin to seat themselves. Miss Mackenna goes to John Corbet and they remain standing.*)

MISS MACKENNA   I am glad that you are a sceptic.

JOHN CORBET   I thought you were a spiritualist.

MISS MACKENNA   I have seen a good many séances and sometimes think it is all coincidence and thought-transference. (*She says this in a low voice.*) Then at other times I think as Doctor Trench does, and then I feel as Job—you know the quotation—the hair of my head stands up. A spirit passed before my face.

MRS. MALLET   Turn the key, Doctor Trench, we don't want anybody blundering in here. (*Doctor Trench locks door.*) Come and sit here, Miss Mackenna.

MISS MACKENNA   No, I am going to sit beside Mr. Corbet. (*Corbet and Miss Mackenna sit down.*)

JOHN CORBET   You feel like Job to-night?

MISS MACKENNA   I feel that something is going to happen, that is why I am glad you are a sceptic.

JOHN CORBET   You feel safer?

MISS MACKENNA   Yes, safer.

MRS. HENDERSON   I am glad to meet all my dear friends again and to welcome Mr. Corbet amongst us. As he is a stranger I must explain that we do not call up spirits; we make the right conditions and they come. I do not know who is going to come; sometimes there are a great many and the guides choose between them. The guides try to send somebody for everybody but do not always succeed. If you want to speak to some dear friend who has passed over, do not be discouraged. If your friend cannot come this time, may-be he can next time. My control is a dear little girl called Lulu who died when she was five or six years old. She describes the spirits present and tells us what spirit wants to speak. Miss Mackenna, a verse of a hymn, please, the same we had last time, and will everyone join in the singing. (*They sing the following lines from Hymn 564, Dublin Church Hymnal, Tune Stillorgan.*)

> Sun of my soul, Thou Saviour dear,
> It is not night if Thou art near:
> O may no earth-born cloud arise
> To hide Thee from Thy servant's eyes.

(*Mrs. Henderson is leaning back in her chair asleep.*)

MISS MACKENNA   (*to John Corbet*) She always snores like that when she is going off.

MRS. HENDERSON   (*in a child's voice*) Lulu so glad to see all her friends.

MRS. MALLET   And we are glad you have come, Lulu.

MRS. HENDERSON   (*in a child's voice*) Lulu glad to see new friend.

MISS MACKENNA   (*to John Corbet*) She is speaking to you.

JOHN CORBET   Thank you, Lulu.

MRS. HENDERSON   (*in a child's voice*) You mustn't laugh at the way I talk.

JOHN CORBET   I am not laughing, Lulu.

MRS. HENDERSON   (*in a child's voice*) Nobody must laugh. Lulu does her best but can't say big long words. Lulu sees a tall man here, lots of hair on face (*Mrs. Henderson passes her hands over her cheeks and chin*), not much on the top of his head (*Mrs. Henderson passes her hand over the top of her head*), red necktie, and such a funny sort of pin.

MRS. MALLET   Yes. . . . Yes . . .

MRS. HENDERSON   (*in a child's voice*) Pin like a horseshoe.

MRS. MALLET   It's my husband.

MRS. HENDERSON   (*in a child's voice*) He has a message.

MRS. MALLET   Yes.

MRS. HENDERSON   (*in a child's voice*) Lulu cannot hear. He is too far off. He has come near. Lulu can hear now. He says. . . . he says, "Drive that man away!" He is pointing to somebody in the corner, that corner over there. He says it is the bad man who spoilt everything last time. If they won't drive him away, Lulu will scream.

MISS MACKENNA   That horrible spirit again.

ABRAHAM JOHNSON   Last time he monopolised the séance.

MRS. MALLET   He would not let anybody speak but himself.

MRS. HENDERSON   (*in a child's voice*) They have driven that bad man away. Lulu sees a young lady.

MRS. MALLET   Is not my husband here?

MRS. HENDERSON   (*in a child's voice*) Man with funny pin gone away. Young lady here—Lulu thinks she must be at a fancy dress party, such funny clothes, hair all in curls—all bent down on floor near that old man with glasses.

DOCTOR TRENCH   No, I do not recognise her.

MRS. HENDERSON   (*in a child's voice*) That bad man, that bad old man in the corner, they have let him come back. Lulu is going to scream. O. . . . O . . . (*in a man's voice*). How dare you write to her? How dare you ask if we were married? How dare you question her?

DOCTOR TRENCH   A soul in its agony—it cannot see us or hear us.

MRS. HENDERSON   (*upright and rigid, only her lips moving, and still in a man's voice*) You sit crouching there. Did you not hear what I said? How dared you question her? I found you an ignorant little girl without intellect, without moral ambition. How many times did I not stay away from great men's houses', how many times forsake the Lord Treasurer's, how many times neglect the business of the State that we might read Plutarch together.

(*Abraham Johnson half rises. Doctor Trench motions him to remain seated.*)

DOCTOR TRENCH   Silence.

ABRAHAM JOHNSON   But, Doctor Trench.

DOCTOR TRENCH   Hush—we can do nothing.

MRS. HENDERSON   (*speaking as before*) I taught you to think in
every situation of life not as Hester Vanhomrigh would think in that
situation but as Cato or Brutus would, and now you behave like some
common slut with her ear against the keyhole.

JOHN CORBET   (*to Miss Mackenna*) It is Swift, Jonathan Swift,
talking to the woman he called Vanessa. She was christened Hester
Vanhomrigh.

MRS. HENDERSON   (*in Vanessa's voice*) I questioned her, Jonathan, because I love. Why have you let me spend hours in your
company if you did not want me to love you? (*In Swift's voice.*)
When I re-built Rome in your mind it was as though I walked its
streets. (*In Vanessa's voice.*) Was that all, Jonathan? Was I nothing
but a painter's canvas? (*In Swift's voice.*) My God, do you think it
was easy? I was a man of strong passions and I had sworn never to
marry. (*In Vanessa's voice.*) If you and she are not married, why
should we not marry like other men and women? I loved you from the
first moment when you came to my mother's house and began to
teach me. I thought it would be enough to look at you, to speak to
you, to hear you speak. I followed you to Ireland five years ago and I
can bear it no longer. It is not enough to look, to speak, to hear.
Jonathan, Jonathan, I am a woman, the women Brutus and Cato
loved were not different. (*In Swift's voice.*) I have something in my
blood that no child must inherit. I have constant attacks of dizziness;
I pretend they come from a surfeit of fruit when I was a child. I had
them in London—there was a great doctor there, Doctor Arbuthnot,
I told him of those attacks of dizziness, I told him of worse things. It
was he who explained.—there is a line of Dryden's. . . . (*In Vanessa's voice.*) O, I know—"Great wits are sure to madness near
allied." If you had children, Jonathan, my blood would make them
healthy. I will take your hand, I will lay it upon my heart—upon the
Vanhomrigh blood that has been healthy for generations. (*Mrs.
Henderson slowly raises her left hand.*) That is the first time you
have touched my body, Jonathan. (*Mrs. Henderson stands up and
remains rigid. In Swift's voice.*) What do I care if it be healthy?
What do I care if it could make mine healthy? Am I to add another
to the healthy rascaldom and knavery of the world? (*In Vanessa's
voice.*) Look at me, Jonathan. Your arrogant intellect separates us.

Give me both your hands. I will put them upon my breast. (*Mrs. Henderson raises her right hand to the level of her left and then raises both to her breast.*) O it is white—white as the gambler's dice—white ivory dice. Think of the uncertainty. Perhaps a mad child—perhaps a rascal—perhaps a knave—perhaps not, Jonathan. The dice of the intellect are loaded, but I am the common ivory dice. (*Her hands are stretched out as though drawing somebody towards her.*) It is not my hands that draw you back. My hands are weak, they could not draw you back if you did not love as I love. You said that you have strong passions; that is true, Jonathan—no man in Ireland is so passionate. That is why you need me, that is why you need children, nobody has greater need. You are growing old. An old man without children is very solitary. Even his friends, men as old as he, turn away, they turn towards the young, their children or their children's children. They cannot endure an old man like themselves. (*Mrs. Henderson moves away from the chair, her movements gradually growing convulsive.*) You are not too old for the dice, Jonathan, but a few years if you turn away will make you an old miserable childless man. (*In Swift's voice.*) O God hear the prayer of Jonathan Swift, that afflicted man, and grant that he may leave to posterity nothing but his intellect that came to him from Heaven. (*In Vanessa's voice.*) Can you face solitude with that mind, Jonathan? (*Mrs. Henderson goes to the door, finds that it is closed.*) Dice, white ivory dice. (*In Swift's voice.*) My God, I am left alone with my enemy. Who locked the door, who locked me in with my enemy? (*Mrs. Henderson beats upon the door, sinks to the floor and then speaks as Lulu.*) Bad old man. Do not let him come back. Bad old man does not know he is dead. Lulu cannot find fathers, mothers, sons that have passed over. Power almost gone. (*Mrs. Mallet leads Mrs. Henderson who seems very exhausted back to her chair. She is still asleep. She speaks again as Lulu.*) Another verse of hymn. Everybody sing. Hymn will bring good influence. (*They sing.*)

> If some poor wandering child of Thine
> Have spurned today the voice divine,
> Now, Lord, the gracious work begin;
> Let him no more lie down in sin.

(*During the hymn Mrs. Henderson has been murmuring "Stella" but the singing has almost drowned her voice. The singers draw one another's attention to the fact that she is speaking. The singing stops.*)

DOCTOR TRENCH   I thought she was speaking.

MRS. MALLET   I saw her lips move.

DOCTOR TRENCH   She would be more comfortable with a cushion but we might wake her.

MRS. MALLET   Nothing can wake her out of a trance like that until she wakes up herself. (*She brings a cushion and she and Doctor Trench put Mrs. Henderson into a more comfortable position.*)

MRS. HENDERSON   (*in Swift's voice*) Stella.

MISS MACKENNA   (*to John Corbet*) Did you hear that? She said Stella.

JOHN CORBET   Vanessa has gone, Stella has taken her place.

MISS MACKENNA   Did you notice the change while we were singing? The new influence in the room?

JOHN CORBET   I thought I did, but it must have been fancy.

MRS. MALLET   Hush!

MRS. HENDERSON   (*in Swift's voice*) Have I wronged you, beloved Stella? Are you unhappy? You have no children, you have no lover, you have no husband. A cross and ageing man for friend—nothing but that. But no, do not answer—you have answered already in that poem you wrote for my last birthday. With what scorn you speak of the common lot of women "with no adornment but a face—

> Before the thirtieth year of life
> A maid forlorn or hated wife."

It is the thought of the great Chrysostom who wrote in a famous passage that women loved according to the soul, loved as saints can love, keep their beauty longer, have greater happiness than women loved according to the flesh. That thought has comforted me, but it is a terrible thing to be responsible for another's happiness. There are moments when I doubt, when I think Chrysostom may have been wrong. But now I have your poem to drive doubt away. You have addressed me in these noble words—

> You taught how I might youth prolong
> By knowing what is right or wrong;
> How from my heart to bring supplies
> Of lustre to my fading eyes;
> How soon a beauteous mind repairs

The loss of chang'd or falling hairs,
How wit and virtue from within
Can spread a smoothness o'er the skin.

JOHN CORBET   The words on the window pane.

MRS. HENDERSON   (*in Swift's voice*) Then, because you understand that I am afraid of solitude, afraid of outliving my friends—and myself—you comfort me in that last verse—you overpraise my moral nature when you attribute to it a rich mantle, but O how touching those words which describe your love—

Late dying may you cast a shred
Of that rich mantle o'er my head;
To bear with dignity my sorrow,
One day alone, then die tomorrow.

Yes, you will close my eyes, Stella, but you will live long after me, dear Stella, for you are still a young woman, but you will close my eyes. (*Mrs. Henderson sinks back in chair and speaks as Lulu.*) Bad old man gone. Power all used up. Lulu can do no more Goodbye, friends. (*Mrs. Henderson speaking in her own voice.*) Go away, go away! (*She wakes.*) I saw him a moment ago, has he spoilt the séance again?

MRS. MALLET   Yes, Mrs. Henderson, my husband came, but he was driven away.

DOCTOR TRENCH   Mrs. Henderson is very tired. We must leave her to rest. (*To Mrs. Henderson.*) You did your best and nobody can do more than that. (*He takes out money.*)

MRS. HENDERSON   No. . . . No. . . . I cannot take any money, not after a séance like that.

DOCTOR TRENCH   Of course you must take it, Mrs. Henderson. (*He puts money on table and Mrs. Henderson gives a furtive glance to see how much it is. She does the same as each sitter lays down his or her money.*)

MRS. MALLET   A bad séance is just as exhausting as a good séance, and you must be paid.

MRS. HENDERSON   No. . . . No. . . . Please don't. It is very wrong to take money for such a failure. (*Mrs. Mallet lays down money.*)

CORNELIUS PATTERSON   A jockey is paid whether he wins or not. (*He lays down money.*)

Miss Mackenna   That spirit rather thrilled me. (*She lays down money.*)

Mrs. Henderson   If you insist, I must take it.

Abraham Johnson   I shall pray for you tonight. I shall ask God to bless and protect your séances. (*He lays down money. All go out except John Corbet and Mrs. Henderson.*)

John Corbet   I know you are tired, Mrs. Henderson, but I must speak to you. I have been deeply moved by what I have heard. This is my contribution to prove that I am satisfied, completely satisfied. (*He puts a note on the table.*)

Mrs. Henderson   A pound note—nobody ever gives me more than ten shillings, and yet the séance was a failure.

John Corbet (*sitting down near Mrs. Henderson*) When I say I am satisfied I do not mean that I am convinced it was the work of spirits. I prefer to think that you created it all, that you are an accomplished actress and scholar. In my essay for my Cambridge doctorate I examine all the explanations of Swift's celibacy offered by his biographers and prove that the explanation you selected was the only plausible one. But there is something I must ask you. Swift was the chief representative of the intellect of his epoch free at last from superstition. He foresaw its collapse. He foresaw democracy, he must have dreaded the future. Did he refuse to beget children because of that dread? Was Swift mad? Or was it the intellect itself that was mad?

Mrs. Henderson   Who are you talking of, sir?

John Corbet   Swift, of course.

Mrs. Henderson   Swift? I do not know anybody called Swift.

John Corbet   Jonathan Swift, whose spirit seemed to be present tonight.

Mrs. Henderson   What? That dirty old man?

John Corbet   He was neither old nor dirty when Stella and Vanessa loved him.

Mrs. Henderson   I saw him very clearly just as I woke up. His clothes were dirty, his face covered with boils. Some disease had made one of his eyes swell up, it stood out from his face like a hen's egg.

John Corbet   He looked like that in his old age. Stella had been dead a long time. His brain had gone, his friends had deserted him. The man appointed to take care of him beat him to keep him quiet.

MRS. HENDERSON   Now they are old, now they are young. They change all in a moment as their thought changes. It is sometimes a terrible thing to be out of the body, God help us all.

DOCTOR TRENCH   (*at doorway*) Come along, Corbet. Mrs. Henderson is tired out.

JOHN CORBET   Good-bye, Mrs. Henderson. (*He goes out with Doctor Trench. All the sitters except Miss Mackenna, who has returned to her room, pass along the passage on their way to the front door. Mrs. Henderson counts the money, finds her purse which is in a vase on the mantelpiece and puts the money in it.*)

MRS. HENDERSON   How tired I am! I'd be the better of a cup of tea. (*She finds the teapot and puts kettle on fire, and then as she crouches down by the hearth suddenly lifts up her hands and counting her fingers, speaks in Swift's voice.*) Five great Ministers that were my friends are gone, ten great Ministers that were my friends are gone. I have not fingers enough to count the great ministers that were my friends and that are gone. (*She wakes with a start and speaks in her own voice.*) Where did I put that tea-caddy? Ah! there it is. And there should be a cup and saucer. (*She finds the saucer.*) But where's the cup? (*She moves aimlessly about the stage and then, letting the saucer fall and break, speaks in Swift's voice.*) Perish the day on which I was born.

.   .
.   .
.   .

If the narrative job is to absorb the reader in a coherent past, drama uses its sensational battery to isolate and intensify those few happenings that are in the act of shaping the crucial future. Dramatic sensation is too intense to last long. Its intensity, rapidity, and powerful sense of immediate consequence compensate for its inability to deal with a complex inner life or with a great variety of scenes, characters, and events. (Its conditions are those of decision-making, and it is perhaps not only the expense of production which locates theater in cities where decision-makers congregate.)

The morphologist must work with the limited material of a script, but he can still remark dramatic condensations, economies of exposition, place, time, and character.

LEAVING THE YELLOW HOUSE

Saul Bellow

The neighbors—there were in all six white people who lived at Sego Desert Lake—told one another that old Hattie could no longer make it alone. The desert life, even with a forced-air furnace in the house and butane gas brought from town in a truck, was still too difficult for her. There were older women in the county. Twenty miles away was Amy Walters, the gold miner's widow. But she was a hardier old girl. Every day of the year she took a bath in the lake. And Amy was crazy about money and knew how to manage it, as Hattie did not. Hattie was not exactly a drunkard, but she hit the bottle pretty hard, and now she was in trouble and there was a limit to the help she could expect from even the best of neighbors.

They were fond of her, though. You couldn't help being fond of Hattie. She was big and cheerful, puffy, comic, boastful, with a big round back and stiff, rather long legs. Before the century began she had graduated from finishing school and studied the organ in Paris. But now she didn't know a note from a skillet; she had tantrums when she played canasta. And all that remained of her fine fair hair was frizzled along her forehead in small grey curls. Her forehead was not much wrinkled, but the skin was bluish, the color of skim milk. She walked with long strides in spite of the heaviness of her hips, pushing on, round-backed, with her shoulders and showing the flat rubber bottoms of her shoes.

Once a week, in the same cheerful, plugging but absent way, she took off her short skirt and the dirty aviator's jacket with the wool collar and put on a girdle, a dress and high-heeled shoes. When she stood on these heels her fat old body trembled. She wore a big brown Rembrandt-like tam with a ten-cent-store brooch, eyelike, carefully centered. She drew a straight line with lipstick on her mouth, leaving part of the upper lip pale. At the wheel of her old turret-shaped car, she drove, seemingly methodical but speeding dangerously, across

228

forty miles of mountainous desert to buy frozen meat pies and whiskey. She went to the Laundromat and the hairdresser, and then had lunch with two Martinis at the Arlington. Afterwards she would often visit Marian Nabot's Silvermine Hotel at Miller Street near skid row and pass the rest of the day gossiping and drinking with her cronies, old divorcées like herself who had settled in the West. Hattie never gambled any more and she didn't care for the movies, and at five o'clock she drove back at the same speed, calmly, partly blinded by the smoke of her cigarette. She was a tough-looking smoker. The fixed cigarette gave her a watering eye.

The Rolfes and the Paces were her only white neighbors at Sego Desert Lake. There was Sam Jervis too, but he was only an old gandy walker who did odd jobs in her garden, and she did not count him. Nor did she count among her neighbors Darly, the dudes' cowboy who worked for the Paces, nor Swede, the telegrapher. Pace had a guest ranch, and Rolfe and his wife were rich and had retired. Thus there were three good houses at the Lake, Hattie's yellow house, Pace's and the Rolfes'. All the rest of the population—Sam, Swede, Watchtah the section foreman, and the Mexicans and Indians and Negroes—lived in shacks and boxcars. You could count all the trees in a minute's time: cottonwoods and box elders. All the rest, down to the shores, was sagebrush and juniper. The lake was what remained of an old sea that had covered the volcanic mountains. To the north there were some tungsten mines; to the south, fifteen miles, was an Indian village built of railroad ties.

In this barren place Hattie had lived for more than twenty years. Her first summer was spent not in a house but in an Indian wikiup on the shore. She used to say that she had watched the stars from this almost roofless shelter. After her divorce she took up with a cowboy named Wicks. Neither of them had any money—it was the Depression—and they had lived on the range, trapping coyotes for a living. Once a month they would come into town and rent a room and go on a bender. Hattie told this sadly, but also gloatingly, and with many trimmings. A thing no sooner happened to her than it was transformed into something else. "We were caught in a storm," she said, "and we rode hard, down to the lake and knocked on the door of the yellow house"—now her house. "Alice Parmenter took us in and let us sleep on the floor." What had actually happened was that the wind was blowing—there had been no storm—and they were not far away

from the house anyway; and Alice Parmenter, who knew that Hattie
and Wicks were not married, offered them separate beds; but Hattie,
swaggering, had said in a loud voice, "Why get two sets of sheets
dirty?" and she and her cowboy had slept in Alice's double bed while
Alice had taken the sofa.

Now Wicks was gone. There was never anybody like him in the
sack; he was brought up in a whorehouse and the girls taught him
everything, said Hattie. She didn't really understand what she was
saying, but believed that she was being Western, and more than
anything else she wanted to be thought of as a rough, experienced
woman of the West. Still, she was a lady, too. She had good silver and
good china and engraved stationery, but she kept canned beans and
A-1 sauce and tunafish and bottles of catsup and fruit salad on the
library shelves of her living room. On the night table was the Bible
her pious brother Angus—her other brother was a heller—had given
her; but behind the little cabinet door was a bottle of bourbon. When
she awoke in the night she tippled herself back to sleep. In the glove
compartment of her old car she kept little sample bottles for
emergencies on the road. Old Darly found them after her accident.

The accident did not happen far out in the desert as she had always
feared, but near her home. She had had a few Martinis with the
Rolfes one evening and as she was driving home over the railroad
crossing she lost control of the car and drove off the crossing onto the
tracks. The explanation she gave was that she had sneezed, and the
sneeze had blinded her and made her twist the wheel. The motor was
killed and all four wheels of the car sat smack on the rails. Hattie
crept down from the door, high off the roadbed. A great fear took
hold of her—for the car, for the future, and not only for the future
but for the past—and she began to hurry on stiff legs through the
sagebrush to Pace's ranch.

Now the Paces were away on a hunting trip and had left old Darly
in charge; he was tending bar in the old cabin that went back to the
days of the pony express when Hattie burst in. There were two customers, a tungsten miner and his girl.

"Darly, I'm in trouble. Help me. I've had an accident," said Hattie.

How the face of a man will alter when a woman has bad news to
tell him! It happened now to lean old Darly; his eyes went flat and
looked unwilling, his jaw moved in and out, his wrinkled cheeks be-

gan to flush, and he said, "What's the matter—what's happened to you now?"

"I'm stuck on the tracks. I sneezed. I lost control of the car. Tow me off, Darly, with the pickup before the train comes."

Darly threw down his towel and stamped his high-heeled boots with anger. "Now what have you gone and done?" he said. "I told you to stay home after dark."

"Where's Pace? Ring the fire bell and fetch Pace."

"There's nobody on the property but me," said the lean old man. "And I'm not supposed to close the bar and you know it as well as I do."

"Please, Darly. I can't leave my car on the tracks."

"Too bad!" he said. Nevertheless he moved from behind the bar. "How did you say it happened?"

"I told you, I sneezed," said Hattie.

Everyone, as she later told it, was as drunk as sixteen thousand dollars: Darly, the miner and the miner's girl.

Darly was limping as he locked the door of the bar. A year before, a kick from one of Pace's mares had broken his ribs as he was loading her into the trailer, and he hadn't recovered from it. He was too old. But he dissembled the pain. The high-heeled narrow boots helped, and his painful bending looked like the ordinary stooping posture of a cowboy on the ground. However, Darly was not a genuine cowboy, like Pace who had grown up in the saddle. He was a late-comer from the East and until the age of forty had never been on horseback. In this respect he and Hattie were alike. They were not the Westerners they seemed to be.

Hattie hurried after him through the ranch yard.

"Damn you!" he said to her, "I got thirty bucks out of that sucker and I would have skinned him out of his whole pay check if you minded your business. Pace is going to be sore as hell."

"You've got to help me. We're neighbors," said Hattie.

"You're not fit to be living out here. You can't do it any more. Besides you're swacked all the time."

Hattie couldn't afford to talk back to him. The thought of her car on the tracks made her frantic. If a freight came now and smashed it, her life at Sego Desert Lake would be finished. And where would she go then? She was not fit to live in this place. She had never made the grade at all; she only seemed to have made it. And Darly—why did he say such hurtful things to her? Because he himself was sixty-eight years old, and he had no other place to go, either; he took bad treatment from Pace besides. Darly stayed because his only alternative was to go to the soldier's home. Moreover, the dude women would crawl into his sack. They wanted a cowboy and they thought he was one. Why, he couldn't even raise himself out of his bunk in the morning. And where else would he get women? "After the season," she wanted to say to him, "you always have to go to the Veterans' Hospital to get yourself fixed up again." But she didn't dare offend him now.

The moon was due to rise. It appeared as they drove over the un-graded dirt road toward the crossing where Hattie's turret-shaped car was sitting on the rails. At great speed Darly wheeled the pickup around, spraying dirt on the miner and his girl who had followed in their car.

"You get behind the wheel and steer," Darly told Hattie.

She climbed into the seat. Waiting at the wheel she lifted up her face and said, "Please, God, I didn't bend the axle or crack the oil pan."

When Darly crawled under the bumper of Hattie's car the pain in his ribs suddenly cut off his breath, so instead of doubling the tow chain he fastened it at full length. He rose and trotted back to the truck on the narrow boots. Motion seemed the only remedy for the pain; not even booze did the trick any more. He put the pickup into towing gear and began to pull. One side of Hattie's car dropped into the roadbed with a heave of springs. She sat with a stormy, frightened, conscience-stricken face, racing the motor until she flooded it.

The tungsten miner yelled, "Your chain's too long."

Hattie was raised high in the air by the pitch of the wheels. She had to roll down the window to let herself out because the door handle had been jammed from the inside for years. Hattie struggled out on the uplifted side crying, "I better call the Swede. I better have him signal. There's a train due."

"Go on, then," said Darly. "You're no good here."

"Darly, be careful with my car. Be careful."

The ancient sea bed at this place was flat and low and the lights of her car and of the truck and of the tungsten miner's Chevrolet were bright and big at twenty miles. Hattie was too frightened to think of this. All she could think was that she was a procrastinating old woman; she had lived by delays; she had meant to stop drinking, she had put off the time, and now she had smashed her car—a terrible end, a terrible judgment on her. She got to the ground and, drawing up her skirt, she started to get over the tow chain. To prove that the chain didn't have to be shortened, and to get the whole thing over with, Darly threw the pickup forward again. The chain jerked up and struck Hattie in the knee and she fell forward and broke her arm.

She cried, "Darly, Darly, I'm hurt. I fell."

"The old lady tripped on the chain," said the miner. "Back up here and I'll double it for you. You're getting nowheres."

Drunkenly the miner lay down on his back in the dark, soft red cinders of the roadbed. Darly had backed up to slacken the chain.

Darly hurt the miner, too. He tore some skin from his fingers by racing ahead before the chain was secure. Uncomplainingly the miner wrapped his hand in his shirttail saying, "She'll do it now." The old car came down from the tracks and stood on the shoulder of the road.

"There's your goddam car," said Darly to Hattie.

"Is it all right?" she said. Her left side was covered with dirt, but she managed to pick herself up and stand, round-backed and heavy, on her stiff legs. "I'm hurt, Darly." She tried to convince him of it.

"Hell if you are," he said. He believed she was putting on an act to escape blame. The pain in his ribs made him especially impatient with her. "Christ, if you can't look after yourself any more you've got no business out here."

"You're old yourself," she said. "Look what you did to me. You can't hold your liquor."

This offended him greatly. He said, "I'll take you to the Rolfes. They let you tie this on in the first place, so let them worry about you. I'm tired of your bunk, Hattie."

He speeded up. Chains, spade and crowbar clashed on the sides of the truck. She was frightened and held her arm and cried. Rolfe's dogs jumped at her to lick her when she went through the gate. She shrank from them crying, "Down, down."

"Darly," she cried in the darkness, "take care of my car. Don't leave it standing there on the road. Darly, take care of it, please."

But Darly in his ten-gallon hat, his chin-bent face wrinkled, small and angry, a furious pain in his ribs, tore away at high speed.

"Oh, God, what will I do," she said.

The Rolfes were having a last drink before dinner, sitting at their fire of pitchy railroad ties, when Hattie opened the door. Her knee was bleeding, her eyes were tiny with shock, her face grey with dust.

"I'm hurt," she said desperately. "I had an accident. I sneezed and lost control of the wheel. Jerry, look after the car. It's on the road."

They bandaged her knee and took her home and put her to bed. Helen Rolfe wrapped a heating pad around her arm.

"I can't have the pad," Hattie complained. "The switch goes on and off and every time it does it starts my generator and uses up the gas."

"Ah, now, Hattie," Rolfe said, "this is not the time to be stingy. We'll take you to town in the morning and have you looked over. Helen will phone Doctor Stroud."

Hattie wanted to say, "Stingy! Why you're the stingy ones. I just haven't got anything. You and Helen are ready to hit each other over two bits in canasta." But the Rolfes were good to her; they were her only real friends here. Darly would have let her lie in the yard all night, and Pace would sell her to the bone man if he had an offer.

So she didn't talk back to the Rolfes, but as soon as they left the yellow house and walked through the super-clear moonlight under the great skirt of branch shadows to their new car, Hattie turned off the switch and the heavy swirling and battering of the generator stopped. Presently she began to have her first real taste of the pain in her arm, and she sat rigid and warmed the injured place with her hand. It seemed to her that she could feel the bone. Before leaving, Helen Rolfe had thrown over her a comforter that had belonged to Hattie's dead friend India, from whom she had inherited the small house and everything in it. Had the comforter lain on India's bed the night she died? Hattie tried to remember, but her thoughts were mixed up. She was fairly sure the death-bed pillow was in the loft, and she believed she had put the rest of the bedding in a trunk. Then how had this comforter got out? She couldn't do anything about it now but draw it away from contact with her skin. It kept her legs warm; this she accepted, but she didn't want it any nearer.

More and more Hattie saw her own life as though from birth to the present every moment had been filmed. Her fancy was that when she died she would see the film shown. Then she would know how she appeared from the back, watering the plants, in the bathroom, asleep, playing the organ, embracing—everything, even tonight, in pain, almost the last pain, perhaps, for she couldn't take much more. How many more turns had life to show her yet? There couldn't be a lot. To lie awake and think such thoughts was the worst thing in the world. Better death than insomnia. Hattie not only loved sleep, she believed in it.

The first attempt to set the bone was not successful. "Look what they've done to me," said Hattie and showed the discolored skin on her breast. After the second operation her mind wandered. The sides of her bed had to be raised, for in her delirium she roamed the wards. She cried at the nurses when they shut her in, "You can't make people prisoners in a democracy without a trial." She cursed them fiercely.

For several weeks her mind was not clear. Asleep, her face was lifeless; her cheeks were puffed out and her mouth, no longer wide and grinning, was drawn round and small. Helen sighed when she saw her.

"Shall we get in touch with her family?" she asked the doctor. "She has a brother in Maine who is very strait-laced. And another one down in Mexico, even older than Hattie."

"No younger relations?" asked the doctor. His skin was white and thick. He had chestnut hair, abundant but very dry. He sometimes explained to his patients, "I had a tropical disease during the war."

"Cousins' children," said Helen. She tried to think who would be called to her own bedside. Rolfe would see that she was cared for. He would hire a nurse. Hattie could not afford one. She had already gone beyond her means. A trust company in Philadelphia paid her eighty dollars a month. She had a small bank account.

"I suppose it will be up to us to get her out of hock," said Rolfe. "Unless the brother down in Mexico comes across."

In the end, no relations had to be called. Hattie began to recover. At last she could recognize some of her friends, though her mind was still in disorder; much that had happened she couldn't recall.

"How much blood did they have to give me," she kept asking. "I seem to remember five, six, eight different times. Daylight, electric light . . ." She tried to smile, but she couldn't make a pleasant face as yet. "How am I going to pay?" she said. "At twenty-five bucks a quart. My little bit of money is just about wiped out."

Blood became her constant topic, her preoccupation. She told everyone who came to see her, "—have to replace all that blood. They poured gallons of the stuff into me. I hope it was all good." And, though very weak, she began to grin and laugh again. There was more of a hiss in her laughter than formerly; the illness had affected her chest.

"No cigarettes, no booze," the doctor told Helen.

"Doctor," Helen asked him, "do you expect her to change?"

"All the same, I am obliged to say it."

"Life may not be much of a temptation to her," said Helen.

Her husband laughed. When his laughter was intense it blinded one of his eyes and his short Irish face turned red except for the bridge of his small, sharp nose where the skin grew white. "Hattie's like me," he said. "She'll be in business till she's cleaned out. And if Sego Lake was all whiskey she'd use her last strength to knock her old yellow house down and build a raft of it. So why talk temperance to her now?"

Hattie recognized the similarity between them. When he came to see her she said, "Jerry, you're the only one I can really talk to about my troubles. What am I going to do for money? I have Hotchkiss Insurance. I paid eight dollars a month."

"That won't do you much good, Hat. No Blue Cross?"

"I let it drop ten years ago. Maybe I could sell some of my valuables."

"What have you got?" he said. His eye began to droop with laughter.

"Why," she said defiantly, "there's plenty. First there's the beautiful, precious Persian rug that India left me."

"Coals from the fireplace have been burning it for years, Hat!"

"The rug is in perfect condition," she said with an angry sway of her shoulders. "A beautiful object like that never loses its value. And the oak table from the Spanish monastery is three hundred years old."

"With luck you could get twenty bucks for it. It would cost fifty to haul it out of here. It's the house you ought to sell."

"The house?" she said. Yes, that had been in her mind. "I'd have to get twenty thousand for it."

"Eight is a fair price."

"Fifteen. . . ." She was offended, and her voice recovered its strength. "India put eight into it in two years. And don't forget that Sego Lake is one of the most beautiful places in the world."

"But where is it? Five hundred and some miles to San Francisco and two hundred to Salt Lake City. Who wants to live way out here in Utah but a few eccentrics like you and India and me?"

"There are things you can't put a price tag on. Beautiful things."

"Oh, bull, Hattie! You don't know what they are any more than I do. I live here because it figures for me, and you because India left you the house. And just in the nick of time, too. Without it you wouldn't have had a pot of your own."

His words offended Hattie; more than that, they frightened her. She was silent and then grew thoughtful, for she was fond of Jerry Rolfe and he of her. He had good sense and moreover he only spoke her own thoughts. He spoke no more than the truth about India's death and the house. But she told herself, *He doesn't know every-thing. You'd have to pay a San Francisco architect ten thousand just to think of such a house. Before he drew a line.*

"Jerry," the old woman said, "what am I going to do about replacing the blood in the blood bank?"

"Do you want a quart from me, Hat?" His eye began to fall shut.

"You won't do. You had that tumor, two years ago. I think Darly ought to give some."

"The old man?" Rolfe laughed at her. "You want to kill him?"

"Why," said Hattie with anger, lifting up her massive face with its fringe of curls which had become frayed by fever and perspiration; at the back of her head the hair had knotted and matted so that it had to be shaved, "he almost killed me. It's his fault that I'm in this condition. He must have blood in him. He runs after all the chicks—all of them—young and old."

"Come, you were drunk, too," said Rolfe.

"I've driven drunk for forty years. It was the sneeze. Oh, Jerry, I feel wrung out," said Hattie, haggard, sitting forward in bed. But her face was cleft by her nonsensically happy grin. She was not one to be miserable for long; she had the expression of a perennial survivor.

Every other day she went to the therapist. The young woman worked her arm for her; it was a pleasure and a comfort to Hattie, who would have been glad to leave the whole cure to her. However, she was given other exercises to do, and these were not so easy. They rigged a pulley for her and Hattie had to hold both ends of a rope and saw it back and forth through the scraping little wheel. She bent heavily from the hips and coughed over her cigarette. But the most important exercise of all she shirked. This required her to put the flat of her hand to the wall at the level of her hips and, by working her fingertips slowly, to make the hand ascend to the height of her shoulder. That was painful; she often forgot to do it, although the doctor warned her, "Hattie, you don't want adhesions, do you?"

A light of despair crossed Hattie's eyes. Then she said, "Oh, Dr. Stroud, buy my house from me."

"I'm a bachelor. What would I do with a house?"

"I know just the girl for you—my cousin's daughter. Perfectly charming and very brainy. Just about got her Ph.D."

"You must get quite a few proposals yourself," said the doctor.

"From crazy desert rats. They chase me. But," she said, "after I pay my bills I'll be in pretty punk shape. If at least I could replace that blood in the blood bank I'd feel easier."

"If you don't do as the therapist tells you, Hattie, you'll need another operation. Do you know what adhesions are?"

She knew. But Hattie thought, *How long must I go on taking care of myself?* It made her angry to hear him speak of another operation. She had a moment of panic, but she veiled it from him. With him, this young man whose skin was already as thick as buttermilk and whose chestnut hair was as dry as death, she always assumed the part of a small child. She said, "Yes, doctor." But her heart was in a fury.

Night and day, however, she repeated, "I was in the Valley of the Shadow. But I'm alive." She was weak, she was old, she couldn't follow a train of thought very easily, she felt faint in the head. But she was still here; here was her body, it filled space, a great body. And though she had worries and perplexities, and once in a while her arm felt as though it was about to give her the last stab of all; and though her hair was scrappy and old, like onion roots, and scattered like nothing under the comb, yet she sat and amused herself with visitors; her great grin split her face; her heart warmed with every kind word.

And she thought, "People will help me out. It never did me any good to worry. At the last minute something turned up, when I wasn't looking for it. Marian loves me. Helen and Jerry love me. Half Pint loves me. They would never let me go to the ground. And I love them. If it were the other way around, I'd never let them go down."

Above a horizon in a baggy vastness which Hattie by herself occasionally visited, the features of India, or her shade, sometimes rose. She was indignant and scolding. Not mean. Not really mean. Few people had ever been really mean to Hattie. But India was annoyed with her. "The garden is going to hell, Hattie," she said. "Those lilac bushes are all shriveled."

"But what can I do? The hose is rotten. It broke. It won't reach."

"Then dig a trench," said the phantom of India. "Have old Sam dig a trench. But save the bushes."

Am I thy servant still? said Hattie to herself. *No*, she thought, *let the dead bury their dead.*

But she didn't defy India now any more than she had done when they lived together. Hattie was supposed to keep India off the bottle, but often both of them began to get drunk after breakfast. They forgot to dress, and in their slips the two of them wandered drunkenly around the house and blundered into each other, and they were in despair at having been so weak. Late in the afternoon they would be sitting in the living room, waiting for the sun to set. It shrank, burning itself out on the crumbling edges of the mountains. When the sun passed, the fury of the daylight ended and the moutain surfaces were more blue, broken, like cliffs of coal. They no longer suggested faces. The east began to look simple, and the lake less inhuman and haughty. At last India would say, "Hattie—it's time for the lights." And Hattie would pull the switch chains of the lamps, several of them, to give the generator a good shove. She would turn on some of the wobbling eighteenth-century-style lamps whose shades stood out from their slender bodies like dragonflies' wings. The little engine in the shed would shuffle, then spit, then charge and bang, and the first weak light would rise unevenly in the bulbs.

"*Hettie!*" cried India. After she drank she was penitent, but her penitence too was a hardship to Hattie, and the worse her temper the more English her accent became. "*Where the hell ah you Het-tie!*" After India's death Hattie found some poems she had written in which she, Hattie, was affectionately and even touchingly mentioned. But Hattie's interest in ideas was very small, whereas India had been all over the world and was used to brilliant society. India wanted her to discuss Eastern religion, Bergson and Proust, and Hattie had no head for this, and so India blamed her drinking on Hattie. "I can't talk to you," she would say. "And I'm here because I'm not fit to be anywhere else. I can't live in New York any more. It's too dangerous for a woman my age to be drunk in the street at night."

And Hattie, talking to her Western friends about India, would say, "She is a lady" (implying that they made a pair). "She is a creative person" (this was why they found each other so congenial). "But helpless? Completely. Why she can't even get her own girdle on."

"Hettie! come here. Het-tie! Do you know what sloth is?"

Undressed, India sat on her bed and with the cigarette in her drunken, wrinkled, ringed hand she burned holes in the blankets. On Hattie's pride she left many small scars, too. She treated her like a servant.

Weeping, India begged her afterward to forgive her. *"Hattie, please, don't condemn me in your heart. Forgive me, dear, I know I am bad. But I hurt myself more in my evil than I hurt you."*

Hattie would keep a stiff bearing. She would lift up her face with its incurved nose and puffy eyes, and say, "I am a Christian person. I never bear a grudge." And by repeating this she actually brought herself to forgive India.

But of course she had no husband, no child, no skill, no savings. And what she would have done if India had not died and left her the yellow house, nobody knows.

Jerry Rolfe said privately to Marian, "Hattie can't do anything for herself. If I hadn't been around during the '44 blizzard she and India both would have starved. She's always been careless and lazy and now she can't even chase a cow out of her yard. She's too feeble. The thing for her to do is go East to her brother. Hattie would have ended at the poor farm if it hadn't been for India. But India should have left her something besides the house. Some dough. India didn't use her head."

When Hattie returned to the lake she stayed with the Rolfes. "Well, old shellback," said Jerry, "there's a little more life in you now."

Indeed, with joyous eyes, the cigarette in her mouth and her hair newly frizzed and overhanging her forehead, she seemed to have triumphed again. She was pale, but she grinned, she chuckled, and she held a bourbon Old-Fashioned with a cherry and a slice of orange in it. She was on rations; the Rolfes allowed her two a day. Her back, Helen noted, was more bent than before. Her knees went outward a little weakly; her feet, however, came close together at the ankles.

"Oh, Helen dear and Jerry dear, I am so thankful, so glad to be back at the lake. I can look after my place again, and I'm here to see the spring. It's more gorgeous than ever."

Heavy rains had fallen while Hattie was away. The Sego lilies, which bloomed only after a wet winter, came up from the loose dust, especially around the marl pit; but even on the burnt granite they seemed to grow. Desert peach was beginning to appear and in Hattie's yard the rosebushes were filling out. The roses were yellow and abundant, and the odor they gave off was like that of damp tea leaves.

"Before it gets hot enough for the rattlesnakes," said Hattie to Helen, "we ought to drive up to Marky's ranch to cut watercress."

Hattie was going to attend to lots of things, but the heat came early that year and, as there was no television to keep her awake, she slept most of the day. She was now able to dress herself, though there was little more that she could do. Sam Jervis rigged the pulley for her on the porch and she remembered once in a while to use it. Mornings when she had her strength she rambled over to her own house, examining things, behaving importantly and giving orders to Sam Jervis and Wanda Gingham. At ninety, Wanda, a Shoshone, was still an excellent seamstress and housecleaner.

Hattie looked over the car, which was parked under a cottonwood tree. She tested the engine. Yes, the old pot would still go. Proudly, happily, she listened to the noise of tappets; the dry old pipe shook as the smoke went out at the rear. She tried to work the shift, turn the wheel. That, as yet, she couldn't do. But it would come soon, she was confident.

At the back of the house the soil had caved in a little over the cesspool and a few of the old railroad ties over the top had rotted. Otherwise things were in good shape. Sam had looked after the garden. He had fixed a new catch for the gate after Pace's horses—maybe because he never could afford to keep them in hay—had broken in and Sam found them grazing and drove them out. Luckily they hadn't damaged many of her plants. Hattie felt a moment of wild rage against Pace. He had brought the horses into her garden, she was sure. But her anger didn't last long. It was reabsorbed into the feeling of golden pleasure that enveloped her. She had little strength, but all that she had was a pleasure to her. So she forgave even Pace, who would have liked to do her out of the house, who had always used her, embarrassed her, cheated her at cards, passed the buck whenever he could. He was a fool about horses. They were ruining him. Breeding horses was a millionaire's amusement.

She saw the animals in the distance, feeding. Unsaddled, the mares appeared undressed; they reminded her of naked women walking with their glossy flanks in the Sego lilies which curled on the ground. The flowers were yellowish, like winter wool, but fragrant; the mares, naked and gentle, walked through them. Their strolling, their perfect beauty, the sound of their hoofs on stone touched a deep place in Hattie's nature. Her love for horses, birds and dogs was well-known. Dogs led the list. And now a piece cut from a green blanket reminded her of Richie. The blanket was one he had torn, and she had cut it into strips and placed them under the doors to keep out the draughts. In the house she found more traces of him: hair he had shed on the furniture. Hattie was going to borrow Helen's vacuum cleaner, but there wasn't really enough current to make it pull as it should. On the doorknob of India's room hung the dog collar.

Hattie had decided to have herself moved into India's bed when she lay dying. Why use two beds? A perilous look came into her eyes while her lips pressed together forbiddingly. "I follow," she said, speaking to India with an inner voice, "so never mind." Presently—before long—she would have to leave the yellow house in her turn. And as she went into the parlor thinking of the will, she sighed. Pretty soon she would have to attend to it. India's lawyer, Claiborne, helped her with such things. She had phoned him in town, while she was staying with Marian, and talked matters over with him. He had promised to try to sell the house for her. Fifteen thousand was her bottom price, she said. If he couldn't find a buyer, perhaps he could find a tenant. Two hundred dollars a month was the rental she set. Rolfe laughed. But Hattie turned toward him one of those proud, dulled looks she always took on when he angered her and said haughtily, "For summer on Sego Lake?"

"You're competing with Pace's ranch."

"Why, the food is stinking down there. He cheats the dudes," said Hattie. "He really cheats them at cards. You'll never catch me playing blackjack with him again."

And what would she do, thought Hattie, if Claiborne could neither rent nor sell the house? This question she shook off as regularly as it returned. *I don't have to be a burden on anybody*, thought Hattie. *It's looked bad many a time before, but when push came to shove, I made it. Somehow I got by.* But she argued with herself. *How many times? How long, O God—an old thing, feeble, no use to anyone?* Who said she had any right to hold a piece of property?

She was sitting on her sofa which was very old, India's sofa, eight feet long, kidney-shaped, puffy and bald. An underlying pink shone through the green; the upholstered tufts were like the pads of dogs' paws; between them rose bunches of hair. Here Hattie slouched, resting, with her knees wide apart and a cigarette in her mouth, eyes half shut but far-seeing. The mountains seemed not fifteen miles but fifteen hundred yards away, the lake a blue band; the tea-like odor of the roses, though they were still unopened, was already in the air, for Sam was watering them in the heat. Gratefully Hattie yelled, "Sam!"

Sam was very old, and all shanks. His feet looked big. His old railroad jacket was made tight across his back by his stoop. A crooked finger with its great broad nail over the mouth of the hose made the water spray and sparkle. Happy to see Hattie he turned his long jaw, empty of teeth, and his blue eyes, which seemed to penetrate his temples with their length (it was his face that turned, not his body), and he said, "Oh, there, Hattie. You've made it back today? Welcome, Hattie."

"Have a beer, Sam. Come around the back and I'll give you a beer."

She never had Sam come in, owing to his skin disease. There were raw patches on his chin and the back of his ears. Hattie feared infection from his touch. She gave him the beer can, never a glass, and she put on gloves before she used the garden tools. Since he would take no money from her—she had to pay Wanda Gingham a dollar a day—she got Marian to find old clothes for him in town and she left food for him at the door of the damp-wood-smelling boxcar where he lived.

"How's the old wing, Hat?" he said.

"It's coming. I'll be driving again before you know it," she told him. "By the first of May I'll be driving again." Every week she moved the date forward. "By Decoration Day I expect to be on my

own again," she said. In mid-June however she was still unable to
drive. Helen Rolfe said to her, "Hattie, Jerry and I are due in Seattle
the first week of July."

"Why, you never told me that," said Hattie.

"You don't mean to tell me this is the first you heard of it," said
Helen. "You've known about it from the first—since Christmas."

It wasn't easy for Hattie to meet her eyes. She presently put her
head down. Her face became very dry, especially the lips. "Well,
don't you worry about me. I'll be all right here," she said.

"Who's going to look after you?" said Jerry. He evaded nothing
himself and tolerated very little evasion in others. Except, as Hattie
knew, he always indulged her. She couldn't count on her friend Half
Pint, she couldn't really count on Marian either. Until now, this very
moment, she had only the Rolfes to turn to. Helen, trying to be
steady, gazed at her and made sad, involuntary movements with her
head, sometimes nodding, sometimes seeming as if she disagreed.
Hattie, with her inner voice, swore at her: *Bitch-eyes. I can't win
because I'm old. Is that fair?* And yet she admired Helen's eyes. Even
the skin about them, slightly wrinkled underneath, was touching,
beautiful. There was a heaviness in her bust that went, as if by
attachment, with the heaviness of her eyes. Her head, her hands and
feet should have taken a more slender body. Helen, said Hattie, was
the nearest thing she had on this earth to a sister. But there was no
reason to go to Seattle—no genuine business. It was only idleness,
only a holiday. The only reason was Hattie herself; this was their way
of telling her that there was a limit to what she could expect them to
do. Helen's head wavered, but her thoughts were steady; she knew
what was passing through Hattie's mind. Like Hattie, she was an idle
woman. Why was her right to idleness better?

Because of money? thought Hattie. Because of age? Because she
has a husband? Because she had a daughter in Swarthmore College?
But a funny thing occurred to her. Helen disliked being idle, whereas
she herself never made any bones that an idle life was all she was ever
good for. But for her it was uphill, all the way, because when
Waggoner divorced her she didn't have a cent. She even had to
support Wicks for seven or eight years. Except with horses, he had no
sense. And then she had to take a ton of dirt from India. *I am the
one,* Hattie asserted to herself. *I would know what to do with Helen's
advantages. She only suffers from them. And if she wants to stop*

being an idle woman why can't she start with me, her neighbor? Her skin, for all its puffiness, burned with anger. She said to Rolfe and Helen: "Don't worry. I'll make out by myself. But if I have to leave the lake you'll be ten times more lonely than before. Now I'm going back to my house."

She lifted up her broad old face and her lips were childlike with suffering. She would never take back what she had said.

But the trouble was no ordinary trouble. Hattie was herself aware that she rambled, forgot names, and answered when no one spoke.

"We can't just take charge of her," Rolfe said. "What's more, she ought to be near a doctor. She keeps her shotgun loaded so she can fire it if anything happens to her in the house. But who knows what she'll do? I don't believe it was Jacamares who killed that Doberman of hers."

He drove into her yard the day after she returned to her house and said, "I'm going into town. I can bring you some chow if you like"

She couldn't afford to refuse his offer, angry though she was, and she said, "Yes, bring me some stuff from the Mountain Street Market. Charge it." She only had some frozen shrimp and a few cans of beer in the icebox. When Rolfe had gone she put out the shrimp to thaw.

People really used to stick by one another in the West. Hattie now saw herself as one of the pioneers. This modern race had come later. After all, she had lived on the range like an old-timer. Wicks had had to shoot their Christmas dinner and she had cooked it—venison. He killed it on the reservation, and if the Paiutes had caught them there would have been hell to pay.

The weather was hot, the clouds were heavy and calm in a large sky. The horizon was so huge that in it the lake must have seemed like a saucer of milk. *Some milk!* Hattie thought. Two thousand feet deep in the middle, so deep no body could ever be recovered. It went around with the currents, and there were rocks like eyeteeth, and hot springs, and colorless fish at the bottom which were never caught. Now that the white pelicans were nesting they patrolled the rocks for snakes and other egg thieves. They were so big and flew so slow you might imagine they were angels. Hattie no longer visited the lake shore; the walk exhausted her. She saved her strength to go to Pace's bar in the afternoon.

She took off her shoes and stockings and walked on bare feet from

one end of her house to the other. On the land side she saw Wanda
Gingham sitting near the tracks while her great-grandson played in
the soft red gravel. Wanda wore a large purple shawl and her black
head was bare. All about her was—was nothing, Hattie thought; for
she had taken a drink, breaking her rule. Nothing but mountains,
thrust out like men's bodies; the sagebrush was the hair on their
chests.

The warm wind blew dust from the marl pit. This white powder
made her sky less blue. On the water side were the pelicans, pure as
spirits, slow as angels, blessing the air as they flew with great wings.

Should she or should she not have Sam do something about the
vine on the chimney? Sparrows nested in it, and she was glad of that.
But all summer long the king snakes were after them and she was
afraid to walk in the garden. When the sparrows scratched the ground
for seed they took a funny bound; they held their legs stiff and flung
back the dust with both feet. Hattie sat down at her old Spanish
table, watching them in the cloudy warmth of the day, clasping her
hands, chuckling and sad. The bushes were crowded with yellow
roses, half of them now rotted. The lizards scrambled from shadow to
shadow. The water was smooth as air, gaudy as silk. The mountains
succumbed, falling asleep in the heat. Drowsy, Hattie lay down on her
sofa; its pads were like dogs' paws. She gave in to sleep and when she
woke it was midnight; she did not want to alarm the Rolfes by
putting on her lights, so took advantage of the moon to eat a few
thawed shrimps and go to the bathroom. She undressed and lifted
herself into bed and lay there feeling her sore arm. Now she knew
how much she missed her dog. The whole matter of the dog weighed
heavily on her soul; she came close to tears in thinking about him and
she went to sleep, oppressed by her secret.

I suppose I had better try to pull myself together a little, thought
Hattie nervously in the morning. *I can't just sleep my way through.*
She knew what her difficulty was. Before any serious question her
mind gave way; it became diffused. She said to herself, *I can see
bright, but I feel dim. I guess I'm not so lively any more. Maybe I'm
becoming a little touched in the head, as mother was.* But she was not
so old as her mother was when she did those strange things. At eighty-
five her mother had to be kept from going naked in the street. *I'm not
as bad as that yet*, thought Hattie. *Thank God. I walked into the
men's wards, but that was when I had a fever, and my nightie was
on.*

She drank a cup of Nescafé and it strengthened her determination to do something for herself. In all the world she had only her brother Angus to go to. Her brother Will had led a rough life; he was an old heller, and now he drove everyone away. He was too crabby, thought Hattie. Besides he was angry because she had lived so long with Wicks. Angus would forgive her. But then he and his wife were not her kind. With them she couldn't drink, she couldn't smoke, she had to make herself small-mouthed, and she would have to wait while they read a chapter of the Bible before breakfast. Hattie could not bear to wait for meals. Besides, she had a house of her own at last; why should she have to leave it? She had never owned a thing before. And now she was not allowed to enjoy her yellow house. *But I'll keep it*, she said to herself rebelliously. *I swear to God I'll keep it. Why, I barely just got it. I haven't had time.* And she went out on the porch to work the pulley and do something about the adhesions in her arm. She was sure now that they were there. *And what will I do?* she cried to herself. *What will I do? Why did I ever go to Rolfe's that night— and why did I lose control on the crossing!* She couldn't say now "I sneezed." She couldn't even remember what had happened, except that she saw the boulders and the twisting blue rails and Darly. It was Darly's fault. He was sick and old himself, and couldn't make it. He envied her the house, and her woman's peaceful life. Since she returned from the hospital he hadn't even come to visit her. He only said, "Hell, I'm sorry for her, but it was her fault." What hurt him most was that she said he couldn't hold his liquor.

Her resolve to pull herself together did not last; she remained the same procrastinating old woman. She had a letter to answer from Hotchkiss Insurance, and it drifted out of sight. She was going to phone Claiborne the lawyer, and it slipped her mind. One morning she announced to Helen that she believed she would apply to an institution in Los Angeles that took over the property of old people and managed it for them. They gave you an apartment right on the ocean, and your meals and medical care. You had to sign over half of your estate. "It's fair enough," said Hattie. "They take a gamble. I may live to be a hundred."

"I wouldn't be surprised," said Helen.

However, Hattie never got around to sending to Los Angeles for the brochure. But Jerry Rolfe took it on himself to write a letter to her brother Angus about her condition. And he drove over also to have a talk with Amy Walters, the gold miner's widow at Fort Walters—as the ancient woman called it. One old tar-paper building was what she owned, plus the mine shafts, no longer in use since the death of her second husband. On a heap of stones near the road a crimson sign *Fort Walters* was placed, and over it a flagpole. The American flag was raised every day. Amy was working in the garden in one of dead Bill's shirts. He had brought water down from the mountains for her in a homemade aqueduct so she could raise her own peaches and vegetables.

"Amy," Rolfe said, "Hattie's back from the hospital and living all alone. You have no folks and neither has she. Not to beat around the bush about it, why don't you live together?"

Amy's face had great delicacy. Her winter baths in the lake and her soups and the waltzes she played for herself alone on the grand piano that stood beside her wood stove and the murder stories she read till darkness made her go to bed had made her remote. She looked delicate, yet her composure couldn't be touched. It was very strange.

"Hattie and me have different habits, Jerry," said Amy. "And Hattie wouldn't like my company. I can't drink with her."

"That's true," said Rolfe, recalling that Hattie referred to Amy as though she were a ghost. He couldn't speak to Amy of the solitary death that was in store for her. There was not a cloud in the arid sky today, and there was not a shadow of death on Amy. She was tranquil, she seemed to be supplied with a sort of pure fluid that would feed her life slowly for years to come.

He said, "All kinds of things could happen to a woman like Hattie in that yellow house, and nobody would know."

"That's a fact. She doesn't know how to take care of herself."

"She can't. Her arm hasn't healed."

Amy didn't say that she was sorry to hear it. In the place of those words came a silence which could have meant that. Then she said, "I might go for a few hours a day, but she would have to pay me."

"Now, Amy, you must know as well as I do that Hattie has never had any money—not much more than her pension. Just the house."

At once Amy said, no pause coming between his words and hers, "I would take care of her if she'd agree to leave the house to me."

"Leave it in your hands, you mean?" said Rolfe. "To manage?"

"In her will. To belong to me."

"Why, Amy, what would you do with Hattie's house?" he said.

"It would be my property, that's all. I'd have it."

"Maybe you would leave Fort Walters to her in your will," he said.

"Oh, no," she answered quickly. "Why should I do that? I'm not asking Hattie for her help. I don't need it. Hattie is a city woman."

Rolfe could not carry this proposal back to Hattie. He was too wise ever to mention her will to her.

But Pace was not so careful of her feelings. By mid-June Hattie had begun to visit the bar regularly. She had so many things to think about she couldn't keep herself at home. When Pace came in from the yard one day—he had been packing the axles of his horse-trailer and was wiping grease from his fingers—he said with his usual bluntness, "How would you like it if I paid you fifty bucks a month for the rest of your life, Hat?"

Hattie was holding her second Old-Fashioned of the day. At the bar she made it appear that she observed the limit; but she had started drinking at home after lunch. She began to grin, expecting Pace to make one of his jokes. But he was wearing his scoop-shaped Western hat as level as a Quaker, and he had drawn down his chin, a sign that he was not fooling. She said, "That would be nice, but what's the catch?"

"No catch," he said. "This is what we'd do. I'd give you five hundred dollars cash, and fifty bucks a month for life, and you'd let me put some dudes in the yellow house, and you'd leave the house to me in your will."

"What kind of a deal is that?" said Hattie, her look changing. "I thought we were friends."

"It's the best deal you'll ever get," he said.

The day was sultry, but Hattie till now had thought that it was nice, that she was dreamy, but comfortable, about to begin to enjoy the cool of the day; but now she felt that such cruelty and injustice had been waiting to attack her, that it would have been better to die in the hospital than be so disillusioned.

She cried, "Everybody wants to push me out. You're a cheater, Pace. God! I know you. Pick on somebody else. Why do you have to pick on me? Just because I happen to be around?"

"Why, no, Hattie," he said, trying now to be careful. "It was just a business offer."

"Why don't you give me some blood for the bank if you're such a friend of mine?"

"Well, Hattie, you drink too much, and you oughtn't have been driving anyway."

"The whole thing happened because I sneezed. Everybody knows it. I wouldn't sell you my house. I'd give it away to the lepers first. You'd let me go and then never send me a cent. You never pay anybody. You can't even buy wholesale in town any more because nobody trusts you. It looks as though I'm stuck, that's all, just stuck. I keep on saying that this is my only home in all the world, this is where my friends are, and the weather is always perfect and the lake is beautiful. I wish the whole damn empty old place were in Hell. It's not human and neither are you. But I'll be here the day the sheriff takes your horses—you never mind."

He told her then that she was drunk again, and so she was, but she was more than that, and though her head was spinning she decided to go back to the house at once and take care of some things she had been putting off. This very day she was going to write to the lawyer, Claiborne, and make sure that Pace never got her property. She wouldn't put it past him to swear in court that India had promised him the yellow house.

She sat at the table with pen and paper, trying to think how to put it.

"I want this on record," she wrote. "I could kick myself in the head when I think how he's led me on. I have been his patsy ten thousand times. As when that drunk crashed his Cub plane on the lake shore. At the coroner's jury he let me take the whole blame. He had instructed me when I was working for him never to take in any drunks. And this flier was drunk. He had nothing on but a T shirt and Bermuda shorts and he was flying from Sacramento to Salt Lake City. At the inquest Pace denied he had ever given me such instructions. The same was true when the cook went haywire. She was a tramp. He never hires decent help. He cheated her on the bar bill and blamed me and she went after me with a meat cleaver. She disliked me because I criticized her for drinking at the bar in her one-piece white bathing suit with the dude guests. But he turned her loose on me. He hints that he did certain things for India. She would never have let him. He was too common for her. It can never be said about India that she was not a lady in every way. He thinks he is the greatest sack-artist in the world. He only loves horses, as a fact. He has no claims at all, oral or written, on this yellow house. I want you to have this over my signature. He was cruel to Pickle-Tits who was his first wife, and he's no better to the charming woman who is his present one. I don't know why she takes it. It must be despair." She said to herself, *I don't suppose I'd better send that.*

She was still angry. Her heart was knocking from within: the deep pulses, as after a hot bath, beat at the back of her thighs. The air outside was dotted with transparent particles. The mountains were red as clinkers. The iris leaves were fan sticks—they stuck out like Jiggs's hair.

She always ended by looking out of the window at the desert and the lake. *They drew you from yourself. But after they had drawn you, what did they do with you? It was too late to find out. I'll never know. I wasn't meant to. I'm not the type,* Hattie reflected. *Maybe something too cruel for women or for any woman, young or old.*

So she stood up and, rising, she had the sensation that she had gradually become a container for herself. *You get old, your heart, your liver, your lungs seem to expand in size, and the walls of the body give way outward,* she thought, *and you take the shape of an old jug, wider and wider toward the top. You swell up with tears and fat.* She no longer even smelled to herself like a woman. Her face with its much-slept-upon skin was only faintly like her own—like a cloud that has changed. It was a face. It became a ball of yarn. It had drifted open. It had scattered.

I was never one single thing anyway, she thought. *Never my own. I was only loaned to myself.*

But the thing wasn't over yet. And in fact she didn't know for certain that it was ever going to be over; she had only had other people's word for it that death was such and such. *How do I know?* she asked herself challengingly. Her anger had sobered her for a little while. Now she was again drunk. *It was strange. It is strange. It may continue being strange.* She further thought, *I used to wish for death more than I do now. Because I didn't have anything at all. I changed when I got a roof of my own over me. And now? Do I have to go? I thought Marian loved me, but she has a sister. And I never thought Helen and Jerry would desert me. And now Pace insulted me. They think I'm not going to make it.*

She went to the cupboard—she kept the bourbon bottle there; she drank less if each time she had to rise and open the cupboard door. And, as if she were being watched, she poured a drink and swallowed it.

The notion that in this emptiness someone saw her was connected with the other fancy that she was being filmed from birth to death. That this was done for everyone. And afterward you could view your life.

Hattie wanted to see some of it now, and she sat down on the dogs' paw cushions of her sofa and, with her knees far apart and a smile of yearning and of fright, she bent her round back, burned a cigarette at the corner of her mouth and saw—the Church of Saint-Sulpice in Paris where her organ teacher used to bring her. It looked like country walls of stone, but rising high and leaning outward were towers. She was very young. She knew music. The sky was grey. After this she saw some entertaining things she liked to tell people about. She was a young wife. She was in Aix-les-Bains with her mother-in-law, and they played bridge in a mud bath with a British general and his aide. There were artificial waves in the swimming pool. She lost her bathing suit because it was a size too big. How did she get out? Ah, you got out of everything.

She saw her husband, James John Waggoner IV. They were snowbound together in New Hampshire. "Jimmy, Jimmy, how can you fling a wife away?" she asked him. "Have you forgotten love? Did I drink too much—did I bore you?" He had married again and had two children. He had gotten tired of her. And though he was a vain man with nothing to be vain about—no looks, not too much intelligence, nothing but an old Philadelphia family—she had loved him. She too had been a snob about her Philadelphia connections. Give up the name of Waggoner? How could she? For this reason she had never married Wicks. "How dare you," she had said to Wicks, "come without a shave in a dirty shirt and muck on you, come and ask me to marry! If you want to propose, go and clean up first." But his dirt was only a pretext. *Trade Waggoner for Wicks?* she asked herself again with a swing of her shoulders. She wouldn't think of it. Wicks was an excellent man. But he was a cowboy. He couldn't even read. But she saw this on her film. They were in Athens Canyon, in a cratelike house, and she was reading aloud to him from *The Count of Monte Cristo*. He wouldn't let her stop. While walking to stretch her legs, she read, and he followed her about to catch each word. After all, he was very dear to her. Such a man! Now she saw him jump from his horse. They were living on the range, trapping coyotes. It was just the second grey of evening, cloudy, moments after the sun had gone down. There was an animal in the trap, and he went toward it to kill it. He wouldn't waste a bullet on the creatures, but killed them with a kick of his boot. And then Hattie saw that this coyote was all white— snarling teeth, white scruff. "Wicks, he's white! White as a polar bear. You're not going to kill him, are you?" The animal flattened to the ground. He snarled and cried. He couldn't pull away because of the heavy trap. And Wicks killed him. What else could he have done? The white beast lay dead. The dust of Wicks' boots hardly showed on its head and jaws. Blood ran from the muzzle.

And now came something on Hattie's film she tried to shun. It was she herself who had killed her dog, Richie. Just as Rolfe and Pace had warned her, he was vicious, his brain was turned. She, because she was on the side of all dumb creatures, defended him when he bit the trashy woman Jacamares was living with. Perhaps if she had had Richie from a puppy he wouldn't have turned on her. When she got him he was already a year and a half old and she couldn't break him of his habits. But she thought only she understood him. And Rolfe had warned her, "You'll be sued, do you know it? The dog will take out after somebody smarter than that Jacamares' woman and you'll be in for it."

Hattie saw herself as she swayed her shoulders and said, "Nonsense."

But what fear she had felt when the dog went for her on the porch. Suddenly she could see by his skull, by his eyes that he was evil. She screamed at him, "Richie!" And what had she done to him? He had lain under the gas range all day growling and wouldn't come out. She tried to urge him out with the broom, and he snatched it in his teeth. She pulled him out and he left the stick and tore at her. Now, as the spectator of this, her eyes opened, beyond the pregnant curtain and the air wave of marl dust, summer's snow, drifting over the water. "Oh, my God! Richie!" Her thigh was snatched by his jaws. His teeth went through her skirt. She felt she would fall. Would she go down? Then the dog would rush at her throat—then black night, bad-odored mouth, the blood pouring from her torn veins. Her heart shriveled as the teeth went in her thigh, and she couldn't delay another second but took her kindling hatchet from the nail, strengthened her grip on the smooth wood and hit the dog. She saw the blow. She saw him die at once. And then in fear and shame she hid the body. And at night she buried him in the yard. Next day she accused Jacamares. On him she laid the blame for the disappearance of her dog.

She stood up; she spoke to herself in silence, as was her habit. *God, what shall I do? I have taken life. I have lied. I have borne false witness. I have stalled. And now what shall I do? Nobody will help me.*

And suddenly she made up her mind that she should go and do what she had been putting off for weeks, namely, test herself with the car, and she slipped on her shoes and went out. Lizards ran before her in the thirsty dust. She opened·the hot, broad door of the car. She lifted her lame hand onto the wheel. Her right hand she reached far to the left and turned the wheel with all her might. Then she started the motor and tried to drive out of the yard. But she could not release the emergency brake with its rasplike rod. She reached with her good hand, the right, under the steering wheel and pressed her bosom on it and strained. No, she could not shift the gears and steer. She couldn't even reach the hand brake. The sweat broke out on her skin. Her efforts were too much. She was deeply wounded by the pain in her arm. The door of the car fell open again and she turned from the wheel and with her stiff legs outside the door she wept. What could she do now? And when she had wept over the ruin of her life she got out of the old car and went back to the house. She took the bottle of bourbon from the cupboard and picked up the ink bottle and a pad of paper and sat down to write her will.

My Will, she wrote, and sobbed to herself.

Since the death of India she had numberless times asked the question, To Whom? Who will get this when I die? She had unconsciously put people to the test to find out whether they were worthy. It made her more severe than before.

Now she wrote, "I, Harriet Simmons Waggoner, being of sound mind and not knowing what may be in store for me at the age of seventy-two (born 1885), living alone at Sego Desert Lake, instruct my lawyer, Harold Claiborne, Paiute County Court Building, to draw my last will and testament upon the following terms."

She sat perfectly still now to hear from within who would be the lucky one, who would inherit the yellow house. For which she had waited. Yes, waited for India's death, choking on her bread because she was a rich woman's servant and whipping girl. But who had done for her, Hattie, what she had done for India? And who, apart from India, had ever held out a hand to her? Kindness, yes. Here and there people had been kind. But the word in her head was not kindness, it was succor. And who had given her that? Only India. If at least, next best after succor, someone had given her a shake and said, "Stop stalling. Don't be such a slow, old, procrastinating sit-stiller." Again, it was only India who had done her good. She had offered her succor. "Het-tie!" said that drunken mask. "Do you know what sloth is? Damn your poky old life!"

But I was waiting, Hattie realized. I was waiting, thinking, "Youth is terrible, frightening. I will wait it out. And men? Men are cruel and strong. They want things I haven't got to give." There were no kids in me, thought Hattie. Not that I wouldn't have loved them, but such my nature was. And who can blame me for having it? My nature?

She drank from an Old-Fashioned glass. There was no orange in it, no ice, no bitters or sugar, only the stinging, clear bourbon.

So then, she continued, looking at the dry sun-stamped dust and the last freckled flowers of red wild peach, to live with Angus and his wife, and have to hear a chapter from the Bible before breakfast; once more in the house—not of a stranger, perhaps, but not far from it either. In other houses, in someone else's house, to wait for mealtimes was her lifelong punishment. She always felt it in the throat and stomach. And so she would again, and to the very end. However, she must think of someone to leave the house to.

And first of all she wanted to do right by her family. None of them had ever dreamed that she, Hattie, would ever have something to bequeath. Until a few years ago it had certainly looked as if she would die a pauper. So now she could keep her head up with the proudest of them. And, as this occurred to her, she actually lifted up her face with its broad nose and victorious eyes; if her hair had become shabby as onion roots, if at the back her head was round and bald as a newel post, what did that matter? Her heart experienced a childish glory, not yet tired of it after seventy-two years. She, too, had amounted to something. I'll do some good by going, she thought. Now I believe I should leave it to, to. . . . She returned to the old point of struggle. She had decided many times and many times changed her mind. She tried to think, Who would get the most out of it? It was a tearing thing to go through. If it had not been the yellow house but instead some brittle thing she could hold in her hand, then the last thing she would do would be to throw and smash it, and so the thing and she herself would be demolished together. But it was vain to think such thoughts. To whom should she leave it? Her brothers? Not they. Nephews? One was a submarine commander. The other was a bachelor in the State Department. Then began the roll call of cousins. Merton? He owned an estate in Connecticut. Anna? She had a face like a hot-water bottle. That left Joyce, the orphaned daughter of her cousin Wilfred. Joyce was the most likely heiress. Hattie had already written to her and had her out to the lake at Thanksgiving, two years ago. But this Joyce was another odd one; over thirty, good, yes, but placid, running to fat, a scholar—ten years in Eugene, Oregon, working for her degree. In Hattie's opinion this was only another form of sloth. Nevertheless, Joyce yet hoped to marry. Whom? Not Dr. Stroud. He wouldn't. And still she had vague hope. Hattie knew how that could be. At least have a man she could argue with.

She was now more drunk than at any time since her accident. Again she filled her glass. *Have ye eyes and see not? Sleepers, awake!*

Knees wide apart she sat in the twilight, thinking. Marian? Marian didn't need another house. Half Pint? She wouldn't know what to do with it. Brother Louis came up for consideration next. He was an old actor who had a church for the Indians at Athens Canyon. Hollywood stars of the silent days sent him their negligées; he altered them and wore them in the pulpit. The Indians loved his show. But when Billy Shawah blew his brains out after his two-week bender, they still tore his shack down and turned it inside out to get rid of his ghost. They had their old religion. No, not Brother Louis. He'd show movies in the yellow house to the tribe or make a nursery of it.

And now she began to consider Wicks. When last heard from he was south of Bishop, California, a handy man in a saloon off toward Death Valley. It wasn't she who heard from him but Pace. Herself, she hadn't actually seen Wicks since—how low she had sunk then!— she had kept the hamburger stand on Route 158. The little lunch-room had supported them both. Wicks hung around on the end stool, rolling cigarettes (she saw it on the film). Then there was a quarrel. Things had been going from bad to worse. He'd begun to grouse now about this and now about that. He complained about the food, at last. She saw and heard him. "Hat," he said, "I'm good and tired of hamburger." "Well, what do you think I eat?" she said with that round, defiant movement of her shoulders which she herself recognized as characteristic (*me all over*, she thought). But he opened the cash register and took out thirty cents and crossed the street to the butcher's and brought back a steak. He threw it on the griddle. "Fry it," he said. She did and watched him eat.

And when he was through she could bear her rage no longer. "Now," she said, "you've had your meat. Get out. Never come back." She kept a pistol under the counter. She picked it up, cocked it, pointed it at his heart. "If you ever come in that door again, I'll kill you," she said.

She saw it all. *I couldn't bear to fall so low*, she thought, *to be slave to a shiftless cowboy.*

Wicks said, "Don't do that, Hat. Guess I went too far. You're right."

"You'll never have a chance to make it up," she cried. "Get out!"

On that cry he disappeared, and since then she had never seen him.

"Wicks, dear," she said. "Please! I'm sorry. Don't condemn me in your heart. Forgive me. I hurt myself in my evil. I always had a thick idiot head. I was born with a thick head."

Again she wept, for Wicks. She was too proud. A snob. Now they might have lived together in this house, old friends, simple and plain.

She thought, *He really was my good friend.*

But what would Wicks do with a house like this, alone, if he was alive and survived her? He was too wiry for soft beds or easy chairs.

And she was the one who had said stiffly to India, "I'm a Christian person. I do not bear a grudge."

Ah, yes, she said to herself. *I have caught myself out too often. How long can this go on?* And she began to think, or try to think of Joyce, her cousin's daughter. Joyce was like herself, a woman alone, getting on, clumsy. She would have given much, now, to succor Joyce.

But it seemed to her now that that too had been a story. First you heard the pure story. Then you heard the impure story. Both stories. She had paid out years, now to one shadow, now to another shadow.

Joyce would come here to the house. She had a little income and could manage. She would live as Hattie had lived, alone. Here she would rot, start to drink, maybe, and day after day read, day after day sleep. See how beautiful it was here? It burned you out. How empty? It turned you into ash.

"How can I doom a young person to the same life?" asked Hattie. "It's for somebody like me. When I was younger it wasn't right. But now it is. Only I fit in here. It was made for my old age, to spend my last years peacefully. If I hadn't let Jerry make me drunk that night— if I hadn't sneezed! My arm! I'll have to live with Angus. My heart will break there away from my only home."

She now was very drunk, and she said to herself, *Take what God brings. He gives no gifts unmixed. He makes loans.*

She resumed her letter of instructions to lawyer Claiborne: "Upon the following terms," she wrote a second time. "Because I have suffered much. Because I only lately received what I have to give away, I can't bear it." The drunken blood was soaring to her head. But her hand was clear enough. She wrote, "It is too soon! Too soon! Because I do not find it in my heart to care for anyone as I would wish. Being cast off and lonely, and doing no harm where I am. Why should it be? This breaks my heart. In addition to everything else, why must I worry about this, which I must leave? I am tormented out of my mind. Even though by my own fault I have put myself into this position. And I am not ready to give up on this. No, not yet. And so I'll tell you what, I leave this property, land, house, garden and water rights, to Hattie Simmons Waggoner. Me! I realize this is bad and wrong. It cannot happen. Yet it is the only thing I really wish to do, so may God have mercy on my soul."

"How can that be?" She studied what she had written and finally she acknowledged that she was drunk. "I'm drunk," she said, "and don't know what I'm doing. I'll die, and end. Like India. Dead as that lilac bush. Only tonight I can't give the house away. I'm drunk and so I need it. But I won't be selfish from the grave. I'll think again tomorrow," she promised herself.

UNCLE MITWALLI

Mahmud Taimur

Uncle Mitwalli was a hawker of peanuts, melon seeds, and sweets, well known to the inhabitants of Hilmiya and the neighboring districts. He went about in a long white turban and a broad-sleeved cloak, with a dignified demeanor, and cried his wares to the children with a Sudanese accent, in a faltering voice weakened by poverty and infirmity yet still retaining something of the ring of command.

The man had grown up in the Sudan and had fought in the armies of the Mahdi with the rank of divisional commander. He had lived all his life alone, with neither wife nor child; and occupied a small dark room in the alley of Abdallah Bey, furnished only with an old trunk and a straw mat with a tattered cushion and blanket. Yet despite his obvious and abject poverty, he and his possessions were spotlessly clean.

He used to return to his room overwhelmed with weariness. When he had recited the evening prayer, he would light his pallid oil lamp, sit by his trunk, and take out an old sword. He would rest it across his knees and sink into long reveries, going over the memories of his past life; and when the memory of the Mahdi passed through his mind, he would lift up his eyes and pray to God to hasten the days of Return, the days of the awaited reappearance of the Mahdi—the Flagbearer of the Faith—who would descend upon the world and cleanse it of its corruptions. Then he would lower his eyes, stroke his tear-stained beard, and take the old sword and kiss it with great passion.

So he would rise for his evening meal and prayer, and when he had completed them he would go to bed, to sink before long into a restful sleep, and to dream of his proud past and of his future made splendid by the Mahdi's return. At dawn he would rise, recite the morning prayer and read the Litanies of Sidi Gulshani and the Praises of the Prophet until, with the first warm shafts of sunlight coming through his narrow window, he would rise slowly, put his basket on his back, and turn toward Hilmiya to begin his daily round.

This had been his way since he had come to Cairo fifteen years earlier, and he had changed nothing in the order of his life. Buildings had fallen and others had risen, men had died and children had grown up, but Uncle Mitwalli knew nothing of Cairo and its outskirts save his accustomed round. He had his resting places on the way, places where he ate and sat awhile. There were two especially where he spent most of his moments of repose. The first was a small mosque, by the door of which he would take his midday meal; when he had finished, he would praise God at length and go into the mosque to pray and sleep. His second halt was before the house of Nur ad-Din Bey in Suyufiya, which he always sought after the sunset prayer. There by the palace gate, the doorkeepers of the neighboring houses and the servants of Nur ad-Din would gather around him and converse of Islam in its former glory and of how it had fallen on evil times. Thereupon Uncle Mitwalli would rise with radiant eyes and tell them tales of the Return that is to come, with measured and awe-inspiring accents and a powerful and captivating eloquence that won all their hearts. They would all sit reverent and contented, listening with rapt attention to this great Saint as he spoke of the appearance of the Mahdi and the cleansing of the world of its corruptions and the return of Islam to its former greatness. At that time Nur ad-Din Bey would come out of the door of his house leaning on his expensive walking stick. He would walk toward Uncle Mitwalli and greet him courteously, bestow his gift upon him, and leave him, emitting a haughty and pompous cough.

Ibrahim Bey, the son of Nur ad-Din Bey, would come, too—a merry and playful youth in his sixteenth year. He would approach Uncle Mitwalli, crying, "Are you still telling of the battles and adventures of the Mahdi and his army?"

"I tell them and I glory in them. I was in command of a thousand warriors."

Ibrahim Bey would roar with laughter, and affecting a posture of reverence, would button his jacket, straighten his fez, and raise his right hand to his head in a military salute. Then he would take a piaster from his pocket and give it to Uncle Mitwalli, saying, "Please give me a piaster's worth of melon seeds and peanuts, O General!"

One day at noon, Uncle Mitwalli went to the house of Nur ad-Din Bey and sat near the gate, as was his custom. The children began to run to him as usual to buy his wares; the servants thronged to him

UNCLE MITWALLI
Mahmud Taimur

from all sides. When they had settled down in a circle to listen, Uncle Mitwalli rose and spoke to them in his accustomed manner. But as they listened enraptured to his enchanting words, Ibrahim Bey appeared and cried, "General Mitwalli—"

The preacher paused and the people turned their eyes in anger and inquiry toward the merry youngster. Without paying any attention to them, Ibrahim came forward and continued, "My father wishes to see you. Would you please follow me?"

The gathering deplored this interruption. Uncle Mitwalli left the circle with his basket on his back and walked calmly toward the door, giving his faithful followers a look of affection and apology. He followed Ibrahim Bey into the garden of the palace, and they walked together for some time along a path leading to the entrance of the visitors' quarters, where Nur ad-Din Bey was waiting for them on a broad divan. He welcomed Uncle Mitwalli, and dismissing his son, bade the old man sit by him on the ground.

A brief silence reigned, during which Uncle Mitwalli repeated in a low voice his thanks to God and his prayers for the Prophet. Then Nur ad-Din informed Uncle Mitwalli, after a brief introduction, that the venerable lady his mother had heard much of him and of his qualities, and desired to meet him and hear his noble religious tales and his wonderful stories of Islam. Uncle Mitwalli's heart quivered with joy that his fame had penetrated the outer walls of houses and reached the ears of secluded ladies.

Nur ad-Din Bey rose and walked toward the women's quarters of the house, Uncle Mitwalli following behind him. They passed through a wide corridor and a huge doorway leading into the garden of the women's quarters. Then they walked up the stairs of a dark passage and into a hall so vast that hardly had Uncle Mitwalli crossed the threshold, when he was overcome by its magnificence and his heart was filled with awe and wonderment. Never had he seen—not even in the castle of the Mahdi—so vast and magnificent a chamber.

Uncle Mitwalli was still lost in wonderment when a weak female voice came to his ears. He turned toward the voice and found the lady of the palace sitting on a large divan not far from him and smoking. He walked toward her until he was near enough to see her clearly. She was a Turkish lady with bent back and wrinkled skin, wearing gold-rimmed spectacles and dark clothes.

Uncle Mitwalli advanced toward her, kissed her thin hand, and wished her long life and good fortune. Introductions were completed, and Nur ad-Din Bey left them and went his way. The lady spoke, expressing her joy at his coming and her desire to hear some of his tales. He lowered his eyes and began to gather his tales and traditions in his mind. Then he raised his head and told his story with a fluency and with moving accents that fascinated the lady. When he had finished his story, she gave him a present, a sum greater than any he had dreamed of, and overwhelmed him with expressions of admiration that embarrassed and confused him. Then he left, repeating words of gratitude and loyalty to her and to her family. No sooner had he reached the garden than a crowd of maidservants began to cluster around him, seeking blessings from him and stroking his sleeves with their hands. They asked him to sell them something of his wares, and he sat happily on the ground, opened his old basket, and sold until he had no more. And so he left and went straight to the mosque, where he prayed with forty prostrations, thanking God for His bounteous gift.

From that day Uncle Mitwalli went often to the house of Nur ad-Din Bey, where he was welcomed with respect and esteem and showered with favors. His condition changed, and he began to bear himself upright, always speaking with a firm voice. He rented a better situated room, with new furniture, and changed his diet from cheese, leeks, and radishes to rice and vegetables every day and meat twice a week. He was able to make his turban bigger and longer, to broaden the sleeves of his cloak, to wrap a cheap cashmere shawl around his shoulders, and to wear bright-red slippers and a silk sash with a long fringe. He gradually gave up hawking, freeing himself from his weary round. He enjoyed long and pleasant slumbers, and began to give alms to the poor and became known among them as a sustainer of the needy. He could go to the mosque at his leisure and listen to the sermons, the preaching and admonition, which he could repeat later to the lady, the mother of Nur ad-Din Bey.

So his fame spread in the neighborhood and men began to whisper to one another and to exchange news about him, and the image of Uncle Mitwalli, the hawker of melon seeds and peanuts, the man of poverty and infirmity, faded before that of a great dervish.

A group of his followers were sitting by the door of Nur ad-Din Bey, awaiting his appearance, when one of them said, "Do you think, my friends, that Uncle Mitwalli is merely a righteous man who can speak well and eloquently of Islam?"

Another asked the first, "What do you think he is?"

The man replied in a whisper, "He is one of the Saints of God, one of the Great Ones of the Faith."

"Who told you?"

"Look into his eyes awhile. You will see a strange light shining from them. This is a sign that he is a Saint. . . . I had an adventure with him which I fear to tell you, lest you disbelieve me!"

The gathering drew near to him, saying, "Tell us! Tell us!"

"I was walking with him once in Sidi Shawish Street and the time was evening. The street was lit only by two oil lamps, giving a weak, pale light. Suddenly a strong gust of wind put them both out, leaving us in pitch darkness. A sudden fear came over me, and I seized Uncle Mitwalli's hand and pressed it, and he murmured, 'Fear nothing, we are in God's keeping!'"

While they were listening to his words, another man began to speak. "Now that I have heard your story, it is easier for me to tell you what I know about this righteous Saint, with whom we have associated much, though we knew but little of his true character."

The group turned their eyes toward him, and one of them said, with avid interest, "And what do you know of his character?"

The man spoke with a constrained voice and a tense face. "He is the Mahdi, the awaited Mahdi!"

They craned their necks forward and whispered to one another, "The Mahdi? The awaited Mahdi?"

The speaker went on in the same tone, his voice trembling with emotion: "I have seen the sword of Prophecy in his trunk, and when I touched it with my hand, I was able to heal my son, my son whom the doctors could not cure, who was on the point of death!"

They vied with one another in questioning the man, and he answered them willingly, with much detail. The clamor grew, and the circle was increased by others who came to ask what was afoot, and to listen to the man who was speaking of the sword of Prophecy and the generosity of the Mahdi, whom God had sent a second time to guide mankind.

At that moment Uncle Mitwalli appeared from afar. The gathering saw him, and the tumult died away. They hastened to open a path for him between their serried ranks.

Uncle Mitwalli came with his deliberate tread, grave and dignified, giving a calm and sweet smile to those who welcomed him. The people gathered reverently around him, thronging to him and kissing his fingers and the hems of his sash. The man who had touched the sword of Prophecy stepped forward and said:

"My Master, my Lord, savior of my son from death! We know you in spite of your concealment. You are the servant of God whom He has sent to guide mankind; you are the vicar of the Prophet; you are the awaited Mahdi . . ."

Uncle Mitwalli stared at the man in astonishment and said, "What are you saying? Are you raving?"

"You can no longer hide your noble character from us. Yes, you are the Mahdi, the vicar of the Prophet, the bearer of the sword of truth amid men!"

"Be silent! Be silent! For I have not this tremendous honor!"

"Did you not save my son from death?"

"I?"

The man who had told the tale of the dark street slipped forward and said, "Did you not light up the street with your resplendent face?"

"I? I?"

The man who had spoken previously said, "The righteous Abu Bakr—may God be pleased with him—visited me in a dream and revealed your character to me."

Uncle Mitwalli murmured in a low voice and leaned on the man standing by him.

"The righteous Abu Bakr revealed my character to you?"

He took refuge in silence awhile, staring about him. Then he began to speak, as if to himself. "My children! The Mahdi is a mighty man, mightier and greater than I. I am but a faithful servant of God . . ."

He did not sit long with them, but returned home early, sunk in dreams.

Uncle Mitwalli was scarcely awake next morning when he heard a knock on his door. He got up to find out what the matter was, and soon a man with a bandaged head and an emaciated body was clinging to his garments, moaning and supplicating.

"Let me touch the sword of Prophecy from your pure hand."

"The sword of Prophecy?"

"Save me from my sufferings, O my master. Have pity on the wretched who seek you, O mighty vicar of the Prophet!"

Uncle Mitwalli let him into his room, and tended him all day. He recited a section of the Litanies over his head. When evening approached, he put him to bed by his side, with the "sword of Prophecy" under his head.

The next day the sun rose on the sick man, and he declared himself to be full of happiness and energy, in a state of health such as he had never known before. He went up to Uncle Mitwalli and pounced on his hands, smothering them with kisses. His voice bellowed thanks and prayers.

The days passed, and the dwelling of Uncle Mitwalli became a place of pilgrimage for men from every part, who came to seek a cure for the ills of their bodies and the whisperings of their souls. Uncle Mitwalli left home rarely, spending all his time straying amid endless dreams. If he awoke from these dreams, he would take out his sword, place it on his knees, and stare at it in bewilderment.

One day Uncle Mitwalli saw the noble lady, the mother of Nur ad-Din Bey, come to visit him amid a crowd of his followers. As soon as she saw him, she knelt before him reverently, took the skirt of his robe and began to kiss it, saying:

"O mighty vicar of the Prophet! I have come to you, submissive and humble, to seek your grace! . . ."

From the day Uncle Mitwalli confined himself to his room. Sometimes he received visitors, and sometimes he locked the door of his room and let none come near him. He would sit leaning his back on the wall, with lowered eyelids, and would spend long hours in this manner. Then suddenly he would start out of his reverie, agitated and feverish, draw his sword from the scabbard, and thrust at the air this way and that, leaping around the room and shouting, bidding the devils avaunt—until he fell senseless to the floor.

The neighbors heard much of this shouting, and they knew that the righteous Saint in his hours of retreat was meditating his mighty mysteries. They gathered around his door with intent ears, with souls full of awe and veneration. Uncle Mitwalli lived in this state for a few weeks.

Then one day he rushed out of his room with disheveled hair and eyes that blazed like burning coals, brandishing his sword right and left. He hurried to the nearby coffeehouse and began to strike with the sword at those who were sitting there, shouting, "Away, O rebels, O evildoers," and people gathered around him to stop him.

At last he fell into the hands of the police, screaming in a weak voice:

"Praise be to God! I have accomplished my mission. I have completed my holy war."

And his strength failed . . .

TRANSLATED BY BERNARD LEWIS

THE ANIMAL GAME

Machado de Assis

Camillo—or Camillinho, as he was affectionately known to his friends—held a position as clerk in one of the arsenals of Rio de Janeiro (Army or Navy). He earned two hundred milreis a month, subject to tax and pension deductions. He was a bachelor, but once, during the holidays, he went to spend Christmas night at the home of a friend in the suburb of Rocha. There he saw a modest little thing, blue dress, appealing eyes. Three months later they were married.

Neither had anything. He, nothing more than his salary; she, her willing hands and energy to take care of the whole house, which was small, and help the old colored woman who had been her nurse and followed her without wages. It was this colored woman who made them get married all the sooner. Not that she gave them any such advice. As a matter of fact, it seemed better to her for the girl to remain with her widowed aunt, without either responsibilities or children. But no one asked her for her opinion. Since, however, she had one day said that if her baby married she would go and work for her without pay, this remark was told to Camillo, and Camillo made up his mind to get married two months later. If he had thought about it a little, perhaps he would not have married right away: the colored woman was old, they were young, and so forth. The idea that the colored woman would work for them without pay was entered as a permanent appropriation in his fiscal estimate.

Germana, the colored woman, was as good as her word. "This little old bag of bones can still cook up a pot of stew," she said.

A year later the couple had a child. And the joy it brought made up for the burdens it would bring. Joanninha, the wife, got along without a wet nurse; she had so much milk, was so strong—not to mention the lack of money, and it is certain they never even thought of that.

The young clerk was all joy, all hope. There was going to be a reorganization at the arsenal, and he would be promoted. While the reorganization was slow in coming, there was a vacancy caused by death, and Camillo joined in his co-worker's funeral procession, almost laughing. At home he did not restrain himself and laughed aloud. He told his wife exactly what would happen, the name of those up for promotion—two, a certain Botelho, favored by General—, and he. The promotions took place, and the choice lighted upon Botelho and another man. Camillo wept bitterly; he beat his fists into the bed, against the table, and himself.

"Have patience," said Joanninha.

"Patience! For five years I've just been marking time . . ." He broke off. That word, of military origin, used by an employee of the arsenal, was oil on troubled waters: it comforted him. Camillo was delighted with himself. He went so far as to repeat it to some of his close friends.

Not long after, when there was again talk of a reorganization, Camillo went to see the minister and said, "Look, Your Excellency, for more than five years now I have just been *marking time.*"

The italics are to convey the emphasis with which he uttered the final phrase. It seemed to him that it made a good impression on the minister, even though all the classes might use the same metaphor— bank clerks, tradesmen, judges, industrialists, and so on.

There was no reorganization: Camillo reconciled himself and went on living. He already had a few debts, was borrowing against his salary, and looking for odd jobs, secretly, on the outside. Since they were young, and in love, the bad weather only made them think of a sky that was everlastingly blue.

Even without this explanation, there was a whole week when Camillo's joy knew no bounds. You shall see. Let posterity hear me! It was when Camillo played the animals for the first time. "Playing the animals" is not a euphemism like "playing ducks and drakes." The player chooses a number that by established custom is identified with a certain animal, and if this number turns out to be the winning number in the lottery all who risked their pennies on it win, and all who placed their trust in other numbers and other animals lose. It began with pennies, and they say it is now up in the millions. But let us get on with our story.

For the first time, Camillo played the animals: he chose the monkey, and with a bet of five *tostões* won I do not know how many times as much. He found this so preposterous that he refused to believe it, but finally he had to believe it and go collect the money. Naturally, he tried the monkey again—two, three, four times—but this animal, half-human, did not live up to its early promise. Camillo threw himself on the mercy of other animals, with no better luck, and all the winnings went into the bookie's cash drawer. He saw it would be better to rest for a while. But there is no eternal rest, not even in the grave. One day, along comes an archaeologist digging up bones and eras.

Camillo had faith. And faith levels mountains. He tried the cat, then the dog, then the ostrich: since he had not bet on them it could be that . . . It could not be. Fortune scattered her favors impartially on all three animals: she saw to it that none of them paid. He was unwilling to follow the tips in the newspapers, as some of his friends did. Camillo asked how half a dozen news hacks could foretell the numbers of the grand prize. Once, to prove the error of their thinking, he agreed to follow a tip, bought on the cat, and won.

"Well?" said his friends.

"You can't always lose," he replied.

"You can end up always winning," said one of them. "It's a question of tenacity, of never weakening."

In spite of this, Camillo went on with his own system of calculations—though he sometimes gave way before certain signs that appeared to come from heaven, like something a child said in the street, "Mother, why don't you bet on the snake?" He would bet on the snake and lose, and explain that fact with the best reasoning in this world; and reason strengthens faith.

Instead of a reorganization in his department, there was an increase in salaries, about sixty *milreis* a month. Camillo decided to baptize his son, and chose as godfather no less a person than the very fellow who sold him the animals—his trusted "banker." There was no family connection between them. It even seems that the man was a bachelor without any relatives. The request was so unexpected that it almost made him laugh; but he saw the young man's earnestness, was honored at being asked, and accepted with pleasure.

"No call for full dress?"

"Full dress! A modest little affair."

"Nor a carriage?"

"Carriage . . ."

"Why bother with a carriage, eh?"

"Yes, we *could* walk. The church is not far, in the next street or so."

"Then let us walk."

People of discernment will have already perceived that Camillo's feeling was that the baptismal party should ride in a carriage. They will have also perceived from his hesitation and manner that the idea of letting the godfather pay for the carriage entered into the feeling, and that if the godfather was not going to pay for the carriage nobody was. The baptism took place, the godfather left a gift for his godchild and promised with a laugh that he would give him a "win" on the eagle.

This silly joke explains the father's choice of godfather. It was his suspicion that the bookmaker shared in the animals' good luck, and he wanted to bind himself to him with a spiritual tie. He did not play the eagle right off, "so as not to startle . . . fate," he said to himself. But he did not forget the promise, and one day he laughingly reminded the bookmaker, "*Compadre*, be sure to warn me when it's to be the eagle."

"The eagle?"

Camillo recalled his remark. The bookmaker burst into a loud laugh. "No, compadre," he said, "I can't foretell the winner. I was only joking. I wish I could give you a prize. The eagle pays, not usually, but it does pay."

"Then why has it never won for me?"

"That I don't know. I can't give advice, but I am inclined to think, compadre, that you don't have enough patience with an animal, you don't play with true constancy. You keep changing. That's the reason you've won only a few times. Tell me now, how many times have you won?"

"Off hand, I can't say. But I have it all written down in my notebook."

"Well, you just look, and you'll see that your whole trouble is in not sticking with the same animal for any length of time. Now, there's a colored man who has been betting on the butterfly for three months: yesterday he won and carried off a pile of money . . ."

Camillo really did keep a written account of his disbursements and receipts, but he never compared them—in order to remain in ignorance of the difference. He did not want to know the deficit. Though methodical, he had a genuine talent for closing his eyes to the truth, so as not to see it and be saddened by it. On the other hand, the suggestion made by his child's godfather was worth considering: perhaps his restlessness, impatience, and not sticking with the same animals was the reason for his never winning anything.

When he got home he found his wife divided between the kitchen and her sewing. Germana was sick in bed, Joanninha was cooking dinner and at the same time finishing a dress for one of her customers. She now took in sewing to help with the household expense and to buy an occasional dress for herself. The husband did not hide his dismay over the situation. He ran in to look at the colored woman. The fever had already gone down; his wife had given her some quinine she had in the house—on a "hunch." And the old colored woman added with a smile, "Nhã* Joanninha's hunches good."

He was sad as he sat down to dinner, at seeing his wife so burdened with work, but her gaiety in the face of everything soon put him in a gay mood too. After dinner he got out the notebook that he kept shut up in a drawer, and began to go over his accounts. He added up the bets and the animals: so many on the snake, so many on the cat, so many on the dog, and on the others—a complete fauna, but so lacking in persistence that it was easy to miss. He was reluctant to total the disbursements and the receipts because he did not want to receive a blow between the eyes, and closed the book. Finally he gave in and began to add the totals—slowly, carefully, so as not to make a mistake: he had spent seven hundred and seven milreis, and had won eighty-four milreis—a deficit of six hundred and twenty-three milreis. He was astounded.

"It's not possible!"

He added the columns a second time, still more slowly, and found the difference to be five milreis less. His hopes rose and he once more added up the amounts spent, and arrived at the original deficit of six hundred and twenty-three milreis. He shut the book up in the drawer. Joanninha, who had seen him gay and lively at dinner, was surprised at the change, and asked what was wrong.

"Nothing."

"Something's wrong. Something you remembered . . ."

"It wasn't anything."

As his wife insisted on knowing, he made up a story out of whole

* Corruption of *senhora*.

cloth—a set-to with the head of his department—a matter of no importance.

"But you were so gay . . ."

"That proves it's of no importance. Just now I happened to remember it . . . and was thinking about it, but it's nothing. . . . How about a game of *bisca?*"

Bisca was their "show," their opera, their Rua do Ouvidor, Petropolis, Tijuca—everything that can convey the idea of amusement, outings, and pleasant idleness. The wife's gaiety returned. As for the husband, if he was not quite so expansive as usual, he found some pleasure, and great hope, in the numbers on the cards. As he played he made calculations, on the basis of the first card dealt, then of the second, then the third; he waited for the last; he made other combinations, to see which animals would come up. And he saw a lot of them, but principally the monkey and the snake; it was in these he put his trust.

"My mind is made up," he concluded on the following day, "I will go as far as seven hundred milreis. If I don't win a good substantial amount by then, I won't bet any more."

He decided to place his trust in the snake, because of its wiliness, and set out in the direction of the godfather's place. He told him he had taken his advice and was going to start by sticking with the snake.

"The snake is a good one," said his child's godfather.

Camillo bet on the snake a whole week without winning a thing. On the seventh day he got the idea of mentally fixing on a certain species, and he chose the coral snake. It lost. The next day he called it a rattlesnake. It lost too. Then it became a twelve-foot bushmaster, a boa constrictor, a viper. None of the varieties escaped the same unhappy fortune. He changed his direction. He was quite capable of changing it without reason, in spite of his promise; but what actually made him do it was that he happened to see a carriage run over a poor little child. A crowd gathered, the police came, the child was taken to a pharmacy, the driver to the station. Camillo saw scarcely anything but the number on the carriage: its final digits were the same as the lamb's. He embraced the lamb. The lamb was no luckier than the snake.

Although Camillo had mastered the system of adopting an animal and betting on it until it was played out, he did not spurn the use of lucky numbers. For example, he would turn a corner with his eyes on the ground, take forty, sixty, eighty steps, suddenly raise his eyes and glance at the house on his right, or left, take down the number, and bet on the corresponding animal. He had already used up the combinations he had written down and placed in his hat, numbers on treasury notes—he rarely saw those any more—and a hundred other methods tried over and over again, or with slight variations. In every case, he always fizzled out into impatience and kept shifting back and forth. One day he made a resolution: he resolved to pin his faith to the lion, and stick by him. When his son's godfather realized that he had made up his mind not to abandon the king of beasts under any circumstance, he gave thanks to God.

"Well, thanks be to God that I should ever see you ready to take this great step. The lion has been disinclined of late, he'll probably knock over everything any day now."

"Disinclined? You don't mean to say . . . ?"

"On the contrary."

Say what? On the contrary what? Dark words, but, for one who has faith and deals with numbers, nothing plainer. Camillo increased the size of his bet. He had almost reached the seven hundred milreis: win or die!

The young wife kept up the cheerful gaiety of their home, however hard life might be, however rude her tasks, however fast their debts and borrowings grew, and the not infrequent times of hunger. The fault did not lie with her, but she was patient none the less. He, when he had lost the seven hundred milreis, would lock the barn door. The lion was unwilling to pay. Camillo considered trading it for another animal, but his child's godfather would become so upset at such weakness that he always ended up in the arms of royalty. The seven hundred milreis were running out, were almost gone.

"Today I can breathe freely," Camillo said to his wife. "This is the last time."

About two o'clock, as he sat at his desk in the government office, copying a serious and weighty document, Camillo's mind ran on numbers as he cursed Lady Luck. The document contained figures, and he kept making mistakes in them because of the stampede of digits in his brain. A slip was easy; the numbers from his brain turned up more often on the paper than those from the original document. And the worst of it was that he did not notice the mistake: he would write down the lion instead of transcribing the proper number of tons of gunpowder.

Suddenly, an errand boy came into the room, went up to Camillo and whispered in his ear that the lion had paid. Camillo dropped his pen; the ink ran out and spoiled the copy, which was almost finished. Under other circumstances it would have been reason to bring his fist down on the paper and break the pen, but the circumstances were these: the lion had paid. Paper and pen escaped the justest acts of violence in this world. The lion had paid. But, since doubt does not die:

"Who told you the lion paid?" Camillo asked in a whisper.

"The fellow who sold me a ticket on the snake."

"Then it was the snake that paid."

"No, senhor. He made a mistake. He came to notify me because he thought I bet on the lion, but it was on the snake."

"You're sure?"

"Positive."

Camillo decided to dash out of there right then, but the ink-blotted paper motioned him back. He went to the head of his department, told him of the mishap, and asked permission to copy it over the next day: he would come early, or take the original home . . .

"What are you talking about? The copy has to be got out today."

"But it's almost three o'clock."

"I'll postpone closing time."

Camillo would like to have postponed the department head into the sea, if such a use of the verb and of the regulation had been permissible. He went back to his desk, took a sheet of paper, and began to write his resignation. The lion had paid; he could send this life of hell to the devil. All this in rapid seconds, scarcely a minute and a half. Since he could not do otherwise, he began to recopy the document, and by four o'clock it was finished. The handwriting came out shaky and uneven—furiously angry, then melancholy, little by little lively and gay, as the lion kept repeating in the clerk's ear, in a softened voice, "I paid! I paid!"

"Well! Come here and give me a hug," said the baby's godfather when Camillo turned up at his place. "At last, Fortune has begun to show some regard for you."

"How much?"

"One hundred and five milreis."

Camillo got hold of himself and took the hundred and five milreis. Not until he was in the street did he remember he had not thanked his child's godfather; he stopped, hesitated, then went on. A hundred and five milreis! He was on fire to get home and tell his wife the good news; but like that . . . nothing more . . . ?

"Yes, one should celebrate this marvelous happening. Today is not just another day. I must give thanks to heaven for the fortune it has bestowed upon me. Something special for dinner . . ."

He saw a pastry shop close by, went in, and ran his eyes over the display without choosing anything. The shopkeeper came to help him, and as Camillo hung uncertain between a meat dish and dessert, decided to sell him both. He began with a meat pie, "a magnificent meat pie that would fill the eyes before it filled one's mouth and stomach." The dessert was "a magnificent pudding" on which was written in white confectionery this indestructible viva: "Long live hope!" Camillo's joy was so great and so evident that the man had no recourse but to suggest wine also—a bottle, or two. Two.

"This calls for port. I'll have a boy deliver it all to your house. It's not far, is it?"

Camillo agreed, and paid the bill. He gave directions to the boy about the address and what he should do. He should not knock at the door but wait outside for him. He might not yet be home. If he was, he would come to the window from time to time. He paid sixteen milreis and went out.

He was so happy with the dinner he was bringing home, and the surprise to his wife, that he never once thought of buying her a gift. This idea did not come to him until he was on the street car. He got off and went back on foot to look for some trinket or other, if only a little gold pin with a precious stone. He found just such a pin, so modest in price—fifty milreis—that he was astonished. He bought it, like that, and flew homeward.

When he arrived, the delivery boy was standing outside with the look of a boy that had already called him some bad names and sent him to the devil. He took the packages from him, and offered him a tip.

"No, senhor, the boss doesn't allow it."

"Then don't tell him. Here! Here's ten tostões. You can buy a ticket on the snake. Bet on the snake!"

His recommending the animal that had not paid, instead of the lion, which had paid, was not from calculation—or meanness. It was, quite likely, confusion. The boy took the ten tostões. Camillo went into the house, with the packages and his whole soul in his arms, and thirty-eight milreis in his pocket.

TRANSLATED BY HELEN CALDWELL

TENANTS

Federigo Tozzi

Marta and Gertrude both had doors on the same dark landing; and people always went to the wrong door.

Marta had been a widow for ten years, and Gertrude was an old maid with gray hair. They had lived there since girlhood, but visited each other only on solemn feast days; between times, neither called on the other. And even these visits lasted only the time it took to speak of the weather and their health, and occurred mornings, after Mass, before they began to get lunch.

Marta would say, "I've bought these shoelaces."

"I needed a skirt that wasn't so dirty."

"Let's hope it's a better new year!"

"Let's hope!"

"Good-by, I won't trouble you any longer."

"I'll put my prayer book up and come to visit you."

"You'll see, I haven't cleaned up yet."

And they would part.

A quarter of an hour later Gertrude would pull at Marta's bell; and Marta, waiting as though for a nuisance, would hurry to the door:

"Come in."

"No, no; it's better that we not waste our time. We've both got things to do."

"You're right. How is your health?"

"The same old aches in my knees, especially in the evening. And your health?"

"I can hardly wait to die. I can't say more."

"Let's hope God will help us, as He always has."

"Let's hope."

"Good-by, Signora Marta. I've stayed even longer than you did with me."

"No matter! No matter! On the contrary, it's been a pleasure."

Nor did they shake hands this time, either; smiling, gay.

And since their rooms had a wall in common, whenever one of them understood what the other was doing, she would take care to move more quietly so that the other would not hear her. Sometimes, avoiding a chair or the bed, it happened that they would strike the wall at the same time, and almost at the same point. Then both of them would stop, motionless for an instant.

Only one night, in all this time, after an earth tremor had woken them, did they call to each other; without getting up, though.

"Signora Marta!"

"Signora Gertrude!"

"Were you frightened?"

"Rather!"

"So was I."

And there they let their exchange end. The morning after, they avoided meeting on the stair.

And yet Gertrude, just like Marta, did nothing but think constantly of the other: if by midday one hadn't heard the other, she would go to the wall to listen.

Gertrude had a handsome she-cat, all white, with sky-blue eyes that reminded her of the color of her glass prayer beads. Whenever Marta saw the cat on the landing, waiting for its mistress to let it in, she would quietly go in her own door, and then admit the cat and get a little piece of bread or cheese for it; because she had mice. But she didn't want Gertrude to find out—not to turn red. The cat, though, was not the least interested in mousing for her, and would miaow to be let out. And Marta would have to open the door again.

Marta's bell rang less well than Gertrude's, and also her door had to be given two hard pushes before putting the inside latch on. And her floor shook, too, when she walked over it; while Gertrude's didn't. Both believed they had the same number of rooms, but, for all their curiosity to make sure, they never inquired.

In fact, their curiosity began to change into a feeling of hostility; but they did everything to contain it, out of good breeding. Marta was small, with cutting blue eyes; she always wore black, and a large pale rose in her bonnet. Gertrude, on the other hand, had a smooth face, and a partly idiotic, partly sinister air about her: tall, with eyes that could only be called green; and yellow hair. But she wasn't bad, either. Of their pasts nothing remained but a residue in their memories; even the grave of Marta's husband had become less and less visible, and its headstone, where no one read any more, was overgrown with thick clumps of succulents. And when it rained the water left cypress leaves on it.

Their pasts had been entirely cut off from them, and they had withered, as though the sap had been cut off, too. They tried to close the gap, in vain.

But now the years were all alike; and the two women, one as much as the other, lived only for the happenings of the day. They were pleased that the same things recurred, and always to be making the same remarks, as if they had had to learn them by heart. If they had had to express a single idea more, they would have been incapable of it. Which is why even their doors looked alike.

But in the end, Gertrude fell ill: she sensed she was about to die: she wanted to die. Only grudgingly would she get up again. Illness gave her a pleasurable feeling of indolence, which one can never be freed from.

She would say to everyone, as if she were going on a most ordinary journey, "At last I'm going to die!"

And, stretched out longer than the bed, she would smile, trying to make the others smile, too. But death hung back. Then she fancied that just by longing for it she could make it come.

Whenever she remembered Marta, she would think: She'll go on living. I'm glad she has to live.

This was a kind of revenge she was able to take, as a person growing richer might say: Not I—it's he who's poor. Still, she felt a languid, loving kindness toward the things she saw and the people who came to call. Also, she was seized by a restlessness to make gifts to everybody.

She was always saying, "I'll give you my ring. Why should I have it put on when I'm dead? . . . And you my silverware. You just have to promise never to sell it. But to Marta, even if she comes to see me, I won't even give my cat; because she's always envied me!"

But she tired of looking at the walls of her room, and her impatience grew and grew; like a fever. In the end, death came truly; without Gertrude's even noticing it.

And Marta, who had never dared enter her flat! At times Marta waited on the steps for the people leaving; to ask after Gertrude. But Gertrude begged them not to say anything.

Marta couldn't sleep any more: on the other side of the wall, she knew, in a room like hers, the oil lamp burned all night.

Also, she had a strong desire to talk about Gertrude and to show pity, thinking up many fine, sweet things to say, and praying for her: she wanted Gertrude to go to heaven.

Now she called the cat not so much to mouse for her as because she wanted to care for it. She felt as if she were always taking it in; making herself its mistress.

But one night she dreamed that Gertrude had got well; she saw Gertrude go by swiftly without moving her legs. Wherever was she going? She tried to do the same, but failed.

The dream left her very envious. By then she hadn't any of the finer feelings; and she left off feeding the cat, lest Gertrude not die. But what if she gave her the cat?

How she disliked living for so long in the same house with her! Why had she met her? Next she got angry because she heard the bell ring at least six or seven times a day.

Her kitchen window filled in a little time, but did not let her forget Gertrude. From the Mangia Tower the hours struck in the silence through all Siena; and an echo, like another clock, repeated them into the countryside, with placid clarity. The trees behind the hospital shaded the patients' large windows, and the round basins in the orchards, at the foot of the walls, shone like tarnished mirrors. In the limpid air the hills had a still sweetness, and the cathedral was so white as to wound the eyes, when the sun was too bright.

Flocks of swallows filled the sky with their screeching, without letup; they flew round behind Marta's house; and then so close, almost grazing it, that the beating of their wings was heard; others dropped away from the Mangia Tower, bent to one side, returned round behind; one lone swallow from another tower went by swiftly, in spurts; a swarm, smaller and less dense, hung for hours and hours in the same spot. Somewhere a bell sounded, and she recognized the church. She could see so many rooftops that from there, from above, they seemed to float in mid-air. The swallows even went up under the eaves troughs to build their nests; rising from the green orchards planted with a few peach trees in blossom, and with rows of cypresses. The spring air called up no memories, but she felt better, and it was a great pleasure knowing that Gertrude was ill and could not see all she saw. But now she understood, without knowing why, the reason one must live; she opened the window, dipping her bread into the scalded milk, holding the handleless cup over the sill, so as to have the serenity before her in full. She chewed slowly, not to finish too quickly, thinking with joy that her husband was dead too. And this could hardly be explained, for she had always loved him.

But for her to feel as she did was a joy. She thought: I can eat at my leisure, because they're not coming for me with a coffin.

Yet she was also strangely sad, in a way that recalled times past; and past things came back to her so vividly as to seem like pictures. Even artificial flowers seem real at times.

Marta heard a former spirit speaking in her stead, and she could not still it. Because her memories had an artificial life of their own.

But she took to looking at the wall on the other side of which Gertrude lay, with an air of defiance, that was a little frightening. Maybe it wasn't thick enough; maybe they could see her anyway. She shook her fist at the wall, in a fury, threatening Gertrude. Was she unable to live without thinking of Gertrude? And when they carried her away, Marta went out; she went to sit on a bench along the public walk of the Lizza; but she cried, though; and it was as if the coffin were going right by before her.

Then she struck up a conversation with a wet nurse, very grateful to the nurse, who talked about quite different things.

And although she was ashamed to have left the house, she did not go back till nightfall.

On the stairs, in the dark, she got a start: as she turned the key in the lock the cat brushed up against her legs, without miaowing. She screamed aloud.

Before going to sleep—but she never drew the shutters, to let the moonlight in—she stared long at the wall, waiting for the corpse to rap with its bare knuckles.

Two days later, when she was climbing the stairs again, the cat ran up against her, miaowing. She locked herself in, slamming the door with a crash that went through the whole house.

But it didn't take much for her to know that the house was no longer for her: as after the visit of a thief. Indeed, it was as if everything were gone: air too. And then she began spending nearly every day outdoors—on the first empty bench she came to, under the branches of the shrubbery in the public garden. She sat for hours and hours, watching people go by, even listening to the buzz of flies. She even stopped placing flowers at her husband's grave—not to have to kneel at Gertrude's. She had to forget Gertrude, as if she had never known her! But Gertrude in death was more alive than before; and between them conversations of exhausting length took place, which left her yawning in the end.

And in the evening she could never avoid the cat, which had grown stunted and scrawny, and so dirty that it must have been grubbing in street sweepings. It was pinched and slack-skinned; its nose not soft and rosy any more, but yellow and sickly. The fur in its ears was coming out. It wanted to follow her in at all costs, and miaowed even after the door was closed; it wouldn't keep quiet all night. The cat that had always been Gertrude's!

Then she went to an apothecary; she asked him—whispering for shame—to sell her some poison. Marta, who under no circumstances would give a two-*centesimo* coin to anyone, spent half a lira. But she was happy. The poor creature! It wouldn't die of hunger!

She cut the fatty part, which she always threw out, from the beef she was going to boil, and dredged it in the white powder. Then she called the cat, her heart throbbing with fear and pleasure. The cat caught hold of the meat, ravening it convulsively, bolting it almost whole.

The scavenger found it lying out at the foot of the stairs and flung it into his cart.

And Marta lived five years longer.

TRANSLATED BY BEN JOHNSON

TIN LIZZIE

John Dos Passos

"Mr. Ford the automobileer," the featurewriter wrote in 1900,

"Mr. Ford the automobileer began by giving his steed three or four sharp jerks with the lever at the righthand side of the seat; that is, he pulled the lever up and down sharply in order, as he said, to mix air with gasoline and drive the charge into the exploding cylinder. . . . Mr. Ford slipped a small electric switch handle and there followed a puff, puff, puff. . . . The puffing of the machine assumed a higher key. She was flying along about eight miles an hour. The ruts in the road were deep, but the machine certainly went with a dreamlike smoothness. There was none of the bumping common even to a streetcar. . . . By this time the boulevard had been reached, and the automobileer, letting a lever fall a little, let her out. Whiz! She picked up speed with infinite rapidity. As she ran on there was a clattering behind, the new noise of the automobile.

For twenty years or more,

ever since he'd left his father's farm when he was sixteen to get a job in a Detroit machineshop, Henry Ford had been nuts about machinery. First it was watches, then he designed a steamtractor, then he built a horseless carriage with an engine adapted from the Otto gasengine he'd read about in *The World of Science*, then a mechanical buggy with a onecylinder fourcycle motor, that would run forward but not back;

at last, in ninetyeight, he felt he was far enough along to risk throwing up his job with the Detroit Edison Company, where he'd worked his way up from night fireman to chief engineer, to put all his time into working on a new gasoline engine,

Henry Ford had ideas about other things than the designing of motors, carburetors, magnetos, jigs and fixtures, punches and dies; he had ideas about sales,

that the big money was in economical quantity production, quick turnover, cheap interchangeable easilyreplaced standardized parts;

it wasn't until 1909, after years of arguing with his partners, that Ford put out the first Model T.

Henry Ford was right.

That season he sold more than ten thousand tin lizzies, ten years later he was selling almost a million a year.

In these years the Taylor Plan was stirring up plantmanagers and manufacturers all over the country. Efficiency was the word. The same ingenuity that went into proving the performance of a machine could go into improving the performance of the workmen producing the machine.

In 1913 they established the assemblyline at Ford's. That season the profits were something like twentyfive million dollars, but they had trouble in keeping the men on the job, machinists didn't seem to like it at Ford's.

Henry Ford had ideas about other things than production.

He was the largest automobile manufacturer in the world; he paid high wages; maybe if the steady workers thought they were getting a cut (a very small cut) in the profits, it would give trained men an inducement to stick to their jobs,

wellpaid workers might save enough money to buy a tin lizzie; the first day Ford's announced that cleancut properlymarried American workers who wanted jobs had a chance to make five bucks a day (of course it turned out that there were strings to it; always there were strings to it)

such an enormous crowd waited outside the Highland Park plant

all through the zero January night

that there was a riot when the gates were opened; cops broke heads, jobhunters threw bricks; property, Henry Ford's own property, was destroyed. The company dicks had to turn on the firehose to beat back the crowd.

The American Plan; automotive prosperity seeping down from above; it turned out there were strings to it.

But that five dollars a day

paid to good, clean American workmen

who didn't drink or smoke cigarettes or read or think,

and who didn't commit adultery
and whose wives didn't take in boarders,
made America once more the Yukon of the sweated workers of the world;
made all the tin lizzies and the automotive age, and incidentally,
made Henry Ford the automobileer, the admirer of Edison, the birdlover,
the great American of his time.

But Henry Ford had ideas about other things besides assemblylines and the livinghabits of his employees. He was full of ideas. Instead of going to the city to make his fortune, here was a country boy who'd made his fortune by bringing the city out to the farm. The precepts he'd learned out of McGuffey's Reader, his mother's prejudices and preconceptions, he had preserved clean and unworn as freshprinted bills in the safe in a bank.

He wanted people to know about his ideas, so he bought the *Dearborn Independent* and started a campaign against cigarettesmoking.

When war broke out in Europe, he had ideas about that too. (Suspicion of armymen and soldiering were part of the midwest farm tradition, like thrift, stickativeness, temperance and sharp practice in money matters.) Any intelligent American mechanic could see that if the Europeans hadn't been a lot of ignorant underpaid foreigners who drank, smoked, were loose about women and wasteful in their methods of production, the war could never have happened.

When Rosika Schwimmer broke through the stockade of secretaries and servicemen who surrounded Henry Ford and suggested to him that he could stop the war,

he said sure they'd hire a ship and go over and get the boys out of the trenches by Christmas.

He hired a steamboat, the *Oscar II*, and filled it up with pacifists and socialworkers,
to go over to explain to the princelings of Europe
that what they were doing was vicious and silly.
It wasn't his fault that Poor Richard's commonsense no longer rules the world and that most of the pacifists were nuts,
goofy with headlines.

When William Jennings Bryan went over to Hoboken to see him
off, somebody handed William Jennings Bryan a squirrel in a cage;
William Jennings Bryan made a speech with the squirrel under his
arm. Henry Ford threw American Beauty roses to the crowd. The
band played *I Didn't Raise My Boy to Be a Soldier*. Practical jokers
let loose more squirrels. An eloping couple was married by a platoon
of ministers in the saloon, and Mr. Zero, the flophouse humanitarian,
who reached the dock too late to sail,

dove into the North River and swam after the boat.

The *Oscar II* was described as a floating Chautauqua; Henry Ford
said it felt like a middlewestern village, but by the time they reached
Christiansand in Norway, the reporters had kidded him so that he
had gotten cold feet and gone to bed. The world was too crazy outside
of Wayne County, Michigan. Mrs. Ford and the management sent an
Episcopal dean after him who brought him home under wraps,

and the pacifists had to speechify without him.

Two years later Ford's was manufacturing munitions, Eagle boats;
Henry Ford was planning oneman tanks, and oneman submarines like
the one tried out in the Revolutionary War. He announced to the
press that he'd turn over his war profits to the government,

but there's no record that he ever did.

One thing he brought back from his trip
was the Protocols of the Elders of Zion.

He started a campaign to enlighten the world in the *Dearborn
Independent*; the Jews were why the world wasn't like Wayne
County, Michigan, in the old horse and buggy days;

the Jews had started the war, Bolshevism, Darwinism, Marxism,
Nietzsche, short skirts and lipstick. They were behind Wall Street
and the international bankers, and the whiteslave traffic and the
movies and the Supreme Court and ragtime and the illegal liquor
business.

Henry Ford denounced the Jews and ran for senator and sued the
Chicago Tribune for libel,

and was the laughingstock of the kept metropolitan press;

but when the metropolitan bankers tried to horn in on his
business

he thoroughly outsmarted them.

In 1918 he had borrowed on notes to buy out his minority stockholders for the picayune sum of seventy-five million dollars.

In February, 1920, he needed cash to pay off some of these notes that were coming due. A banker is supposed to have called on him and offered him every facility if the bankers' representative could be made a member of the board of directors. Henry Ford handed the banker his hat,

and went about raising the money in his own way:

he shipped every car and part he had in his plant to his dealers and demanded immediate cash payment. Let the other fellow do the borrowing had always been a cardinal principle. He shut down production and canceled all orders from the supplyfirms. Many dealers were ruined, many supplyfirms failed, but when he reopened his plant,

he owned it absolutely,

the way a man owns an unmortgaged farm with the taxes paid up.

In 1922 there started the Ford boom for President (high wages, waterpower, industry scattered to the small towns) that was skillfully pricked behind the scenes

by another crackerbarrel philosopher,

Calvin Coolidge;

but in 1922 Henry Ford sold one million three hundred and thirtytwo thousand two hundred and nine tin lizzies; he was the richest man in the world.

Good roads had followed the narrow ruts made in the mud by the Model T. The great automotive boom was on. At Ford's production was improving all the time; less waste, more spotters, strawbosses, stoolpigeons (fifteen minutes for lunch, three minutes to go to the toilet, the Taylorized speedup, everywhere, reach under, adjust washer, screw down bolt, shove in cotterpin, reachunder adjustwasher, screwdown bolt, reachunderadjustscrewdownreachunderadjust until every ounce of life was sucked off into production and at night the workmen went home grey shaking husks).

Ford owned every detail of the process from the ore in the hills until the car rolled off the end of the assemblyline under its own power, the plants were rationalized to the last tenthousandth of an inch as measured by the Johansen scale;

in 1926 the production cycle was reduced to eightyone hours from

the ore in the mine to the finished salable car proceeding under its
own power,
    but the Model T was obsolete.

    New Era prosperity and the American Plan
    (there were strings to it, always there were strings to it)
    had killed Tin Lizzie.
    Ford's was just one of many automobile plants.
    When the stockmarket bubble burst,
    Mr. Ford the crackerbarrel philosopher said jubilantly,
    "I told you so.
    Serves you right for gambling and getting in debt.
    The country is sound."
    But when the country on cracked shoes, in frayed trousers, belts
tightened over hollow bellies,
    idle hands cracked and chapped with the cold of that coldest
March day of 1932,
    started marching from Detroit to Dearborn, asking for work and
the American Plan, all they could think of at Ford's was machine-
guns.
    The country was sound, but they mowed the marchers down.
    They shot four of them dead.

    Henry Ford as an old man
    is a passionate antiquarian,
    (lives besieged on his father's farm embedded in an estate of
thousands of millionaire acres, protected by an army of servicemen,
secretaries, secret agents, dicks under orders of an English ex-
prizefighter,
    always afraid of the feet in broken shoes on the roads, afraid the
gangs will kidnap his grandchildren,
    that a crank will shoot him,
    that Change and the idle hands out of work will break through the
gates and the high fences;
    protected by a private army against
    the new America of starved children and hollow bellies and cracked
shoes stamping on souplines,
    that has swallowed up the old thrifty farmlands
    of Wayne County, Michigan,

as if they had never been).
Henry Ford as an old man
is a passionate antiquarian.

He rebuilt his father's farmhouse and put it back exactly in the state he remembered it in as a boy. He built a village of museums for buggies, sleighs, coaches, old plows, waterwheels, obsolete models of motorcars. He scoured the country for fiddlers to play old-fashioned squaredances.

Even old taverns he bought and put back into their original shape, as well as Thomas Edison's early laboratories.

When he bought the Wayside Inn near Sudbury, Massachusetts, he had the new highway where the newmodel cars roared and slithered and hissed oilily past (*the new noise of the automobile*),
moved away from the door,
put back the old bad road,
so that everything might be
the way it used to be,
in the days of horses and buggies.

.   .
.   .
.   .

The beautiful, rapid biographies which Dos Passos stuffed like truffles into his fictional trilogy U.S.A. could hardly exist outside that grand spread. Too brief for "the real thing," too rich for serial consumption, they need the banquet largesse and variety of his panorama. Each is a brilliant construct, the compression of life matter by dominant notions packaged by a variety of poetic devices, repetitions, quick transitions, in medias res beginnings, and the physical make-up of sentences and pages for rhythmic reinforcement.

Henry Ford may have been more, less, or other than a tinkering, corn-fed Dr. Frankenstein, but it will take a thousand duller pages to dislodge Dos Passos' gleaming portrait from his readers' galleries.

THE WALKER-THROUGH-WALLS

Marcel Aymé

There lived in Montmartre, on the third floor of No. 75*bis*, Rue d'Orchampt, an excellent man named Dutilleul who possessed the singular gift of being able to walk through walls without experiencing any discomfort. He wore *pince-nez* and a little black beard, and he was a third-grade clerk in the Ministry of Registration. In winter he went by bus to his office, and in summer he went on foot, under his bowler-hat.

Dutilleul had just entered his forty-third year when his especial aptitude was revealed to him. One evening, having been caught by a brief failure of the electricity in the vestibule of his small bachelor apartment, he fumbled for a moment in the darkness, and when the lights went on again found himself on the third-floor landing. Since his front door was locked on the inside the incident caused him to reflect, and despite the protests of his reason he resolved to go in as he had come out, by walking through the wall. This strange attainment, which seemed to correspond to none of his aspirations, preyed slightly on his mind, and on the following day, a Saturday, he took advantage of the weekend to call on a neighbouring doctor and put the case to him. The doctor, after convincing himself of the truth of his story, discovered upon examination that the cause of the trouble lay in the helicoidal hardening of the strangulatory wall of the thyroid vesicle. He prescribed a regime of intensive exertion, and, at the rate of two cachets a year, the absorption into the system of tetravalent reintegration powder, a mixture of rice flour and centaur's hormones.

After taking the first cachet Dutilleul put the rest away in a drawer and thought no more about them. As for the intensive exertion, his work as a civil servant was ordered by custom which did not permit of any excess; neither did his leisure hours, which were devoted to the daily paper and his stamp collection, call for any unreasonable

290

expenditure of energy. So that at the end of a year his knack of walking through walls remained unimpaired; but he never made use of it, except inadvertently, having little love of adventure and being non-receptive to the lures of the imagination. It did not even occur to him to enter his own apartment otherwise than by the door, after duly turning the key in the lock. Perhaps he would have grown old in his sedate habits, without ever being tempted to put his gift to the test, had not an extraordinary event suddenly occurred to revolutionise his existence. M. Mouron, the head of his sub-section at the ministry, was transferred to other duties and replaced by a M. Lécuyer, who was brisk of speech and wore a small military moustache. From the first day this newcomer manifested the liveliest disapproval of the *pince-nez* which Dutilleul wore attached to a short chain, and of his little black beard, and he elected to treat him as a tiresome and not over-clean elderly encumbrance. Worst of all, he saw fit to introduce into the work of his sub-section certain far-reaching reforms which were well calculated to trouble the peace of mind of his subordinate. Dutilleul was accustomed to begin his letters with the following formula: "With reference to your esteemed communication of the such-and-such instant, and having regard to our previous exchange of letters on this subject, I have the honour to inform you . . ." For which M. Lécuyer proposed to substitute a more trans-Atlantic form of words: "Yours of the such-and-such. I beg to state . . ." Dutilleul could not accustom himself to this epistolary terseness. Despite himself he reverted with a machine-like obstinacy to the traditional form, thereby incurring the increasing animosity of his superior. The atmosphere of the Ministry of Registration became almost oppressive to him. He went apprehensively to work in the morning, and at night, after going to bed, he would often lie brooding for as much as a quarter of an hour before falling asleep.

Outraged by a reactionary stubbornness which threatened to undermine the success of his reforms. M. Lécuyer relegated Dutilleul to a small and sombre room, scarcely more than a cupboard, next door to his own office. It was entered by a low, narrow door giving on to the corridor, and which bore in capital letters the legend: "BACK FILES." Dutilleul resignedly acquiesced in this unprecedented humiliation, but when he read some more than usually sanguinary story in his newspaper he found himself dreaming that M. Lécuyer was the victim.

One day his chief burst into his cupboard brandishing a letter and bellowing:

"This must be done again! I insist upon your rewriting this unspeakable document which is a disgrace to my sub-section!"

Dutilleul was about to protest, but in a voice of thunder M. Lécuyer informed him that he was a routine-besotted mole and crumpling the letter flung it in his face. Dutilleul was a modest man, but proud. Left alone in his cupboard he felt his temperature rising, and suddenly he was seized with an inspiration. Leaving his seat he passed into the wall between his chief's room and his own, but he did so with caution, so that only his head emerged on the other side. M. Lécuyer, seated again at his desk, his pen still quivering, was in the act of striking out a comma from the text of a letter submitted by a subordinate for his approval, when he heard the sound of a cough in his room. Looking up he perceived with unspeakable dismay the head of Dutilleul, seemingly affixed to the wall like a trophy of the chase. But this head was alive. Through the *pince-nez*, with their length of chain, the eyes glared balefully at him. What is more, the head spoke.

"Sir," it said, "you are a scoundrel, a blockhead and a mountebank."

M. Lécuyer, his mouth gaping with horror, had difficulty in withdrawing his gaze from the apparition. At length he heaved himself out of his chair, plunged into the corridor and flung open the door of the cupboard. Dutilleul, pen in hand, was seated in his accustomed place, in an attitude of tranquil and devoted industry. M. Lécuyer stared at him for some time in silence, and then, after muttering a few words, returned to his office. Scarcely had he resumed his seat than the head again appeared on the wall.

"Sir, you are a scoundrel, a blockhead and a mountebank."

In the course of that day alone the terrifying head manifested itself twenty-three times, and on the following days it appeared with a similar frequency. Having acquired a certain skill at the game, Dutilleul was no longer content merely to abuse his chief. He uttered obscure threats, for example proclaiming in a sepulchral voice punctuated with truly demoniac laughter:

"The werewolf is here, the end is near! (*laughter*). Flesh creeps and terror fills the air! (*laughter*)."

Hearing which, the unhappy sub-section chief grew yet more pale,

THE WALKER-THROUGH-WALLS
Marcel Aymé

yet more breathless, while the hairs stood rigid on his head and the sweat of anguish trickled down his spine. During the first day he lost a pound in weight. In the course of the ensuing week, besides almost visibly melting away, he developed a tendency to eat soup with a fork and to greet the guardians of the law with a military salute. At the beginning of the second week an ambulance called at his dwelling and bore him off to a mental home.

Being thus delivered from the tyranny of M. Lécuyer, Dutilleul could return to his cherished formula—"With reference to your esteemed communication of the such-and-such . . ." Yet he was not satisfied. There was now a yearning in him, a new, imperious impulse which was nothing less than the need to walk through walls. It is true that he had ample opportunities of doing so, in his apartment for example, of which he did not neglect to avail himself. But the man possessing brilliant gifts cannot long be content to squander them on trifles. Moreover, the act of walking through a wall cannot be said to constitute an end in itself. It is a mere beginning, the start of an adventure calling for an outcome, a realisation—calling, in short, for a reward. Dutilleul was well aware of this. He felt an inner need to expand, a growing desire to fulfil and surpass himself, and a restless hankering which was in some sort the call of the other side of the wall. But an objective, alas, was lacking. He sought inspiration in his daily paper, particularly in the columns devoted to politics and sport, both of which seemed to him commendable activities; but perceiving finally that these offered no outlet for persons capable of walking through walls, he fell back on the crime columns, which proved to be rich in suggestion.

Dutilleul's first burglary took place in a large credit establishment on the right bank of the Seine. After passing through a dozen walls and partitions he thrust his hand into a number of strong-boxes, filled his pockets with banknotes and before leaving signed his crime in red chalk, using the pseudonym of "The Werewolf," adorned with a handsome flourish which was reproduced in all the papers next day. By the end of a week "The Werewolf" had achieved an extraordinary celebrity. The heart of the public went out unreservedly to this phenomenal burglar who so prettily mocked the police. He drew attention to himself each night by a fresh exploit carried out at the expense, now of a bank, now of a jeweller's shop or of some wealthy individual. In Paris, as in the provinces, there was no woman with romance in her heart who had not a fervent desire to belong body and soul to the terrible Werewolf. After the theft of the famous Burdigala diamond and the robbing of the Crédit Municipal, which occurred during the same week, the enthusiasm of the crowd reached the point of delirium. The Minister of the Interior was compelled to resign, dragging with him in his fall the Minister of Registration. Nevertheless, Dutilleul, now one of the richest men in Paris, never failed to arrive punctually at the office, and was spoken of as a candidate for the *palmes académiques*. And every morning, at the Ministry of Registration, he had the pleasure of hearing his colleagues discuss his exploits of the previous night. "This Werewolf," they said, "is a stupendous fellow, a superman, a genius." Hearing such praise, Dutilleul turned pink with embarrassment and behind the *pince-nez* his eyes shone with friendship and gratitude. A day came when the atmosphere of sympathy so overwhelmed him that he felt he could keep the secret no longer. Surveying with a last twinge of shyness the group of his colleagues arrayed round a newspaper containing an account of the robbery of the Banque de France, he said in a diffident voice: "As a matter of fact, *I'm* the Werewolf." The confession was received with a huge and interminable burst of laughter, and the nickname of "Werewolf" was at once mockingly bestowed on him. That evening, at the time of leaving the ministry, he was the object of endless pleasantries on the part of his fellow-workers, and life seemed to him less rosy.

A few days later the Werewolf allowed himself to be caught by a police patrol in a jeweller's shop on the Rue de la Paix. He had inscribed his signature on the safe and was singing a drinking-song while smashing windows with a massive gold tankard. It would have been a simple matter for him to escape by merely slipping through a wall, but everything leads one to suppose that he wished to be arrested, probably for the sole purpose of confounding the colleagues whose incredulity had so mortified him. These were indeed greatly astonished when the newspapers next day published Dutilleul's picture on the front page. They bitterly regretted having underrated their inspired *confrère*, and did him homage by growing little beards. Some of them, carried away by remorse and admiration, went so far as to try to get their hands on the wallets or watches of their friends and relations.

It may well be considered that to allow oneself to be caught by the police in order to impress a few colleagues is to display an extreme frivolity unworthy of an eminent public figure; but the apparent exercise of free-will plays little part in a resolution of this kind. In sacrificing his liberty Dutilleul thought he was yielding to an arrogant desire for revenge, whereas in fact he was merely following the ineluctable course of his destiny. No man who walks through walls can consider his career even moderately fulfilled if he has not had at least one taste of prison. When Dutilleul entered the precincts of the Santé he had a feeling of being the spoilt child of fortune. The thickness of the walls was to him a positive delight. On the very day following his incarceration the warders discovered to their stupefaction that he had driven a nail into the wall of his cell and had hung from it a gold watch belonging to the prison Governor. He either could not or would not disclose how the article had come into his possession. The watch was restored to its owner and the next day was again found at the bedside of the Werewolf, together with the first volume of *The Three Musketeers*, borrowed from the Governor's library. The whole staff of the prison was on edge. The warders complained, moreover, of receiving kicks on the bottom coming from some inexplicable source. It seemed that the walls no longer had ears but had feet instead. The detention of the Werewolf had lasted a week when the Governor, entering his office one morning, found the following letter on his desk:

SIR:
    With reference to our interview of the 17th instant, and having regard to your general instruction of May 15th of last year, I have the honour to inform you that I have just concluded my perusal of *The Three Musketeers*, Vol. II, and that I propose to escape tonight between 11:25 P.M. and 11:35 P.M.

                    I beg to remain, Sir,
                        With expressions of the deepest respect,
                            Your obedient servant,
                                THE WEREWOLF.

Despite the extremely close watch kept upon him that night, Dutilleul escaped at 11:30. The news, when it became known to the public on the following day, occasioned an outburst of tremendous enthusiasm. Nevertheless, Dutilleul, having achieved another burglary which set the seal on his popularity, seemed to have little desire to hide himself and walked freely about Montmartre without taking any precautions. Three days after his escape he was arrested in the Café du Rêve on the Rue Clignancourt, where he was drinking a *vin blanc citron* with a few friends.

Being taken back to the Santé and secured behind triple locks in a gloomy dungeon, the Werewolf left it the same evening and passed the night in the guest-room of the Governor's apartment. At about nine the next morning he rang for his *petit déjeuner* and allowed himself to be captured in bed, without offering any resistance, by the warders summoned for the purpose. The outraged Governor caused a special guard to be posted at the door of his cell and put him on bread and water. Towards midday he went out and had lunch at a neighbouring restaurant, and, having finished his coffee, telephoned the Governor as follows:

"My dear Governor, I am covered with confusion. When I left the prison a short time ago I omitted to take your wallet, so that I am now penniless in a restaurant. Will you be so good as to send someone to pay my bill?"

The Governor hurried to the spot in person, and so far forgot himself as to utter threats and abuse. Wounded in his deepest feelings, Dutilleul escaped the following night, never to return. This time he took the precaution of shaving his black tuft of beard and substituting hornrimmed spectacles for the *pince-nez* and chain. A sports cap and a suit of plus-fours in a loud check completed his transformation. He established himself in a small apartment in the Avenue Junot where, during the period preceding his first arrest, he had installed a part of his furniture and the possessions which he most valued. The notoriety attaching to his name was beginning to weary him, and since his stay in the Santé he had become rather blasé in the matter of walking through walls. The thickest, the proudest of them seemed to him no more than the flimsiest of screens, and he dreamed of thrusting his way into the very heart of some massive pyramid. While meditating on the project of a trip to Egypt he lived the most tranquil of lives, divided between his stamp collection, the cinema and prolonged strolls about Montmartre. So complete was his metamorphosis that, clean-shaven and hornrimmed-spectacled, he passed his best friends in the street without being recognised. Only the painter, Gen Paul, whom no detail escaped of any change in the physiognomy of an old resident of the quarter, succeeded in the end in penetrating his disguise. Finding himself face to face with Dutilleul at the corner of the Rue de l'Abreuvoir, he could not restrain himself from remarking in his crude slang:

"*Dis donc, je vois que tu t'es miché en gigolpince pour tétarer ceux de la sûrepige*"—which roughly means, in common speech: "I see you've got yourself up like a man of fashion to baffle the inspectors of the Sûreté."

"Ah!" murmured Dutilleul. "So you've recognised me!"

He was perturbed by this and resolved to hasten his departure for Egypt. But it was on the afternoon of this very day that he fell in love with a ravishing blonde whom he twice encountered in the Rue Lepic, at a quarter of an hour's interval. He instantly forgot his stamp collection, Egypt and the Pyramids. The blonde, for her part, had gazed at him with considerable interest. Nothing stirs the imagination of the young women of the present day more than plus-fours and horn-rimmed spectacles: they have a flavour of film scripts, they set one dreaming of cocktails and Californian nights. Unfortunately the lady—so Dutilleul was informed by Gen Paul—was married to a violent and jealous man. This suspicious husband, who himself led a dissolute life, regularly forsook his wife between the hours of ten at night and four in the morning; but before doing so he locked her in her bedroom and padlocked all the shutters. During the daytime he kept a close eye on her, even going so far on occasions as to follow her as she went along the streets of Montmartre.

"Always snooping, you see. He's one of those coarse-minded so-and-so's that don't stand for anyone poaching on their preserves."

But Gen Paul's warning served only to inflame Dutilleul's ardour. Encountering the young woman in the Rue Tholozé on the following day, he boldly followed her into a *crémerie*, and while she was awaiting her turn to be served he told her of his respectful passion and that he knew all—the villainous husband, the locked door and the padlocked shutters—but that he proposed nevertheless to visit her that same evening. The blonde flushed scarlet while the milk-jug trembled in her hand. Her eyes melting with tenderness she murmured weakly: "Alas, Monsieur, it is impossible."

On the evening of that glorious day, towards ten o'clock, Dutilleul was at his post in the Rue Norvins, keeping watch on a solid outer wall behind which was situated a small house of which he could see nothing except the weather-cock and the chimney-stack. A door in this wall opened and a man emerged who, after locking it carefully behind him, went down the hill towards the Avenue Junot. Dutilleul waited until he saw him vanish in the far distance at the turn of the road, after which he counted ten. Then he darted forward, skipped lightly with an athlete's stride into the wall, and running through all obstacles penetrated into the bedroom of the beautiful captive. She received him with transports of delight and they made love till an advanced hour.

The next day Dutilleul had the vexation to suffer from a severe headache. It was a matter of no importance, and he had no intention of failing to keep his rendezvous for so little. However, chancing to discover a few cachets scattered at the bottom of a drawer, he swallowed one in the morning and another in the afternoon. By the evening his headache was bearable, and his state of exaltation caused him to forget it. The young woman was awaiting him with all the impatience to which her recollections of the previous evening had given rise, and that night they made love until three in the morning. Upon his departure, as he passed through the inner and outer walls of the house, Dutilleul had a sense of unaccustomed friction at his hips and shoulders. However, he did not think this worthy of any particular attention. Only when he came to penetrate the surrounding wall did he become definitely aware of a feeling of resistance. He seemed to be moving in a substance that was still fluid, but which was thickening so that it seemed to gain in consistency with every movement that he made. Having succeeded in thrusting the whole of his body into the thickness of the wall, he found that he could no longer progress, and in terror he recalled the two cachets he had taken during the day. These cachets, which he had mistaken for aspirin, had in reality contained the tetravalent reintegration powder prescribed by the doctor a year before. The medicine, aided by his intensive exertions, was suddenly having its intended effect.

Dutilleul was, as it were, petrified in the interior of the wall. He is there to this day, incorporated in the stone. Nightbirds descending the Rue Norvins at the hour when the clamour of Paris had died down, may sometimes hear a stifled voice seeming to come from beyond the tomb, which they take to be the moaning of the wind as it whistles at the crossroads of the Butte. It is Werewolf Dutilleul mourning for his glorious career and his too-brief love. Occasionally on a winter's night the painter, Gen Paul, taking down his guitar, ventures forth into the echoing solitude of the Rue Norvins to console the unhappy prisoner with a song; and the notes, flying from his benumbed fingers, pierce to the heart of the stone like drops of moonlight.

TRANSLATED BY NORMAN DENNY

THE MANY MEN SO BEAUTIFUL

David Jones

> Men marched, they kept equal step . . .
> Men marched, they had been nurtured together.

'49 Wyatt, 01549 Wyatt.

Coming sergeant.

Pick 'em up, pick 'em up—I'll stalk within yer chamber.

Private Leg . . . sick.

Private Ball . . . absent.

'01 Ball, '01 Ball, Ball of No. 1.

Where's Ball, 25201 Ball—you corporal,

Ball of your section.

Movement round and about the Commanding Officer.

Bugler, will you sound "Orderly Sergeants."

A hurrying of feet from three companies converging on the little group apart where on horses sit the central command. But from "B" Company there is no such darting out. The Orderly Sergeant of "B" is licking the stub end of his lead pencil; it divides a little his fairish moist moustache.

Heavily jolting and sideway jostling, the noise of liquid shaken in a small vessel by a regular jogging movement, a certain clinking ending in a shuffling of the feet sidelong—all clear and distinct in that silence peculiar to parade grounds and to refectories. The silence of a high order, full of peril in the breaking of it, like the coming on parade of John Ball.

He settles between numbers 4 and 5 of the rear rank. It is as ineffectual as the ostrich in her sand. Captain Gwynn does not turn or move or give any sign.

Have that man's name taken if you please, Mr. Jenkins.

Take that man's name, Sergeant Snell.

Take his name, corporal.

Take his name take his number—charge him—late on parade—the Battalion being paraded for overseas—warn him for Company Office.

Have you go his name Corporal Quilter.

Temporary unpaid Lance-Corporal Aneirin Merddyn Lewis had somewhere in his Welsh depths a remembrance of the nature of man, of how a lance-corporal's stripe is but held vicariously and from on high, is of one texture with an eternal economy. He brings in a manner, baptism, and metaphysical order to the bankruptcy of the occasion.

'01 Ball is it—there was a man in Bethesda late for the last bloody judgment.

Corporal Quilter on the other hand knew nothing of these things.

Private Ball's pack, ill adjusted and without form, hangs more heavily on his shoulder blades, a sense of ill-usage pervades him. He withdraws within himself to soothe himself—the inequity of those in high places is forgotten. From where he stood heavily, irksomely at ease, he could see, half-left between 7 and 8 of the front rank, the profile of Mr. Jenkins and the elegant cut of his war-time rig and his flax head held front; like San Romano's foreground squire, un-helmeted; but we don't have lances now nor banners nor trumpets. It pains the lips to think of bugles—and did they blow Defaulters on the Uccello horns.

He put his right hand behind him to ease his pack, his cold knuckles find something metallic and colder.

No mess-tin cover.

Shining sanded mess-tin giving back the cold early light. *Improperly dressed, the Battalion being paraded for overseas.* His imaginings as to the precise relationship of this general indictment from the book to his own naked mess-tin were with suddenness and most imperatively impinged upon, as when an animal hunted, stopping in some ill-chosen convert to consider the wickedness of man, is started into fresh effort by the cry and breath of dogs dangerously and newly near. For the chief huntsman is winding his horn, the officer commanding is calling his Battalion by name—whose own the sheep are.

55th Battalion!
Fifty-fifth Bat-tal-i-on
'talion!!

From "D" to "A" his eyes knew that parade. He detected no movement. They were properly at ease.

Reverberation of that sudden command broke hollowly upon the emptied huts behind "D" Company rear platoons. They had only in them the rolled mattresses, the neatly piled bed-boards and the empty tea-buckets of the orderly-men, emptied of their last gun-fire.

Stirrups taut and pressing upward in the midst of his saddle he continues the ritual words by virtue of which a regiment is moved in column of route:

. . . the Battalion will move in column of fours to the right—"A" Company—"A" Company leading.

Words lost, yet given continuity by that thinner command from in front of No. 1. Itself to be wholly swallowed up by the concerted movement of arms in which the spoken word effected what it signified.

"A" Company came to the slope, their files of four turn right. The complex of command and heel-iron turned confuse the morning air. The rigid structure of their lines knows a swift mobility, patterns differently for those sharp successive cries.

Mr. P. D. I. Jenkins who is twenty years old has now to do his business:

No. 7 Platoon—number seven.

number seven—right—by the right.

How they sway in the swing round for all this multiplicity of gear.

Keept'y'r dressing.

Sergeant Snell did his bit.

Corporal Quilter intones:

Dress to the right—no—other right.

Keep those slopes.

Keep those sections of four.

Pick those knees up.

Throw those chests out.

Hold those heads up.

Stop that talking.

Keep those chins in.

Left left lef'—lef' righ' lef'—you Private Ball it's you I'v got me glad-eye on.

So they came outside the camp. The liturgy of a regiment departing has been sung. Empty wet parade ground. A camp-warden, some unfit men and other details loiter, dribble away, shuffle off like men whose ship has sailed.

The long hutment lines stand. Not a soul. It rains harder: torn felt lifts to the wind about Hut 10, Headquarter Company; urinal concrete echoes for a solitary whistler. Corrugated iron empty—no one. Chill gust slams the vacant canteen door.

Miss Veronica Best who runs the hut for the bun-wallahs stretches on her palliasse, she's sleepy, she can hear the band: We've got too many buns—and all those wads—you knew they were going—why did you order them—they won't be in after rouse-parade even—they're gone.

Know they've gone—shut up—Jocks from Bardown move in Monday. Violet turns to sleep again.

Horses' tails are rather good—and the way this one springs from her groomed flanks.

He turns slightly in his saddle.

You may march at ease.

No one said march easy Private Ball, you're bleedin' quick at some things ain't yer.

The Squire from the Rout of San Romano smokes Melachrino No. 9.

The men may march easy and smoke, Sergeant Snell.

Some like tight belts and some like loose belts—trussed-up pockets—cigarettes in ammunition pouches—rifle-bolts, webbing, buckles and rain—gotta light mate—give us a match chum. How cold the morning is and blue, and how mysterious in cupped hands glow the match-lights of a concourse of men, moving so early in the morning.

The body of the high figure in front of the head of the column seemed to change his position however so slightly. It rains on the transparent talc of his map-case.

The Major's horse rubs noses with the horse of the superior officer. Their docked manes brush each, as two friends would meet. The dark horse snorts a little for the pulling at her bridle rein.

In "D" Company round the bend of the road in the half-light is movement, like a train shunting, when the forward coaches buffer the rear coaches back. The halt was unexpected. How heavy and how top-heavy is all this martial panoply and how the ground seems to press upward to afflict the feet.

The bastard's lost his way already.

Various messages are passed.

Some lean on their rifles as aged men do on sticks in stageplays. Some lean back with the muzzle of the rifle supporting the pack in the position of gentlewomen at field sports, but not with so great assurance.

It's cold when you stop marching with all this weight and icy down the back.

Battalion cyclists pass the length of the column. There is fresh stir in "A" Company.

Keep your column distance.

The regular rhythm of the march has re-established itself.

The rain increases with the light and the weight increases with the rain. In all that long column in brand-new overseas boots weeping blisters stick to the hard wool of grey government socks.

I'm a bleedin' cripple already Corporal, confides a limping child.

Kipt' that step there.

Keep that proper distance.

Keept' y'r siction o' four—can't fall out me little darlin'. Corporal Quilter subsides, he too retreats within himself, he has his private thoughts also.

It's a proper massacre of the innocents in a manner of speaking, no so-called seven ages o' man only this bastard military age.

Keep that step there.

Keep that section distance.

Hand us thet gas-pipe young Saunders—let's see you shape—you too, little Benjamin—hang him about like a goddam Chris'us tree—use his ample shoulders for an armoury-rack—it is his part to succour the lambs of the flock.

With some slackening of the rain the band had wiped their instruments. Broken catches on the wind-gust came shrilly back:

Of Hector and Lysander and such great names as these
—the march proper to them.

So they went most of that day and it rained with increasing vigour until night-fall. In the middle afternoon the outer parts of the town of embarkation were reached. They halted for a brief while; adjusted puttees, straightened caps, fastened undone buttons, tightened rifle-slings and attended each one to his own bedraggled and irregular condition. The band recommenced playing; and at the attention and in excellent step they passed through the suburbs, the town's centre, and so towards the docks. The people of that town did not acclaim them, nor stop about their business—for it was late in the second year.

By some effort of a corporate will the soldierly bearing of the text books maintained itself through the town, but with a realisation of the considerable distance yet to be covered through miles of dock, their frailty reasserted itself—which slackening called for fresh effort from the Quilters and the Snells, but at this stage with a more persuasive intonation, with almost motherly concern.

Out of step and with a depressing raggedness of movement and rankling of tempers they covered another mile between dismal sheds, high and tarred. Here funnels and mastheads could be seen. Here the influence of the sea and of the tackle and ways of its people fell upon them. They revived somewhat, and for a while. Yet still these interminable ways between—these incessant halts at junctions. Once they about-turned. Embarkation officers, staff people of all kinds and people who looked as though they were in the Navy but who were not, consulted with the Battalion Commander. A few more halts, more passing of messages,—a further intensifying of their fatigue. The platoons of the leading company unexpectedly wheel. The spacious shed is open at either end, windy and comfortless. Multi-farious accoutrements, metal and cloth and leather sink with the perspiring bodies to the concrete floor.

Certain less fortunate men were detailed for guard, John Ball amongst them. The others lay, where they first sank down, wet with rain and sweat. They smoked; they got very cold. They were given tins of bully beef and ration biscuits for the first time and felt like real expeditionary soldiers. Sometime between midnight and 2 A.M. they were paraded. Slowly, and with every sort of hitch, platoon upon platoon formed single file and moved toward an invisible gangway. Each separate man found his own feet stepping in the darkness on an inclined plane, the smell and taste of salt and machinery, the texture of rope, and the glimmer of shielded light about him.

So without sound of farewell or acclamation, shrouded in a dense windy darkness, they set toward France. They stood close on deck and beneath deck, each man upholstered in his life-belt. From time to time a seaman would push between them about some duty belonging to his trade.

Under a high-slung arc-light whose cold clarity well displayed all their sea weariness, their long cramped-upness and fatigue, they stumblingly and one by one trickled from the ship on to French land. German prisoners in green tunics, made greener by the light, heavily unloading timber at a line of trucks—it still rained, and a bitter wind in from the sea.

A young man, comfortable in a short fleece jacket, stood smoking, immediately beneath the centre of the arc—he gave orders in a pleasant voice, that measured the leisure of his circumstances and his class. Men move to left and right within the orbit of the light, and away into the half darkness, undefined, beyond it.

"B" Company were conducted by a guide, through back ways between high shuttered buildings, to horse-stalls, where they slept. In the morning, they were given Field Service postcards—and sitting in the straw they crossed out what did not apply, and sent them to their mothers, to their sweethearts.

Toward evening on the same day they entrained in cattle trucks; and on the third day, which was a Sunday, sunny and cold, and French women in deep black were hurrying across flat land—they descended from their grimy, littered, limb restricting, slatted vehicles, and stretched and shivered at a siding. You feel exposed and apprehensive in this new world.

THE FARMER'S WIFE

The Panchatantra

There was once a farmer who lived with his wife in a certain place. And because the husband was old, the wife was forever thinking of lovers, and could not possibly be contented at home. Her one idea was strange men.

Now a rogue who lived by pilfering, noticed her and said: "You lovely creature, my wife is dead, and I am smitten with love at the sight of you. Pray enrich me with love's perfect treasure."

And she said: "You beautiful man, if you feel that way, my husband has a great deal of money, and he is so old that he cannot stir. I will bring it, so that I may go somewhere with you and enjoy the delights of love."

"That is satisfactory to me," he replied. "Suppose you hasten to this spot at dawn, so that we may go together to some fascinating city where life may bear for me its perfect fruit." "Very well," she agreed, and went home with laughing countenance.

Then at night, while her husband slept, she took all the money, and reached the rendezvous at dawn. The rogue, for his part, put her in front, started south, and traveled two leagues, gaily enjoying the delights of conversation with her. But when he saw a river ahead, he reflected: "What am I to do with this middle-aged female? Besides, someone might perhaps pursue her. I will just take her money and be off."

So he said to her: "My dear, this is a great river, hard to cross. I will just take the money and put it safe on the far bank, then return to carry you alone on my back, and so transport you in comfort." "Do so, my beloved," said she.

So he took the money to the last penny, and then he said: "Dearest, hand me your dress and your wrap, too, so that you may travel through the water unembarrassed." And when she did so, the rogue took the money and the two garments and went to the place he had in mind.

Then the farmer's wife sat down woebegone on the river-bank, digging her two hands into her throat. At that moment a she-jackal came to the spot, carrying a piece of meat. As she came up and peered about, a great fish leaped from the water and was stranded on the bank. On spying him, she dropped the meat and darted at the fish. Whereupon a vulture swooped from the sky and flew off with the meat. And the fish, perceiving the jackal, struggled into the river. So the she-jackal had her pains for nothing, and as she gazed after the vulture, the naked woman smiled and said:

"You poor she-jackal!

> The vulture has your meat;
>   The water holds your fish:
> Of fish and flesh forlorn,
>   What further do you wish?"

And the she-jackal, perceiving that the woman was equally forlorn, having lost her husband's money and her lover, said with a sneer:

"You naked thing!

> Your cleverness is twice
>   As great as mine, 'twould seem;
> Lover and husband lost,
>   You sit beside the stream."

While the crocodile was telling this story, a second water-beast arrived and reported: "Alas! Your house has been occupied by another crocodile—a big fellow." And the crocodile became despondent on hearing this, anxiously considering how to drive him from the house. "Alas, my friends!" said he. "See how unlucky I am. For you must know,

> A stranger occupies my house;
>   My friend is sadly vexed;
> On top of that, my wife is dead.
>   Oh, what will happen next?

"How true it is that misfortunes never come singly! Well, shall I fight him? Or shall I address him with soft conciliation, and get him out of the house? Or shall I try intrigue? Or bribery? Ah, here is my monkey friend. I will ask him. For the proverb says:

> Ask aid of kindly teachers, man,
>   The kind you ought to ask.

> Their counsel leads to sure success,
>   Whatever be your task."

After these reflections, he put the question to the monkey, who had climbed back into the rose-apple tree. "Oh, my friend," said he, "see how unlucky I am. For now my very house is seized and held by a powerful crocodile. Therefore I put it to you. Tell me, what am I to do? Is this the place for soft conciliation or one of the other three devices?"

But the monkey said: "You ungrateful wretch! Why do you still pursue me, though I asked you not to? You are a fool, therefore I will not even give you good advice. For the proverb says:

> Give counsel only when it fits
>   To such as seek the best.
> The foolish monkey broke to bits
>   The sparrow's cozy nest."

TRANSLATED BY ARTHUR W. RYDER

. .
.   .
. .

The morphologist will be amused to read a version of this tale which is some two thousand years younger (and two hundred dollars too costly for inclusion in this collection), Flannery O'Connor's "The Life You Save May Be Your Own" from A Good Man is Hard to Find.

I'M TELLING YOU THE TRUTH

Juan José Arreola

Everybody who is interested in seeing the camel pass through the eye of the needle should inscribe his name on the list of patrons for the Niklaus Experiment.

Disassociated from a group of death-dealing scientists, the kind who manipulate uranium, cobalt, and hydrogen, Arpad Niklaus is guiding his present research toward a charitable and radically humanitarian end: the salvation of the souls of the rich.

He proposes a scientific plan to disintegrate a camel and make it pass in a stream of electrons through a needle's eye. A receiving apparatus (very similar to the television screen) will organize the electrons into atoms, the atoms into molecules, and the molecules into cells, immediately reconstructing the camel according to its original scheme. Niklaus has already managed to make a drop of heavy water change its position without touching it. He has also been able to evaluate, up to the point where the discretion of the material permits, the quantum energy discharged by a camel's hoof. It seems pointless here to burden the reader with that astronomical figure.

The only serious difficulty Professor Niklaus has run into is the lack of his own atomic plant. Such installations, extensive as cities, are incredibly expensive. But a special committee is already busy solving the problem by means of a world-wide subscription drive. The first contributions, still rather anemic, are serving to defray the cost of thousands of pamphlets, bonds, and explanatory prospectuses, as well as to assure Professor Niklaus the modest salary permitting him to continue with his calculations and theoretical investigations while the immense laboratories are being built.

At present, the committee can count only on the camel and the needle. As the societies for the prevention of cruelty to animals approve the project, which is inoffensive and even healthful for any camel (Niklaus speaks of a probable regeneration of all the cells), the country's zoos have offered a veritable caravan. New York City has not hesitated to risk its very famous white dromedary.

As for the needle, Arpad Niklaus is very proud of it and considers it the keystone of the experiment. It is not just any needle, but a marvelous object discovered by his assiduous talent. At first glance, it might be confused with a common ordinary needle. Mrs. Niklaus, displaying a fine sense of humor, takes pleasure in mending her husband's clothes with it. But its value is infinite. It is made from an extraordinary, as yet unclassified, metal, whose chemical formula, scarcely hinted at by Niklaus, seems to indicate that it involves a base composed exclusively of isotopes of nickel. This mysterious substance has made scientists ponder a great deal. There was even one who sustained the laughable hypothesis of a synthetic osmium or an abnormal molybdenum, or still another who dared to proclaim in public the words of an envious professor who was sure he had recognized Niklaus' metal in the form of tiny crystalline clusters encysted in dense masses of siderite. What is known with certainty is that Niklaus' needle can resist the friction of a stream of electrons flowing at ultrasonic speed.

In one of those explanations so pleasing to abstruse mathematicians, Professor Niklaus compares the camel in its transit to a spider's thread. He tells us that if we were to use that thread to weave a fabric, we would need all of sidereal space to stretch it out in, and that the visible and invisible stars would be caught in it like sprays of dew. The skein in question measures millions of light years, and Niklaus is offering to wind it up in about three-fifths of a second.

As can be seen, the project is completely viable, and, we might even say, overly scientific. It can already count on the sympathy and moral support (not officially confirmed yet) of the Interplanetary League, presided over in London by the eminent Olaf Stapledon.

In view of the natural expectation and anxiety that Niklaus' project has provoked everywhere, the committee is manifesting a special interest by calling the world powers' attention to it, so they will not let themselves be surprised by charlatans who are passing dead camels through subtle orifices. These individuals, who do not hesitate to call themselves scientists, are simply swindlers on the lookout for imprudent optimists. They proceed by an extremely vulgar method, dissolving the camel in sulphuric acid solutions each time lighter than the last. Then they distil the liquid through the needle's eye, using a steam clepsydra, believing that they have performed the miracle. As one can see, the experiment is useless, and there is no reason to finance it. The camel must be alive before and after the impossible transfer.

Instead of melting down tons of candle wax and spending money on indecipherable works of charity, persons interested in the eternal life who have more capital than they know what to do with should subsidize the disintegration of the camel, which is scientific, colorful, and, ultimately, lucrative. To speak of generosity in such a case is totally unnecessary. One must shut one's eyes and open one's purse generously, knowing full well that all expenses will be met pro rata. The reward for all the contributors will be the same; what is urgent is to hasten the date of payment as much as possible.

The total capital necessary cannot be known until the unpredictable end, and Professor Niklaus, in all honesty, refuses to work with a budget that is not fundamentally elastic. The subscribers should pay out their investment quotas patiently over the years. It is necessary to contract for thousands of technicians, managers, and workers. Regional and national subcommittees must be established. And the statute founding a school of successors for Professor Niklaus must not only be foreseen, but budgeted for in detail, since the experiment might reasonably extend over several generations. In this respect, it is not beside the point to indicate the ripe old age of the learned Niklaus.

Like all human plans, Experiment Niklaus offers two probable results: failure and success. Besides simplifying the problem of personal salvation, a success by Niklaus will convert the promoters of such a mystical experience into stockholders of a fabulous transport company. It will be very easy to develop the disintegration of human beings in a practical and economical way. The men of tomorrow will travel great distances in an instant and without danger, dissolved in electronic flashes.

But the possibility of a failure is even more attractive. If Arpad Niklaus is a maker of chimeras and is followed at his death by a whole line of imposters, his humanitarian work will only have increased in grandeur, like a geometric progression or the texture of a chicken bred by Carrel. Nothing will keep him from passing into history as the glorious innovator of the universal disintegration of capital. And the rich, impoverished en masse by the draining investments, will easily enter the kingdom of heaven by the narrow gate (the eye of the needle), though the camel may not pass through.

TRANSLATED BY GEORGE D. SCHADE

PARZIVAL AND SIGUNE

Wolfram von Eschenbach

"Open up!"

To whom? Who are you?

"I want to come into your heart to you."

Then it is a small space you wish.

"What does that matter? Though I scarcely find room, you will have no need to complain of crowding. I will tell you now of wondrous things."

Oh, it is *you*, Lady Adventure? How fares that lovable knight? I mean the noble Parzival whom Cundrie with harsh words drove forth to seek the Grail. Many a lady there did lament that he could not be spared that journey. From Arthur, the Briton, he rode away then—how is he faring now?

Take up that tale again and say whether he despairs of joy, or whether he has won great honor, or whether his unmarred renown has grown in length and breadth, or has it grown short and scant? Tell us all that his hands have done. Has he seen Munsalvaesche since that time, and the gentle Anfortas whose heart was then so full of sighs? For your mercy's sake give us comfort and say if he be released from suffering. Let us hear if Parzival was there, your lord and also mine. Reveal to me how he has fared, sweet Herzeloyde's child and son of Gahmuret, since he rode away from Arthur. Has he won joy or affliction in battle since then? Does he ride out to the open field, or has he tarried at his ease since then? Tell me how he lives and all that he does.

The adventure tells us now that he had wandered through many lands, on horseback and in ships on the sea, and that no one save a fellow countryman or kinsman ever vied with him in a joust and kept his seat. Thus the weight of his scale can sink and cause his own fame to rise, but the fame of the others to fall. In many hard fights he had guarded himself against defeat, exerting himself so unsparingly in

314

combat that he who wished to borrow fame from him tried it to his
sorrow. The sword that Anfortas had given him when he was with the
Grail snapped later when he was attacked, but the power of the spring
of Karnant, called Lac, made it whole again. This sword helped him
win fame. Whoever does not believe this, commits a sin.

The adventure tells us now that Parzival the bold warrior came
riding into a forest, I do not know at what time, where his eyes found
a hermit's cell, newly built, with a swift stream flowing through it.
One side of it jutted out over the water. The dauntless young warrior
was riding in search of adventure. Then God took thought for his
guidance, and Parzival found a hermitess, who for love of God had
dedicated to Him her maidenhood and renounced her joy. From its
roots in her woman's heart sorrow put forth fresh flowers each day, yet
the troth from which it sprang was old.

Schianatulander and Sigune he found there. Inside the cell the hero
lay buried and dead, and she, bowed down upon his coffin, suffered a
life of anguish. Sigune *la duchesse* heard no Mass, yet her whole life
was a kneeling in prayer. Her lips, once so full and warm and red, were
blanched and pale since the day when worldly joy entirely forsook her.
Never did a maid suffer such cruel pain. It was to cry out her grief that
she lived alone.

For the sake of the love which had died with him—for the prince
had had no pleasure from it—she loved and cherished his dead body.
Had she become his wife, Lady Lunete would have been slow to offer
such speedy counsel as she gave her own mistress. We still often see
today Lady Lunetes come riding up with all too hasty advice. The
woman who, joined with her husband in true companionship and
ruled by the power of self-restraint, refuses alien love, if as long as he
lives she shuns such love, that man, to my mind, has received in her
the crown of his desires. Such constancy becomes a woman as nothing
else. —To that I shall gladly bear witness if I am asked. —After his
death let her do as she pleases. Yet if she still preserves his honor, she
wears a garland brighter than if she went, wreathed and merry, to the
dance.

How can I speak of joy in the presence of such suffering as Sigune's
faithfulness imposed on her? Let me say no more about it.

Over fallen tree trunks, where there was no path, Parzival rode up
to the window—too near, he was sorry for that later. He wanted to
ask about the forest and the direction he should take.

Hoping for an answer, he asked, "Is anyone within?"

She answered, "Yes."

When he heard that it was a woman's voice, he quickly wheeled the horse aside upon untrodden grass. Yet he felt that even in this he was too slow, and he smarted with shame that he had not dismounted before.

He tethered his horse to the branch of a fallen tree and hung his hole-ridden shield there too. When for courtesy's sake the bold yet gentle man had also removed his sword, he went to the window in the wall to ask what he wished to know. The cell was empty of joy, bare of all gaiety. He found nothing there but great sorrow. He asked her to come to the window, and the pale maiden rose courteously from her knees. Even then he did not know who she was nor who she might possibly be. She wore a hair shirt next to her skin, under her gown of grey. Great sorrow was her dearest companion; it had crushed her high spirits and had pressed from her heart many sighs.

Politely the maid came to the window and greeted him with friendly words. She carried a psalter in her hand, and Parzival the warrior noticed a little ring which in all her misery she had never taken off, but wore it still, as true love counseled her. The stone in it was a garnet which gleamed out through the darkness like a little spark of fire. The band that held her hair was proof of her sorrowing love.

"Out there by the wall, Sir," she said, "there is a bench. Have a seat there if you like and if your affairs permit. For the greeting which you have given me may God reward you, as He rewards all true courtesy."

The hero did as she advised him and sat down by the window, asking her too to be seated inside.

"Seldom have I sat here with a man," she said.

The hero began to question her about what she did here and how she lived. "It seems to me strange, Lady, that you live so far from the road in this wilderness. What do you live from when all around you there is not one human dwelling?"

"My food comes here to me directly from the Grail," she said. "Cundrie *la sorcière*, as she herself arranged, brings me every Saturday night food enough for the whole week." And she added, "If only all else were well with me, I would take little thought for food—of that I have enough."

Then Parzival thought she was lying and that she wished to mislead him in other ways too. So he said to her jokingly, "For whom are you wearing that ring? I've always heard it said that hermitess and hermit were not allowed to have *amours*."

She said, "If your words had the power, you would like to dishonor me. If I ever learn to deal falsely, reproach me with it if you are present. God willing, I am free from all dishonor, and far from any ill will." And she added, "This betrothal ring I wear for the sake of a beloved man, whose love in the *human* sense I never possessed. It is my virgin heart that bids me love him so." And again she spoke, "I have him here within, whose token I have worn ever since Orilus' spear struck him down. All the years of my life of mourning I will dedicate to my love for him. True love will I give to him, who with shield and spear and with knightly hand wooed me until he died in my service. I am a maid, and unmarried, yet in the sight of God he is my husband. If thoughts are the same as deeds, then I have nothing to conceal which would sever my marriage bond. His death brought grief to my life. This true marriage ring shall go with me into God's presence. The tears that stream from my heart are the bolts and bars of my fidelity. Here within I am not alone. Schianatulander is the one, and I am the other."

Then Parzival understood that it was Sigune, and her grief weighed heavy on him. Before he spoke to her again, he went to the trouble of removing his coif of mail, leaving his head uncovered.

The maiden, perceiving how his skin shone fair through the grime of the iron, at once recognized the sturdy warrior. "Is it you, Sir Parzival?" she said. "How fares it with your search for the Grail? Have you at last discovered its true nature? How has your journey been?"

He said to the highborn maiden, "Great joy I lost there, and sorrow enough does the Grail bring me. I left a land where I wore the crown, and the loveliest wife as well—never on this earth was one more beautiful born of human kind. I long for her gentle courtesy, and for her love I sorely mourn—yet even more for the high goal, to behold Munsalvaesche and the Grail. That has not yet come to pass. Cousin Sigune, it is cruel of you to bear me such ill will when you know how many are my cares."

The maid replied, "All of my censure of you, cousin, I shall withdraw. You have indeed lost much joy through being so slow and not asking the precious question when the sweet Anfortas was your host and your happiness. Your question then would have gained you the supreme reward. Now your joy must languish and your noble spirit go lame. Your heart has tamed care, which would be wild and alien to you, had you but asked your question then."

"I did as one who is bound to be the loser," he said. "Dear cousin, give me counsel. Remember how close we are of kin, and tell me too how things stand with you. I would lament for your sorrow, save that I bear a grief greater than any man has ever borne. My misery is beyond all measure."

She said, "Now may help come to you from the hand of Him who knows all sorrow. You may perhaps succeed in finding a track which will lead you to Munsalvaesche, where, as you say, your joy abides. Cundrie *la sorcière* just now rode away from here. I am sorry I did not ask whether she meant to return there or to some other place. Always when she comes, her mule stands there where the spring flows out of the rock. I advise you to ride after her. She may not be so far ahead but that you could soon overtake her."

Then there was no tarrying more. The hero bade farewell, and turned to the fresh hoof track, the way Cundrie's mule had gone. But misfortune and the pathless woods prevented him from pursuing the track he had seen. And so, once more, the Grail was lost to him, and his joy was then forgot. I think, if he had come then to Munsalvaesche, he would have done better at questioning than you heard of him before. Well, let him ride, but where shall he go?

There came riding toward him a man, his head bare, wearing a rich and costly surcoat, and under it armor shining bright. Except for his head he was fully armed. He rode straight toward Parzival and said, "Sir, I do not like it that you thus invade my lord's forest. You will speedily get a rebuke you will feel very painfully. Munsalvaesche is not accustomed to let anyone come so near unless he were ready to face perilous strife or make the atonement which outside this forest is known as Death."

In his hand he carried a helmet with ties of silken cord and a sharp spearhead on a fresh shaft. Angrily the hero bound the helmet on his head. His threats and his fighting too were soon to cost him dear. No matter, he readied himself for the joust.

But Parzival too had splintered many a spear just as costly. He thought to himself, "It would be my death if I rode over this man's crops. What could avail me then against his wrath? But here, after all, I am trampling down only wild fern. If my hands and both arms do not fail me, I'll pay him a price for my journey so that his hand will not stop me."

Both set their horses at a gallop, spurring them on to full career, and neither joust missed its aim. But many a thrust of spear had Parzival's sturdy chest confronted, and training and impulse both taught him to aim his thrust straight at the knot in the helmet cords —he struck him just where one holds the shield in knightly sport. The templar from Munsalvaesche fell from his horse and rolled far down into a ravine so steep that he scarce found place for sleeping.

Parzival rushed ahead. His horse was going too fast to stop. It plunged into the chasm and was dashed to pieces. Parzival gripped the branch of a cedar tree with his hands. Now please don't hold it against him that, lacking a hangman, he hanged himself. With his feet he caught hold of the hard rock beneath him. Down below, in the pathless waste, his horse lay dead.

The knight was hastily escaping up the opposite slope. Did he intend to share his winnings from the fight with Parzival? He would do better to get a donation at home from the Grail.

Parzival climbed back again. The templar's horse had caught its feet in the reins, which were dragging on the ground, and it stood there as if it had been ordered to wait, an order which that knight had quite forgotten to give. Parzival swung himself on its back. Nothing was missing but his spear, and the find of the horse outweighed that loss. I think that neither the strong Lehelin nor the proud Kingrisin, neither *le roi* Gramoflanz nor *le comte* Lascoyt, *le fils de* Gurnemanz, ever rode a better joust than the one in which this horse was won.

Then Parzival rode away, he knew not where . . .

TRANSLATED BY HELEN M. MUSTARD
AND CHARLES E. PASSAGE

THOUGHTS IN THE DARK

Tatsuzo Ishikawa

"If you really go blind, I won't be able to stand it, seeing you fumbling and helpless. Not a very bright future, is it? Maybe we'd be better off dead," his wife would say sometimes. And he wasn't sure she was joking. She would say it almost passionately.

"Really," she might add, "let's kill ourselves. It's horrible to go on living like this, a little more miserable every day."

And sometimes he would agree with her, half in earnest. But other times he would say something like this:

"I had an idea in bed last night. I was thinking what work I could do even if I did go blind. There's not much—even music's out—I wouldn't have time to learn to play the *koto* well enough to give lessons. But what about detective stories? I'm going to try and think one up. I can dictate it to you. Detective stories, even I should be able to do."

He sat there facing her, the white bandage over his eyes, his back against the post, and the spring sunshine from the window on his shoulders. Pitiful. She tried to imagine him as a blind mystery-writer. Fat for lack of exercise. Pale for want of sunlight. And those shut eyes gazing into darkness, everlasting darkness. In that darkness he would see the scenes of his mystery. Murder, blood, a knife, the criminal fighting hand-to-hand with the detective. That's all he would see, those gruesome scenes. In his own darkness he would be creating an even darker society. She shuddered and shook her head.

"No, not that! I don't like it. It *would* be better to die."

He smiled gently under the bandage.

It wasn't certain yet that he would go blind. His sight had become very weak suddenly, and then growths had appeared on his corneas. It was dangerous because the pupils were affected. Even if the growths

320

healed, there would be irregular scars, and if they didn't heal, he might never be able to see again.

All day long he listened to the radio. In the morning and evening his wife read the newspapers to him. And the hours when there was nothing on the radio he spent thinking what to do if he went blind.

Once or twice he had really thought of killing himself as his wife suggested. He had even been serious about the mystery stories for a while. He had been in a panic at first and had thought up fantastic schemes for making a living. But as time passed his ideas became more conservative. And in the depths of that conservatism he found a stagnant calm. Now, he wasn't trying to plan ahead any longer. When and if he knew for certain that he was going to be blind, something would turn up, probably. It wasn't easy to think about. It was in trying to foresee what would happen that he ran the risk of delusion.

He ate like a child. She was watching him as he let the grains of rice pour over the rim of his bowl. She bent over and collected them and threw them into the brazier. She was irritated.

"Don't you know how to eat yet?"

He didn't answer. He wasn't used to being blind and even feeding himself was a chore. And he felt that his wife was more distant than ever. That made him unbearably lonely. The more wretched he became the closer he wanted to get to her. So he was all the more conscious of her irritable remoteness. There was a gap between them. How unaware of it he had been when he was healthy and able to do what he wanted! Health dulled one's senses.

His wife picked all the bones out of the fish before she put it on his plate and gave it to him. A sorry business, just like caring for a four-year-old. He ate the fish with no sign of enjoyment, expressionless as a machine. Only his mouth was in lively motion. He finished all the fish, but kept groping at the plate with his chopsticks. He was trying to close them on the white spots in the dish. White things he could make out vaguely, but nothing else.

His wife put down her own chopsticks and watched his futile efforts. She burst into tears.

"That's the pattern on your plate."

"No more?"

"You've eaten it all, haven't you?"

He didn't answer. He gulped the rice left in his bowl, and hurled his chopsticks down on his tray. He felt a tremendous rage.

Every day she had to take him by the sleeve, lead him out to the street, put him in a cab, and ride with him to the doctor. The doctor spoke with less and less conviction.

"Surgery is successful sometimes. But even if we try it, we can't tell how it'll turn out. So . . ."

She felt alone. She had no one left to turn to.

Every day, as she got ready to go to the doctor, she would keep thinking about whether to use make-up. It seemed a little silly to make herself beautiful when her husband couldn't see her. But she did use make-up. Was it for other people? She knew perfectly well it was wrong of her, but she couldn't help getting angry at his pathetic helplessness.

She would sit down in front of him, her knees next to his, and open her right hand suddenly about three feet from his face. "Can you see it?"

"I can tell there's something there."

"How many fingers?" She put out three. He was silent. He's worse than yesterday, she thought angrily.

"I don't know."

"Try now!" Her voice was fierce. She brought her hand to within two feet of his face. He still couldn't see.

"Two fingers?"

That day he couldn't tell the number until she put her fingers close enough to touch his nose. He was beaten. He couldn't fight back against her sternness and irritation. He slumped down on his back.

"Please get the bed ready."

"You're sleepy?"

"What's the use of staying up?"

She looked closely at his fat cheeks and chin. His beard had grown horribly. She boiled water, stood behind him, and shaved his tough whiskers, clumsily.

"Come here a minute." He called her and she came over and stood in front of him. He began to run his hands over her feet.

"What do you want?"

He laughed and said, "I was listening to your walk. It's a very

THOUGHTS IN THE DARK
Tatsuzo Ishikawa

unusual sound. A series of different sounds, really. I thought you must be flat-footed, and so you are." It was the first time he had noticed the shape of her feet since his vision had started to go.

He put a lot of bowls and plates in a row and rapped on them and said that if you set up a full scale that way you'd have a regular piano.

It was strange that a man in his condition should still have healthy desires. As she yielded her body to his lovemaking, she couldn't get rid of the idea that it was another man she was going to feel. There was a sad and desperate violence in his manner. Her own existence would become a dream floating through his darkness, but that, she suddenly knew, was no reason for despair on her part, none at all. Perhaps, if she too could go blind, another life might start for her, with new sensations, abstracted and purified in a world of quiet. A world liberated from color and outline, in which there were only touch and taste and sound. She shut her eyes and looked. And a world of mystery and illusion she had never sensed through all the nights before seemed to rise vaguely before her.

One morning, he hugged her gently and said, "I can't see at all any more."

She stiffened for a moment and looked in his face.

"There's no difference between light and dark."

"Open your eyes for a minute."

Both eyes were bleared dead white. They were like the eyes of those blind masseurs you often saw. She was terrified; he frightened her as he never had before.

He tightened his embrace and spoke quietly.

"It's all right. We've got to make our minds up to it now. . . . Let's try to think of a good job a blind man can work at. We're not so badly off. There's still lots of happiness in store for us."

She hid her face against his shoulder and cried softly, silently. But she didn't think of dying. Blindness was less of a disaster than she'd feared. And then she folded her two hands coaxingly around her husband's neck, as she had done so frequently before all this began.

TRANSLATED BY BREWSTER HORWITZ

A DISTANT EPISODE

Paul Bowles

The September sunsets were at their reddest the week the Professor decided to visit Aïn Tadouirt, which is in the warm country. He came down out of the high, flat region in the evening by bus, with two small overnight bags full of maps, sun lotions and medicines. Ten years ago he had been in the village for three days; long enough, however, to establish a fairly firm friendship with a café-keeper, who had written him several times during the first year after his visit, if never since. "Hassan Ramani," the Professor said over and over, as the bus bumped downward through ever warmer layers of air. Now facing the flaming sky in the west, and now facing the sharp mountains, the car followed the dusty trail down the canyons into air which began to smell of other things besides the endless ozone of the heights: orange blossoms, pepper, sun-baked excrement, burning olive oil, rotten fruit. He closed his eyes happily and lived for an instant in a purely olfactory world. The distant past returned—what part of it, he could not decide.

The chauffeur, whose seat the Professor shared, spoke to him without taking his eyes from the road. "*Vous êtes géologue?*"

"A geologist? Ah, no! I'm a linguist."

"There are no languages here. Only dialects."

"Exactly. I'm making a survey of variations on Moghrebi."

The chauffeur was scornful. "Keep on going south," he said. "You'll find some languages you never heard of before."

As they drove through the town gate, the usual swarm of urchins rose up out of the dust and ran screaming beside the bus. The Professor folded his dark glasses, put them in his pocket; and as soon as the vehicle had come to a standstill he jumped out, pushing his way through the indignant boys who clutched at his luggage in vain, and walked quickly into the Grand Hotel Saharien. Out of its eight rooms there were two available—one facing the market and the other, a smaller and cheaper one, giving onto a tiny yard full of refuse and barrels, where two gazelles wandered about. He took the smaller room, and pouring the entire pitcher of water into the tin basin, began to wash the grit from his face and ears. The afterglow was nearly gone from the sky, and the pinkness in objects was disappearing, almost as he watched. He lit the carbide lamp and winced at its odor.

After dinner the Professor walked slowly through the streets to Hassan Ramani's café, whose back room hung hazardously out above the river. The entrance was very low, and he had to bend down slightly to get in. A man was tending the fire. There was one guest sipping tea. The *qaouaji* tried to make him take a seat at the other table in the front room, but the Professor walked airily ahead into the back room and sat down. The moon was shining through the reed latticework and there was not a sound outside but the occasional distant bark of a dog. He changed tables so he could see the river. It was dry, but there was a pool here and there that reflected the bright night sky. The *qaouaji* came in and wiped off the table.

"Does this café still belong to Hassan Ramani?" he asked him in the Moghrebi he had taken four years to learn.

The man replied in bad French: "He is deceased."

"Deceased?" repeated the Professor, without noticing the absurdity of the word. "Really? When?"

"I don't know," said the *qaouaji*. "One tea?"

"Yes. But I don't understand . . ."

The man was already out of the room, fanning the fire. The Professor sat still, feeling lonely, and arguing with himself that to do so was ridiculous. Soon the *qaouaji* returned with the tea. He paid him and gave him an enormous tip, for which he received a grave bow.

"Tell me," he said, as the other started away. "Can one still get those little boxes made from camel udders?"

The man looked angry. "Sometimes the Reguibat bring in those things. We do not buy them here." Then insolently, in Arabic: "And why a camel-udder box?"

"Because I like them," retorted the Professor. And then because he was feeling a little exalted, he added, "I like them so much I want to make a collection of them, and I will pay you ten francs for every one you can get me."

"*Khamstache*," said the *qaouaji*, opening his left hand rapidly three times in succession.

"Never. Ten."

"Not possible. But wait until later and come with me. You can give me what you like. And you will get camel-udder boxes if there are any."

He went out into the front room, leaving the Professor to drink his tea and listen to the growing chorus of dogs that barked and howled as the moon rose higher in the sky. A group of customers came into the front room and sat talking for an hour or so. When they had left, the *qaouaji* put out the fire and stood in the doorway putting on his burnous. "Come," he said.

Outside in the street there was very little movement. The booths were all closed and the only light came from the moon. An occasional pedestrian passed, and grunted a brief greeting to the *qaouaji*.

"Everyone knows you," said the Professor, to cut the silence between them.

"Yes."

"I wish everyone knew me," said the Professor, before he realized how infantile such a remark must sound.

"No one knows you," said his companion gruffly.

They had come to the other side of the town, on the promontory above the desert, and through a great rift in the wall the Professor saw the white endlessness, broken in the foreground by dark spots of oasis. They walked through the opening and followed a winding road between rocks, downward toward the nearest small forest of palms. The Professor thought: "He may cut my throat. But his café—he would surely be found out."

"Is it far?" he asked, casually.

"Are you tired?" countered the *qaouaji*.

"They are expecting me back at the Hotel Saharien," he lied.

"You can't be there and here," said the *qaouaji*.

The Professor laughed. He wondered if it sounded uneasy to the other.

"Have you owned Ramani's café long?"

"I work there for a friend." The reply made the Professor more unhappy than he had imagined it would.

"Oh. Will you work tomorrow?"

"That is impossible to say."

The Professor stumbled on a stone, and fell, scraping his hand. The *qaouaji* said: "Be careful."

The sweet black odor of rotten meat hung in the air suddenly.

"Agh!" said the Professor, choking. "What is it?"

The *qaouaji* had covered his face with his burnous and did not answer. Soon the stench had been left behind. They were on flat ground. Ahead the path was bordered on each side by a high mud wall. There was no breeze and the palms were quite still, but behind the walls was the sound of running water. Also, the odor of human excrement was almost constant as they walked between the walls.

The Professor waited until he thought it seemed logical for him to ask with a certain degree of annoyance: "But where are we going?"

"Soon," said the guide, pausing to gather some stones in the ditch.

"Pick up some stones," he advised. "Here are bad dogs."

"Where?" asked the Professor, but he stooped and got three large oncs with pointed edges.

They continued very quietly. The walls came to an end and the bright desert lay ahead. Nearby was a ruined marabout, with its tiny dome only half standing, and the front wall entirely destroyed. Behind it were clumps of stunted, useless palms. A dog came running crazily toward them on three legs. Not until it got quite close did the Professor hear its steady low growl. The *qaouaji* let fly a large stone at it, striking it square in the muzzle. There was a strange snapping of jaws and the dog ran sideways in another direction, falling blindly against rocks and scrambling haphazardly about like an injured insect.

Turning off the road, they walked across the earth strewn with sharp stones, past the little ruin, through the trees, until they came to a place where the ground dropped abruptly away in front of them.

"It looks like a quarry," said the Professor, resorting to French for the word "quarry," whose Arabic equivalent he could not call to mind at the moment. The *qaouaji* did not answer. Instead he stood still and turned his head, as if listening. And indeed, from somewhere down below, but very far below, came the faint sound of a low flute. The *qaouaji* nodded his head slowly several times. Then he said: "The path begins here. You can see it well all the way. The rock is white and the moon is strong. So you can see well. I am going back now and sleep. It is late. You can give me what you like."

Standing there at the edge of the abyss which at each moment looked deeper, with the dark face of the *qaouaji* framed in its moonlit burnous close to his own face, the Professor asked himself exactly what he felt. Indignation, curiosity, fear, perhaps, but most of all relief and the hope that this was not a trick, the hope that the *qaouaji* would really leave him alone and turn back without him.

He stepped back a little from the edge, and fumbled in his pocket for a loose note, because he did not want to show his wallet. Fortunately there was a fifty-franc bill there, which he took out and handed to the man. He knew the *qaouaji* was pleased, and so he paid no attention when he heard him saying: "It is not enough. I have to walk a long way home and there are dogs. . . ."

"Thank you and good night," said the Professor, sitting down with his legs drawn up under him, and lighting a cigarette. He felt almost happy.

"Give me only one cigarette," pleaded the man.

"Of course," he said, a bit curtly, and he held up the pack.

The *qaouaji* squatted close beside him. His face was not pleasant to see. "What is it?" thought the Professor, terrified again, as he held out his lighted cigarette toward him.

The man's eyes were almost closed. It was the most obvious registering of concentrated scheming the Professor had ever seen. When the second cigarette was burning, he ventured to say to the still-squatting Arab: "What are you thinking about?"

The other drew on his cigarette deliberately, and seemed about to speak. Then his expression changed to one of satisfaction, but he did not speak. A cool wind had risen in the air, and the Professor shivered. The sound of the flute came up from the depths below at intervals, sometimes mingled with the scraping of nearby palm fronds one against the other. "These people are not primitives," the Professor found himself saying in his mind.

"Good," said the *qaouaji*, rising slowly. "Keep your money. Fifty francs is enough. It is an honor." Then he went back into French: "*Ti n'as qu'à discendre, to' droit.*" He spat, chuckled (or was the Professor hysterical?), and strode away quickly.

The Professor was in a state of nerves. He lit another cigarette, and found his lips moving automatically. They were saying: "Is this a situation or a predicament? This is ridiculous." He sat very still for several minutes, waiting for a sense of reality to come to him. He stretched out on the hard, cold ground and looked up at the moon. It was almost like looking straight at the sun. If he shifted his gaze a little at a time, he could make a string of weaker moons across the sky. "Incredible," he whispered. Then he sat up quickly and looked about. There was no guarantee that the *qaouaji* really had gone back to town. He got to his feet and looked over the edge of the precipice. In the moonlight the bottom seemed miles away. And there was nothing to give it scale; not a tree, not a house, not a person. . . . He listened for the flute, and heard only the wind going by his ears. A sudden violent desire to run back to the road seized him, and he turned and looked in the direction the *qaouaji* had taken. At the same time he felt softly of his wallet in his breast pocket. Then he spat over the edge of the cliff. Then he made water over it, and listened intently, like a child. This gave him the impetus to start down the path into the abyss. Curiously enough, he was not dizzy. But prudently he kept from peering to his right, over the edge. It was a steady and steep downward climb. The monotony of it put him into a frame of mind not unlike that which had been induced by the bus ride. He was murmuring "Hassan Ramani" again, repeatedly and in rhythm. He stopped, furious with himself for the sinister overtones the name now suggested to him. He decided he was exhausted from the trip. "And the walk," he added.

He was now well down the gigantic cliff, but the moon, being directly overhead, gave as much light as ever. Only the wind was left behind, above, to wander among the trees, to blow through the dusty streets of Aïn Tadouirt, into the hall of the Grand Hotel Saharien, and under the door of his little room.

It occurred to him that he ought to ask himself why he was doing this irrational thing, but he was intelligent enough to know that since he was doing it, it was not so important to probe for explanations at that moment.

Suddenly the earth was flat beneath his feet. He had reached the bottom sooner than he had expected. He stepped ahead distrustfully still, as if he expected another treacherous drop. It was so hard to know in this uniform, dim brightness. Before he knew what had happened the dog was upon him, a heavy mass of fur trying to push him backwards, a sharp nail rubbing down his chest, a straining of muscles against him to get the teeth into his neck. The Professor thought: "I refuse to die this way." The dog fell back; it looked like an Eskimo dog. As it sprang again, he called out, very loud: "Ay!" It fell against him, there was a confusion of sensations and a pain somewhere. There was also the sound of voices very near to him, and he could not understand what they were saying. Something cold and metallic was pushed brutally against his spine as the dog still hung for a second by his teeth from a mass of clothing and perhaps flesh. The Professor knew it was a gun, and he raised his hands, shouting in Moghrebi: "Take away the dog!" But the gun merely pushed him forward, and since the dog, once it was back on the ground, did not leap again, he took a step ahead. The gun kept pushing; he kept taking steps. Again he heard voices, but the person directly behind him said nothing. People seemed to be running about; it sounded that way, at least. For his eyes, he discovered, were still shut tight against the dog's attack. He opened them. A group of men was advancing toward him. They were dressed in the black clothes of the Reguibat. "The Reguiba is a cloud across the face of the sun." "When the Reguiba appears the righteous man turns away." In how many shops and market-places he had heard these maxims uttered banteringly among friends. Never to a Reguiba, to be sure, for these men do not frequent towns. They send a representative in disguise, to arrange with shady elements there for the disposal of captured goods. "An opportunity," he thought quickly, "of testing the accuracy of such statements." He did not doubt for a moment that the adventure would prove to be a kind of warning against such foolishness on his part—a warning which in retrospect would be half sinister, half farcical.

Two snarling dogs came running from behind the oncoming men and threw themselves at his legs. He was scandalized to note that no one paid any attention to this breach of etiquette. The gun pushed him harder as he tried to sidestep the animals' noisy assault. Again he cried: "The dogs! Take them away!" The gun shoved him forward with great force and he fell, almost at the feet of the crowd of men facing him. The dogs were wrenching at his hands and arms. A boot kicked them aside, yelping, and then with increased vigor it kicked the Professor in the hip. Then came a chorus of kicks from different sides, and he was rolled violently about on the earth for a while. During this time he was conscious of hands reaching into his pockets and removing everything from them. He tried to say: "You have all my money; stop kicking me!" But his bruised facial muscles would

not work; he felt himself pouting and that was all. Someone dealt him
a terrific blow on the head, and he thought: "Now at least I shall lose
consciousness, thank Heaven." Still he went on being aware of the
guttural voices he could not understand, and of being bound tightly
about the ankles and chest. Then there was black silence that opened
like a wound from time to time, to let in the soft, deep notes of the
flute playing the same succession of notes again and again. Suddenly
he felt excruciating pain everywhere—pain and cold. "So I have been
unconscious, after all," he thought. In spite of that, the present
seemed only like a direct continuation of what had gone before.

It was growing faintly light. There were camels near where he was
lying; he could hear their gurgling and their heavy breathing. He
could not bring himself to attempt opening his eyes, just in case it
should turn out to be impossible. However, when he heard someone
approaching, he found that he had no difficulty in seeing.

The man looked at him dispassionately in the gray morning light.
With one hand he pinched together the Professor's nostrils. When
the Professor opened his mouth to breathe, the man swiftly seized his
tongue and pulled on it with all his might. The Professor was gagging
and catching his breath; he did not see what was happening. He could
not distinguish the pain of the brutal yanking from that of the sharp
knife. Then there was an endless choking and spitting that went on
automatically, as though he were scarcely a part of it. The word
"operation" kept going through his mind; it calmed his terror
somewhat as he sank back into darkness.

The caravan left sometime toward midmorning. The Professor, not
unconscious, but in a state of utter stupor, still gagging and drooling
blood, was dumped doubled-up into a sack and tied at one side of a
camel. The lower end of the enormous amphitheater contained a
natural gate in the rocks. The camels, swift *mehara*, were lightly laden
on this trip. They passed through single file, and slowly mounted the
gentle slope that led up into the beginning of the desert. That night,
at a stop behind some low hills, the men took him out, still in a state
which permitted no thought, and over the dusty rags that remained of
his clothing they fastened a series of curious belts made of the
bottoms of tin cans strung together. One after another of these bright
girdles was wired about his torso, his arms and legs, even across his
face, until he was entirely within a suit of armor that covered him
with its circular metal scales. There was a good deal of merriment

during this decking-out of the Professor. One man brought out a flute and a younger one did a not ungraceful caricature of an Ouled Naïl executing a cane dance. The Professor was no longer conscious; to be exact, he existed in the middle of the movements made by these other men. When they had finished dressing him the way they wished him to look, they stuffed some food under the tin bangles hanging over his face. Even though he chewed mechanically, most of it eventually fell out onto the ground. They put him back into the sack and left him there.

Two days later they arrived at one of their own encampments. There were women and children here in the tents, and the men had to drive away the snarling dogs they had left there to guard them. When they emptied the Professor out of his sack, there were screams of fright, and it took several hours to convince the last woman that he was harmless, although there had been no doubt from the start that he was a valuable possession. After a few days they began to move on again, taking everything with them, and traveling only at night as the terrain grew warmer.

Even when all his wounds had healed and he felt no more pain, the Professor did not begin to think again; he ate and defecated, and he danced when he was bidden, a senseless hopping up and down that delighted the children, principally because of the wonderful jangling racket it made. And he generally slept through the heat of the day, in among the camels.

Wending its way southeast, the caravan avoided all stationary civilization. In a few weeks they reached a new plateau, wholly wild and with a sparse vegetation. Here they pitched camp and remained, while the *mehara* were turned loose to graze. Everyone was happy here; the weather was cooler and there was a well only a few hours away on a seldom-frequented trail. It was here they conceived the idea of taking the Professor to Fogara and selling him to the Touareg.

It was a full year before they carried out this project. By this time the Professor was much better trained. He could do a handspring, make a series of fearful growling noises which had, nevertheless, a certain element of humor; and when the Reguibat removed the tin from his face they discovered he could grimace admirably while he danced. They also taught him a few basic obscene gestures which never failed to elicit delighted shrieks from the women. He was now brought forth only after especially abundant meals, when there was music and festivity. He easily fell in with their sense of ritual, and evolved an elementary sort of "program" to present when he was called for: dancing, rolling on the ground, imitating certain animals, and finally rushing toward the group in feigned anger, to see the resultant confusion and hilarity.

When three of the men set out for Fogara with him, they took four *mehara* with them, and he rode astride his quite naturally. No precautions were taken to guard him, save that he was kept among them, one man always staying at the rear of the party. They came within sight of the walls at dawn, and they waited among the rocks all day. At dusk the youngest started out, and in three hours he returned with a friend who carried a stout cane. They tried to put the Professor through his routine then and there, but the man from Fogara was in a hurry to get back to town, so they all set out on the *mehara*.

In the town they went directly to the villager's home, where they had coffee in the courtyard sitting among the camels. Here the Professor went into his act again, and this time there was prolonged merriment and much rubbing together of hands. An agreement was reached, a sum of money paid, and the Reguibat withdrew, leaving the Professor in the house of the man with the cane, who did not delay in locking him into a tiny enclosure off the courtyard.

The next day was an important one in the Professor's life, for it was then that pain began to stir again in his being. A group of men came to the house, among whom was a venerable gentleman, better clothed than those others who spent their time flattering him, setting fervent kisses upon his hands and the edges of his garments. This person made a point of going into classical Arabic from time to time, to impress the others, who had not learned a word of the Koran. Thus his conversation would run more or less as follows: "Perhaps at In Salah. The French there are stupid. Celestial vengeance is approaching. Let us not hasten it. Praise the highest and cast thine anathema against idols. With paint on his face. In case the police wish to look close." The others listened and agreed, nodding their heads slowly and solemnly. And the Professor in his stall beside them listened, too. That is, he was *conscious* of the sound of the old man's Arabic. The words penetrated for the first time in many months. Noises, then: "Celestial vengeance is approaching." Then: "It is an honor. Fifty francs is enough. Keep your money. Good." And the *quaouaji* squatting near him at the edge of the precipice. Then "anathema

against idols" and more gibberish. He turned over panting on the
sand and forgot about it. But the pain had begun. It operated in a
kind of delirium, because he had begun to enter into consciousness
again. When the man opened the door and prodded him with his
cane, he cried out in a rage, and everyone laughed.

They got him onto his feet, but he would not dance. He stood
before them, staring at the ground, stubbornly refusing to move. The
owner was furious, and so annoyed by the laughter of the others that
he felt obliged to send them away, saying that he would await a more
propitious time for exhibiting his property, because he dared not show
his anger before the elder. However, when they had left he dealt the
Professor a violent blow on the shoulder with his cane, called him
various obscene things, and went out into the street, slamming the
gate behind him. He walked straight to the street of the Ouled Naïl,
because he was sure of finding the Reguibat there among the girls,
spending the money. And there in a tent he found one of them still
abed, while an Ouled Naïl washed the tea glasses. He walked in and
almost decapitated the man before the latter had even attempted to
sit up. Then he threw his razor on the bed and ran out.

The Ouled Naïl saw the blood, screamed, ran out of her tent into
the next, and soon emerged from that with four girls who rushed
together into the coffee house and told the *quaouaji* who had killed
the Reguiba. It was only a matter of an hour before the French
military police had caught him at a friend's house, and dragged him
off to the barracks. That night the Professor had nothing to eat, and
the next afternoon, in the slow sharpening of his consciousness caused
by increasing hunger, he walked aimlessly about the courtyard and the
rooms that gave onto it. There was no one. In one room a calendar
hung on the wall. The Professor watched nervously, like a dog watching a fly in front of its nose. On the white paper were black objects that
made sounds in his head. He heard them: "*Grande Epicerie du Sahel.
Juin. Lundi, Mardi, Mercredi.* . . ."

The tiny inkmarks of which a symphony consists may have been
made long ago, but when they are fulfilled in sound they become
imminent and mighty. So a kind of music of feeling began to play in
the Professor's head, increasing in volume as he looked at the mud
wall, and he had the feeling that he was performing what had been
written for him long ago. He felt like weeping; he felt like roaring
through the little house, upsetting and smashing the few breakable

objects. His emotion got no further than this one overwhelming desire. So, bellowing as loud as he could, he attacked the house and its belongings. Then he attacked the door into the street, which resisted for a while and finally broke. He climbed through the opening made by the boards he had ripped apart, and still bellowing and shaking his arms in the air to make as loud a jangling as possible, he began to gallop along the quiet street toward the gateway of the town. A few people looked at him with great curiosity. As he passed the garage, the last building before the high mud archway that framed the desert beyond, a French soldier saw him. *"Tiens,"* he said to himself, "a holy maniac."

Again it was sunset time. The Professor ran beneath the arched gate, turned his face toward the red sky, and began to trot along the Piste d'In Salah, straight into the setting sun. Behind him, from the garage, the soldier took a pot shot at him for good luck. The bullet whistled dangerously near the Professor's head, and his yelling rose into an indignant lament as he waved his arms more wildly, and hopped high into the air at every few steps, in an access of terror.

The soldier watched a while, smiling, as the cavorting figure grew smaller in the oncoming evening darkness, and the rattling of the tin became a part of the great silence out there beyond the gate. The wall of the garage as he leaned against it still gave forth heat, left there by the sun, but even then the lunar chill was growing in the air.

THREE REFLECTED VISIONS

Alain Robbe-Grillet

1. The Dressmaker's Dummy

The coffee pot is on the table.

It is a round table with four legs, covered with an oilcloth checkered red and gray on a neutral background—a yellowish-white that was once ivory, perhaps, or just white. In the middle of the table is a porcelain tile instead of the usual table mat: the design on the tile is completely covered, or at least made unrecognizable, by the coffee pot that is standing on it.

The coffee pot is made of brown earthenware. It is in the form of a sphere surmounted by a cylindrical percolator and a mushroom-shaped lid. The spout is an S with flattened sides, slightly more rounded at the base. The handle has more or less the shape of an ear, or rather of the outer rim of an ear. Even so, it would be a deformed ear—too round and without enough lobe: more or less an ear shaped like a pot handle. The spout, the handle, and the mushroom-shaped lid are cream color. The rest of the pot is a bright, shiny, even shade of brown.

There is nothing else on the table except the oilcloth, the tile and the coffee pot.

To the right, in front of the window, stands the dressmaker's dummy.

Behind the table, on the mantlepiece, is a large rectangular mirror in which can be seen half the french window (the right half), and, to the left (that is, to the left of the window, the reflection of the mirrored wardrobe. In the mirror of the wardrobe the window can be seen again, all of it this time, and the right way around (that is, the right half on the right, the left half on the left).

Thus, above the mantlepiece there are actually three halves of the window that can be successively distinguished without a break in continuity—they are, respectively (from left to right), the left half seen the right way around, the right half, also seen the right way around, and the right half seen in reverse. Since the wardrobe is standing exactly in the corner of the room, extending as far as the edge of the window, the two right halves of the window appear to be separated only by a narrow upright of the wardrobe, which could also be part of the window frame (the right upright of the left half exactly overlaps the left upright of the right half). The three halves make it possible to see, on the other side of the window screen, the leafless trees of the garden.

In this way, the window occupies the entire surface of the mirror except for the upper portion, in which can be seen a strip of the ceiling and the top of the mirrored wardrobe.

Also in the mirror on the mantlepiece can be seen two other dummies, one in front of the first, narrowest section of the window, all the way to the left; and the other in front of the third half (the one farthest to the right). The dummies are neither facing toward nor away from one another; the one on the right is turned so that its right side is facing toward the one on the left, which is slightly smaller and standing with its left side turned to face the one on the right. But this is hard to discern at first glance, for the two reflections are actually facing the same way and both therefore seem to be showing the same side—probably the left one.

The three dummies are standing in a row. The one in the middle, placed on the right side of the mirror, and about as much larger than the one on its right as it is smaller than the other one on its left, is facing in exactly the same direction on the table.

On the spherical part of the coffee pot there is a distorted reflection of the window, a more or less quadrilateral figure with its sides composed of circular arcs. The line formed by the wooden uprights between the two halves of the window suddenly spreads out at the bottom of this reflection into a rather shapeless blotch. This is certainly the shadow of the dummy.

The room is very bright, for the window is exceptionally large, although it has only two sections.

A good smell of hot coffee is coming out of the coffee pot on the table.

The dummy is not where it belongs: usually it is kept in the angle of the window, on the side opposite the mirrored wardrobe. The wardrobe has been put where it is to make fittings more convenient.

The design on the tile is an owl with two huge, almost frightening eyes. But, for the moment, nothing can be seen because of the coffee pot.

2. THE SUBSTITUTE

The high-school student stepped back a little and lifted his head toward the lowest branches. Then he moved forward to catch hold of a twig that seemed to be within his reach; he stood on tiptoe and stretched out his hand as high as he could, but did not manage to reach it. After several fruitless attempts he appeared to give up. He lowered his arm and continued merely staring at something in the foliage.

Then he returned to the foot of the tree, where he stood in the same position as at first: his knees slightly bent, his body inclined toward the right, his head leaning toward his shoulder. He was still holding his satchel in his left hand. His other hand couldn't be seen, but he was doubltess holding it against the trunk, next to his face, which was almost touching the bark, as if he were looking very closely at some minute detail about four feet from the ground.

The child had stopped reading again, but this time there must have been a period, perhaps even an indentation, and he was probably trying to indicate the end of a paragraph. The high-school student straightened up to inspect the bark a little higher.

Whispering broke out in several parts of the classroom. The teacher turned his head and noticed that most of the students had raised their eyes instead of following the reading in their texts: the reader himself was looking toward the rostrum with a vaguely questioning, perhaps timorous expression. The teacher said severely, "Why don't you go on? What are you waiting for?"

Every head was lowered in silence, and the child continued in the same diligent tone, without intonation and a trifle too slowly, giving each word an identical weight, spacing them all uniformly: " 'That evening, Joseph de Hagen, one of Phillip's lieutenants, presented himself at the archbishop's palace, supposedly as an act of courtesy. As we have said above the two brothers . . .' "

On the other side of the street, the student was staring into the low branches again. The teacher rapped on the desk with the flat of his hand. "As we have said above, comma, the two brothers . . ." He found the passage again in his own book and read it aloud, exaggerating the punctuation: "Repeat after me, 'As we have said above, the two brothers were there already, in order to be able, should the occasion arise, to shield themselves behind this alibi.' And pay attention to what you are reading."

After a pause the child began the sentence again, " 'As we have said above, the two brothers were there already, in order to be able, should the occasion arise, to shield themselves behind this alibi—which was, in truth, a dubious one, but, nevertheless, the best they could devise in the situation—to prevent their suspicious cousin . . .' "

The monotonous voice suddenly came to a stop in the middle of a sentence. The other students, who were already lifting their heads toward the paper jumping-jack hanging on the wall, immediately plunged back into their books. The teacher turned his eyes away from the window toward the reader, who was sitting opposite him in the first row of chairs, near the door. "Well, go on. There's no period there. You don't seem to understand what you are reading!"

The child looked at the teacher, and past him, a little to the right, at the white paper jumping-jack. "Do you understand what you are reading—yes or no?"

"Yes," said the child in a shaky voice.

"Yes, *sir*," corrected the teacher.

"Yes, sir," repeated the child.

The teacher looked down at his book and asked, "What do you think the word 'alibi' means?"

The child looked at the clown cut out of white paper, then at the blank wall straight in front of him, then at the book on his desk; then at the wall again, for almost a minute.

"Well?"

"I don't know, sir," said the child.

The teacher slowly inspected the class. One student near the window at the back of the room raised his hand. The teacher pointed his finger at him and the boy stood up from his bench. "So people would think they were there, sir."

"Who were there? What do you mean?"

"The two brothers, sir."

"Where did they want people to think they were?"

"In the city, sir, at the archbishop's palace."

"And where were they, actually?"

The child reflected a moment before answering. "They were really there, sir, but they wanted to go somewhere else and make everyone believe they were *still* there. 'Late at night, hidden behind black masks and wrapped up in huge capes, the two brothers let themselves down into a deserted alley by means of a rope ladder.' "

The teacher nodded several times, his head on one side, as if half approving. After several seconds of silence he said, "Good. Now give a resumé of the rest of the story for those students who have not understood it."

The child looked toward the window. Then he lowered his eyes to the book, immediately lifting them again in the direction of the rostrum. "Where should I begin, sir?"

"Begin at the beginning of the chapter."

Without sitting down again, the child turned the pages of his book, and after a short silence began to tell the story of the conspiracy of Phillip of Coburg. In spite of frequent hesitations and repetitions, he managed to make it a more or less coherent account, though he accorded far too much importance to secondary facts and, on the other hand, scarcely mentioned certain events of vital significance— sometimes omitting them altogether. Since the child continually emphasized actions themselves rather than their political causes, an uninformed listener would have had considerable difficulty unraveling the meaning of the story and the links that connected the actions thus described with each other as well as with the various characters involved. The teacher gradually shifted his attention toward the windows. The high-school student was standing under the lowest branch again; he had set his satchel at the foot of the tree, and was jumping up from where he stood, one arm raised. When he saw that all his efforts were in vain, he stood perfectly still once more, contemplating the inaccessible leaves. Phillip of Coburg and his mercenaries were encamped on the banks of the Neckar. The students, who no longer had to follow the printed text, had all lifted their heads again and were silently considering the paper jumping-jack on the wall. It had neither hands nor feet, merely four crudely indicated limbs and a round head, too fat for its body, to which a string was attached. Three inches higher, at the other end of the string, was a rough pellet of blotting paper which held it on the wall.

But the narrator had lost himself in a series of minor complications, and at last the teacher interrupted him. "That's fine," he said, "we know quite enough as it is. Sit down and continue reading at the top of the page: 'But Phillip and his partisans . . .' "

All the students leaned over their desks at the same moment, and the new reader began, his voice as inexpressive as his predecessor's, although conscientiouly stressing all commas and periods. " 'But Phillip and his partisans did not choose to interpret the matter in this fashion. If the majority of the members of the Diet—or even the party of the barons alone—renounced the privileges that had been granted, to him as well as to themselves, in return for the inestimable support they had provided the archducal cause at the time of the revolt, neither he nor they, in the future, would ever again be able to demand that any man they accused be arraigned or deprived of his seignorial rights without benefit of trial. It was essential that these negotiations, which appeared to him to be undertaken in a manner so prejudicial to his cause, be interrupted at any cost before the fateful date. That evening, Joseph de Hagen, one of Phillip's lieutenants, presented himself at the archbishop's palace, supposedly as an act of courtesy. As we have said above, the two brothers were there already . . .' "

The heads remained dutifully bowed over the desks. The teacher turned his eyes toward the window. The student was leaning against the tree again, absorbed in his inspection of the bark. He leaned down very slowly, lower and lower, as if he were tracing a line drawn on the trunk—on the side of the tree not visible from the schoolroom windows. At about four feet from the ground he stopped moving and leaned his head to one side, in precisely the same position that he had assumed before. One by one, in the classroom, the heads rose from their desks.

The children looked at the teacher, then at the windows. But the lower panes were of ground glass, and through the upper ones they could see only treetops and the sky. Not a single bee or butterfly could be seen against the glass. Soon every pair of eyes were contemplating once again the white paper jumping-jack.

3. The Wrong Direction

Rain water has accumulated in the bottom of a shallow depression, forming among the trees a great pool roughly circular in shape and about thirty feet across. The soil is black around the edges of the pool, without showing the slightest trace of vegetation between the straight, tall trunks. In this part of the forest there are no thickets, no underbrush of any kind. The ground is covered instead by an even layer of felt, composed of twigs and leaves crumbled to veiny skeletons upon which, here and there, a few patches of half-rotten moss are barely discernible. High above the boles the bare branches stand out sharply against the sky.

The water is quite transparent, although brownish in color. Tiny fragments that have fallen from the trees—twigs, empty pods, strips of bark—accumulate at the bottom and steep there all winter long. But nothing is floating on the water, nothing breaks the uniformly polished surface. There is not the slightest breath of wind to disturb its perfection.

The weather has cleared. The day is drawing to its close. The sun is low on the left, behind the tree trunks. Its weakly slanting rays describe a few narrow, luminous stripes across the surface of the pool, alternating with wider bands of shadow.

Parallel to these stripes, a row of huge trees stands at the edge of the water on the opposite bank; perfectly cylindrical, without any low branches, they extend themselves downward to meet their reflections which are far more vivid than the trunks themselves; by contrast the trees seem almost indistinct, perhaps even blurred. In the black water the symmetrical boles gleam as if they were varnished, and on the sides facing the setting sun a last touch of light confirms their contours.

However, this admirable landscape is not only upside down, but discontinuous as well. The rays of the sun that cross-hatch the mirror-like surface interrupt the reflection at regular intervals perpendicular to the trunks; one's vision is obscured by the very intensity of the light which reveals innumerable particles suspended in the upper layer of the water. It is only in the zones of shadow, where these tiny particles are invisible, that the brilliance of the reflection can now be remarked. Thus each trunk is interrupted at apparently equal intervals by a series of uncertain rings (something like the rings on the trees themselves), so that this whole forest "in depth" has the appearance of a checkerboard.

Within reach of one's hand, near the southern bank, the branches of the reflection overlap some old, sunken leaves, rust-colored but still whole, whose perfect outlines contrast sharply with the background of mud—they are oak leaves.

Someone walking noiselessly on this carpet of humus has appeared at the right, heading for the water. He walks to the edge and stops. The sun is in his eyes and he has to step to one side to be able to make out anything at all.

Then he sees the striped surface of the pool. But from where he is standing the reflection of the trunks coincides with their shadows— partially at least, for the trees in front of him are not perfectly straight. The light in his eyes keeps him from seeing anything clearly, and there are certainly no oak leaves at his feet.

This was the place toward which he was walking. Or has he just discovered that he came the wrong way? After a few uncertain glances around him, he turns back toward the east, walking through the woods as silently as before along the path by which he had come.

The place is deserted again. The sun is still at the same height on the left; the light has not changed. Across the pool, the sleek, straight boles are reflected in the unrippled water, perpendicular to the rays of the setting sun.

At the bottom of the bands of darkness gleam the truncated reflections of the columns—upside down and black, miraculously washed.

TRANSLATED BY RICHARD HOWARD

. .
. .
. .

Modern urban life requires large doses of refined ennui. Much recent French literature not only treats this subject but satisfies the requirement.

For a hundred and fifty years, France has been the laboratory for modern fiction, and many French poems and stories are written in the experimental vein, written, that is, to be explained and compared with other test-tube products.

The barer the stage, the more room for critical furniture. Recent French literature has enjoyed an immense amount of subtle criticism. It would seem incomplete without it, and, knowing this, the writers frequently put on neckties and write the criticism themselves. Michel Butor, Robbe-Grillet, Claude Ollier, and Nathalie Sarraute are all delightful and subtle people who write fine French prose. The world would be poorer in their absence and undoubtedly in the absence of their work.

LIUMPA

Yuri Olyesha

The little boy Alexander was planing planks in the kitchen. The small cuts on his fingers were covered with edible-looking golden scabs. He recalled how they used to put kvass on his cuts and he drew his cheeks in sharply.

The kitchen opened onto the courtyard; it was springtime, the doors were not closed and grass was growing in the doorway; spilt water shone on a stone. A rat made its appearance in the garbage pail. In the kitchen a finely chopped potato was frying. The kerosene stove had been lit. The stove came to life exuberantly, flaming like a torch toward the ceiling. It died a small blue flame. Eggs bounced in the saucepan. One of the tenants was cooking crabs, picking them up alive in his fingers. The crabs were greenish, the color of pipe water. Suddenly, one after another, two or three little drops dripped out of the tap. The tap snuffled quietly. Then the pipes up above started conversing in several voices. All at once it was dusk. A single glass continued to shine on the window sill. Through the gate it caught the last rays of the sun. The tap chattered away. Around and about the stove rustlings and squeakings started up.

It was a wonderful twilight. People in their lovingly built houses were holding sunflower seeds, songs rang out, the yellow room-light fell on the sidewalk, a bright light shone from the local food store.

In a room beside the kitchen Ponamarev was lying very ill. He was alone in the room, a candle was burning, a bottle of medicine stood beside his head with the prescription attached to the bottle.

When friends came to see Ponamarev he would say, "Congratulate me, I am dying."

Toward evening he became feverish. The bottle watched him. The prescription extended itself like a train. The bottle was married to a duchess, one addressed the bottle as "your Grace." The sick man

345

became delirious. He wanted to write a thesis. He talked to the comforter.

"Well, aren't you ashamed?" he whispered.

The comforter sat beside him, lay down beside him, left the room, told him the news.

The sick man had a few things around him: medicine, a spoon, the light, wallpaper. The other things had gone. When he understood that he was seriously ill and would die, he realized how grand and varied is the world of things and how few of those things he still controlled. Every day the number of things decreased. Such an intimate thing as a railway ticket had already become irretrievably remote. At first the number of things decreased on the outskirts, far away from him, then the loss came closer and approached the center —him, his heart, into the yard, the house, the corridor, the room.

At first the disappearance of things didn't distress the sick man.

Countries disappeared, America, the possibility of being handsome, or rich, of a family (he was a bachelor). . . . His illness had nothing at all to do with the disappearance of these things—they slipped away as he grew older—but the real ache began when he realized that those things that continually moved along with him were also beginning to withdraw. Thus he was deserted in one day by the street, the office, the post office. And then in a rush things near him disappeared: the corridor had already gone from his grasp—and in the room itself, under his very eyes, his coat had lost its meaning, the door bolts, his boots. Of the whole enormous and irrelevant number, death left him only a few, and those were things which he would never have allowed to come into his home, if he had had any say in the matter. He was given a bedpan. He received fearful visits and looks from his friends. He realized that he was not in a position to defend himself against the invasion of these unasked and useless—as they always seemed to him —things. But they were the only ones and inevitable. He had lost his right to choose things.

The little boy Alexander was making a model airplane.

He was a far more complex and serious boy than others thought. He cut his fingers, blood flowed, dripping onto the shavings smeared with glue. He coaxed a piece of silk, cried, was boxed on the ears. Grownups considered themselves perfectly justified. But meanwhile the boy behaved in a completely adult way; more than that: he acted

Liumpa
Yuri Olyesha

in a way that few adults do, he worked in complete accord with nature. The model was built on a design, calculations were necessary —the boy knew the rules. He was able to relate the attacks of grownups to an empiric law, a demonstration of experiences, but he was silent because he did not consider it was right to show himself more serious-minded than grownups.

Littered around the boy were strips of rubber, wire, bits of metal, a finely woven silk cloth, the smell of glue. The sky was bright. Insects moved across a stone. Inside the stone a shell was petrifying.

Another boy, quite naked, came up to the boy who was working. He fiddled with things and got in the way. Alexander drove him away. The naked boy wandered about the house, through the corridor, where a bicycle was standing. (The bicycle was leaning against the wall by its pedal. On the wallpaper the pedal had made a groove. By means of this notch the bicycle somehow or other held onto the wall.)

The small boy approached Ponamarev. The child's head showed dimly at the end of the bed. The sick man's temples were white like a blind man's. The boy came right up to the head and examined it. He thought to himself that in the world it always was and always would be like this: the bearded man lying in bed. The boy had only just become aware of things. He could not yet see the different places they occupied in time.

The boy turned around and began to walk about the room. He saw the parquet floor, the dust on the baseboard, the cracks in the plaster. About him lines composed and distributed themselves, forms materialized. Suddenly there was a light. The boy ran toward it but had hardly moved a step before the altered distance destroyed the reflection—and the boy looked around, looked behind the stove, high and low, waving his arms distractedly at not finding it. Every second created something new for him. The spider was a marvel. The spider disappeared at the boy's first thought to touch it with his hand.

The disappearing things left the dying man only their names.

In the world there was an apple. It shone among the leaves, gently revolving, catching and throwing back scraps of the day, the blueness of the garden, the frame of the window. The law of gravity lay waiting for it under the tree, in the black earth; beady ants scurried in the lumpy earth. Newton was sitting in the garden. In the apple was hidden a multitude of qualities, earnest of a still greater number of

discoveries. But not one of these discoveries was destined for Ponamarev. The apple had become an abstraction for him. And the fact that
the body of the thing had gone from him, and yet the idea remained,
tormented him.

"I thought that the world of appearances did not exist," he
pondered. "I thought that my eyes and hearing controlled things. I
thought the world would cease to exist when I ceased to exist. But
now . . . I see that everything turns its back on me while I am still
living. After all, I am still alive! Why do things no longer exist? I
thought that my brain gave them form, weight and color—but there,
they have gone away and left me, and only their names, having lost
their masters, swarm in my brain. And what are these names to
me?"

Ponamarev looked sadly at the child. He was walking around.
Things rushed to meet him. He smiled at them, not knowing a single
name. He walked out and the splendid train of things fluttered about
him.

"Listen," called the invalid to the child, "listen. . . . You know
that when I die nothing will be left. Of the courtyard, or the tree, nor
Daddy or Mummy. I am taking everything with me."

The rat had made its way through to the kitchen. Ponamarev
listened: the rat had taken over, rattling the plates, turning on a tap,
rustling in the pail.

"Well, I never! She is a washer-up," thought Ponamarev. Just then
a disturbing thought struck him—that the rat might have its own
name, unknown to people. He began to invent such a name. He was
delirious. As he thought, he was struck by a more and more
overpowering fear. He realized that whatever happened he must stop
and not think about what name the rat might be called—and all the
same he kept on, knowing that the instant that he invented this sole,
senseless and terrifying name, he would die.

"Liumpa!" he shrieked suddenly in a ghastly voice.

The house slept. It was early morning—just past five. The boy
Alexander was not asleep. The door from the kitchen opened onto the
courtyard. The sun was still somewhere down below.

The dead man crossed the kitchen, bent at the middle and holding
his arms stretched out with their protruding bones. He was on his way
collecting things.

The boy Alexander ran across the courtyard, the model flying in front of him. It was the last thing Ponamarev saw.

He did not take it. It flew away.

During the day they brought the coffin into the kitchen, blue with yellow decorations. The naked boy watched from the corridor, clasping his hands behind his back. It took a long time and a lot of maneuvering to turn the coffin around so as to get it through the door. They scraped it against the stove, the saucepans; plaster crumbled. The boy Alexander climbed onto the stove and helped, supporting the box from underneath. When they finally got the coffin through, into the corridor, which immediately turned black, the naked boy, shuffling in his sandals, ran on ahead.

"Grandpa, Grandpa," he cried, "they've brought you a coffin."

TRANSLATED BY CAMILLA GRAY

SIGNS AND SYMBOLS

Vladimir Nabokov

I

For the fourth time in as many years they were confronted with the problem of what birthday present to bring a young man who was incurably deranged in his mind. He had no desires. Man-made objects were to him either hives of evil, vibrant with a malignant activity that he alone could perceive, or gross comforts for which no use could be found in his abstract world. After eliminating a number of articles that might offend him or frighten him (anything in the gadget line for instance was taboo), his parents chose a dainty and innocent trifle: a basket with ten different fruit jellies in ten little jars.

At the time of his birth they had been married already for a long time: a score of years had elapsed, and now they were quite old. Her drab grey hair was done anyhow. She wore cheap black dresses. Unlike other women of her age (such as Mrs. Sol, their next-door neighbour, whose face was all pink and mauve with paint and whose hat was a cluster of brookside flowers), she presented a naked white countenance to the fault-finding light of spring days. Her husband, who in the old country had been a fairly successful business man, was now wholly dependent on his brother Isaac, a real American of almost forty years standing. They seldom saw him and had nicknamed him "the Prince."

That Friday everything went wrong. The Underground train lost its life current between two stations, and for a quarter of an hour one could hear nothing but the dutiful beating of one's heart and the rustling of newspapers. The bus they had to take next kept them waiting for ages; and when it did come, it was crammed with garrulous high-school children. It was raining hard as they walked up the brown path leading to the sanitarium. There they waited again; and instead of their boy shuffling into the room as he usually did (his poor face blotched with acne, ill-shaven, sullen, and confused), a nurse they knew, and did not care for, appeared at last and brightly explained that he had again attempted to take his life. He was all right, she said, but a visit might disturb him. The place was so miserably understaffed, and things got mislaid or mixed up so easily, that they decided not to leave their present in the office but to bring it to him next time they came.

She waited for her husband to open his umbrella and then took his arm. He kept clearing his throat in a special resonant way he had when he was upset. They reached the bus-stop shelter on the other side of the street and he closed his umbrella. A few feet away, under a swaying and dripping tree, a tiny half-dead unfledged bird was helplessly twitching in a puddle.

During the long ride to the Underground station, she and her husband did not exchange a word; and every time he glanced at his old hands (swollen veins, brown-spotted skin), clasped and twitching upon the handle of his umbrella, she felt the mounting pressure of tears. As she looked around trying to hook her mind on to something, it gave her a kind of soft shock, a mixture of compassion and wonder, to notice that one of the passengers, a girl with dark hair and grubby red toenails, was weeping on the shoulder of an older woman. Whom did that woman resemble? She resembled Rebecca Borisovna, whose daughter had married one of the Soloveichiks—in Minsk, years ago.

The last time their son had tried to take his life, his method had been, in the doctor's words, a masterpiece of inventiveness; he would have succeeded, had not an envious fellow patient thought he was learning to fly—and stopped him. What he really wanted to do was to tear a hole in his world and escape.

The system of his delusions had been the subject of an elaborate paper in a scientific monthly, but long before that she and her husband had puzzled it out for themselves. "Referential mania," Herman Brink had called it. In these very rare cases the patient imagines that everything happening around him is a veiled reference to his personality and existence. He excludes real people from the conspiracy—because he considers himself to be so much more intelligent than other men. Phenomenal nature shadows him wherever he goes. Clouds in the staring sky transmit to one another, by means of slow signs, incredibly detailed information regarding him. His inmost thoughts are discussed at nightfall, in manual alphabet, by darkly gesticulating trees. Pebbles or stains or sun flecks form patterns representing in some awful way messages which he must intercept.

Everything is a cipher and of everything he is the theme. Some of the spies are detached observers, such as glass surfaces and still pools; others, such as coats in store windows, are prejudiced witnesses, lynchers at heart; others again (running water, storms) are hysterical to the point of insanity, have a distorted opinion of him and grotesquely misinterpret his actions. He must be always on his guard and devote every minute and module of life to the decoding of the undulation of things. The very air he exhales is indexed and filed away. If the only interest he provokes were limited to his immediate surroundings—but alas it is not! With distance the torrents of wild scandal increase in volume and volubility. The silhouettes of his blood corpuscles, magnified a million times, flit over vast plains; and still farther, great mountains of unbearable solidity and height sum up in terms of granite and groaning firs the ultimate truth of his being.

II

When they emerged from the thunder and foul air of the Underground railway, the last dregs of the day were mixed with the street lights. She wanted to buy some fish for supper, so she handed him the basket of jelly jars, telling him to go home. He walked up to the third landing and then remembered he had given her the keys earlier in the day.

In silence he sat down on the steps and in silence rose when some ten minutes later she came, heavily trudging upstairs, wanly smiling, shaking her head in deprecation of her silliness. They entered their two-room flat and he at once went to the mirror. Straining the corners of his mouth apart by means of his thumbs, with a horrible masklike grimace, he removed his new hopelessly uncomfortable dental plate and severed the long tusks of saliva connecting him to it. He read his Russian-language newspaper while she laid the table. Still reading, he ate the pale victuals that needed no teeth. She knew his moods and was also silent.

When he had gone to bed, she remained in the living-room with her pack of soiled cards and her old albums. Across the narrow yard where the rain tinkled in the dark against some battered ash cans, windows were blandly alight and in one of them a black-trousered man with his bare elbows raised could be seen lying supine on an untidy bed. She pulled the blind down and examined the photographs. As a baby he looked more surprised than most babies. From a fold in the album, a German maid they had had in Leipzig and her fat-faced fiancé fell out. Minsk, the Revolution, Leipzig, Berlin, Leipzig, a slanting house front badly out of focus. Four years old, in a park: moodily, shyly, with puckered forehead, looking away from an eager squirrel as he would from any other stranger. Aunt Rosa, a fussy, angular, wild-eyed old lady, who had lived in a tremulous world of bad news, bankruptcies, train accidents, cancerous growths—until the Germans put her to death, together with all the people she had worried about. Age six—that was when he drew wonderful birds with human hands and feet, and suffered from insomnia like a grown-up man. His cousin, now a famous chess player. He again, aged about eight, already difficult to understand, afraid of the wallpaper in the passage, afraid of a certain picture in a book which merely showed an idyllic landscape with rocks on a hillside and an old cart wheel hanging from the branch of a leafless tree. Aged ten: the year they left Europe. The shame, the pity, the humiliating difficulties, the ugly, vicious, backward children he was with in that special school. And then came a time in his life, coinciding with a long convalescence after pneumonia, when those little phobias of his which his parents had stubbornly regarded as the eccentricities of a prodigiously gifted child hardened as it were into a dense tangle of logically interacting illusions, making him totally inaccessible to normal minds.

This, and much more, she accepted—for after all living did mean accepting the loss of one joy after another, not even joys in her case— mere possibilities of improvement. She thought of the endless waves of pain that for some reason or other she and her husband had to endure; of the invisible giants hurting her boy in some unimaginable fashion; of the incalculable amount of tenderness contained in the world; of the fate of this tenderness, which is either crushed, or wasted, or transformed into madness; of neglected children humming to themselves in unswept corners; of beautiful weeds that cannot hide from the farmer and helplessly have to watch the shadow of his simian stoop leave mangled flowers in its wake, as the monstrous darkness approaches.

III

It was past midnight when from the living-room she heard her husband moan; and presently he staggered in, wearing over his night-

gown the old overcoat with astrakhan collar which he much preferred
to the nice blue bathrobe he had.

"I can't sleep," he cried.

"Why," she asked, "why can't you sleep? You were so tired."

"I can't sleep because I am dying," he said and lay down on the
couch.

"Is it your stomach? Do you want me to call Dr. Solov?"

"No doctors, no doctors," he moaned: "To the devil with doctors!
We must get him out of there quick. Otherwise we'll be responsible.
Responsible!" he repeated and hurled himself into a sitting position,
both feet on the floor, thumping his forehead with his clenched fist.

"All right," she said quietly, "we shall bring him home tomorrow
morning."

"I would like some tea," said her husband and retired to the
bathroom.

Bending with difficulty, she retrieved some playing cards and a
photograph or two that had slipped from the couch to the floor:
knave of hearts, nine of spades, ace of spades. Elsa and her bestial
beau.

He returned in high spirits, saying in a loud voice:

"I have it all figured out. We will give him the bedroom. Each of us
will spend part of the night near him and the other part on this
couch. By turns. We will have the doctor see him at least twice a
week. It does not matter what the Prince says. He won't have to say
much anyway because it will come out cheaper."

The telephone rang. It was an unusual hour for the telephone to
ring. His left slipper had come off and he groped for it with his heel
and toe as he stood in the middle of the room, and childishly,
toothlessly, gaped at his wife. Having more English than he did, it
was she who attended to calls.

"Can I speak to Charlie," said a girl's dull little voice.

"What number you want? No. That is not the right number."

The receiver was gently cradled. Her hand went to her old tired
heart.

"It frightened me," she said.

He smiled a quick smile and immediately resumed his excited
monologue. They would fetch him as soon as it was day. Knives
would have to kept in a locked drawer. Even at his worst he presented
no danger to other people.

The telephone rang a second time. The same toneless anxious young voice asked for Charlie.

"You have the incorrect number. I will tell you what you are doing: you are turning the letter O instead of the zero."

They sat down to their unexpected festive midnight tea. The birthday present stood on the table. He sipped noisily; his face was flushed; every now and then he imparted a circular motion to his raised glass so as to make the sugar dissolve more thoroughly. The vein on the side of his bald head where there was a large birthmark stood out conspicuously and, although he had shaved that morning, a silvery bristle showed on his chin. While she poured him another glass of tea, he put on his spectacles and re-examined with pleasure the luminous yellow, green, red little jars. His clumsy moist lips spelled out their eloquent labels: apricot, grape, beech plum, quince. He had got to crab apple, when the telephone rang again.

THE CABBAGES IN THE CEMETERY

Pio Baroja

The house was on the way out of town, to the left of the highway: an ancient, one-story house, upon whose rain blackened walls various letters majestically formed the following phrase: "BLASIDO'S WINE SHOP."

The artist who had done the letters, not content with the elegant tone imparted to each letter, had striven to exceed himself, and above the lintel of the wide door he had painted a rooster with long, erect feathers, balancing its two claws upon a large heart, wounded and shot through by a treacherous arrow: a mysterious hieroglyphic whose significance no one knew.

The spacious entranceway to the house was narrowed by two great wine casks at each side, which left a small passage between. Behind them was the shop, which, in addition to being a tavern, was a tobacconist's, a stationer's, an establishment dispensing hot chocolate, and a few other things besides. In back of the house a few tables stood under a bower, and there the worshipers of Bacchus gathered on Sunday afternoons to drink and play nine-pins, while those of the cult of Venus dropped in to assuage their ardors with refreshing blackberries.

Justa, the owner's wife and barmaid, would have made out well enough if she had not been burdened with a lazy husband, a wastrel and loafer, who, besides treating all the spirits his wife dispensed with sentimental familiarity, also possessed the fertility of a stud horse.

"*Arrayua*, Blasido! Whoa!" his friends would yell at him. "You mean your wife is that way again! How the devil do you do it . . ."

"What do you expect?" he would reply. "Women! They're just like sows. And mine. . . . The mere smell of it, a whiff . . . eh? All I have to do is hang my underpants on the bedpost, and she's pregnant. The soil's good, the seed's good, the season's good."

"Drunkard! Pig!" his wife would scream when she heard him. "It would be better for you if you worked instead of talked."

"Work! What ideas these women get in their heads!"

One day in January, Blasido, who was drunk, fell into the river, and though his friends hauled him out in time to save him from drowning, he had to go to bed as soon as he got home because he was having chills. Later he developed double pneumonia. While he was sick he sang all the *zortzicos* he knew. And finally, one morning, when he heard the drummer talking in the tavern, he called out:

"Chomín, will you bring in your fife and drum?"

"All right."

Because he thought highly of Blasido, Chomín brought in his fife and drum.

"What shall I play?"

"The *Aurrescu*," said Blasido.

But then, halfway through the drum roll, Blasido turned around and said: "The end, Chomín, play the end, for I'm going now."

And Blasido turned his head back to the wall and died.

The next day, Pachi, the gravedigger, dug a magnificent and commodious grave, three feet deep, for his old friend. Justa, the barmaid, who was pregnant, struggled on, with her seven little ones and her tavern, and the advice of her dead husband's friends.

Of these friends, the most devoted was Pachi-zurra, or Pachi-hell as some called him. Pachi was a man who might have seemed tall if he had not been so heavy; seen from the rear he was square, from the front he was round, and in profile he was simply big-bellied. His face, carefully clean shaven, was of a hue between red and violet. His eyes, small and joyous, were circled with fleshy borders. His nose, which, it must be confessed, was not Greek, might have been handsome, if it had not been so large, wide, and highly colored. His mouth contained no teeth, but even his enemies could not do less than admit that his lips parted to produce the most sumptuous of smiles, and that his beret, wide as a platter and always pulled down over his head, was in exquisite good taste.

Evil tongues, the eternal old ladies, said that Pachi had had a stormy and dubious youth. Who could have guessed, said some, that those hands (aided by a modest blunderbuss), had stripped travelers of their wealth, over toward La Rioja, when the railroad line to the North was being built? Others detected in him the classical escaped

convict; still others, a seaman from a pirate ship; and there were even
those who, following logically from deduction to deduction, supposed
that Pachi had petitioned for the job of gravedigger in order to melt
down and render the fat of dead children. But all these suppositions
(for the sake of the truth we must admit it) were not true.

Pachi, on returning to his native town after lengthy travels in
America, found that on some property of his—a bit of land on a
hillside, land that had come down to him by inheritance—a cemetery
had been established. In the town they had thought Pachi dead.
When Pachi demanded the return of his land, the municipality made
attempts to buy it from him. But Pachi would not accept the offers
made him and proposed in turn that the deeding of the land to the
municipality be made conditional on his being given the post of
gravedigger and the right to construct a small house in one of the
walled angles of the cemetery, where he, with his beret and pipe,
could go and live.

His proposition accepted, Pachi built a little house and went to live
in it and watch over the cemetery. The dead surely must not have
minded that Pachi had been given charge of their tombs, for he
decorated them with fragrant plants and beautiful flowers.

Despite the care lavished on the tombs by the good Pachi, the
townspeople looked upon him as a reprobate; all because some
Sundays he would forget to go to mass, and because whenever he
heard the village vicar eulogized he would wink his eye and say:
"*Esaguna laguna*," which in Basque literally means: "I know you, my
friend"; with which phrase it was assumed he was making sly
reference to a false tale—though the story was not without its vestiges
of truth—which recounted the details of how the vicar had fathered
two or three children in the neighboring town.

Such was the terror Pachi inspired that mothers, in order to frighten
their children, would say to them: "If you don't keep quiet, *matitia*,
Pachi-hell is going to come and get you, and take you away with
him."

The aristocracy of the town treated Pachi with scorn, and the
druggist, who thought himself a clever fellow, attempted to make
mock of him.

Pachi and the young village-doctor got along splendidly; whenever
the doctor performed an autopsy, the gravedigger acted as his
assistant, and if some curious rubberneck got too close and then gave

sudden signs of horror or repugnance, Pachi would wink knowingly at the doctor, as if to say: "This fellow's frightened because he's not in on the secret. . . . He, he!"

Pachi paid little attention to what was said about him; he was satisfied with being the oracle of Justa's tavern. His audience was made up of the road-mender, who was the only liberal in town, the substitute judge, who when he was not substituting for anyone kept busy making rope-soled sandals, Don Ramón, the former school-master, who brought his supper and a bottle of his own to the tavern, the drummer, one of the workers in the public granary, and a handful of others. Pachi's words attracted and held them.

When, having outlined his views of the *ignis fatuus*, the will-o'-the-wisp, he added, "No one need be frightened of them; it's simply a matter of 'electricity,'" everyone would turn to his neighbor, searching each others' eyes to see whether or not the other had plumbed the profundity of this phrase.

And Pachi was the man for a phrase—not all great men have the gift—and he gave vent to aphorisms worthy of Hippocrates. His philosophy was encompassed in these words: "Men are like weeds: they are because they are, they appear for no reason; some weeds have red flowers and others yellow, and just so are there good men and bad; and whoever is a drunkard is fated to be one."

He would moisten his lips with water, and, as if this act of daring had frightened him, he would immediately follow it with a giant swallow of brandy; for the gravedigger always had his water served in a small shot glass and his brandy in a large tumbler—it was a standing joke on his part.

At repartee, Pachi was a phenomenon. One day, a mine operator, a wealthy young man who gave himself airs as a Don Juan, was recounting his conquests.

"I have a child in Olozábal," he was saying, "and another in the house of Zubiaurre, and one in Gaztelu's house."

"You'd be alright now, if you had one in your own house," said Pachi philosophically, "and if your wife's children were your own."

When Pachi recounted his adventures in South America, the smoke of his pipe warming his red nose, his words met with a chorus of exclamations and roars of laughter.

Pachi's adventures in America were of the highest interest. He had been a gambler, merchant, stockbreeder, soldier, and a dozen other

things besides. As a soldier he had been forced to burn alive a goodly
number of Indians. But it was as lover that Pachi's stories took on a
truly suggestive air, when he told of his amorous adventures with
Negresses, Indian and Negro half-breeds, mulatto women, and yellow
damsels. He could say, without exaggeration, that his love had run the
chromatic scale of women.

The barmaid and now tavern-owner was of such a lively disposition
that a week after giving birth to her eighth child she was up and about
as if nothing had happened. But that night she was forced to return to
her bed with a fever, which turned out to be puerperal, and which
carried her to the cemetery. The widow had fallen behind in her
accounts, and so the tavern was sold, and the eight children were left
in the street.

"*Hay que hacel algo por esoz niñoz,*" said the mayor, speaking
almost in Andalusian to cover up his Basque accent: "Something will
have to be done with those children."

"With those children something will have to be done," murmured
the vicar in his suave voice, lifting his eyes to heaven.

"There's no alternative," said the pharmacist resolutely, "something will have to be done about those children."

"Children. . . . Charity . . ." added the town secretary.

And the days passed and the weeks passed, the older girl had gone
to serve as a maid in the postman's house, where she was happy
enough, and the infant in arms was being nursed with great ill-will by
the farrier's wife.

The other six—Chomín, Shanti, Martiñacho, Joshe, Maru, and
Gaspar—ran barefoot about the highway, begging.

One day in the morning, the gravedigger came into town with a
little cart, put the six children in it, took the suckling infant from the
farrier's wife and tucked him into his arms, and led the entire troupe
to the cemetery. On the way, he stopped at the general store and
bought a nursing bottle for the infant.

"What a humbug!" said the Mayor.

"What an imbecile!" exclaimed the pharmacist.

The vicar modestly lifted his eyes to heaven, withdrawing them
from the sight of such misery.

"He'll abandon them," prognosticated the secretary.

But Pachi has not abandoned them, and he is bringing them up.

And, since he now has so many mouths to feed, he has left off the brandy. On the other hand, he is filling up the cemetery with garden produce and covering hallowed ground with crops in a lamentable fashion. And since there is now a market in town, Pachi has contracted with a friend of his, who owns the farm nearest the cemetery, to sell his cabbages and artichokes for him in the public square.

The cabbages of Pachi's friend, which are the cabbages from the cemetery, have a reputation in the public market for being delicious and especially tasty. What the people that buy them don't know is that they are quietly feeding on the substance of their grandfathers.

TRANSLATED BY ANTHONY KERRIGAN

THE TWO FACES

Henry James

The servant, who, in spite of his sealed, stamped look, appeared to have his reasons, stood there for instruction, in a manner not quite usual, after announcing the name. Mrs. Grantham, however, took it up—"Lord Gwyther?"—with a quick surprise that for an instant justified him even to the small scintilla in the glance she gave her companion, which might have had exactly the sense of the butler's hesitation. This companion, a shortish, fairish, youngish man, clean-shaven and keen-eyed, had, with a promptitude that would have struck an observer—which the butler indeed was—sprung to his feet and moved to the chimney-piece, though his hostess herself, mean-while, managed not otherwise to stir. "Well?" she said, as for the visitor to advance; which she immediately followed with a sharper "He's not there?"

"Shall I show him up, ma'am?"

"But of course!" The point of his doubt made her at last rise for impatience, and Bates, before leaving the room, might still have caught the achieved irony of her appeal to the gentleman into whose communion with her he had broken. "Why in the world not——? What a way——!" she exclaimed, as Sutton felt beside his cheek the passage of her eyes to the glass behind him.

"He wasn't sure you'd see anyone."

"I don't see 'anyone,' but I see individuals."

"That's just it; and sometimes you don't see them."

"Do you mean ever because of *you?*" she asked as she touched into place a tendril of hair. "That's just his impertinence, as to which I shall speak to him."

"Don't," said Shirley Sutton. "Never notice anything."

"That's nice advice from you," she laughed, "who notice every-thing!"

"Ah, but I speak of nothing."

She looked at him a moment. "You're still more impertinent than Bates. You'll please not budge," she went on.

"Really? I must sit him out?" he continued as, after a minute, she had not again spoken—only glancing about, while she changed her place, partly for another look at the glass and partly to see if she could improve her seat. What she felt was rather more than, clever and charming though she was, she could hide. "If you're wondering how you seem, I can tell you. Awfully cool and easy."

She gave him another stare. She was beautiful and conscious. "And if you're wondering how *you* seem——"

"Oh, I'm not!" he laughed from before the fire; "I always perfectly know."

"How you seem," she retorted, "is as if you didn't!"

Once more for a little he watched her. "You're looking lovely for him—extraordinarily lovely, within the market limits of your range. But that's enough. Don't be clever."

"Then who *will* be?"

"There you are!" he sighed with amusement.

"Do you know him?" she asked as, through the door left open by Bates, they heard steps on the landing.

Sutton had to think an instant, and produced a "No" just as Lord Gwyther was again announced, which gave an unexpectedness to the greeting offered him a moment later by this personage—a young man, stout and smooth and fresh, but not at all shy, who, after the happiest rapid passage with Mrs. Grantham, put out a hand with a frank, pleasant "How d'ye do?"

"Mr. Shirley Sutton," Mrs. Grantham explained.

"Oh, yes," said her second visitor, quite as if he knew; which, as he couldn't have known, had for her first the interest of confirming a perception that his lordship would be—no, not at all, in general, embarrassed, only was now exceptionally and especially agitated. As it is, for that matter, with Sutton's total impression that we are particularly and almost exclusively concerned, it may be further mentioned that he was not less clear as to the really handsome way in which the young man kept himself together and little by little— though with all proper aid indeed—finally found his feet. All sorts of things, for the twenty minutes, occurred to Sutton, though one of them was certainly not that it would, after all, be better he should go. One of them was that their hostess was doing it in perfection—

simply, easily, kindly, yet with something the least bit queer in her
wonderful eyes; another was that if he had been recognized without
the least ground, it was through a tension of nerves on the part of his
fellow guest that produced inconsequent motions; still another was
that, even had departure been indicated, he would positively have felt
dissuasion in the rare promise of the scene. This was in especial after
Lord Gwyther not only had announced that he was now married, but
had mentioned that he wished to bring his wife to Mrs. Grantham for
the benefit so certain to be derived. It was the passage immediately
produced by that speech that provoked in Sutton the intensity, as it
were, of his arrest. He already knew of the marriage as well as Mrs.
Grantham herself, and as well also as he knew of some other things;
and this gave him, doubtless, the better measure of what took place
before him and the keener consciousness of the quick look that, at a
marked moment—though it was ‘not absolutely meant for him any
more than for his companion—Mrs. Grantham let him catch.

She smiled, but it had a gravity. "I think, you know, you ought to
have told me before."

"Do you mean when I first got engaged? Well, it all took place so
far away, and we really told, at home, so few people."

Oh, there might have been reasons; but it had not been quite right.
"You were married at Stuttgart? That wasn't too far for *my* interest,
at least, to reach."

"Awfully kind of you—and of course one knew you *would* be kind.
But it wasn't at Stuttgart; it was over there, but quite in the country.
We should have managed it in England but that her mother naturally
wished to be present, yet was not in health to come. So it was really,
you see, a sort of little hole-and-corner German affair."

This didn't in the least check Mrs. Grantham's claim, but it started
a slight anxiety. "Will she be—a, then, German?"

Sutton knew her to know perfectly what Lady Gwyther would
"be," but he had by this time, while their friend explained, his
independent interest. "Oh dear, no! My father-in-law has never
parted with the proud birthright of a Briton. But his wife, you see,
holds an estate in Würtemberg from *her* mother, Countess Kremnitz,
on which, with the awful condition of his English property, you
know, they've found it for years a tremendous saving to live. So that
though Valda was luckily born at home, she has practically spent her
life over there."

"Oh, I see." Then, after a slight pause, "Is Valda her pretty name?" Mrs. Grantham asked.

"Well," said the young man, only wishing, in his candor, it was clear, to be drawn out—"well, she has, in the manner of her mother's people about thirteen; but that's the one we generally use."

Mrs. Grantham hesitated but an instant. "Then may I generally use it?"

"It would be too charming of you; and nothing would give her—as, I assure you, nothing would give *me*, greater pleasure." Lord Gwyther quite glowed with the thought.

"Then I think that instead of coming alone you might have brought her to see me."

"It's exactly what," he instantly replied, "I came to ask your leave to do." He explained that for the moment Lady Gwyther was not in town, having as soon as she arrived gone down to Torquay to put in a few days with one of her aunts, also her godmother, to whom she was an object of great interest. She had seen no one yet, and no one—not that *that* mattered—had seen her; she knew nothing whatever of London and was awfully frightened at facing it and at what—however little—might be expected of her. "She wants someone," he said, "someone who knows the whole thing, don't you see? And who's thoroughly kind and clever, as you would be, if I may say so, to take her by the hand." It was at this point and on these words that the eyes of Lord Gwyther's two auditors inevitably and wonderfully met. But there was nothing in the way he kept it up to show that he caught the encounter. "She wants, if I may tell you so, for the great labyrinth, a real friend; and asking myself what I could do to make things ready for her, and who would be absolutely the best woman in London——"

"You thought, naturally, of *me*?" Mrs. Grantham had listened with no sign but the faint flash just noted; now, however, she gave him the full light of her expressive face—which immediately brought Shirley Sutton, looking at his watch, once more to his feet.

"She is the best woman in London!" He addressed himself with a laugh to the other visitor, but offered his hand in farewell to their hostess.

"You're going?"

"I must," he said without scruple.

"Then we do meet at dinner?"

"I hope so." On which, to take leave, he returned with interest to

Lord Gwyther the friendly clutch he had a short time before received.

II

They did meet at dinner, and if they were not, as it happened, side by side, they made that up afterward in the happiest angle of the drawing room that offered both shine and shadow and that was positively much appreciated, in the circle in which they moved, for the favorable "corners" created by its shrewd mistress. Her face, charged with something produced in it by Lord Gwyther's visit, had been with him so constantly for the previous hours that, when she instantly challenged him on his "treatment" of her in the afternoon, he was on the point of naming it as his reason for not having remained with her. Something new had quickly come into her beauty; he couldn't as yet have said what, nor whether on the whole to its advantage or its loss. Till he could make up his mind about that, at any rate, he would say nothing; so that, with sufficient presence of mind, he found a better excuse. If in short he had in defiance of her particular request left her alone with Lord Gwyther, it was simply because the situation had suddenly turned so exciting that he had fairly feared the contagion of it—the temptation of its making him, most improperly, put in his word.

They could now talk of these things at their ease. Other couples, ensconced and scattered, enjoyed the same privilege, and Sutton had more and more the profit, such as it was, of feeling that his interest in Mrs. Grantham had become—what was the luxury of so high a social code—an acknowledged and protected relation. He knew his London well enough to know that he was on the way to be regarded as her main source of consolation for the trick that, several months before, Lord Gwyther had publicly played her. Many persons had not held that, by the high social code in question, his lordship could have "reserved the right" to turn up in that way, from one day to another, engaged. For himself London took, with its short cuts and its cheap psychology, an immense deal for granted. To his own sense he was never—could in the nature of things never be—any man's "successor." Just what had constituted the predecessorship of other men was apparently that they had been able to make up their minds. He, worse luck, was at the mercy of her face, and more than ever at the mercy of it now, which meant, moreover, not that it made a slave of him, but

THE TWO FACES
Henry James

that it made, disconcertingly, a skeptic. It was the absolute perfection
of the handsome; but things had a way of coming into it. "I felt," he
said, "that you were there together at a point at which you had a right
to the ease that the absence of a listener would give. I reflected that
when you made me promise to stay you hadn't guessed——"

"That he could possibly have come to me on such an extraordinary
errand? No, of course, I hadn't guessed. Who *would?* But didn't you
see how little I was upset by it?"

Sutton demurred. Then with a smile, "I think *he* saw how little."

"You yourself didn't, then?"

He again held back, but not, after all, to answer. "He was
wonderful, wasn't he?"

"I think he was," she replied after a moment. To which she added:
"Why did he pretend that way he knew you?"

"He didn't pretend. He felt on the spot as if we were friends."
Sutton had found this afterward, and found truth in it. "It was an
effusion of cheer and hope. He was so glad to see me there, and to find
you happy."

"Happy?"

"Happy. Aren't you?"

"Because of *you?*"

"Well—according to the impression he received as he came in."

"That was sudden then," she asked, "and unexpected?"

Her companion thought. "Prepared in some degree, but confirmed
by the sight of us, there together, so awfully jolly and sociable over
your fire."

Mrs. Grantham turned this round. "If he knew I was 'happy' then
—which, by the way, is none of his business, nor of yours either—why
in the world did he come?"

"Well, for good manners, and for his idea," said Sutton.

She took it in, appearing to have no hardness of rancor that could
bar discussion. "Do you mean by his idea his proposal that I should
grandmother his wife? And, if you do, is the proposal your reason for
calling him wonderful?"

Sutton laughed. "Pray, what's yours?" As this was a question,
however, that she took her time to answer or not to answer—only
appearing interested for a moment in a combination that had formed
itself on the other side of the room—he presently went on. "What's
his?—that would seem to be the point. His, I mean, for having

decided on the extraordinary step of throwing his little wife, bound hands and feet, into your arms. Intelligent as you are, and with these three or four hours to have thought it over, I yet don't see how that can fail still to mystify you."

She continued to watch their opposite neighbors. " 'Little,' you call her. Is she so very small?"

"Tiny, tiny—she *must* be; as different as possible in every way—of necessity—from you. They always *are* the opposite pole, you know," said Shirley Sutton.

She glanced at him now. "You strike me as of an impudence——!"

"No, no. I only like to make it out with you."

She looked away again and, after a little, went on. "I'm sure she's charming, and only hope one isn't to gather that he's already tired of her."

"Not a bit! He's tremendously in love, and he'll remain so."

"So much the better. And if it's a question," said Mrs. Grantham, "of one's doing what one can for her, he has only, as I told him when you had gone, to give me the chance."

"Good! So he *is* to commit her to you?"

"You use extraordinary expressions, but it's settled that he brings her."

"And you'll really and truly help her?"

"Really and truly?" said Mrs. Grantham, with her eyes again upon him. "Why not? For what do you take me?"

"Ah, isn't that just what I still have the discomfort, every day I live, of asking myself?"

She had made, as she spoke, a movement to rise, which, as if she was tired of his tone, his last words appeared to determine. But, also getting up, he held her, when they were on their feet, long enough to hear the rest of what he had to say. "If you do help her, you know, you'll show him that you've understood."

"Understood what?"

"Why, his idea—the deep, acute train of reasoning that has led him to take, as one may say, the bull by the horns; to reflect that as you might, as you probably *would*, in any case, get at her, he plays the wise game, as well as the bold one, by assuming your generosity and placing himself publicly under an obligation to you."

Mrs. Grantham showed not only that she had listened, but that she had for an instant considered. "What is it you elegantly describe as my getting 'at' her?"

"He takes his risk, but puts you, you see, on your honor."

She thought a moment more. "What profundities indeed then over the simplest of matters! And if your idea is," she went on, "that if I do help her I shall show him I've understood them, so it will be that if I don't——"

"You'll show him"—Sutton took her up—"that you haven't? Precisely. But in spite of not wanting to appear to have understood *too* much——"

"I may still be depended on to do what I can? Quite certainly. You'll see what I may still be depended on to do." And she moved away.

III

It was not, doubtless, that there had been anything in their rather sharp separation at that moment to sustain or prolong the interruption; yet it definitely befell that, circumstances aiding, they practically failed to meet again before the great party at Burbeck. This occasion was to gather in some thirty persons from a certain Friday to the following Monday, and it was on the Friday that Sutton went down. He had known in advance that Mrs. Grantham was to be there, and this perhaps, during the interval of hindrance, had helped him a little to be patient. He had before him the certitude of a real full cup—two days brimming over with the sight of her. He found, however, on his arrival that she was not yet in the field, and presently learned that her place would be in a small contingent that was to join the party on the morrow. This knowledge he extracted from Miss Banker, who was always the first to present herself at any gathering that was to enjoy her, and whom, moreover—partly on that very account—the wary not less than the speculative were apt to hold themselves well-advised to engage with at as early as possible a stage of the business. She was stout, red, rich, mature, universal—a massive, much-fingered volume, alphabetical, wonderful, indexed, that opened of itself at the right place. She opened for Sutton instinctively at G——, which, happened to be remarkably convenient. "What she's really waiting over for is to bring down Lady Gwyther."

"Ah, the Gwythers are coming?"

"Yes; caught, through Mrs. Grantham, just in time. *She'll* be the feature—everyone wants to see her."

Speculation and wariness met and combined at this moment in Shirley Sutton. "Do you mean—a—Mrs. Grantham?"

"Dear no! Poor little Lady Gwyther, who, but just arrived in England, appears now literally for the first time in her life in any society whatever, and whom (don't you know the extraordinary story? you ought to—*you!*) she, of all people, has so wonderfully taken up. It will be quite—here—as if she were 'presenting' her."

Sutton, of course, took in more things than even appeared. "I never know what I ought to know; I only know, inveterately, what I oughtn't. So what is the extraordinary story?"

"You really haven't heard——?"

"Really," he replied without winking.

"It happened, indeed, but the other day," said Miss Banker, "yet everyone is already wondering. Gwyther has thrown his wife on her mercy—but I won't believe you if you pretend to me you don't know why he shouldn't."

Sutton asked himself then what he *could* pretend. "Do you mean because she's merciless?"

She hesitated. "If you don't know, perhaps I oughtn't to tell you."

He liked Miss Banker and found just the right tone to plead. "*Do* tell me."

"Well," she sighed, "it will be your own fault——! They had been such friends that there could have been but one name for the crudity of his original *procédé*. When I was a girl we used to call it throwing over. They call it in French to *lâcher*. But I refer not so much to the act itself as to the manner of it, though you may say indeed, of course, that there is in such cases, after all, only one manner. Least said, soonest mended."

Sutton seemed to wonder. "Oh, he said too much?"

"He said nothing. That was it."

Sutton kept it up. "But was *what?*"

"Why, what she must, like any woman in her shoes, have felt to be his perfidy. He simply went and *did* it—took to himself this child, that is, without the preliminary of a scandal or a rupture—before she could turn round."

"I follow you. But it would appear from what you say that she *has* turned round now."

"Well," Miss Banker laughed, "we shall see for ourselves how far. It will be what everyone will try to see."

"Oh, then we've work cut out!" And Sutton certainly felt that he himself had—an impression that lost nothing from a further talk with Miss Banker in the course of a short stroll in the grounds with her the next day. He spoke as one who had now considered many things.

"Did I understand from you yesterday that Lady Gwyther's a 'child'?"

"Nobody knows. It's prodigious the way she has managed."

"The way Lady Gwyther has——?"

"No; the way May Grantham has kept her till this hour in her pocket."

He was quick at his watch. "Do you mean by 'this hour' that they're due now?"

"Not till tea. All the others arrive together in time for that." Miss Banker had clearly, since the previous day, filled in gaps and become, as it were, revised and enlarged. "She'll have kept a cat from seeing her, so as to produce her entirely herself."

"Well," Sutton mused, "that will have been a very noble sort of return——"

"For Gwyther's behavior? Very. Yet I feel creepy."

"Creepy?"

"Because so much depends for the girl—in the way of the right start or the wrong start—on the signs and omens of their first appearance. It's a great house and a great occasion, and we're assembled here, it strikes me, very much as the Roman mob at the circus used to be to see the next Christian maiden brought out to the tigers."

"Oh, if she *is* a Christian maiden——!" Sutton murmured. But he stopped at what his imagination called up.

It perhaps fed that faculty a little that Miss Banker had the effect of making out that Mrs. Grantham might individually be, in any case, something of a Roman matron. "She has kept her in the dark so that we may only take her from her hand. She will have formed her for us."

"In so few days?"

"Well, she will have prepared her—decked her for the sacrifice with ribbons and flowers."

"Ah, if you only mean that she will have taken her to her dressmaker——!" And it came to Sutton, at once as a new light and as a check, almost, to anxiety, that this was all poor Gwyther, mistrustful probably of a taste formed by Stuttgart, might have desired of their friend.

There were usually at Burbeck many things taking place at once; so that wherever else, on such occasions, tea might be served, it went forward with matchless pomp, weather permitting, on a shaded stretch of one of the terraces and in presence of one of the prospects. Shirley Sutton, moving, as the afternoon waned, more restlessly about and mingling in dispersed groups only to find they had nothing to keep him quiet, came upon it as he turned a corner of the house—saw it seated there in all its state. It might be said that at Burbeck it was, like everything else, made the most of. It constituted immediately, with multiplied tables and glittering plate, with rugs and cushions and ices and fruit and wonderful porcelain and beautiful women, a scene of splendor, almost an incident of grand opera. One of the beautiful women might quite have been expected to rise with a gold cup and a celebrated song.

One of them did rise, as it happened, while Sutton drew near, and he found himself a moment later seeing nothing and nobody but Mrs. Grantham. They met on the terrace, just away from the others, and the movement in which he had the effect of arresting her might have been that of withdrawal. He quickly saw, however, that, if she had been about to pass into the house, it was only on some errand—to get something or to call someone—that would immediately have restored her to the public. It somehow struck him on the spot—and more than ever yet, though the impression was not wholly new to him—that she felt herself a figure for the forefront of the stage and indeed would have been recognized by anyone at a glance as the *prima donna assoluta*. She caused, in fact, during the few minutes he stood talking to her, an extraordinary series of waves to roll extraordinarily fast over his sense, not the least mark of the matter being that the appearance with which it ended was again the one with which it had begun. "The face—the face," as he kept dumbly repeating; that was at last, as at first, all he could clearly see. She had a perfection resplendent, but what in the world had it done, this perfection, to her beauty? It was her beauty, doubtless, that looked out at him, but it was into something else that, as their eyes met, he strangely found himself looking.

It was as if something had happened in consequence of which she had changed, and there was that in this swift perception that made him glance eagerly about for Lady Gwyther. But as he took in the recruited group—identities of the hour added to those of the previous twenty-four—he saw, among his recognitions, one of which was the husband of the person missing, that Lady Gwyther was not there. Nothing in the whole business was more singular than his consciousness that, as he came back to his interlocutress after the nods and smiles and handwaves he had launched, she knew what had been his thought. She knew for whom he had looked without success; but why should this knowledge visibly have hardened and sharpened her, and precisely at a moment when she was unprecedentedly magnificent? The indefinable apprehension that had somewhat sunk after his second talk with Miss Banker and then had perversely risen again —this nameless anxiety now produced on him, with a sudden sharper pinch, the effect of a great suspense. The action of that, in turn, was to show him that he had not yet fully known how much he had at stake on a final view. It was revealed to him for the first time that he "really cared" whether Mrs. Grantham were a safe nature. It was too ridiculous by what a thread it hung, but something was certainly in the air that would definitely tell him.

What was in the air descended the next moment to earth. He turned round as he caught the expression with which her eyes attached themselves to something that approached. A little person, very young and very much dressed, had come out of the house, and the expression in Mrs. Grantham's eyes was that of the artist confronted with her work and interested, even to impatience, in the judgment of others. The little person drew nearer, and though Sutton's companion, without looking at him now, gave it a name and met it, he had jumped for himself at certitude. He saw many things— too many, and they appeared to be feathers, frills, excrescences of silk and lace—massed together and conflicting, and after a moment also saw struggling out of them a small face that struck him as either scared or sick. Then, with his eyes again returning to Mrs. Grantham, he saw another.

He had no more talk with Miss Banker till late that evening—an evening during which he had felt himself too noticeably silent; but something had passed between this pair, across dinner table and drawing room, without speech, and when they at last found words it was in the needed ease of a quiet end of the long, lighted gallery, where she opened again at the very paragraph.

"You were right—that *was* it. She did the only thing that, at such short notice, she *could* do. She took her to her dressmaker."

Sutton, with his back to the reach of the gallery, had, as if to banish a vision, buried his eyes for a minute in his hands. "And oh, the face —the face!"

"Which?" Miss Banker asked.

"Whichever one looks at."

"But May Grantham's glorious. She has turned herself out——"

"With a splendor of taste and a sense of effect, eh? Yes." Sutton showed he saw far.

"She *has* the sense of effect. The sense of effect as exhibited in Lady Gwyther's clothes——!" was something Miss Banker failed of words to express. "Everybody's overwhelmed. Here, you know, that sort of thing's grave. The poor creature's lost."

"Lost?"

"Since on the first impression, as we said, so much depends. The first impression's made—oh, made! I defy her now ever to unmake it. Her husband, who's proud, won't like her the better for it. And I don't see," Miss Banker went on, "that her prettiness *was* enough—a mere little feverish, frightened freshness; what *did* he see in her?—to be so blasted. It has been done with an atrocity of art——"

"That supposes the dressmaker then also a devil?"

"Oh, your London women and their dressmakers!" Miss Banker laughed.

"But the face—the face!" Sutton woefully repeated.

"May's?"

"The little girl's. It's exquisite."

"Exquisite?"

"For unimaginable pathos."

"Oh!" Miss Banker dropped.

"She has at last begun to see." Sutton showed again how far *he* saw. "It glimmers upon her innocence, she makes it dimly out—what has been done with her. She's even worse this evening—the way, my eye, she looked at dinner!—than when she came. Yes"—he was confident

—"it has dawned (how couldn't it, out of all of you?) and she knows."

"She ought to have known before!" Miss Banker intelligently sighed.

"No; she wouldn't in that case have been so beautiful."

"Beautiful?" cried Miss Banker; "overloaded like a monkey in a show!"

"The face, yes; which goes to the heart. It's that that makes it," said Shirley Sutton. "And it's that"—he thought it out—"that makes the other."

"I see. Conscious?"

"Horrible!"

"You take it hard," said Miss Banker.

Lord Gwyther, just before she spoke, had come in sight and now was near them. Sutton on this, appearing to wish to avoid him, reached, before answering his companion's observation, a door that opened close at hand. "So hard," he replied from that point, 'that I shall be off tomorrow morning."

"And not see the rest?" she called after him.

But he had already gone, and Lord Gwyther, arriving, amiably took up her question. "The rest of what?"

Miss Banker looked him well in the eyes. "Of Mrs. Grantham's clothes."

.   .
.   .
.   .

Of this Jamesian jewel, the jeweler remarked: "The value of 'The Two Faces' . . . is . . . peculiarly an economic one. It may conceal rather than exhale its intense little principle of calculation; but the neat evolution, as I call it, the example of the turn of the whole coach and pair in the contracted court, without the 'spill' of a single passenger or the derangement of a single parcel, is only in three or four cases (where the coach is fuller still) more appreciable."

THE FIRST CONSUL IN HIS BATH

Henry Adams

Monroe arrived in sight of the French coast April 7, 1803; but while he was still on the ocean, Bonaparte without reference to him or his mission, opened his mind to Talleyrand in regard to ceding Louisiana to the United States. The First Consul a few days afterward repeated to his Finance Minister, Barbé Marbois, a part of the conversation with Talleyrand; and his words implied that Talleyrand opposed Bonaparte's scheme, less because it sacrificed Louisiana than because its true object was not a war with England, but conquest of Germany. "He alone knows my intentions," said Bonaparte to Marbois. "If I attended to his advice, France would confine her ambition to the left bank of the Rhine, and would make war only to protect the weak States and to prevent any dismemberment of her possessions; but he also admits that the cession of Louisiana is not a dismemberment of France." In reality, the cession of Louisiana meant the overthrow of Talleyrand's influence and the failure of those hopes which had led to the coalition of the 18th Brumaire.

Easter Sunday, April 10, 1803, arrived, and Monroe was leaving Havre for Paris, when Bonaparte, after the religious ceremonies of the day at St. Cloud, called to him two of his ministers, of whom Barbé Marbois was one. He wished to explain his intention of selling Louisiana to the United States; and he did so in his peculiar way. He began by expressing the fear that England would seize Louisiana as her first act of war. "I think of ceding it to the United States. I can scarcely say that I cede it to them, for it is not yet in our possession. If, however, I leave the least time to our enemies, I shall only transmit an empty title to those republicans whose friendship I seek. They ask of me only one town in Louisiana; but I already consider the colony as entirely lost; and it appears to me that in the hands of this growing Power it will be more useful to the policy, and even to the commerce, of France than if I should attempt to keep it."

To this appeal the two ministers replied by giving two opposite opinions. Marbois favored the cession, as the First Consul probably expected him to do; for Marbois was a republican who had learned republicanism in the United States, and whose attachment to that country was secured by marriage to an American wife. His colleague, with equal decision, opposed the scheme. Their arguments were waste of breath. The First Consul said no more, and dismissed them; but the next morning, Monday, April 11, at daybreak, summoning Marbois, he made a short oration of the kind for which he was so famous:

Irresolution and deliberation are no longer in season; I renounce Louisiana. It is not only New Orleans that I cede; it is the whole colony, without reserve. I know the price of what I abandon. I have proved the importance I attach to this province, since my first diplomatic act with Spain had the object of recovering it. I renounce it with the greatest regret; to attempt obstinately to retain it would be folly. I direct you to negotiate the affair. Have an interview this very day with Mr. Livingston.

The order so peremptorily given was instantly carried out; but not by Marbois. Talleyrand, in an interview a few hours afterward, startled Livingston with the new offer.

M. Talleyrand asked me this day, when pressing the subject, whether we wished to have the whole of Louisiana. I told him no; that our wishes extended only to New Orleans and the Floridas; that the policy of France, however, should dictate (as I had shown in an official note) to give us the country above the River Arkansas, in order to place a barrier between them and Canada. He said that if they gave New Orleans the rest would be of little value, and that he would wish to know "what we would give for the whole." I told him it was a subject I had not thought of, but that I supposed we should not object to twenty millions [francs], provided our citizens were paid. He told me that this was too low an offer, and that he would be glad if I would reflect upon it and tell him to-morrow. I told him that as Mr. Monroe would be in town in two days, I would delay my further offer until I had the pleasure of introducing him. He added that he did not speak from authority, but that the idea had struck him.

The suddenness of Bonaparte's change disconcerted Livingston. For months he had wearied the First Consul with written and verbal arguments, remonstrances, threats—all intended to prove that there was nothing grasping or ambitious in the American character; that

France should invite the Americans to protect Louisiana from the Canadians; that the United States cared nothing for Louisiana, but wanted only West Florida and New Orleans—"barren sands and sunken marshes," he said; "a small town built of wood; . . . about seven thousand souls"; a territory important to the United States because it contained "the mouths of some of their rivers," but a mere drain of resources to France. To this rhapsody, repeated day after day for weeks and months, Talleyrand had listened with his imperturbable silence, the stillness of a sceptical mind into which such professions fell meaningless; until he suddenly looked into Livingston's face and asked: "What will you give for the whole?" Naturally Livingston for a moment lost countenance.

The next day, Tuesday, April 12, Livingston, partly recovered from his surprise, hung about Talleyrand persistently, for his chance of reaping alone the fruit of his labors vanished with every minute that passed. Monroe had reached St. Germain late Monday night, and at one o'clock Tuesday afternoon descended from his postchaise at the door of his Paris hotel. From the moment of his arrival he was sure to seize public attention at home and abroad. Livingston used the interval to make one more effort with Talleyrand:

He then thought proper to declare that his proposition was only personal, but still requested me to make an offer; and upon my declining to do so, as I expected Mr. Monroe the next day, he shrugged up his shoulders and changed the conversation. Not willing, however, to lose sight of it, I told him I had been long endeavoring to bring him to some point, but unfortunately without effect; and with that view had written him a note which contained that request. . . . He told me he would answer my note, but that he must do it evasively, because Louisiana was not theirs. I smiled at this assertion, and told him that I had seen the treaty recognizing it. . . . He still persisted that they had it in contemplation to obtain it, but had it not.

An hour or two afterward came a note from Monroe announcing that he would wait upon Livingston in the evening. The two American ministers passed the next day together, examining papers and preparing to act whenever Monroe could be officially presented. They entertained a party at dinner that afternoon in Livingston's apartments, and while sitting at table Livingston saw Barbé Marbois strolling in the garden outside. Livingston sent to invite Marbois to join the party at table. While coffee was served, Marbois came in and entered into conversation with Livingston, who began at once to tell him of Talleyrand's "extraordinary conduct." Marbois hinted that he knew something of the matter, and that Livingston had better come to his house as soon as the dinner company departed. The moment Monroe took leave, Livingston acted on Marbois's hint, and in a midnight conversation the bargain was practically made. Marbois told a story, largely of his own invention, in regard to the First Consul's conduct on Easter Sunday, three days before. Bonaparte mentioned fifty million francs as his price for Louisiana; but as Marbois reported the offer to Livingston, Bonaparte said: "Well! you have charge of the Treasury. Let them give you one hundred millions of francs, and pay their own claims, and take the whole country." The American claims were estimated at about twenty-five millions, and therefore Marbois's price amounted to at least one hundred and twenty-five million francs.

Yet twenty-four or twenty-five million dollars for the whole west bank of the Mississippi, from the Lake of the Woods to the Gulf of Mexico, and indefinitely westward, was not an extortionate price, especially since New Orleans was thrown into the bargain, and indirect political advantages which could not be valued at less than the cost of a war, whatever it might be. Five million dollars were to be paid in America to American citizens, so that less than twenty millions would come to France. Livingston could hardly have been blamed for closing with Marbois on the spot, especially as his instructions warranted him in offering ten millions for New Orleans and the Floridas alone; but Livingston still professed that he did not want the west bank. "I told him that the United States were anxious to preserve peace with France; that for that reason they wished to remove them to the west side of the Mississippi; that we would be perfectly satisfied with New Orleans and the Floridas, and had no disposition to extend across the river; that of course we would not give any great sum for the purchase. . . . He then pressed me to name the sum." After a little more fencing, Marbois dropped at once from one hundred millions to sixty, with estimated claims to the amount of twenty millions more. "I told him that it was vain to ask anything that was so greatly beyond our means; that true policy would dictate to the First Consul not to press such a demand; that he must know it would render the present government unpopular." The conversation closed by Livingston's departure at midnight with a final protest: "I told him that I would consult Mr. Monroe, but that neither he nor I could accede to his ideas on the subject." Then he went home; and

sitting down to his desk wrote a long despatch to Madison, to record
that without Monroe's help he had won Louisiana. The letter closed
with some reflections:—

As to the quantum, I have yet made up no opinion. The field open to
us is infinitely larger than our instructions contemplated, the revenue increasing, and the land more than adequate to sink the capital, should we
even go the sum proposed by Marbois,—nay, I persuade myself that the
whole sum may be raised by the sale of the territory west of the Mississippi, with the right of sovereignty, to some Power in Europe whose
vicinity we should not fear. I speak now without reflection and without
having seen Mr. Monroe, as it was midnight when I left the Treasury
Office, and it is now near three o'clock. It is so very important that you
should be apprised that a negotiation is actually opened, even before Mr.
Monroe has been presented, in order to calm the tumult which the news
of war will renew, that I have lost no time in communicating it. We shall
do all we can to cheapen the purchase; but my present sentiment is that
we shall buy.

A week was next passed in haggling over the price. Livingston did
his utmost to beat Marbois down, but without success. Meanwhile he
ran some risk of losing everything; for when Bonaparte offered a favor
suitors did well to waste no time in acceptance. A slight weight might
have turned the scale; a divulgence of the secret, a protest from Spain,
a moment of irritation at Jefferson's coquetry with England or at the
vaporings of the American press, a sudden perception of the disgust
which every true Frenchman was sure sooner or later to feel at this
squandering of French territory and enterprise—any remonstrance
that should stir the First Consul's pride or startle his fear of posterity,
might have cut short the thread of negotiation. Livingston did not
know the secrets of the Tuileries, or he would not have passed time in
cheapening the price of his purchase. The voice of opposition was
silenced in the French people, but was still so high in Bonaparte's
family as to make the Louisiana scheme an occasion for scenes so
violent as to sound like the prelude to a tragedy.

One evening when Talma was to appear in a new *rôle*, Lucien
Bonaparte, coming home to dress for the theatre, found his brother
Joseph waiting for him. "Here you are at last!" cried Joseph; "I was
afraid you might not come. This is no time for theatre-going; I have
news for you that will give you no fancy for amusement. The General
wants to sell Louisiana."

Lucien, proud of having made the treaty which secured the retrocession, was for a moment thunderstruck; then recovering confidence, he said, "Come, now! if he were capable of wishing it, the Chambers would never consent."

"So he means to do without their consent," replied Joseph. "This is what he answered me, when I said to him, like you, that the Chambers would not consent. What is more, he added that this sale would supply him the first funds for the war. Do you know that I am beginning to think he is much too fond of war?"

History is not often able to penetrate the private lives of famous men, and catch their words as they were uttered. Although Lucien Bonaparte's veracity was not greatly superior to that of his brother Napoleon, his story agreed with the known facts. If his imagination here and there filled in the gaps of memory—if he was embittered and angry when he wrote, and hated his brother Napoleon with Corsican passion, these circumstances did not discredit his story, for he would certainly have told the truth against his brother under no other conditions. The story was not libellous, but Napoleonic; it told nothing new of the First Consul's character, but it was honorable to Joseph, who proposed to Lucien that they should go together and prevent their brother from committing a fault which would rouse the indignation of France, and endanger his own safety as well as theirs.

The next morning Lucien went to the Tuileries; by his brother's order he was admitted, and found Napoleon in his bath, the water of which was opaque with mixture of *eau de Cologne*. They talked for some time on indifferent matters. Lucien was timid, and dared not speak until Joseph came. Then Napoleon announced his decision to sell Louisiana, and invited Lucien to say what he thought of it.

"I flatter myself," replied Lucien, "that the Chambers will not give their consent."

"You flatter yourself!" repeated Napoleon in a tone of surprise; then murmuring in a lower voice, "that is precious, in truth!" (*c'est précieux, en vérité!*)

"And I too flatter myself, as I have already told the First Consul," cried Joseph.

"And what did I answer?" said Napoleon warmly, glaring from his bath at the two men.

"That you would do without the Chambers."

"Precisely! That is what I have taken the great liberty to tell Mr. Joseph, and what I now repeat to the Citizen Lucien—begging him at the same time to give me his opinion about it, without taking into consideration his paternal tenderness for his diplomatic conquest." Then, not satisfied with irony, he continued in a tone of exasperating contempt: "And now, gentlemen, think of it what you will; but both of you go into mourning about this affair—you, Lucien, for the sale itself; you, Joseph, because I shall do without the consent of any one whomsoever. Do you understand?"

At this Joseph came close to the bath, and rejoined in a vehement tone: "And you will do well, my dear brother, not to expose your project to parliamentary discussion; for I declare to you that if necessary I will put myself first at the head of the opposition which will not fail to be made against you."

The First Consul burst into a peal of forced laughter, while Joseph, crimson with anger and almost stammering his words, went on: "Laugh, laugh, laugh, then! I will act up to my promise; and though I am not fond of mounting the tribune, this time you will see me there!"

Napoleon, half rising from the bath, rejoined in a serious tone: "You will have no need to lead the opposition, for I repeat that there will be no debate, for the reason that the project which has not the fortune to meet your approval, conceived by me, negotiated by me, shall be ratified and executed by me alone, do you comprehend?—by me, who laugh at your opposition!"

Hereupon Joseph wholly lost his self-control, and with flashing eyes shouted: "Good! I tell you, General, that you, I, and all of us, if you do what you threaten, may prepare ourselves soon to go and join the poor innocent devils whom you so legally, humanely, and especially with such justice, have transported to Sinnamary."

At this terrible rejoinder Napoleon half started up, crying out: "You are insolent! I ought—" then threw himself violently back in the bath with a force which sent a mass of perfumed water into Joseph's flushed face, drenching him and Lucien, who had the wit to quote, in a theatrical tone, the words which Virgil put into the mouth of Neptune reproving the waves,—

"Quos ego . . ."

Between the water and the wit the three Bonapartes recovered their tempers, while the valet who was present, overcome by fear, fainted and fell on the floor. Joseph went home to change his clothes, while Lucien remained to pass through another scene almost equally amusing. . . .

. .
. .
. .

For Adams' own family, Reason and Its Scribe, History, were present in Quincy as well as Washington. Perhaps the discrepancy between such self-consciousness and the comic oblivion of the Corsican squabblers makes this scene from Adams' History so wonderful. The morphologist may read such French novels as La Princesse de Clèves, Les Liaisons dangereuses, and Lucien Leuwen for full accounts of the collision between public and private affairs. Their powers are beyond both Adams and Napoleon himself, who, as he wrote Josephine in April, 1814, was substituting the plume for the épée, but who, like Adams, was too much affected by the collisions to describe them. It is of ancillary but powerful interest that the toga in which Napoleon swathed his actions has in our time become a fog of such smothering intimacy that one wonders if the rulers themselves can discover the actual sources of their own decisions.

FANNY AND ANNIE

D. H. Lawrence

Flame-lurid his face as he turned among the throng of flame-lit and dark faces upon the platform. In the light of the furnace she caught sight of his drifting countenance, like a piece of floating fire. And the nostalgia, the doom of home-coming went through her veins like a drug. His eternal face, flame-lit now! The pulse and darkness of red fire from the furnace towers in the sky, lighting the desultory, industrial crowd on the wayside station, lit him and went out.

Of course he did not see her. Flame-lit, and unseeing! Always the same, with his meeting eyebrows, his common cap, and his red-and-black scarf knotted round his throat. Not even a collar to meet her! The flames had sunk, there was shadow.

She opened the door of her grimy, branch-line carriage, and began to get down her bags. The porter was nowhere, of course, but there was Harry, obscure, on the outer edge of the little crowd, missing her, of course.

"Here! Harry!" she called, waving her umbrella in the twilight. He hurried forward.

"Tha's come, has ter?" he said, in a sort of cheerful welcome. She got down, rather flustered, and gave him a peck of a kiss.

"Two suit-cases!" she said.

Her soul groaned within her, as he clambered into the carriage after her bags. Up shot the fire in the twilight sky, from the great furnace behind the station. She felt the red flame go across her face. She had come back, she had come back for good. And her spirit groaned dismally. She doubted if she could bear it.

There, on the sordid little station under the furnaces, she stood, tall and distinguished, in her well-made coat and skirt and her broad grey velour hat. She held her umbrella, her bead chatelaine, and a little leather case in her grey-gloved hands, while Harry staggered out of the ugly little train with her bags.

"There's a trunk at the back," she said in her bright voice. But she was not feeling bright. The twin black cones of the iron foundry blasted their sky-high fires into the night. The whole scene was lurid. The train waited cheerfully. It would wait another ten minutes. She knew it. It was all so deadly familiar.

Let us confess it at once. She was a lady's maid, thirty years old, come back to marry her first-love, a foundry worker: after having kept him dangling, off and on, for a dozen years. Why had she come back? Did she love him? No. She didn't pretend to. She had loved her brilliant and ambitious cousin, who had jilted her, and who had died. She had had other affairs which had come to nothing. So here she was, come back suddenly to marry her first-love, who had waited—or remained single—all these years.

"Won't a porter carry those?" she said, as Harry strode with his workman's stride down the platform towards the guard's van.

"I can manage," he said.

And with her umbrella, her chatelaine, and her little leather case, she followed him.

The trunk was there.

"We'll get Heather's greengrocer's cart to fetch it up," he said.

"Isn't there a cab?" said Fanny, knowing dismally enough that there wasn't.

"I'll just put it aside o' the penny-in-the-slot, and Heather's greengrocers 'll fetch it about half-past eight," he said.

He seized the box by its two handles and staggered with it across the level-crossing, bumping his legs against it as he waddled. Then he dropped it by the red sweetmeats machine.

"Will it be safe there?" she said.

"Ay—safe as houses," he answered. He returned for the two bags. Thus laden, they started to plod up the hill, under the great long black building of the foundry. She walked beside him—workman of workmen he was, trudging with that luggage. The red lights flared over the deepening darkness. From the foundry came the horrible, slow clang, clang, clang of iron, a great noise, with an interval just long enough to make it unendurable.

Compare this with the arrival at Gloucester: the carriage for her mistress, the dog-cart for herself with the luggage; the drive out past the river, the pleasant trees of the carriage-approach; and herself sitting beside Arthur, everybody so polite to her.

She had come home—for good! Her heart nearly stopped beating as she trudged up that hideous and interminable hill, beside the laden figure. What a come-down! What a come-down! She could not take it with her usual bright cheerfulness. She knew it all too well. It is easy to bear up against the unusual, but the deadly familiarity of an old stale past!

He dumped the bags down under a lamp-post, for a rest. There they stood, the two of them, in the lamp-light. Passers-by stared at her, and gave good-night to Harry. Her they hardly knew, she had become a stranger.

"They're too heavy for you, let me carry one," she said.

"They begin to weigh a bit by the time you've gone a mile," he answered.

"Let me carry the little one," she insisted.

"Tha can ha'e it for a minute, if ter's a mind," he said, handing over the valise.

And thus they arrived in the streets of shops of the little ugly town on top of the hill. How everybody stared at her; my word, how they stared! And the cinema was just going in, and the queues were tailing down the road to the corner. And everybody took full stock of her. "Night, Harry!" shouted the fellows, in an interested voice.

However, they arrived at her aunt's—a little sweet-shop in a side street. They "pinged" the door-bell, and her aunt came running forward out of the kitchen.

"There you are, child! Dying for a cup of tea, I'm sure. How are you?"

Fanny's aunt kissed her, and it was all Fanny could do to refrain from bursting into tears, she felt so low. Perhaps it was her tea she wanted.

"You've had a drag with that luggage," said Fanny's aunt to Harry.

"Ay—I'm not sorry to put it down," he said, looking at his hand which was crushed and cramped by the bag handle.

Then he departed to see about Heather's green-grocery cart.

When Fanny sat at tea, her aunt, a grey-haired, fair-faced little woman, looked at her with an admiring heart, feeling bitterly sore for her. For Fanny was beautiful: tall, erect, finely coloured, with her delicately arched nose, her rich brown hair, her large lustrous grey eyes. A passionate woman—a woman to be afraid of. So proud, so inwardly violent! She came of a violent race.

It needed a woman to sympathise with her. Men had not the courage. Poor Fanny! She was such a lady, and so straight and magnificent. And yet everything seemed to do her down. Every time she seemed to be doomed to humiliation and disappointment, this handsome, brilliantly sensitive woman, with her nervous, over-wrought laugh.

"So you've really come back, child?" said her aunt.

"I really have, Aunt," said Fanny.

"Poor Harry! I'm not sure, you know, Fanny, that you're not taking a bit of an advantage of him."

"Oh, Aunt, he's waited so long, he may as well have what he's waited for." Fanny laughed grimly.

"Yes, child, he's waited so long, that I'm not sure it isn't a bit hard on him. You know, I *like* him, Fanny— though as you know quite well, I don't think he's good enough for you. And I think he thinks so himself, poor fellow."

"Don't you be so sure of that, Aunt. Harry is common, but he's not humble. He wouldn't think the Queen was any too good for him, if he'd a mind to her."

"Well— It's as well if he has a proper opinion of himself."

"It depends what you call proper," said Fanny. "But he's got his good points——"

"Oh, he's a nice fellow, and I like him, I do like him. Only, as I tell you, he's not good enough for you."

"I've made up my mind, Aunt," said Fanny, grimly.

"Yes," mused the aunt. "They say all things come to him who waits——"

"More than he's bargained for, eh, Aunt?" laughed Fanny rather bitterly.

The poor aunt, this bitterness grieved her for her niece.

They were interrupted by the ping of the shop-bell, and Harry's call of "Right!" But as he did not come in at once, Fanny, feeling solicitous for him presumably at the moment, rose and went into the shop. She saw a cart outside, and went to the door.

And the moment she stood in the doorway, she heard a woman's common vituperative voice crying from the darkness of the opposite side of the road:

"Tha'rt theer, are ter? I'll shame thee, Mester. I'll shame thee, see if I dunna."

Startled, Fanny stared across the darkness, and saw a woman in a black bonnet go under one of the lamps up the side street.

Harry and Bill Heather had dragged the trunk off the little dray, and she retreated before them as they came up the shop step with it.

"Wheer shalt ha'e it?" asked Harry.

"Best take it upstairs," said Fanny.

She went up first to light the gas.

When Heather had gone, and Harry was sitting down having tea and pork pie, Fanny asked:

"Who was that woman shouting?"

"Nay, I canna tell thee. To somebody, I's'd think," replied Harry. Fanny looked at him, but asked no more.

He was a fair-haired fellow of thirty-two, with a fair moustache. He was broad in his speech, and looked like a foundry-hand, which he was. But women always liked him. There was something of a mother's lad about him—something warm and playful and really sensitive.

He had his attractions even for Fanny. What she rebelled against so bitterly was that he had no sort of ambition. He was a moulder, but of very commonplace skill. He was thirty-two years old, and hadn't saved twenty pounds. She would have to provide the money for the home. He didn't care. He just didn't care. He had no initiative at all. He had no vices—no obvious ones. But he was just indifferent, spending as he went, and not caring. Yet he did not look happy. She remembered his face in the fire-glow: something haunted, abstracted about it. As he sat there eating his pork pie, bulging his cheek out, she felt he was like a doom to her. And she raged against the doom of him. It wasn't that he was gross. His *way* was common, almost on purpose. But he himself wasn't really common. For instance, his food was not particularly important to him, he was not greedy. He had a charm, too, particularly for women, with his blondness and his sensitiveness and his way of making a woman feel that she was a higher being. But Fanny knew him, knew the peculiar obstinate limitedness of him, that would nearly send her mad.

He stayed till about half-past nine. She went to the door with him.

"When are you coming up?" he said, jerking his head in the direction presumably, of his own home.

"I'll come to-morrow afternoon," she said brightly. Between Fanny ar. d Mrs. Goodall, his mother, there was naturally no love lost.

Again she gave him an awkward little kiss, and said good-night.

"You can't wonder, you know, child, if he doesn't seem so very keen," said her aunt. "It's your own fault."

"Oh, Aunt, I couldn't stand him when he was keen. I can do with him a lot better as he is."

The two women sat and talked far into the night. They understood each other. The aunt, too, had married as Fanny was marrying: a man who was no companion to her, a violent man, brother of Fanny's father. He was dead, Fanny's father was dead.

Poor Aunt Lizzie, she cried woefully over her bright niece, when she had gone to bed.

Fanny paid the promised visit to his people the next afternoon. Mrs. Goodall was a large woman with smooth-parted hair, a common, obstinate woman, who had spoiled her four lads and her one vixen of a married daughter. She was one of those old-fashioned powerful natures that couldn't do with looks or education or any form of showing off. She fairly hated the sound of correct English. She *thee'd* and *tha'd* her prospective daughter-in-law, and said:

"I'm none as ormin' as I look, seest ta."

Fanny did not think her prospective mother-in-law looked at all orming, so the speech was unnecessary.

"I towd him mysen," said Mrs. Goodall, " 'Er's held back all this long, let 'er stop as 'er is. 'E'd none ha' had thee for *my* tellin'—tha hears. No, 'e's a fool, an' I know it. I says to him, 'Tha looks a man, doesn't ter, at thy age, goin' an' openin' to her when ter hears her scrat' at th' gate, after she's done gallivantin' round wherever she'd a mind. Tha looks rare an' soft.' But it's no use o' any talking: he answered that letter o' thine and made his own bad bargain."

But in spite of the old woman's anger, she was also flattered at Fanny's coming back to Harry. For Mrs. Goodall was impressed by Fanny—a woman of her own match. And more than this, everybody knew that Fanny's Aunt Kate had left her two hundred pounds: this apart from the girl's savings.

So there was high tea in Princes Street when Harry came home back from work, and a rather acrid odour of cordiality, the vixen Jinny darting in to say vulgar things. Of course Jinny lived in a house whose

garden end joined the paternal garden. They were a clan who stuck together, these Goodalls.

It was arranged that Fanny should come to tea again on the
Sunday, and the wedding was discussed. It should take place in a
fortnight's time at Morley Chapel. Morley was a hamlet on the edge
of the real country, and in its little Congregational Chapel Fanny and
Harry had first met.

What a creature of habit he was! He was still in the choir of
Morley Chapel—not very regular. He belonged just because he had a
tenor voice, and enjoyed singing. Indeed his solos were only spoilt to
local fame because, when he sang he handled his aitches so hopelessly.

> *And I saw 'eaven hopened*
> *And be'old, a wite 'orse* ——

This was one of Harry's classics, only surpassed by the fine outburst
of his heaving:

> *Hangels—hever bright an' fair* ——

It was a pity, but it was inalterable. He had a good voice, and he
sang with a certain lacerating fire, but his pronunciation made it all
funny. And *nothing* could alter him.

So he was never heard save at cheap concerts and in the little,
poorer chapels. The others scoffed.

Now the month was September, and Sunday was Harvest Festival
at Morley Chapel, and Harry was singing solos. So that Fanny was to
go to afternoon service, and come home to a grand spread of Sunday
tea with him. Poor Fanny! One of the most wonderful afternoons had
been a Sunday afternoon service, with her cousin Luther at her side,
Harvest Festival at Morley Chapel. Harry had sung solos then—ten
years ago. She remembered his pale blue tie, and the purple asters and
the great vegetable marrows in which he was framed, and her cousin
Luther at her side, young, clever, come down from London, where he
was getting on well, learning his Latin and his French and German so
brilliantly.

However, once again it was Harvest Festival at Morley Chapel, and
once again, as ten years before, a soft, exquisite September day, with

the last roses pink in the cottage gardens, the last dahlias crimson, the last sunflowers yellow. And again the little old chapel was a bower, with its famous sheaves of corn and corn-plaited pillars, its great bunches of grapes, dangling like tassels from the pulpit corners, its marrows and potatoes and pears and apples and damsons, its purple asters and yellow Japanese sunflowers. Just as before, the red dahlias round the pillars were dropping, weak-headed among the oats. The place was crowded and hot, the plates of tomatoes seemed balanced perilous on the gallery front, the Rev. Enderby was weirder than ever to look at, so long and emaciated and hairless.

The Rev. Enderby, probably forewarned, came and shook hands with her and welcomed her, in his broad northern, melancholy singsong before he mounted the pulpit. Fanny was handsome in a gauzy dress and a beautiful lace hat. Being a little late, she sat in a chair in the side-aisle wedged in, right in the front of the chapel. Harry was in the gallery above, and she could only see him from the eyes upwards. She noticed again how his eyebrows met, blond and not very marked, over his nose. He was attractive too: physically lovable, very. If only—if only her *pride* had not suffered! She felt he dragged her down.

> *Come, ye thankful people, come,*
> *Raise the song of harvest-home.*
> *All is safely gathered in*
> *Ere the winter storms begin ——*

Even the hymn was a falsehood, as the season had been wet, and half the crops were still out, and in a poor way.

Poor Fanny! She sang little, and looked beautiful through that inappropriate hymn. Above her stood Harry—mercifully in a dark suit and a dark tie, looking almost handsome. And his lacerating, pure tenor sounded well, when the words were drowned in the general commotion. Brilliant she looked, and brilliant she felt, for she was hot and angrily miserable and inflamed with a sort of fatal despair. Because there was about him a physical attraction which she really hated, but which she could not escape from. He was the first man who had ever kissed her. And his kisses, even while she rebelled from them, had lived in her blood and sent roots down into her soul. After all this time she had come back to them. And her soul groaned, for she felt dragged down, dragged down to earth, as a bird which some dog has got down in the dust. She knew her life would be unhappy. She knew that what she was doing was fatal. Yet it was her doom. She had to come back to him.

He had to sing two solos this afternoon: one before the "address" from the pulpit and one after. Fanny looked at him, and wondered he was not too shy to stand up there in front of all the people. But no, he was not shy. He had even a kind of assurance on his face as he looked down from the choir gallery at her: the assurance of a common man deliberately entrenched in his commonness. Oh, such a rage went through her veins as she saw the air of triumph, laconic, indifferent triumph which sat so obstinately and recklessly on his eyelids as he looked down at her. Ah, she despised him! But there he stood up in that choir gallery like Balaam's ass in front of her, and she could not get beyond him. A certain winsomeness also about him. A certain physical winsomeness, and as if his flesh were new and lovely to touch. The thorn of desire rankled bitterly in her heart.

He, it goes without saying, sang like a canary this particular afternoon, with a certain defiant passion which pleasantly crisped the blood of the congregation. Fanny felt the crisp flames go through her veins as she listened. Even the curious loud-mouthed vernacular had a certain fascination. But oh, also, it was so repugnant. He would triumph over her, obstinately he would drag her right back into the common people: a doom, a vulgar doom.

The second performance was an anthem, in which Harry sang the solo parts. It was clumsy, but beautiful, with lovely words.

> *They that sow in tears shall reap in joy,*
> *He that goeth forth and weepeth, bearing precious seed*
> *Shall doubtless come again with rejoicing, bringing his sheaves with*
> *   him ——*

"Shall doubtless come, Shall doubtless come—" softly intoned the altos—"Bringing his she-e-eaves with him," the trebles flourished brightly, and then again began the half-wistful solo:

> *They that sow in tears shall reap in joy ——*

Yes, it was effective and moving.

But at the moment when Harry's voice sank carelessly down to his close, and the choir, standing behind him were opening their mouths for the final triumphant outburst, a shouting female voice rose up from the body of the congregation. The organ gave one startled trump, and went silent; the choir stood transfixed.

"You look well standing there, singing in God's holy house," came the loud, angry female shout. Everybody turned electrified. A stoutish, red-faced woman in a black bonnet was standing up denouncing the soloist. Almost fainting with shock, the congregation realised it. "You look well, don't you, standing there singing solos in God's holy house, you, Goodall. But I said I'd shame you. You look well, bringing your young woman here with you, don't you? I'll let her know who she's dealing with. A scamp as won't take the consequences of what he's done." The hard-faced, frenzied woman turned in the direction of Fanny. "*That's* what Harry Goodall is, if you want to know."

And she sat down again in her seat. Fanny, startled like all the rest, had turned to look. She had gone white, and then a burning red, under the attack. She knew the woman: a Mrs. Nixon, a devil of a woman, who beat her pathetic, drunken, red-nosed second husband, Bob, and her two lanky daughters, grown-up as they were. A notorious character. Fanny turned round again, and sat motionless as eternity in her seat.

There was a minute of perfect silence and suspense. The audience was open-mouthed and dumb; the choir stood like Lot's wife; and Harry, with his music-sheet, stood there uplifted, looking down with a dumb sort of indifference on Mrs. Nixon, his face naïve and faintly mocking. Mrs. Nixon sat defiant in her seat, braving them all.

Then a rustle, like a wood when the wind suddenly catches the leaves. And then the tall, weird minister got to his feet, and in his strong, bell-like, beautiful voice—the only beautiful thing about him —he said with infinite mournful pathos:

"Let us unite in singing the last hymn on the hymn-sheet; the last hymn on the hymn-sheet, number eleven.

> *Fair waved the golden corn,*
> *In Canaan's pleasant land.*

The organ tuned up promptly. During the hymn the offertory was taken. And after the hymn, the prayer.

Mr. Enderby came from Northumberland. Like Harry, he had never been able to conquer his accent, which was very broad. He was a little simple, one of God's fools, perhaps, an odd bachelor soul, emotional, ugly, but very gentle.

"And if, O our dear Lord, beloved Jesus, there should fall a shadow of sin upon our harvest, we leave it to Thee to judge, for Thou art judge. We lift our spirits and our sorrow, Jesus, to Thee, and our mouths are dumb. O Lord, keep us from froward speech, restrain us from foolish words and thoughts, we pray Thee, Lord Jesus, who knowest all and judgest all."

Thus the minister said in his sad, resonant voice, washed his hands before the Lord. Fanny bent forward open-eyed during the prayer. She could see the roundish head of Harry, also bent forward. His face was inscrutable and expressionless. The shock left her bewildered. Anger perhaps was her dominating emotion.

The audience began to rustle to its feet, to ooze slowly and excitedly out of the chapel, looking with wildly-interested eyes at Fanny, at Mrs. Nixon, and at Harry. Mrs. Nixon, shortish, stood defiant in her pew, facing the aisle, as if announcing that, without rolling her sleeves up she was ready for anybody. Fanny sat quite still. Luckily the people did not have to pass her. And Harry, with red ears, was making his way sheepishly out of the gallery. The loud noise of the organ covered all the downstairs commotion of exit.

The minister sat silent and inscrutable in his pulpit, rather like a death's-head, while the congregation filed out. When the last lingerers had unwillingly departed, craning their necks to stare at the still seated Fanny, he rose, stalked in his hooked fashion down the little country chapel, and fastened the door. Then he returned and sat down by the silent young woman.

"This is most unfortunate, most unfortunate!" he moaned. "I am so sorry, I am so sorry, indeed, indeed, ah, indeed!" he sighed himself to a close.

"It's a sudden surprise, that's one thing," said Fanny brightly.

"Yes—yes—indeed. Yes, a surprise, yes. I don't know the woman, I don't know her."

"I know her," said Fanny. "She's a bad one."

"Well! Well!" said the minister. "I don't know her. I don't understand. I don't understand at all. But it is to be regretted, it is very much to be regretted. I am very sorry."

Fanny was watching the vestry door. The gallery stairs communicated with the vestry, not with the body of the chapel. She knew the choir members had been peeping for information.

At last Harry came—rather sheepishly—with his hat in his hand.

"Well!" said Fanny, rising to her feet.

"We've had a bit of an extra," said Harry.

"I should think so," said Fanny.

"A most unfortunate circumstance—a most *unfortunate* circumstance. Do you understand it, Harry? I don't understand it at all."

"Ay, I understand it. The daughter's goin' to have a childt, an' 'er lays it on to me."

"And has she no occasion to?" asked Fanny, rather censorious.

"It's no more mine than it is some other chap's," said Harry, looking aside.

There was a moment of pause.

"Which girl is it?" asked Fanny.

"Annie—the young one——"

There followed another silence.

"I don't think I know them, do I?" asked the minister.

"I shouldn't think so. Their name's Nixon—mother married old Bob for her second husband. She's a tanger—'s driven the gel to what she is. They live in Manners Road."

"Why, what's amiss with the girl?" asked Fanny sharply. "She was all right when I knew her."

"Ay—she's all right. But she's always in an' out o' th' pubs, wi' th' fellows," said Harry.

"A nice thing!" said Fanny.

Harry glanced towards the door. He wanted to get out.

"Most distressing indeed!" The minister slowly shook his head.

"What about to-night, Mr. Enderby?" asked Harry, in rather a small voice. "Shall you want me?"

Mr. Enderby looked up painedly, and put his hand to his brow. He studied Harry for some time, vacantly. There was the faintest sort of a resemblance between the two men.

"Yes," he said. "Yes, I think. I think we must take no notice, and cause as little remark as possible."

Fanny hesitated. Then she said to Harry:

"But *will* you come?"

He looked at her.

"Ay, I s'll come," he said.

Then he turned to Mr. Enderby.

"Well, good-afternoon, Mr. Enderby," he said.

"Good-afternoon, Harry, good-afternoon," replied the mournful minister. Fanny followed Harry to the door, and for some time they walked in silence through the late afternoon.

"And it's yours as much as anybody else's?" she said.

"Ay," he answered shortly.

And they went without another word, for the long mile or so, till they came to the corner of the street where Harry lived. Fanny hesitated. Should she go on to her aunt's? Should she? It would mean leaving all this, forever. Harry stood silent.

Some obstinacy made her turn with him along the road to his own home. When they entered the house-place, the whole family was there, mother and father and Jinny, with Jinny's husband and children and Harry's two brothers.

"You've been having your ears warmed, they tell me," said Mrs. Goodall grimly.

"Who telled thee?" asked Harry shortly.

"Maggie and Luke's both been in."

"You look well, don't you!" said interfering Jinny.

Harry went and hung his hat up, without replying.

"Come upstairs and take your hat off," said Mrs. Goodall to Fanny, almost kindly. It would have annoyed her very much if Fanny had dropped her son at this moment.

"What's 'er say, then?" asked the father secretly of Harry, jerking his head in the direction of the stairs whence Fanny had disappeared.

"Nowt yet," said Harry.

"Serve you right if she chucks you now," said Jinny. "I'll bet it's right about Annie Nixon an' you."

"Tha bets so much," said Harry.

"Yi—but you can't deny it," said Jinny.

"I can if I've a mind."

His father looked at him enquiringly.

"It's no more mine than it is Bill Bower's, or Ted Slaney's, or six or seven on 'em," said Harry to his father.

And the father nodded silently.

"That'll not get you out of it, in court," said Jinny.

Upstairs Fanny evaded all the thrusts made by his mother, and did not declare her hand. She tidied her hair, washed her hands, and put the tiniest bit of powder on her face, for coolness, there in front of Mrs. Goodall's indignant gaze. It was like a declaration of independence. But the old woman said nothing.

They came down to Sunday tea, with sardines and tinned salmon and tinned peaches, besides tarts and cakes. The chatter was general. It concerned the Nixon family and the scandal.

"Oh, she's a foul-mouthed woman," said Jinny of Mrs. Nixon. "She may well talk about God's holy house, *she* had. It's first time she's set foot in it, ever since she dropped off from being converted. She's a devil and she always was one. Can't you remember how she treated Bob's children, mother, when we lived down in the Buildings? I can remember when I was a little girl, she used to bathe them in the yard, in the cold, so that they shouldn't splash the house. She'd half kill them if they made a mark on the floor, and the language she'd used. And one Saturday I can remember Garry, that was Bob's own girl, she ran off when her step-mother was going to bathe her—ran off without a rag of clothes on—can you remember, mother? And she hid in Smedley's close—it was the time of mowing-grass—and nobody could find her. She hid out there all night, didn't she, mother? Nobody could find her. My word, there was a talk. They found her on Sunday morning——"

"Fred Coutts threatened to break every bone in the woman's body, if she touched the children again," put in the father.

"Anyhow, they frightened her," said Jinny. "But she was nearly as bad with her own two. And anybody can see that she's driven old Bob till he's gone soft."

"Ah, soft as mush," said Jack Goodall. " 'E'd never addle a week's wage, nor yet a day's, if th' chaps didn't make it up to him."

"My word, if he didn't bring her a week's wage, she'd pull his head off," said Jinny.

"But a clean woman, and respectable, except for her foul mouth," said Mrs. Goodall. "Keeps to herself like a bull-dog. Never lets anybody come near the house, and neighbours with nobody."

"Wanted it thrashed out of her," said Mr. Goodall, a silent, evasive sort of man.

"Where Bob gets the money for his drink from is a mystery," said Jinny.

"Chaps treats him," said Harry.

"Well, he's got the pair of frightenedest rabbit-eyes you'd wish to see," said Jinny.

"Ay, with a drunken man's murder in them, *I* think," said Mrs. Goodall.

So the talk went on after tea, till it was practically time to start off to chapel again.

"You'll have to be getting ready, Fanny," said Mrs. Goodall.

"I'm not going to-night," said Fanny abruptly. And there was a sudden halt in the family. "I'll stop with *you* to-night, Mother," she added.

"Best you had, my gel," said Mrs. Goodall, flattered and assured.

ODOR

Saadat Hasan Manto

It was again the monsoon season.

Drops of rain had begun their patter on the leaves of the pipal tree near the window. Inside lay the teak bed on which a Ghatan girl had slept with Randhir.

Beyond the window, in the night's milky darkness, the pipal leaves bathed in the rain, quivering like earrings.

On the spring mattress of the bed, the Ghatan girl had clung to Randhir like gooseflesh. Some hours earlier, he had seen her under the tamarind tree, sheltering from the downpour. She probably worked in the rope factory nearby. Randhir had watched her from his balcony, where he had come for a change from the mustiness of his room. He had wanted a diversion, for all afternoon he had done nothing but read the same newspaper again and again. He had cleared his throat and coughed. This had attracted her attention and he had beckoned her to come up.

For several days he had been feeling very lonely and dejected. One reason was the war, which had put beyond his reach those Anglo-Indian girls who used to come out with him for the evening and even for the night. They were not expensive and because of his English education he had preferred to date them rather than go to the brothels. With the coming of the war, some of them had enlisted in the Women's Auxiliary Corps, others had joined the newly opened dancing schools in the Fort area. As only Tommies were admitted to these schools, Randhir had felt frustrated. His favorite girls had gone off the market. The only ones available were in the dancing schools, where white skin was the passport for admission; nothing else mattered. This had made Randhir very bitter, for he had felt that he was better educated, more refined, and healthier than the average Tommy.

Before the war Randhir had had many a rendezvous with his girl

friends of the Nagpada and Taj Mahal Hotel areas. He knew more
about these girls, physically, than did the Christian boys with whom
they flirted, until they married the most gullible of them.

Randhir had called the Ghatan girl over to his flat because he had
been hurt by the airs Hazel had put on since her enlistment. Every
morning he would see her leave her flat, directly below his own, in her
uniform, her khaki cap set at a rakish angle, walking as if all passers-by
were only waiting to spread themselves out, like sacking on the
pavement, for her to walk on.

Randhir had often wondered why he was so attracted by girls like
Hazel. Was it because they made themselves physically attractive by
accentuating their curves and contours, or was it for their lack of
inhibitions? They never felt abashed at referring to their menstrual
irregularities, they told stories about their former lovers, their feet
automatically tapped the floor on hearing a dance tune, and in bed
they were like patent medicines with directions for use.

When Randhir had beckoned the Ghatan girl, he did not have any
intention of taking her to bed. Noticing her drenched clothes, he had
thought that the poor girl might get pneumonia, and had said, "Take
off these wet clothes, you may catch a cold."

She had understood him, though she did not know his language.
Red webs of shame had suddenly floated in her eyes. When Randhir
had handed her a fresh white dhoti, she had hesitated for a moment,
and then abruptly she had loosened her dirty coarse *kashta*, made
filthier by the rain. As the soaked garment collapsed around her legs,
she had swiftly covered her thighs with the dhoti. She had then tried
to take off her tight choli by opening a tiny knot, almost embedded in
the deep and narrow hollow between her breasts.

Her worn-out nails had pecked at the tiny wet knot several times
but had failed to loosen it. In despair, she had said something to
Randhir in Marathi which meant, "What am I to do; it won't
open?"

Randhir had sat down beside her and investigated the knot. But
soon he had lost his patience, and gripping the strings on either side
of the knot, he had given a sudden jerk. At once the string had
snapped, and his hands had brushed over her breasts, which had come
trembling into view. For a moment Randhir had felt like a potter,
using freshly kneaded clay, who had suddenly molded two cups on the
Ghatan girl's chest. Her breasts had the pliancy, the moist roughness,

O<small>DOR</small>
Saadat Hasan Manto

and the cooling warmth of vessels that have just come off the potter's wheel. Spotless and mud-colored, they had shone dully with a strange glow which seemed to come from a luminous layer beneath her translucent skin. Her uplifted breasts had looked like lamps lit at the bottom of a muddy pool.

It was again the season of rains.

Beyond the window the pipal leaves had dripped with rain. The Ghatan girl's soaked, two-piece dress was on the floor in a filthy heap. The girl had clung to Randhir. The warmth of her nude, unwashed body had reminded him of a hot bath in winter in a filthy public *hamam.*

All night she had clung to Randhir, as if they were one. They had hardly exchanged a word or two, for their panting was as eloquent as their lips and hands were expressive. All night Randhir's hands had fondled her breasts, like the caress of the breeze. Occasionally, her dark areolas, with their coarse grain and the tiny nipples, had stiffened and started a tremor that would streak through her body and communicate itself even to Randhir.

Randhir had experienced such tremors hundreds of times, and was familiar with the delicious sensation they imparted. He had spent many nights with girls, clasping their taut or soft breasts against his own. He had slept with all sorts of girls, simple and talkative ones who gave him information about their families that no stranger should know, and the type who bore all the physical burden in bed and would not let him exert himself. But this Ghatan girl, who had come up to his flat from her shelter under the tamarind tree, had been quite different.

All night Randhir had inhaled a strange odor from her body, an odor both unpleasant and pleasant. He had sought for it in her armpits, her hair, breasts, navel, and in every other part of her body where it could pervade his nose. He had thought that he would never have felt the nearness of the girl but for this odor which had penetrated every layer of his mind and had seeped through his memories, new and old.

For one night Randhir and the girl had been fused together by this odor; they had merged into each other and slipped down to fathomless depths where they had been transformed into pure ecstasy, a state which they thought would be perpetual in spite of its evanescence, and still and stable even though there were fluctuations. They had

been like a little bird that soars into the blueness of the sky, higher
and higher, until it becomes a motionless dot.

Randhir was familiar with the odor that had exhaled from every
pore of the Ghatan girl's body, but he had not been able to analyze it.
It was like the fresh smell of earth sprinkled with water—but no, this
odor was different. It was not an artificial smell like that of lavender
or attar, but something natural and eternal, like the relationship that
has existed between man and woman since the beginning of time.

Randhir hated perspiration. After a bath he usually powdered his
armpits or used deodorants. It was surprising that he had kissed the
hairy armpits of the Ghatan girl many times—yes, many times—and
had felt no aversion. In fact, it had given him a peculiar feeling of
pleasure. The tiny hair in the armpits, bedewed with perspiration, had
given off the same odor that had been obvious and yet so incomprehensible. Randhir had felt that he knew this odor, that he recognized
it, understood it, but he could not describe it to anyone else.

The monsoons were back again.

Randhir looked out of the window and saw the swaying pipal leaves
bathing in the rain, the sound of their rustle and patter merging in the
atmosphere. The night was dark, not pitch dark but of the darkness
that seemed to have absorbed some subdued pearly light washed
down from the stars by the raindrops. The season was the same when
there was only one teak bed in the room, but now another lay beside
it. In the corner stood a new dressing table.

It was again the season of rains, the season of marriages.

The raindrops were flushing the stars of their milky light, but the
atmosphere was filled with the strong perfume of henna. One of
the beds was empty. On the other lay Randhir, looking beyond the
window at the dance of the raindrops on the swaying pipal leaves. By
his side was a milky-white girl who had fallen asleep trying unsuccess-
fully to cover her nakedness. Her red silk shalwar lay on the other bed,
one end of its dark-red cord dangling by its side. Also flung on this bed
were the other clothes of which she had been stripped, her green shirt
with red flowers to match the shalwar, her brassière, underwear, and
dupatta. All were red, marriage red, and scented with henna.

Gold powder lay in the girl's black hair, like dust. The blurred
make-up on her face, a mixture of gold dust, powder, and rouge, was

like a pallid mask of death. Her creamy breasts were blotched with the color of her red brassière.

Her breasts were as white as milk, a whiteness that has a faint tinge of blue. Randhir glanced at the girl several times and thought; "It seems as if I have just pulled out the nails from a crate and lifted her out," for she had scratches on her body like packing marks on books and crockery. When Randhir had unknotted the cord of her tight-fitting brassière, he had felt the ribbing on the soft flesh of her back and bosom, and the creased imprint left around her waist by the cord of her shalwar. A heavy and sharp-edged gold necklace, set with jewels, had bruised her breast as if it had been scratched wildly with nails.

It was the same season of the monsoons.

Countless raindrops were falling again on the soft, delicate pipal leaves. Randhir heard the familiar patter throughout the night. It was a pleasant season. A cool breeze was blowing, but it carried with it the scent of henna. For a long time Randhir's hands stroked the girl's bosom, white as fresh milk. They brushed her breasts gently, like the caress of the breeze. His fingers roving over her soft, milky body felt racing tremors and stirred suppressed passions. When he pressed his breast to the girl's bosom, every pore of his body heard the twanging of the girl's strummed emotions—but where was that note, that call of the Ghatan girl's odor, which had been more compelling than the cry of a suckling baby, that cry which had gone beyond the limits of sound and for him, somehow, had become a nameless perfume.

Randhir was looking out through the bars of the window. Close by, the pipal leaves were rustling, but he was trying to look beyond, far beyond them, at the luminous gray clouds. They had a strange glow like the one that had lurked in the Ghatan girl's breasts, a glow that was hidden like a secret object but yet was discernible.

By his side lay a girl whose body was as white as flour kneaded with milk and ghee. Her sleeping body gave off the perfume of henna, which had now grown faint. Randhir felt a sudden aversion for this dying perfume. It had a peculiar tang, like the taste of the mouth after belching—unsavory and insipid.

Randhir looked at the girl by his side. He found her skin covering her body like whitish curdled grains of sour milk floating without life in a colorless liquid. His senses were permeated with the odor which had exhaled effortlessly from the body of the Ghatan girl. It was an odor lighter but more penetrating than the attar of henna, reaching the olfactory organs without even the intake of the breath.

Randhir rallied and again stroked the milky body of the girl. His hand countered numbness; there was no responsive tremor. His new bride, the daughter of a magistrate, a graduate, the heartthrob of the boys of her college, had failed to kindle his masculine interest. In the dying perfume of henna attar, he continue to grope for the odor of the Ghatan girl, the odor he had inhaled from her unwashed body in these very days of the monsoons, when the pipal leaves had bathed in the rain.

TRANSLATED BY HAMID JALAL

THE FRYING-PAN

Frank O'Connor

Father Fogarty's only real friends in Kilmulpeter were the Whittons. Whitton was the teacher there. He had been to the seminary and college with Fogarty, and, like him, intended to be a priest, but when the time came for him to take the vow of celibacy, he had contracted scruples of conscience and married the principal one. Fogarty, who had known her too, had to admit that she wasn't without justification, and now, in this lonely place where chance had thrown them together again, she formed the real centre of what little social life he had. With Tom Whitton he had a quiet friendship compounded of exchanges of opinion about books or wireless talks. He had the impression that Whitton didn't really like him and considered him a man who would have been better out of the Church. When they went to the races together, Fogarty felt that Whitton disapproved of having to put on bets for him and thought that priests should not bet at all. Like other outsiders, he knew perfectly what priests should be, without the necessity for having to be that way himself. He was sometimes savage in the things he said about the parish priest, old Father Whelan. On the other hand, he had a pleasant sense of humour and Fogarty enjoyed retailing his cracks against the cloth. Men as intelligent as Whitton were rare in country schools, and soon, too, he would grow stupid and wild for lack of educated society.

One evening Father Fogarty invited them to dinner to see some films he had taken at the races. Films were his latest hobby. Before this it had been fishing and shooting. Like all bachelors, he had a mania for adding to his possessions, and his lumber-room was piled high with every possible sort of junk from chest-developers to field-glasses, and his library cluttered with works on everything from Irish history to Freudian psychology. He passed from craze to craze, each the key to the universe.

He sprang up at the knock, and found Una at the door, all in furs, her shoulders about her ears, her big, bony, masculine face, blue with

cold but screwed up in an amiable monkey-grin. Tom, a handsome
man, was tall and self-conscious. He had greying hair, brown eyes, a
prominent jaw, and was quiet-spoken in a way that concealed passion.
He and Una disagreed a lot about the way the children should be
brought up. He thought she spoiled them.

"Come in, let ye, come in!" cried Fogarty hospitably, showing the
way into his warm study with its roaring turf fire, deep leather chairs,
and the Raphael print above the mantelpiece; a real bachelor's room.
"God above!" he exclaimed, holding Una's hand a moment longer
than was necessary. "You're perished! What'll you have to drink,
Una?"

"Whi-hi-hi—" stammered Una excitedly, her eyes beginning to
pop. "I can't say the bloody word."

"Call it malt, girl," said the priest.

"That's enough! That's enough!" she cried laughingly, snatching
the glass from him. "You'll send me home on my ear, and then I'll
hear about it from this fellow."

"Whisky, Tom?"

"Whisky, Jerry," Whitton said quietly with a quick conciliatory
glance. He kept his head very stiff and used his eyes a lot instead.

Meanwhile Una, unabashably inquisitive, was making the tour of
the room with the glass in her hand, to see if there was anything new
in it. There usually was.

"Is this new, father?" she asked, halting before a pleasant eight-
eenth-century print.

"Ten bob," the priest said promptly. "Wasn't it a bargain?"

"I couldn't say. What is it?"

"The old courthouse in town."

"Go on!" said Una.

Whitton came and studied the print closely. "That place is gone
these fifty years and I never saw a picture of it," he said. "This is a
bargain all right."

"I'd say so," Fogarty said with quiet pride.

"And what's the sheet for?" Una asked, poking at a tablecloth
pinned between the windows.

"That's not a sheet, woman!" Fogarty exclaimed. "For God's sake,
don't be displaying your ignorance!"

"Oh, I know," she cried girlishly. "For the pictures! I'd forgotten
about them. That's grand!"

Then Bella, a coarse, good-looking country girl, announced dinner, and the curate, with a self-conscious, boyish swagger, led them into the dining-room and opened the door of the sideboard. The dining-room was even more ponderous than the sitting-room. Everything in it was large, heavy, and dark.

"And now, what'll ye drink?" he asked over his shoulder, studying his array of bottles. "There's some damn good Burgundy—'pon my soul, 'tis great!"

"How much did it cost?" Whitton asked with poker-faced humour. "The only way I have of identifying wines is by the price."

"Eight bob a bottle," Fogarty replied at once.

"That's a very good price," said Whitton with a nod. "We'll have some of that."

"You can take a couple of bottles home with you," said the curate, who, in the warmth of his heart, was always wanting to give his treasures away. "The last two dozen he had—wasn't I lucky?"

"You have the appetite of a canon on the income of a curate," Whitton said in the same tone of grave humour, but Fogarty caught the scarcely perceptible note of criticism in it. He did not allow this to upset him.

"Please God, we won't always be curates," he said sunnily.

"Bella looks after you well," said Una when the meal was nearly over. The compliment was deserved so far as it went, though it was a man's meal rather than a woman's.

"Doesn't she, though?" Fogarty exclaimed with pleasure. "Isn't she damn good for a country girl?"

"How does she get on with Stasia?" asked Una—Stasia was Father Whelan's old housekeeper, and an affliction to the community.

"They don't talk. Stasia says she's an immoral woman."

"And is she?" Una asked hopefully.

"If she isn't, she's wasting her own time and my whisky," said Fogarty. "She entertains Paddy Coakley in the kitchen every Saturday night. I told her I wouldnt' keep her unless she got a boy. And wasn't I right? One Stasia is enough for any parish. Father Whelan tells me I'm going too far."

"And did you tell him to mind his own business?" Whitton asked with a penetrating look.

"I did, to be sure," said Fogarty, who had done nothing of the sort.

"Ignorant, interfering old fool!" Whitton said quietly, the ferocity of his sentiments belied by the mildness of his manner.

"That's only because you'd like to do the interfering yourself," said Una good-humouredly. She frequently had to act as peacemaker between the parish priest and her husband.

"And a robber," Tom Whitton added to the curate, ignoring her. "He's been collecting for new seats for the church for the last ten years. I'd like to know where that's going."

"He had a collection for repairing my roof," said the curate, "and 'tis leaking still. He must be worth twenty thousand."

"Now, that's not fair, father," Una said flatly. "You know yourself there's no harm in Father Whelan. It's just that he's certain he's going to die in the workhouse. It's like Bella and her boy. He had nothing more serious to worry about, and he worries about that."

Fogarty knew there was a certain amount of truth in what Una said, and that the old man's miserliness was more symbolic than real, and at the same time he felt in her words criticism of a different kind from her husband's. Though Una wasn't aware of it she was implying that the priest's office made him an object of pity rather than blame. She was sorry for old Whelan, and, by implication, for him.

"Still, Tom is right, Una," he said with sudden earnestness. "It's not a question of what harm Father Whelan intends, but what harm he does. Scandal is scandal, whether you give it deliberately or through absent-mindedness."

Tom grunted, to show his approval, but he said no more on the subject, as though he refused to enter into an argument with his wife about subjects she knew nothing of. They returned to the study for coffee, and Fogarty produced the film projector. At once the censoriousness of Tom Whitton's manner dropped away, and he behaved like a pleasant and intelligent boy of seventeen. Una, sitting by the fire with her legs crossed, watched them with amusement. Whenever they come to the priest's house, the same sort of thing happened. Once it had been a microscope, and the pair of them had amused themselves with it for hours. Now they were kidding themselves that their real interest in the cinema was educational. She knew that within a month the cinema, like the microscope, would by lying in the lumber-room with the rest of the junk.

Fogarty switched off the light and showed some films he had taken at the last race meeting. They were very patchy, mostly out of focus, and had to be interpreted by a running commentary, which was always a shot or two behind.

"I suppose ye wouldn't know who that is?" he said as the film showed Una, eating a sandwich and talking excitedly and demonstratively to a couple of wild-looking country boys.

"It looks like someone from the County Club," her husband said dryly.

"But wasn't it good?" Fogarty asked innocently as he switched on the lights again. "Now, wasn't it very interesting?" He was exactly like a small boy who had performed a conjuring trick.

"Marvellous, father," Una said with a sly and affectionate grin.

He blushed and turned to pour them out more whisky. He saw that she had noticed the pictures of herself. At the same time, he saw she was pleased. When he had driven them home, she held his hand and said they had had the best evening for years—a piece of flattery so gross and uncalled-for that it made her husband more tongue-tied than ever.

"Thursday, Jerry?" he said with a quick glance.

"Thursday, Tom," said the priest.

The room looked terribly desolate after her; the crumpled cushions, the glasses, the screen and the film projector, everything had become frighteningly inert, while outside his window the desolate countryside had taken on even more of its supernatural animation; bogs, hills, and fields, full of ghosts and shadows. He sat by the fire, wondering what his own life might have been like with a girl like that, all furs and scent and laughter, and two bawling, irrepressible brats upstairs. When he tiptoed up to his bedroom he remembered that there would never be children there to wake, and it seemed to him that with all the things he bought to fill his home, he was merely trying desperately to stuff the yawning holes in his own big, empty heart.

On Thursday, when he went to their house, Ita and Brendan, though already in bed, were refusing to sleep till he said good-night to them. While he was taking off his coat the two of them rushed to the banisters and screamed: "We want Father Fogey." When he went upstairs they were sitting bolt-upright in their cots, a little fat, fair-haired rowdy boy and a solemn baby girl.

"Father," Brendan began at once, "will I be your altar boy when I grow up?"

"You will to be sure, son," replied Fogarty.

"Ladies first! Ladies first!" the baby shrieked in a frenzy of rage. "Father, will I be your altar boy?"

"Go on!" Brendan said scornfully. "Little girls can't be altar boys, sure they can't, father?"

"I can," shrieked Ita, who in her excitement exactly resembled her mother. "Can't I, father?"

"We might be able to get a dispensation for you," said the curate. "In a pair of trousers, you'd do fine."

He was in a wistful frame of mind when he came downstairs again. Children would always be a worse temptation to him than women. Children were the devil! The house was gay and spotless. They had no fine mahogany suite like his, but Una managed to make the few coloured odds and ends they had seem deliberate. There wasn't a cigarette end in the ashtrays; the cushions had not been sat on. Tom, standing before the fireplace (not to disturb the cushions, thought Fogarty), looked as if someone had held his head under the tap, and was very self-consciously wearing a new brown tie. With his greying hair plastered flat, he looked schoolboyish, sulky, and resentful, as though he were meditating ways of restoring his authority over a mutinous household. The thought crossed Fogarty's mind that he and Una had probably quarrelled about the tie. It went altogether too well with his suit.

"We want Father Fogey!" the children began to chant monotonously from the bedroom.

"Shut up!" shouted Tom.

"We want Father Fogey," the chant went on, but with a groan in it somewhere.

"Well, you're not going to get him. Go to sleep!"

The chant stopped. This was clearly serious.

"You don't mind if I drop down to a meeting tonight, Jerry?" Tom asked in his quiet, anxious way. "I won't be more than half an hour."

"Not at all, Tom," said Fogarty heartily. "Sure, I'll drive you."

"No, thanks," Whitton said with a smile of gratitude. "It won't take me ten minutes to get there."

It was clear that a lot of trouble had gone to the making of supper, but out of sheer perversity Tom let on not to recognize any of the dishes. When they had drunk their coffee, he rose and glanced at his watch.

"I won't be long," he said.

"Tom, you're not going to that meeting?" Una asked appealingly.

"I tell you I have to," he replied with unnecessary emphasis.

"I met Mick Mahoney this afternoon, and he said they didn't need you."

"Mick Mahoney knows nothing about it."

"I told him to tell the others you wouldn't be coming, that Father Fogarty would be here," she went on desperately, fighting for the success of her evening.

"Then you had no business to do it," her husband retorted angrily, and even Fogarty saw that she had gone the worst way about it, by speaking to members of his committee behind his back. He began to feel uncomfortable. "If they come to some damn fool decision while I'm away, it'll be my responsibility."

"If you're late, you'd better knock," she sang out gaily to cover up his bad manners. "Will we go into the sitting-room, father?" she asked over-eagerly. "I'll be with you in two minutes. There are fags on the mantelpiece, and you know where to find the whi-hi-hi—blast that word!"

Fogarty lit a cigarette and sat down. He felt exceedingly uncomfortable. Whitton was an uncouth and irritable bastard, and always had been so. He heard Una upstairs, and then someone turned on the tap in the bathroom. "Bloody brute!" he thought indignantly. There had been no need for him to insult her before a guest. Why the hell couldn't he have finished his quarrelling while they were alone? The tap stopped and he waited, listening, but Una didn't come. He was a warm-hearted man and could not bear the thought of her alone and miserable upstairs. He went softly up the stairs and stood on the landing. "Una!" he called softly, afraid of waking the children. There was a light in the bedroom; the door was ajar and he pushed it in. She was sitting at the end of the bed and grinned at him dolefully.

"Sorry for the whine, father," she said, making a brave attempt to smile. And then, with the street-urchin's humour which he found so attractive: "Can I have a loan of your shoulder, please?"

"What the blazes ails Tom?" he asked, sitting beside her.

"He—he's jealous," she stammered, and began to weep again with her head on his chest. He put his arm about her and patted her awkwardly.

"Jealous?" he asked incredulously, turning over in his mind the half-dozen men whom Una could meet at the best of times. "Who the blazes is he jealous of?"

"You!"

"Me?" Fogarty exclaimed indignantly, and grew red, thinking of how he had given himself away with his pictures. "He must be mad! I never gave him any cause for jealousy."

"Oh, I know he's completely unreasonable," she stammered. "He always was."

"But you didn't say anything to him, did you?" Fogarty asked anxiously.

"About what?" she asked in surprise, looking up at him and blinking back her tears.

"About me?" Fogarty mumbled in embarrassment.

"Oh, he doesn't know about that," Una replied frantically. "I never mentioned that to him at all. Besides, he doesn't care that much about me."

And Fogarty realized that in the simplest way in the world he had been brought to admit to a married woman that he loved her and she to imply that she felt the same about him, without a word being said on either side. Obviously, these things happened more innocently than he had ever thought possible. He became more embarrassed than ever.

"But what is he jealous of so?" he added truculently.

"He's jealous of you because you're a priest. Surely, you saw that?"

"I certainly didn't. It never crossed my mind."

Yet at the same time he wondered if this might not be the reason for the censoriousness he sometimes felt in Whitton against his harmless bets and his bottles of wine.

"But he's hardly ever out of your house, and he's always borrowing your books, and talking theology and Church history to you. He has shelves of them here—look!" And she pointed at a plain wooden bookcase, filled with solid-looking works. "In my b-b-bedroom! That's why he really hates Father Whelan. Don't you see, Jerry," she said, calling him for the first time by his Christian name, "you have all the things he wants."

"I have?" repeated Fogarty in astonishment. "What things?"

"Oh, how do I know?" she replied with a shrug, relegating these to the same position as Whelan's bank-balance and his own gadgets, as things that meant nothing to her. "Respect and responsibility and freedom from the worries of a family, I suppose."

"He's welcome to them," Fogarty said with wry humour. "What's that the advertisements say?—owner having no further use for same."

"Oh, I know," she said with another shrug, and he saw that from the beginning she had realized how he felt about her and been sorry for him. He was sure that there was some contradiction here which he should be able to express to himself, between her almost inordinate piety and her light-hearted acceptance of his adoration for her— something that was exclusively feminine, but which he could not isolate with her there beside him, willing him to make love to her, offering herself to his kiss.

"It's a change to be kissed by someone who cares for you," she said after a moment.

"Ah, now, Una, that's not true," he protested gravely, the priest in him getting the upper hand of the lover who had still a considerable amount to learn. "You only fancy that."

"I don't, Jerry," she replied with conviction. "It's always been the same, from the first month of our marriage—always! I was a fool to marry him at all."

"Even so," Fogarty said manfully, doing his duty by his friend with a sort of schoolboy gravity, "You know he's still fond of you. That's only his way."

"It isn't, Jerry," she went on obstinately. "He wanted to be a priest and I stopped him."

"But you didn't."

"That's how he looks at it. I tempted him."

"And damn glad he was to fall!"

"But he did fall, Jerry, and that's what he can never forgive. In his heart he despises me and despises himself for not being able to do without me."

"But why should he despise himself? That's what I don't understand."

"Because I'm only a woman, and he wants to be independent of me and every other woman as well. He has to teach to keep a home for me, and he doesn't want to teach. He wants to say Mass and hear confessions, and be God Almighty for seven days of the week."

Fogarty couldn't grasp it, but he realized that there was something in what she said, and that Whitton was really a lonely, frustrated man who felt he was forever excluded from the only things which interested him.

"I don't understand it," he said angrily. "It doesn't sound natural to me."

"It doesn't sound natural to you because you have it, Jerry," she said. "I used to think Tom wasn't normal, either, but now I'm beginning to think there are more spoiled priests in the world than ever went into seminaries. You see, Jerry," she went on in a rush, growing very red, "I'm a constant reproach to him. He thinks he's a terrible blackguard because he wants to make love to me once a month. . . . I can talk like this to you because you're a priest."

"You can, to be sure," said Fogarty with more conviction than he felt.

"And even when he does make love to me," she went on, too full of her grievance even to notice the anguish she caused him, "he manages to make me feel that I'm doing all the love-making."

"And why shouldn't you?" asked Fogarty gallantly, concealing the way his heart turned over in him.

"Because it's a sin!" she cried tempestuously.

"Who said it's a sin?"

"He makes it a sin. He's like a bear with a sore head for days after. Don't you see, Jerry," she cried, springing excitedly to her feet and shaking her head at him, "it's never anything but adultery with him, and he goes away and curses himself because he hasn't the strength to resist it."

"Adultery?" repeated Fogarty, the familiar word knocking at his conscience as if it were Tom Whitton himself at the door.

"Whatever you call it," Una rushed on. "It's always adultery, adultery, adultery, and I'm always a bad woman, and he always wants to show God that it wasn't him but me, and I'm sick and tired of it. I want a man to make me feel like a respectable married woman for once in my life. You see, I feel quite respectable with you, although I know I shouldn't." She looked in the mirror of the dressing-table and her face fell. "Oh, Lord!" she sighed. "I don't look it. . . . I'll be down in two minutes now, Jerry," she said eagerly, thrusting out her lips to him, her old, brilliant, excitable self.

"You're grand," he muttered.

As she went into the bathroom, she turned in another excess of emotion and threw her arms about him. As he kissed her, she pressed herself close to him till his head swam. There was a mawkish, girlish grin on her face. "Darling!" she said in an agony of passion, and it was as if their loneliness enveloped them like a cloud.

As he went downstairs, he was very thoughtful. He heard Tom's key in the lock and looked at himself in the mirror over the fireplace. He heard Tom's step in the hall, and it sounded in his ears as it had never sounded before, like that of a man carrying a burden too great for him. He realized that he had never before seen Whitton as he really was, a man at war with his animal nature, longing for some high, solitary existence of the intellect and imagination. And he knew that the three of them, Tom, Una, and himself, would die as they had lived, their desires unsatisfied.

CONFESSING

Guy de Maupassant

The noon sun poured fiercely down upon the fields that lay in undulating folds around the clumps of trees that marked each farmstead. Ripe rye and yellowing wheat, pale-green oats, dark-green clover, spread a vast striped cloak, soft and rippling, over the bare body of the earth.

In the distance, on the crest of a slope, the horizon was broken by an endless line of cows, that were like soldiers at ease, some lying down, others on their feet, their great eyes blinking in the burning light, chewing the cud and grazing in a field of clover as broad as a lake.

Two women, mother and daughter, were walking with a swinging step, one behind the other, towards this regiment of cattle. Each carried two zinc pails, slung outwards from the body on the hoop of a cask; at each step the metal sent out a dazzling white flash under the sun that struck full upon it.

The women did not speak. They were on their way to milk the cows. When they arrived, each set down one of her pails and approached a cow. With a kick in the ribs from her wooden shoe she forced the cow to struggle to its feet. The beast rose slowly, first on its forelegs, then with more difficulty it raised its large hind quarters, which seemed to be weighed down by the enormous udder of livid pendulous flesh.

The two Malivoires, mother and daughter, kneeling beneath the animal's belly, tugged swiftly at the swollen teat, which at each squeeze sent a slender pet of milk into the pail. The yellowish froth mouted to the brim, and the women went from cow to cow until they reached the end of the long line.

As soon as they finished milking a beast, they changed its position, giving it a fresh patch of grass on which to graze.

416

Then they started on their way home, more slowly now, weighed down by the load of milk, the mother in front, the daughter behind.

Abruptly the daughter stopped, put down her burden, sat on the ground, and began to cry.

Madame Malivoire, missing the sound of steps behind her, turned round amazed.

"What's the matter with you?" she said.

Her daughter Céleste, a tall girl with bright red hair and flaming cheeks, flecked with freckles as though sparks of fire had fallen upon her face one day as she worked in the sun, moaned and murmured like a beaten child:

"I can't carry the milk any further."

Her mother looked at her suspiciously.

"What's the matter with you?" she repeated.

"It drags too heavy, I can't," replied Céleste. She had collapsed and was lying on the ground between the two pails, hiding her eyes in her apron.

"What's the matter with you, now?" said her mother for the third time. The girl moaned:

"I think there's a baby on the way." And she broke into sobs.

The older woman in her turn set down her load, so amazed that she could find nothing to say. At last she stammered:

"You . . . you . . . you're going to have a baby, you idiot! How can that be?"

The Malivoires were prosperous farmers, well-off and of a certain position, widely respected, good business folk, of some importance in the district.

"I think I am, all the same," faltered Céleste.

The frightened mother looked at the weeping girl groveling at her feet. After a moment she cried:

"You're going to have a baby! A baby! Where did you get it, you slut?"

Céleste, shaken with emotion, murmured:

"I think it was in Polyte's wagon."

The old woman tried to understand, tried to imagine, who could have brought this misfortune upon her daughter. If the lad was well-off and of decent position, an arrangement might be come to. The damage could still be repaired. Céleste was not the first to be in the family way, but it was a nuisance, just the same, considering their position and the way people talked.

"And who was it, you slut?" she repeated.

Céleste, resolved to make a clean breast of it, stammered:

"I think it was Polyte."

At that Madame Malivoire, mad with rage, rushed upon her daughter and began to beat her with such fury that her hat fell off.

With great blows of the fist she struck the girl on the head, on the back, all over her body; Céleste, prostrate between the two pails, which afforded her some slight protection, shielded her face with her hands.

All the cows, disturbed by the noise of the row, had stopped grazing and turned round, staring with their great eyes. The last one mooed, stretching out its muzzle towards the women.

After beating her daughter till she was out of breath, Madame Malivoire stopped, exhausted; her spirits reviving a little, she tried to get a thorough understanding of the situation.

"—— Polyte! Lord save us, it's not possible! How could you, with a bus driver! You must have lost your wits. He must have played you a trick, the good-for-nothing!"

Céleste, still prostrate, murmured in the dust:

"I didn't pay my fare!"

This was something the old Norman woman could understand.

Every week, on Wednesday and on Saturday, Céleste went to town with the farm produce—poultry, cream, and eggs.

She started at seven with her two huge baskets on her arms, the dairy produce in one, the chickens in the other, and went down to the main road to wait for the wagon to Yvetot.

She set down her wares and sat in the ditch, while the chickens with their short pointed beaks and the ducks with their broad flat bills thrust their heads between the wicker slats and looked about them with their round, stupid, surprised eyes.

Soon the bus, a sort of yellow box with a black leather cap on top, came up, jerking and quivering with the trotting of the old white horse.

Polyte the coachman, a big, jolly fellow, stout though still young, and so burnt by sun and wind, soaked by rain, and colored with brandy that his face and neck were brick-red, cracked his whip and shouted from the distance: "Morning, Mam'selle Céleste. In good health, I hope?"

She gave him her baskets, one after the other, which he stowed in the boot; then she got in, stepping very high to reach the bus, and exposing a sturdy leg clad in a blue stocking.

Every time Polyte repeated the same joke: "Well, it's not got any thinner."

She laughed, thinking this funny.

Then he uttered a "Gee up, old girl!" which started off the thin horse. Then Céleste, reaching for her purse in the depths of her pocket, slowly took out ten sous, six for herself and four for the baskets, and handed them to Polyte over his shoulder.

He took them, saying:

"Aren't we going to have our little bit of sport today?"

And he laughed heartily, turning round towards her so as to stare at her at his ease.

She thought it a great expense, this half-franc for a journey of two miles. And when there were no coppers in her purse she felt it still more keenly; it was hard to make up her mind to part with a silver coin.

One day, as she was paying, she asked:

"You ought not ask more than six sous from a good customer like me."

He burst out laughing.

"Six sous, my beauty; why, you're worth more than that."

She insisted:

"But you make a good two francs a month out of me."

He whipped up his horse and exclaimed:

"Look here, I'm an obliging fellow! We'll call it quits for a bit of sport."

"What do you mean?" she asked innocently.

He was so amused that he laughed till he coughed.

"A bit of sport is a bit of sport, damn it; a game for a lad and a lass, a dance for two without music."

She understood, blushed and declared:

"I don't care for that sort of game, Monsieur Polyte."

But he was in no way abashed, and repeated merrily:

"You'll come to it some day, my beauty, a bit of sport for a lad and a lass!"

Ever since that day he had taken to asking her, each time that she paid her fare:

"Aren't we going to have our bit of sport today?"

She, too, joked about it by this time, and replied:

"Not today, Monsieur Polyte, but Saturday, for certain!"

And amid peals of laughter he answered:

"Saturday, then, my beauty."

But inwardly she calculated that, during the two years that this had been going on, she had paid Polyte forty-eight whole francs, and in the country forty-eight francs is not a sum which can be picked up on the roadside; she also calculated that in two more years she would have paid nearly a hundred francs.

To such purpose she meditated that, one spring day as they jogged on alone, when he made his customary inquiry, "Aren't we going to have our bit of sport yet?" she replied:

"Yes, if you like, Monsieur Polyte."

He was not at all surprised, and clambered over the back of his seat, murmuring with a complacent air:

"Come along, then. I knew you'd come to it some day."

The old white horse trotted so gently that she seemed to be dancing upon the same spot, deaf to the voice which cried at intervals, from the depths of the vehicle: "Gee up, old girl! Gee up, there!"

Three months later Céleste discovered that she was going to have a child.

All this she had told her mother in a tearful voice. Pale with fury, the old woman asked:

"Well, what did it cost?"

"Four months; that makes eight francs, doesn't it?" replied Céleste.

At that the peasant woman's fury was utterly unleashed, and, falling once more upon her daughter, she beat her a second time until she was out of breath. Then she rose and said:

"Have you told him about the baby?"

"No, of course not."

"Why haven't you told him?"

"Because very likely he'd have made me pay for all the free rides!"

The old woman pondered a while, then picked up her milk-pails.

"Come on, get up, and try to walk home," she said. After a pause she spoke again:

"And don't tell him as long as he doesn't notice anything. We'll make six or eight months' fares out of him."

Céleste, who had risen, still crying, disheveled and swollen round the eyes, started off again with dragging steps, murmuring:

"Of course I won't tell him."

TRANSLATED BY ERNEST BOYD AND STORM JAMESON

DYING

Richard Stern

Dreben's first call came while Bly was in the laboratory. Mrs. Shearer's pale coniform budded with announcement: "He says it's urgent."

"Can't come." Watching the smear of kineton coax soluble nitrogens from the right leaf bulge, a mobilization of nutrient which left the ravaged context sere, yellow, senescent. "What kinda urgent?"

"Wouldn't say. An odd one." Her bud, seamed, cracked, needful of a good smear itself, trichloro-hydroxyphenyl, petrolatums, lipids: a chapstick; or lip-stick to mask its aging.

"Get the number." Eyes on the ravenous patch of leaf. Molisch, Curtis, and Clark had shown that mobilizing forces were strongest in flowers and fruits, less strong in growing points, still less strong in lateral buds, weakest in roots. Bly was checking on partial senescence, revving up one section of a tobacco leaf at the expense of another.

Two hours later, he drew the yellow Message Slip from his box: Name: F. Dorfman Dreben; Number: Bl 6-4664; Message: Please return call; Message Taken By: LES.

He knew no Dorfman Dreben, needed nothing from Bl 6-4664. The yellow slip floated toward the waste basket.

The second call came that night while he read President Kennedy's favorite book—he was going through the *Life* magazine list one by one—*John Quincy Adams and the State of the Union*, by Samuel F. Bemis. "Professor Bly?"

"*Der spricht.*"

"Professor Bly?"

"I am Bly."

"F. Dorfman Dreben, F. Dorfman Dreben Enterprises, I called you at 2:40 this afternoon."

"My boss wouldn't let me go to the phone, Mr. Dreben. What can

422

I do you for?" Bly held the receiver a foot away, six pock marks in the auditing cup, six at the center of the speaker's circular rash. A great machine. From the solitary six, as much of F. Dorfman Dreben as could be electrically transmitted from voice box A to Ear Drum Y appealed. "It was your poem in *Harper's*, right, Professor?"

The forty-fourth poem he'd written since high school, the eleventh since his appointment as Instructor in Plant Physiology, Division of the Biological Sciences, The University of Chicago, the seventh reproduced for public satisfaction (cf. Raleigh *News and Observer*, December 1954, "Blackie! Thy very name meant life!"; the Wake Forest *Lit*, "Sonnet on Your Easter Bonnet," Fall, 1956, and four others in the same publication) and the only one which had brought him money ($35.00) and fame (notice in the Chicago *Maroon*, a call from the U. of Chicago Public Relations Office resulting in six lines in the Chicago *Sun-Times*, four comments from students, bemused, pleased, uneasy, mocking, even, stupefyingly, joyous, responses from colleagues, one letter from a lady in Milledgeville, Georgia, declaring the poem "the most beautiful I have read in years" requesting a manuscript copy for the Milledgeville Pantosocratic Society, and today, one, then a second, call from F. Dorfman Dreben, F. Dorfman Dreben Enterprises). "All mine."

"A great poem," said the six pock marks. Seven lines unrhymed, iambic tetrameter with frequent substitutions, title, "In Defense of Decrepitude," epigraph, "A characteristic consequence of senescence is the occurrence of death," theme, "O death, thy sting is life." "Which explains, besides congratulations, my call, Professor."

"You're too kind." 2 cubed plus 4 squared equals my age, the square root of 576, a dayful of years.

"Not kind, Professor. Needy. I need your help."

You? And I, and my tobacco leaves, and Plant Physiology, students, the University, *Harper's*, girls—mostly unknown—children—unconceived.

"Though perhaps it will be of help to you too, Professor. Your helping me."

And the greatest of these. "Explain, Mr. Dreben."

"Easily. Here is our situation. My mother, may her soul, lies on her death bed. A week, a month, who knows, a day, will no longer be with us."

"I'm very sorry." His right eye, nose bone, and right cheek leaked—

not sorrow—upon a curl of purple violets (*V. cucullata*) filling a six-by-eight print, glassed-over, above the phone, a retreat of flesh towards hollow, though not sorrowful, limpidity. He was mostly eye. Bly the Eye. Eye had mobilized the nutrient that might have fleshed his flesh, made him at twenty-four husband, father, house-holder, mortgage-payer. Assistant Professor of Plant Physiology ("Get a loada Bly. Claims he looks like a violet").

"Thank you sincerely, Professor. I can tell you're a man of feeling. It showed in the poem, and that's why I call. Because more than a man of feeling, you're a master of words." No. Master of Science. Doctor of Philosophy, but no M.W., except honorary, University of Dorfman-Dreben. "We are in need. Sister and I. What we want to do is to put on mother's stone, already purchased, a short verse, original in nature, only for her. For such a verse, we are inaugurating a contest, prize two hundred dollars. I am officially inviting you to enter the contest with a verse suitable for permanent inscription." The *cucullata* smeared its fuzzy purple into his small jaw, bruised his neck. He was being mobilized for the assault on stone. Bly the Eye reporting. M.W., O.N. (Original in Nature). "A month ago, I wrote this Robert Frost. Saw him on the Inaugural Day. One month and haven't had a line from him. Not even a 'no'. Once they get into politics they're through."

"Through?"

"Poets. Two weeks ago, I wrote Sandburg. Same result. Negative. They're not interested in a business man's dollar. I tried writing one on my own. Failure My sister tried. Also. Then my sister saw your poem in *Harper's*. 'Right in Chicago,' she said. 'A sign.' "

"I was in politics," said Bly. Treasurer of the Arista, Binyon High School. John Quincy Adams, defeated by Jackson, turned to poetry. *Duncan Macmorrogh* or *The Conquest of Ireland*. Epic in four cantos.

"If my mother could have read it, she would say, 'This is the poet for my stone.' "

Bly's mother, "Mother Bly," as his sister's husband, Lember, the John Bircher, called her, had carried the sonnet "Blackie" around in her wallet until its shreds had married those of the Brussel's streetcar stub, souvenir of the European week which was the product of her mother's death and legacy. He had sent his mother neither a copy of *Harper*'s nor notice of his poem's presence there; evil communication corrupteth good parents. The viper generation that sent no sign. But he could use two hundred dollars, no doubt of it. The summer at the Oceanographic Institute at Wood's Hole was stale for him. He wanted his own week in Europe. He wanted to marry—girl unknown —though he had his nourished eye on a couple in Plant Physiology 263. A new suit. A car.

"Just a short poem, Professor. Maybe four lines. Rhymed."

"Rhymed'll cost you two-fifty."

The pock marks paused. "Who knows? I'll expect to hear from you then? F. Dorfman Dreben, 342 Wacker Drive. Bl 6-4664. Any time, day or night. Messages will be taken. I'm very grateful."

Bly sat down under the violets, took up the telephone pad and wrote non-stop:

> Claramae Dreben droops like a leaf.
> Her chest is still heaving, her boy's full of grief.

He pushed the eraser laterally on his forehead, once, twice.

> When she is nothing but dried skin and bone
> Two hundred smackers will carve grief in stone.

Two errors, "Claramae," odds against, one in two thousand, and "Two hundred smackers," which would not buy Bly's rhymed lines. No, a third error: the whole thing.

Bly threw the quatrain under the couch and picked up *John Quincy Adams* who was thinking of going into Congress despite his son's assertion that it would be beneath an ex-president's dignity. An hour later, in bed, he thought first of the kineton smear and the alpha aminoisobutyne acid he would apply to it tomorrow, then of Miss Gammon, a wiry little number in Pl. Phys. 263.

He didn't think of Dorfman Dreben until the third call, five days later. He was home eating the Tai Gum How he had sent up from Sixty-Third Street twice a week. "I called you last night, Professor. Failed to get you."

"Forgive me."

"F. Dorfman Dreben. Mother is sinking."

"I was out, Mr. D." The weekly meeting of the instructors in zoology and botany, papers read, discussion, a good meeting.

Bly sat down under the *cucullata*, the Tai Gum How crawling with porcine force up his stomach cavity. "Mr. Dreben. I must have led you astray. I'm no poet. I've written very few poems. Even if I were a poet, I couldn't take the time to work on a poem now. After all, I didn't even know your mother. Not even her name."

The pock marks were silent. Then, softly, "Clarissa, Professor. A beautiful name."

Bly got up. Almost one in two thousand. A sign. "Yes."

"You are a poet, Professor. No doubt of it. We are not looking for epics. A simple verse, original in nature. Any minute will be her last. I could feel so comforted telling her her resting place will be honored."

At lunch, a joke about the Irishman on his deathbed, sniffing ham cooking in the kitchen, managing to call to his wife for a piece, being refused. "You know better than that, Flaherty. It's for the wake."

"A simple verse at fifty, maybe sixty-one dollars a line. That's not a bad rate in any business."

Cottonwood brushed against the wire screen, the fluff comas breaking off, falling. Behind a violet shield of cotton cloud, the day's sun bowed good night. "Maybe I can try, Mr. Dreben. But listen, if you don't get a note from me this week, you'll know I couldn't do it. I'm not much on elegies. Not exactly a speciality of the house." Tai Gum How/Hot off the sow/One man's meat/Another man's Frau. Dermot O'Flaherty, Epic in Four Graves.

"You'll try then, Professor?"

"I'll try, Mr. D. If I send it on, please remit the two-fifty by certified cheque. Also, my name is not to be signed to or be associated with the verse. The Division might not approve. And finally, we must never communicate again."

"Wel——"

"Not au revoir but good-bye, Mr. D. You either will or will not hear from me within a hundred-and-sixty-eight hours." The pock marks chattered as the receiver plunged.

That evening, Bly sat back in his easy chair and thought about dying. In some ways, he was an expert. There was dying en masse, annually, dying deciduously, dying from the top—tulips, spring wheat, Dean Swift—dying from the bottom—he, Bly, nearly died there from the need to live there five or six times a week. Molisch in Der Lebensauer der Pflanzen showed that the century plant (Agave americana, L.) is a centenarian only when it can't become reproductive for a hundred years. "The most conspicuous factor associated with plant senescence is reproduction." The nutrient was mobilized into the fruit, and the rest suffered. Clarissa Dreben had conceived and spawned F. Dorfman, and who knows if it didn't kill her? Filial sentiments of a matricide. He, Bly, would at times have sold ten of his dayful of years for a few hours with even Mrs. Shearer's dying buds. People dying, Drebens dying. What to say? "Nuts." (Indehiscent, polycarpellary, one-seeded fruits, woodily pericarped. "Fine examination there, Bly.")

He picked up *The State of the Union*, then put it down, ran around the corner to the Trebilcocks and suggested that there was still enough light for a quick badminton game. He and Oscar tied the net cords to the apple trees, laid out the boundary stones, and whacked the birdie till the dark wouldn't even let them guess where it was. He told them his assignment, and, telling it, laughed at its absurdity. The next day, he told it at the physiologists' table, elaborating it with echoes of the Flaherty story. That was it. May passed, and thoughts of the dying Clarissa died with it. Teaching, the study of senescence, the preparation of a paper to be given at the June meetings of the American Association of Plant Physiologists, and then Phyllis Gammon, drove the drebitis from his system.

He had traversed the difficult teacher-student chasm between "Miss Gammon" and "Phyllis." There'd been coffee, then Tai Gum How, then intimate conversation, then amorous relations with the wiry young physiologist from Cumberland, Maryland, who herself remarked about, and thus arrested, the humorous notice of hot gammons and Cumberland Gaps. A girl after if not Bly's heart, at least his mobilizing centers. Even the thought of sacramental union entered his orderly mind without disordering it. Not that there had to be a crash program. Phyllis was no raving beauty, no sex-pot. Her discernible virtues were not those prized in the Bedsheet Derby. She was his, more or less for the asking, a splendid alteration in his life.

He was playing badminton with her at the Trebilcocks when Dreben showed up. A June Sunday that squeezed heat from the stones and thickened the air with summer sounds. They played in shorts, Bly shirtless, asweat. The apple trees were misty with green, their branches wild with the coming weight of the rosy balls busy now sucking nutrient from the sap. The yard ran with children, four Trebilcocks, five Grouts, assorted derivations from China, Ireland, the Baltic, Africa, a running sea of life, rising in the trees, covering the flower borders, drifting through the Jungle Gym and miniature geodesic dome in the yard. Bly and Phyllis—a little wiry for shorts but a great pull on him—whacked the feathered cork over the net while Trebilcock and his wife poured a gallon of Savoia Red back and forth toward their glasses. Bly and Phyllis swigged away between points, so that by the time the dark, bald, bespectacled man in the hound's-tooth winter overcoat strode through the yards, through the quieting children, he was drunk enough almost to disbelieve his presence. "Professor Bly?" Bly saw the black eyes scoot up and down behind the spectacles, and the thinking, "This? A professor? A poet? A sweaty squirt slapping a piece of cork at a sweaty girl, boozing on a run-down lawn. What gives?"

"Yes, I'm Bly. What can I do for you?" though he knew it was Dreben.

Hand out of the hound's-tooth sleeve, shaken by Bly. "F. Dorfman Dreben, Professor. You remember. A month back. Excuse my bother· ing you here Sunday. Your landlady directed——"

"Over here, Mr. Dreben," and Bly led the man by the hound's-tooth elbow to a corner where a rickety bench leaned on an elm. "You want to talk with me about the poetry, even though I told you that silence meant inability to bring back the bacon." His bare chest, both narrow and puffy, a snake of hair winding sweatily down toward his shorts, did not enforce the harsh chill of voice, blue eyes, nostrils, shivering with hauteur.

Dreben's rear sank to the bench, the dark, bald skull lowered to the hound-toothed sternum. In the Renoir blaze of yard, he was a funereal smear. Sobered, easier, Bly said, "I'm sorry, Mr. Dreben. If I could have done the job, I'd have done it. Has, is——?"

"Two weeks ago. Smiling." Spoken to his bright Oxfords. "She rests under two thousand dollars worth of granite. Bare. Waiting the expression of our love." The head was up, spectacles catching the gold thrusts of light.

"What can I do, Mr. Dreben? I don't have time. I'm a full-time physiologist." He spread his hands, or rather one hand and one badminton raquet. Then, blushed for the latter, and for the guzzled Savoia, for the lawn, for Phyllis, for—as a matter of fact—life. "Except for sheer physical relaxation, every now and then. I don't have the thinking energy for poetry, and poetry takes energy and time. Took me eight works—I mean weeks—to write the one you read."

The head, a darkly golden Arp egg, appealed. "Please," it said. "We know you're the one for us. Two hundred and fifty dollars, a prize in a contest, permanent commemoration on granite."

He'd almost forgotten the gold. On the grass, wiry legs folded against each other, strong knees raised toward an assuredly pointed dickey, straw-head apple-rosy with its own and the sun's heat, his hot gammon. Two hundred and fifty would give them a hot little week or two up on the Michigan Dunes. "In the mail by Tuesday, Mr. Dreben. Something will be in the mail. You send the cheque by return mail."

Dreben was up, hound-toothed arms churning, off. Not a word. Was silence a contractual ceremony? At the net, he ducked, head deploying for a half-second stare at the three staring guzzlers, then sideswiping half a dozen racing children, he disappeared.

Five hours later, in Michener's Book Store, Bly skimmed a volume on burials and funeral customs. He learned: that in common law, one is responsible for persons dying under one's roof; that corpses were considered sinfully infectious by Persians who placed them in Dakmas, "towers of silence," where birds defleshed them; that West African Negroes wear white at funerals; that the Roman funeral dresses—black—were called *lugubria*; that Patagonians interred horses, Vikings ships, Hindus and Wends widows, and the Egyptians books with their dead. Books, thought Bly. This was about where he came in with Dreben. Though for the Egyptians, the books were for the dead's guidance, whereas his poem was for display, the display of expensive devotion which could summon something "original in nature," a freshly created object to bury with a freshly-uncreated subject.

Bly walked home in the hot streets, past the humming student taverns, the boarded store fronts, the waste lands of the Land Clearance Commission, the crazy blue whirl-lights of the police cars, the cottonwood elms sighing in the heat. Life, such as it was, mobilized in the growing points. In Michener's he'd been down where the forces were weakest, in the roots of custom, history, meaning, the roots of death, where only an odd Dreben, dark in his hound's-tooth winter coat, mobilized for them.

Out of the gashed window of what had been, three weeks ago, a TASTEE FREEZE BAR, the idea for his mortuary poem came to him.

"Systems in internal equilibrium approach states of perfect order as the temperature lowers toward absolute zero." The third law of thermodynamics which Oscar Trebilcock was using as base for research into frozen protozoa; out of the defunct ice-creamery it slipped and made for the granite above Clarissa Dreben. "Yes," said Bly, Master of Science, to Bly, Master of Words. "Death is perfect order, life disorder." Dodging a lump of dog dung in the cracked pavement, Bly, the Word-Master, thought.

> Clarissa Dreben, know at last,
> Your disorder's been and past.

He stepped off a lawn signed "No dogs. Grass chemically treated," and finished:

> Showing others why they die,
> Under granite, perfect lie.

A great breath in his small chest and a proud look at the prinked-out sky. He'd done it. He ran up the block, up his stairs, called Phyllis and recited it to her. Her response did not dampen him; she was no flatterer. He typed it out on Department of Plant Physiology station-ery, just stopped himself from putting an air-mail stamp on the envelope, and ran downstairs and two blocks to the Fifty-Third Street mailbox, pick-up at 6:45 A.M.

He must have lain awake till pick-up time, drenched in thoughts of gods and death as perfect systems, the former discarded by his mind's razor, Occam's, the latter retained, warmly, the spur to research, poetry, the ordering of disorder. His President's hero, Quincy Adams, filled volumes dodging the subject. That's what one did. One wasn't dragged by the beast, one saddled it and rode elsewhere. He was grate-ful to Clarissa and F. Dorfman, and went to sleep thinking well of them, the sun firing itself through the soot smears on his window.

The next week he gave his Senescence paper at the Plant Physiology Meetings in the Palmer House. A minor triumph which brought him two job offers which he brought to his department chairman for squeezing out a raise and promotion. He saw no one but physiologists and Phyllis, the latter at supper, though one supper extended to breakfast.

At the end of June, the Trebilcocks left for their yearly month in Wisconsin, and Bly remembered the Michigan cabin that he'd planned to rent with his Dreben money. It had not been sent, nor had there been any word at all from F. Dorfman. "Call the man," said Phyllis from the bed, where she lay, covered, with his sweat and her own. He didn't have to look up the number, Bl 6-4664. He dialed and reached a message service, left his name, number and any hope of getting through to Dreben.

Half an hour later, though, the phone rang.

"Hello, Mr. Dreben. I called to find out why I haven't heard from you."

"Yes. I was going to call. We've been considering the entries until just this afternoon, Professor. We've reached our decision. I was going to call. As I said. I'm afraid that the decision has gone against your fine poem."

Bly held the phone off for two or three seconds, the six pock marks whirling in the heat. "What are you doing, Leon?" Phyllis in white socks, the bare remainder curved toward him like an interrogation mark.

He said, "You'd invited other—there were other poets writing verses for you?"

"Two others, Professor. Bladwin Kerner, editor of the Township School year-book, a fine young poet, and then a dear friend of my sister's, Mrs. Reiser."

"Which won?"

"I have only one."

"Who won the contest?"

"Baldwin. His poem was not quite so forcibly expressed as yours, but it was beautiful and true to nature and mother. Of course, he knew her."

"Is there a second prize?"

Pause. "Yes. You won honorable mention."

Bly lay the phone on the tiny rubber towers, reached behind him to touch Phyllis, who reached around to touch him. No plant in evolutionary history had ever contrived such mingling. Then the animal spirits mobilized in the reproductive centers, and he and Phyllis faced each other.

.   .
.   .
.   .

It requires a certain insensitivity to a charge of self-assertion to include one's own work in a selection of international literary real estate. The present inclusion must be defended on the grounds that the collector wants to include an account he can trust of the origin and formation of a story. Not that he tells all, but he does know what he consciously excludes, and this is not the case with those "stories of the story" which can be found both in (Proust, Joyce) and out (James, Gide) of modern fictions.

The story was written in the winter of 1962–63 and was launched by reading an article on plant senescence in a technical journal. Death is a theme to which few writers are not alive. Coupled with an old desire to put a scientist in a sensible story, the theme and article conjured up Bly, and soon (though whether it was minutes or days, I can't say now) he was grafted onto my own Dreben experience. Two years before, a Chicago businessman had called up to request of me the precise service Dreben asks of Bly. I said that I was sorry, I could not help him, but he kept after me until I sent him a sentimental quatrain. Which was the last I heard of him.

I decided early that the Dreben-Bly story should have layers of reference controlled by a number of related themes, but that instead of presenting layers in the conspicuous fashion of say Mann's Felix Krull, I'd make them as inconspicuous a part of the unfolding as was consonant with the telling. They unroll then in Bly's mind. He is reading—as I then was—Bemis' book on Adams, and I tender him some of my observations. The fact that Adams wrote verse belonged to the story. Whether Adams initiated the political references or whether he enriched a layer initiated by Dreben's mention of Frost at the Inaugural I don't know. I do remember thinking that John Quincy Adams may have been a model for the then President, John Kennedy. The chief thematic control stemmed from the article on senescence, but I do not remember much strain in its application. Indeed, the story was written a good deal more easily than stories which do not "assemble themselves" into thematic layers.

I don't believe I ever thought of taking what now seems to me an obvious option, which was to make the surface tone of the story, or indeed the whole story a pathetic, sad or even tragic one as opposed to a more or less serious comedy or farce. It would not have been difficult to make Bly less of a wise guy, Dreben less of a fool. It would not have been difficult to have linked their troubles (Bly's loneliness, his lack of success or perhaps his ignored success, with Dreben's love for his mother). Dreben could have been a poor man, a sympathetic one, Bly could have been without a Phyllis or anyone else (a man who took his dinners alone in the automat). He could have become a friend of Mrs. Dreben; or his own mother could die. These and a hundred other possibilities existed. Yet my mood was what it was as my spine of concern was the difference between the scientific study of a phenomenon and the decayed ritual of its commemoration.

BIOGRAPHICAL DATA

Henry Adams (1838–1918)

Juan José Arreola (1918–   ) a fine Mexican writer who, like Borges in Argentina, faces Europe (specifically Prague) rather than his native capital.

Marcel Aymé (1902–   )

Isaac Babel (1894– ?)

Pio Baroja (1872–1956)

Saul Bellow (1915–   )

Paul Bowles (1910–   ) a composer whose best fiction is blood descendant of Poe-Gothic.

Jacques Casanova de Seingalt (1725–1798)

Anton Chekhov (1860–1904)

Danilo Dolci (1924–   ) one of the twentieth-century saints (Gandhi, Schweitzer, King), professional men who, in mid-career, plunge into a secular swamp; Dolci, an architect from Trieste, went to Sicily because of temples in Agrigento and remained because of misery in Palermo.

John Dos Passos (1896–   )

John Howard Griffin (1920–   ) one of that valuable subdivision of modern letters, the Responsible Reporter; the printed selection

435

is from *Black Like Me* (1961), an account of his experience as a temporary Negro in Alabama and Mississippi.

Heinrich Heine (1797–1856)

Tatsuzo Ishikawa (1905–   ) one of the twentieth-century writers who've done the Balzac-Stendhal-Flaubert graft onto Japanese literature.

Henry James (1843–1916)

David Jones (1895–   ) like another novelist-pyrotechnician, Wyndham Lewis, Jones is primarily an artist.

James Joyce (1882–1941)

Søren Kierkegaard (1813–1855)

Rudyard Kipling (1865–1936)

Ring Lardner (1885–1933)

D. H. Lawrence (1885–1930)

Machado de Assis (1839–1908)

Saadat Hasan Manto (1913–1955) the leading Urdu short-story writer.

Masuccio Salernitano (Tommaso Guardati) (1420?–1500?) the Boccaccio bush's finest bloom; fifty of his stories were collected in 1475 under the title *Il Novellino*.

Guy de Maupassant (1850–1893)

Michel de Montaigne (1533–1592)

Henry de Montherlant (1896–   )

Vladimir Nabokov (1899–   )

Frank O'Connor (Michael O'Donovan) (1903–1966)

Yuri Olyesha (1899–   )

The Panchatantra (*pancha* = five, *tantra* = devices) contains stories
known for five thousand years; the collection itself is two thousand
years old.

Ezra Pound (1885–   )

Marcel Proust (1871–1922)

Alain Robbe-Grillet (1922–   )

Franz Schubert (1797–1828)

Richard Stern (1928–   )

Mahmud Taimur (Mahmoud Teymour) (1894–   ) the most
famous Arabic storyteller of recent times.

Federigo Tozzi (1883–1920) died too young to be Verga's pecr, but,
like Verga, he belongs in the reconnaissance section of Italy's
mid-century revival.

Wolfram von Eschenbach (1170?–1220) one of the glories of the
poetic springtime (German *Abteilung*) of 1200 A.D.

William Butler Yeats (1865–1939) most of Yeats's plays are poetic
coagulations of Celtic gloom and Celtic whimsey; the one printed
here (1934) is of the iron with which Yeats constructed the later
poems and the *Autobiography*.

ACKNOWLEDGMENTS

Danilo Dolci: "Gino O." From *Inchiesta A Palermo,* © 1956 by Einaudi Editore, S.P.A., Turin. English translation © 1959 by MacGibbon and Kee, London, under the title *To Feed the Hungry: Enquiry in Palermo.* U.S. edition © 1959 by Orion Press, Inc., under the title *Report From Palermo.* Reprinted with the permission of Einaudi Editore, S.P.A., Turin; MacGibbon and Kee, London; and Grossman Publishers, Inc., New York.

Anton Chekhov: "A Boring Story." From *Lady With Lapdog and Other Stories.* English translation © 1964 by David Magarshack. Reprinted with the permission of Penguin Books, Ltd.

Henry de Montherlant: "Mademoiselle de Plémeur: Champion of the 'Three hundred metres.'" From *Les Olympiques,* © 1924 by Henry de Montherlant. Included in *Selected Essays,* translated by John Weightman, edited by Peter Quennell. English translation © 1960 by George Weidenfeld and Nicolson, Ltd., London. Reprinted with the permission of Librairie Gallimard, Paris; George Weidenfeld and Nicolson, Ltd., London; and The Macmillan Company, New York.

Ring Lardner: "A Caddy's Diary." © 1922 Curtis Publishing Company; renewal copyright 1950 Ellis A. Lardner. Reprinted with the permission of Charles Scribner's Sons from *How to Write Short Stories* by Ring Lardner.

Søren Kierkegaard: "My Relation to 'Her.'" Reprinted from *A Kierkegaard Anthology,* edited by Robert Bretall, by permission of Princeton University Press. © 1946 by Princeton University Press.

James Joyce: "Joyce on Joyce" (Letter to Harriet Shaw Weaver). From *The Letters of James Joyce,* edited by Stuart Gilbert. © 1957 by The Viking Press, Inc. Reprinted by permission of The Viking Press, Inc., New York, and Faber and Faber, Ltd., London.

Michel de Montaigne: "Of the Disadvantage of Greatness." Reprinted from *The Complete Works of Montaigne,* translated by Donald M. Frame, with the permission of the publishers, Stanford University Press. © Copyright 1948, 1957, 1958 by the Board of Trustees of the Leland Stanford Junior University.

440

John Howard Griffin: "Into Mississippi." From *Black Like Me*, by John Howard Griffin, © 1960, 1961 by John Howard Griffin. Reprinted by permission of the author and Houghton Mifflin Company.

Ezra Pound: "Canto LXXXIII." From *The Cantos of Ezra Pound*, © 1934, 1937, 1940, 1948 by Ezra Pound. Reprinted by permission of the publishers, New Directions, New York; Faber and Faber, Ltd., London; and Arthur V. Moore.

Jacques Casanova de Seingalt: "Voltaire." From *The Memoirs of Casanova*, translated by Arthur Machen (New York: Dover Publications, Inc., 1961). English translation first published in the United States by Albert & Charles Boni, 1932. An unabridged and unaltered republication of the Arthur Machen translation, as slightly revised and edited by Frederick A. Blossom, published in the United States by Dover Publications, Inc., 1961. English edition published by Elek Books, Ltd., London, © in Berne Convention countries by Elek Books, Ltd. Published with the permission of Elek Books, Ltd., London, and Dover Publications, Inc., New York.

Marcel Proust: "Filial Sentiments of a Parricide." Translated by Barbara Anderson. English translation first published in *Partisan Review*, Vol. XV, No. 1, January, 1948, © 1948 by *Partisan Review*. Later reprinted in *Great Short Stories From the World's Literature*, edited by Charles Neider (Rinehart & Company, 1950), © 1950 by Charles Neider. Reprinted with the permission of *Partisan Review*, New York, and Holt, Rinehart and Winston, Inc., New York.

Isaac Babel: "Guy de Maupassant." Translated by Raymond Rosenthal and Waclow Solski. English translation first published in *Partisan Review*, Vol. XVII, No. 1, January, 1950, © 1950 by *Partisan Review*. Later reprinted in *The Collected Stories of Isaac Babel*, © 1955 by Criterion Books, Inc., New York. Reprinted with the permission of *Partisan Review*, New York; S. G. Phillips, Inc., Publisher, Great Meadow, New Jersey; and Methuen & Co., Ltd., London.

Rudyard Kipling: "A Wayside Comedy." From *Wee Willie Winkie and Other Stories* by Rudyard Kipling, by permission of Mrs. George Bambridge; Macmillan & Co., Ltd., London; The Macmillan Company of Canada, Ltd.; The Macmillan Company, New York. Copyright 1895, The Macmillan Company; copyright 1897, Rudyard Kipling. Later published in *The Works of Rudyard Kipling* (Charles Scribner's Sons, 1907).

Masuccio Salernitano: "The Sainted Breeches of Fra Nicolo." Reprinted by permission of Capricorn Books, G. P. Putnam's Sons, New York, from *The Palace of Pleasure: An Anthology of the Novella*, edited by

ACKNOWLEDGMENTS 441

Maurice Valency and Harry Levtow, a Capricorn Original, © 1960 by Capricorn Books.

William Butler Yeats: "The Words Upon the Window Pane." Printed and published in an edition of 350 copies by Elizabeth Corbet Yeats at The Cuala Press, 133 Lower Baggot Street, Dublin, Ireland, in January, 1934. Included in the volume *Wheels and Butterflies*, published in *The Collected Plays of William Butler Yeats* (U.S. edition published by The Macmillan Company, New York, 1935; new edition, with additional plays, published 1953). Copyright 1934 by The Macmillan Company, New York; copyright renewed 1962 by Bertha Georgie Yeats. Reprinted by permission of Mr. M. B. Yeats; The Macmillan Company, New York; Macmillan & Co., Ltd., London; The Macmillan Company of Canada, Ltd.

Saul Bellow: "Leaving the Yellow House." Copyright © 1958, 1966, by Saul Bellow. First published in *Esquire*, January, 1958. Reprinted with the permission of the author.

Mahmud Taimur: "Uncle Mitwalli." English translation by Bernard Lewis, published in *Land of Enchanters*, edited by Bernard Lewis (The Harvill Press, Ltd., London). The story, slightly revised, was reprinted in *A Treasury of Modern Asian Stories*, edited by Daniel L. Milton and William Clifford, © 1961 by the editors, and published as a Mentor Book by The New American Library of World Literature, Inc. Reprinted by permission of the author, Mahmoud Teymour; the translator, Bernard Lewis; the editor, William Clifford; and the publishers, The Harvill Press, Ltd., London, and The New American Library, Inc., New York.

Machado de Assis: "The Animal Game." English translation by Helen Caldwell, included in *The Psychiatrist and Other Stories* by Machado de Assis (University of California Press, 1963), copyright 1963 by the Regents of the University of California. Reprinted by permission of the University of California Press.

Federigo Tozzi: "Tenants." From *Stories of Modern Italy*, edited, translated, and with an Introduction by Ben Johnson (Random House, 1960). Copyright 1960 by Random House, Inc. Reprinted by permission of Random House, Inc., and Vallecchi Editore, S.P.A., Florence.

John Dos Passos: "Tin Lizzie." From *The Big Money* (Houghton Mifflin Company, 1936), © 1936 by John Dos Passos; copyright renewed 1964 by John Dos Passos. *The Big Money* is the third volume of the trilogy *U.S.A.* Reprinted with the permission of the author.

Marcel Aymé: "The Walker-Through-Walls." From *Across Paris and Other Stories* (Harper & Brothers, 1958), © 1943 by Librairie Gallimard,

442   ACKNOWLEDGMENTS

Paris. English translation by Norman Denny. Reprinted by permission of Librairie Gallimard, Paris; The Bodley Head, Ltd., London; and Harper & Row, Publishers, New York.

David Jones: "The Many Men So Beautiful," Part I of *In Parenthesis* (Faber and Faber, Ltd., 1937), © 1937 by David Jones. U.S. edition published in 1961 by Chilmark Press, Inc., and distributed by Random House, Inc. Reprinted by permission of Faber and Faber, Ltd., London, and Chilmark Press, Inc., New York.

"The Farmer's Wife." From *The Panchatantra*, translated by Arthur W. Ryder (University of Chicago Press, 1956), © 1956 by Mary E. and Winifred Ryder. Reprinted by permission of the copyright owners.

Juan José Arreola: "I'm Telling You the Truth." From *Confabulario and Other Inventions*, by Juan José Arreola, translated by George D. Schade (University of Texas Press, 1964). Copyright © 1964 by Juan José Arreola. Reprinted by permission of the University of Texas Press.

Wolfram von Eschenbach: "Parzival and Sigune." Translated by Helen M. Mustard and Charles E. Passage. From *Parzival* (Random House, Inc., 1961). Copyright 1961 by Helen M. Mustard and Charles E. Passage. Reprinted by permission of the publishers, Random House, Inc.

Tatsuzo Ishikawa: "Thoughts in the Dark." Translated by Brewster Horwitz. Translation first published in *New World Writing #4*, October, 1953. Copyright 1953 by Tatsuzo Ishikawa. Reprinted by permission of the author and New American Library, Inc., New York.

Paul Bowles: "A Distant Episode." From *The Delicate Prey and Other Stories* (Random House, 1950). Copyright © 1945, 1946, 1947, 1948, 1949, 1950 by Paul Bowles. Reprinted by permission of Random House, Inc., the William Morris Agency, Inc., and Laurence Pollinger, Ltd., London. The story appeared in England in a volume titled *A Little Stone*, published by John Lehmann, Ltd.

Alain Robbe-Grillet: "Three Reflected Visions." From *Instantanés*, © 1962 by Les Editions de Minuit. Translated by Richard Howard. Translation first published in *Evergreen Review*, Vol. 1, No. 3. Reprinted by permission of Editions de Minuit, Paris; Grove Press, Inc., New York; and Georges Borchardt. An English translation of *Instantanés* by Barbara Wright is included in *Snapshots and Towards a New Novel* (London: Calder S. Boyars, Ltd., 1966). We acknowledge the permission of Calder S. Boyars, Ltd., to publish Richard Howard's translation of "Three Reflected Visions."

Yuri Olyesha: "Liumpa." Translated by Camilla Gray. Translation first published in *New World Writing #14*, © 1958 by The New American Library of World Literature, Inc. Reprinted by permission of the Am-Rus Literary Agency, New York, and New American Library, Inc., New York.

Vladimir Nabokov: "Signs and Symbols." From *Nabokov's Dozen* (Doubleday & Co., Inc., 1958). Copyright © 1948 by Vladimir Nabokov. Collection copyright © 1958 by the author. The story originally appeared in *The New Yorker* in 1948. The collection was published in England in 1959 by William Heinemann, Ltd. Reprinted by permission of Doubleday & Company, Inc., and William Heinemann, Ltd.

Pio Baroja: "The Cabbages in the Cemetery." Translated by Anthony Kerrigan. From *The Restlessness of Shanti Andia and Other Writings* by Pio Baroja (University of Michigan Press, 1959). © The University of Michigan, 1959. Reprinted from *The Restlessness of Shanti Andia and Other Writings* by Pio Baroja by permission of The University of Michigan Press.

Henry James: "The Two Faces." First published, *Harper's Bazaar*, XXXIII (15 December 1900), with the title "The Faces." Reprinted in *The Better Sort* (London: Methuen, 1903; New York: Scribner's, 1903). Reprinted in Vol. XII of the New York Edition, *The Novels and Tales of Henry James* (Scribner's, 1907–09).

Henry Adams: "The First Consul in His Bath." From Chapter II, *A History of the United States of America*, Vol. II, by Henry Adams (Charles Scribner's Sons, 1889). Copyright 1889 by Charles Scribner's Sons; copyright renewed 1917 by Henry Adams. Reprinted by permission of Charles Scribner's Sons.

D. H. Lawrence: "Fanny and Annie." First published in *England My England and Other Stories*, by D. H. Lawrence (Thomas Seltzer, 1922). Copyright 1922 by Thomas Seltzer, Inc. Copyright renewed 1950 by Frieda Lawrence. Reprinted in *The Complete Short Stories of D. H. Lawrence* (Viking Press, Compass Edition, 1961). Reprinted by permission of The Viking Press, Inc., New York; Laurence Pollinger, Ltd., London; and the Estate of the late Mrs. Frieda Lawrence.

Saadat Hasan Manto: "Odor." English translation by Hamid Jalal. Included in *A Treasury of Modern Asian Stories*, edited by Daniel L. Milton and William Clifford, © 1961 by the editors, and published as a Mentor Book by The New American Library of World Literature, Inc. Reprinted by permission of the author's literary executor, Hamid Jalal; the editor, William Clifford; and the publisher, The New American Library, Inc., New York.

Frank O'Connor: "The Frying-Pan." From *More Stories by Frank O'Connor* (Alfred A. Knopf, Inc., 1954). An earlier version of this story appeared in *The Common Chord* (Alfred A. Knopf, Inc., 1948), copyright 1948 by Alfred A. Knopf, Inc. Reprinted by permission of Random House, Inc., and Alfred A. Knopf, Inc., New York, and the author's agent, Cyrilly Abels, New York.

Guy de Maupassant: "Confessing." From *The Novels and Tales of Guy de Maupassant* (Alfred A. Knopf, Inc., 1922), copyright 1922 by Alfred A. Knopf, Inc. Translated by Ernest Boyd and Storm Jameson. Reprinted with the permission of Alfred A. Knopf, Inc., in *The Portable Maupassant* (Viking Press, Inc., 1947), edited, and with an Introduction, by Lewis Galantière. Copyright 1947 by The Viking Press, Inc. For the Viking edition, Lewis Galantière revised in part the translations of Ernest Boyd and Storm Jameson. Reprinted by permission of Random House, Inc., and Alfred A. Knopf, Inc., New York.

Richard Stern: "Dying." From *Teeth, Dying and Other Matters* by Richard G. Stern (Harper & Row, 1964). Copyright © 1964 by Richard G. Stern. Reprinted by permission of Harper & Row, Publishers, New York; MacGibbon & Kee, London; and Russell & Volkening, Inc., New York.